FAIRY TAIL

フェアリーテイル

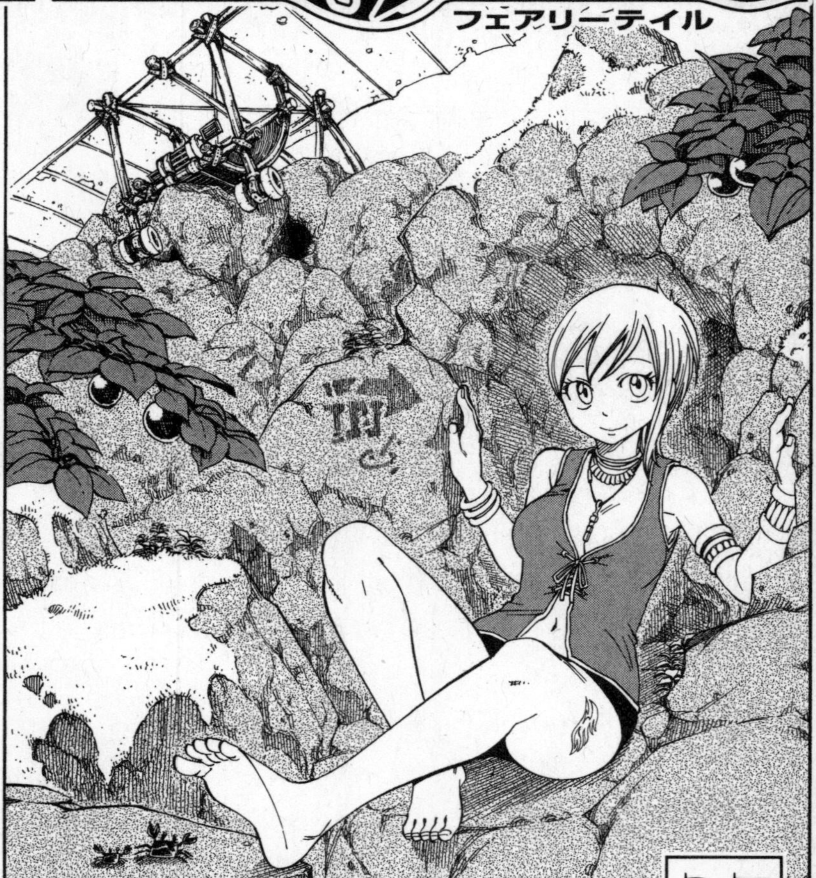

27

HIRO MASHIMA

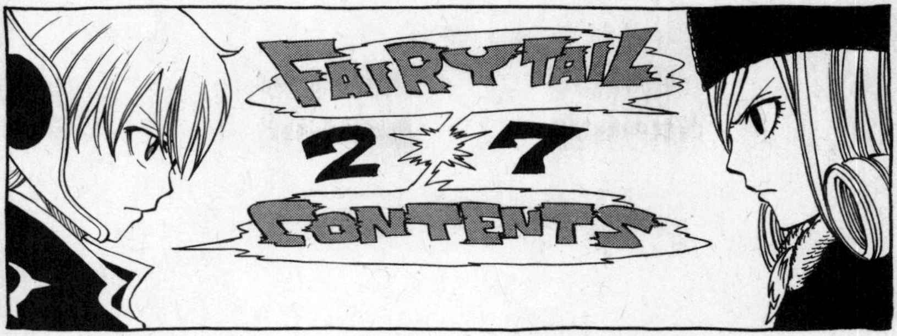
FAIRY TAIL
27
CONTENTS

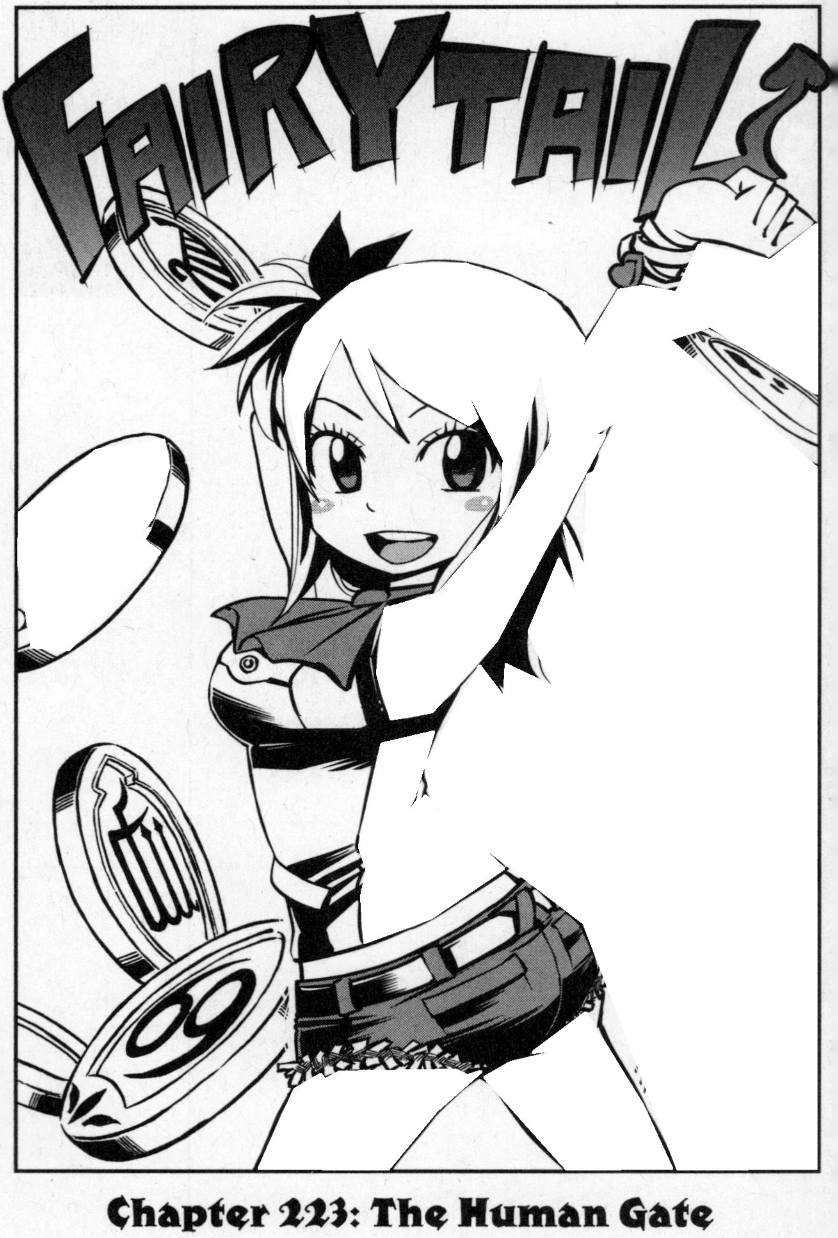
FAIRY TAIL

Chapter 223: The Human Gate

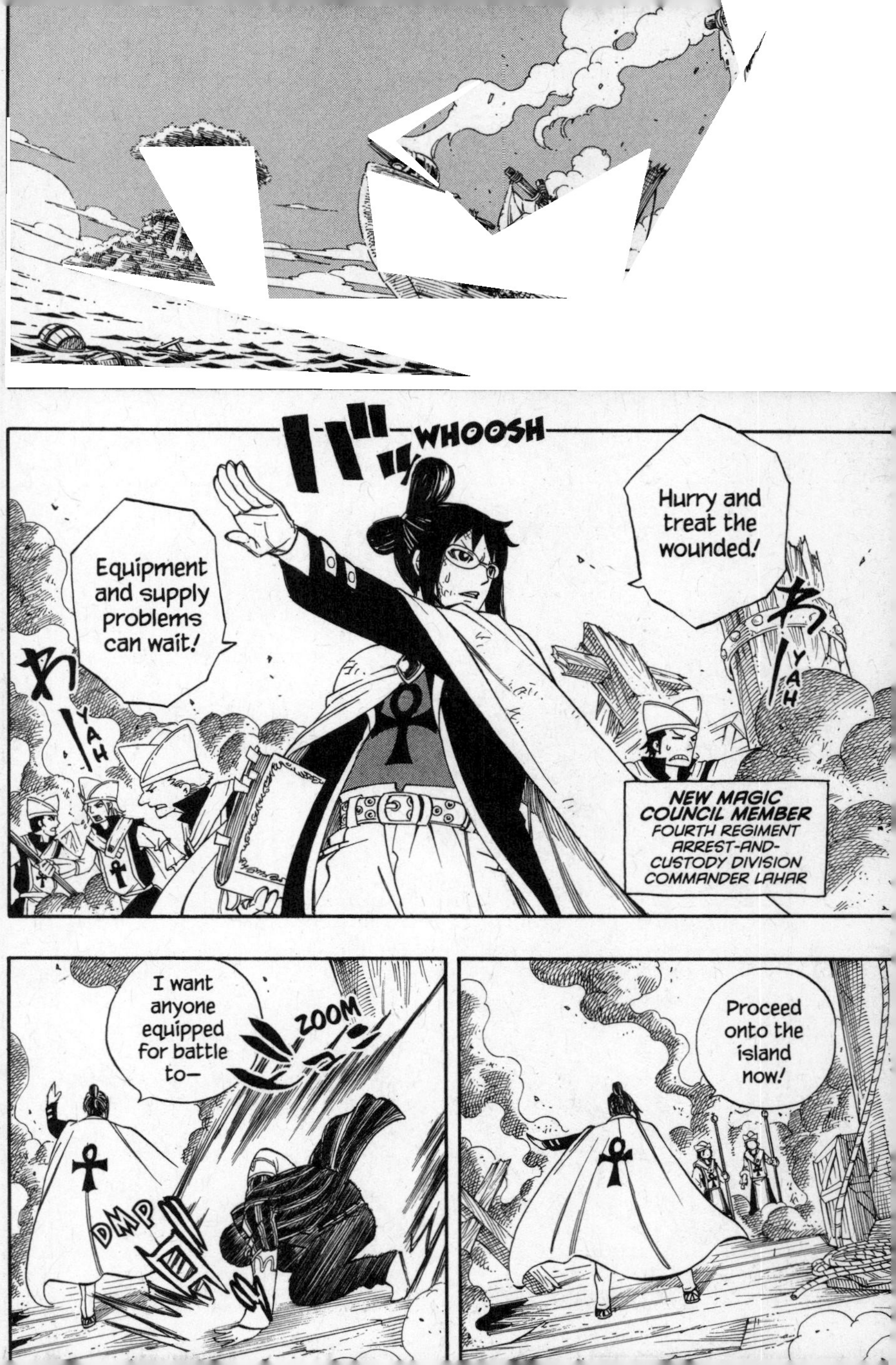
Hurry and treat the wounded!
WHOOSH
YAH
NEW MAGIC COUNCIL MEMBER FOURTH REGIMENT ARREST-AND-CUSTODY DIVISION COMMANDER LAHAR
Equipment and supply problems can wait!
YAH
Proceed onto the island now!
I want anyone equipped for battle to—
ZOOM
DMP

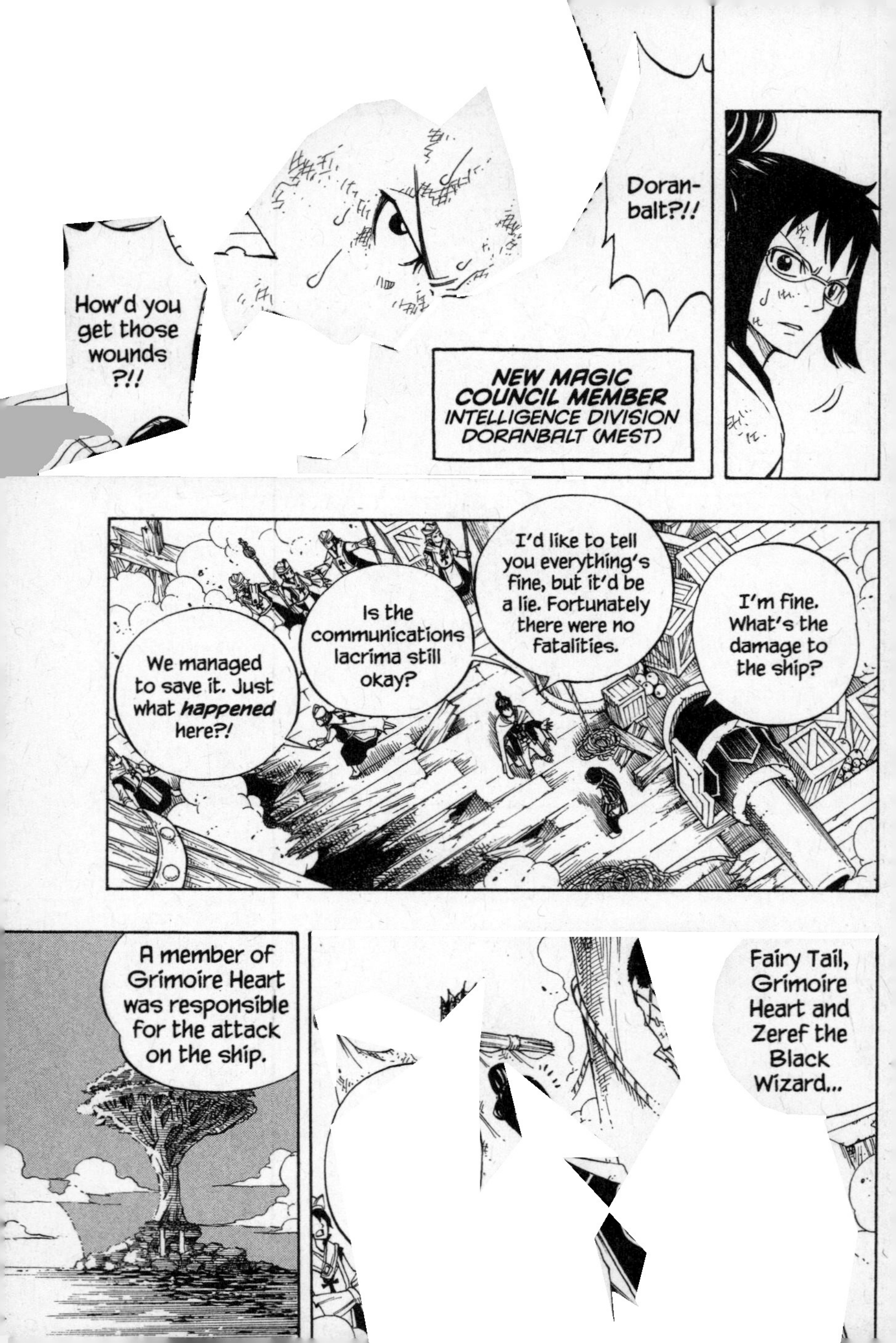

Doran-balt?!!
NEW MAGIC COUNCIL MEMBER INTELLIGENCE DIVISION DORANBALT (MEST)
How'd you get those wounds ?!!
I'm fine. What's the damage to the ship?
I'd like to tell you everything's fine, but it'd be a lie. Fortunately there were no fatalities.
Is the communications lacrima still okay?
We managed to save it. Just what *happened* here?!
Fairy Tail, Grimoire Heart and Zeref the Black Wizard...
A member of Grimoire Heart was responsible for the attack on the ship.

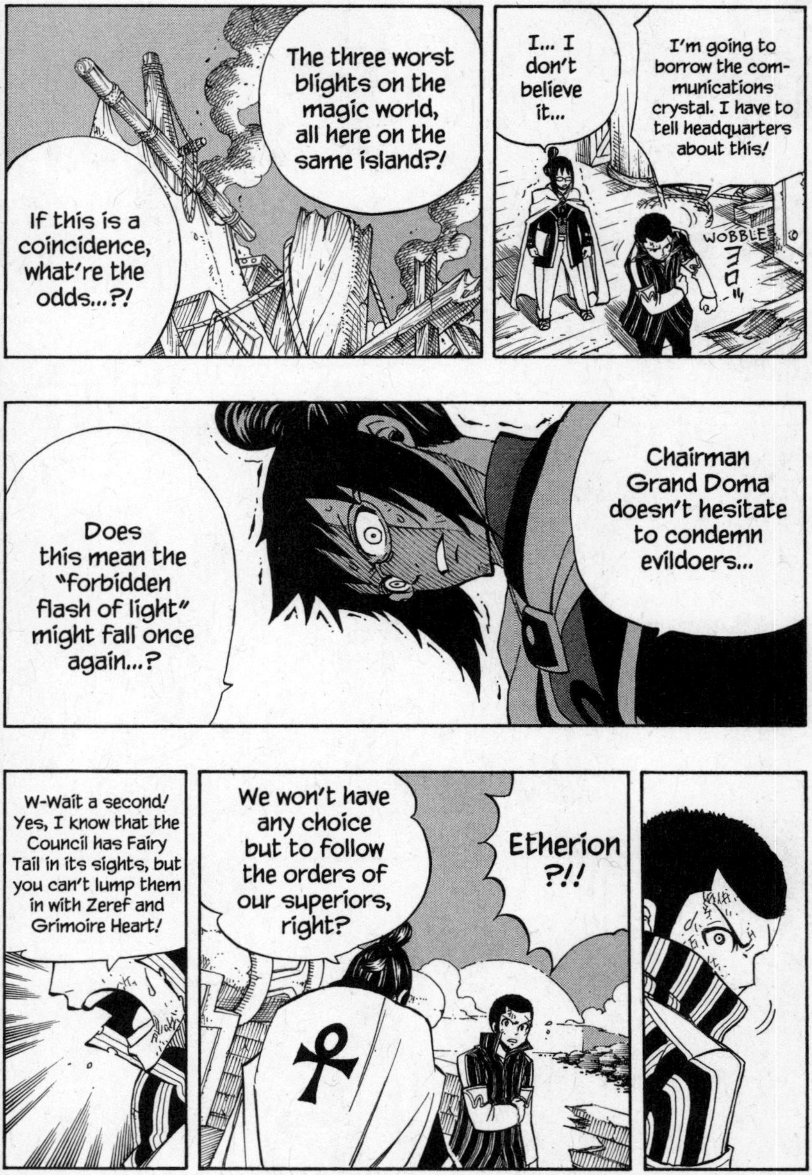
I'm going to borrow the communications crystal. I have to tell headquarters about this!
I... I don't believe it...
WOBBLE
The three worst blights on the magic world, all here on the same island?!
If this is a coincidence, what're the odds...?!
Chairman Grand Doma doesn't hesitate to condemn evildoers...
Does this mean the "forbidden flash of light" might fall once again...?
Etherion ?!!
We won't have any choice but to follow the orders of our superiors, right?
W-Wait a second! Yes, I know that the Council has Fairy Tail in its sights, but you can't lump them in with Zeref and Grimoire Heart!

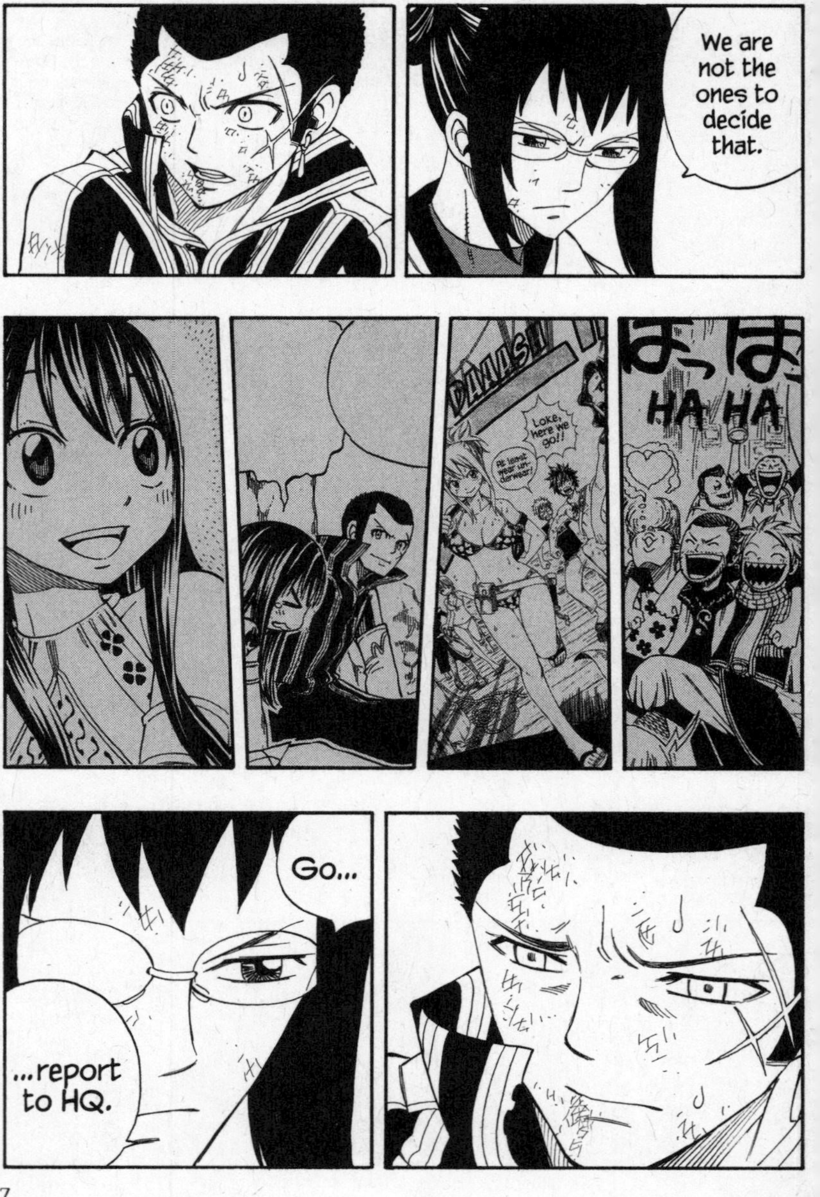
We are not the ones to decide that.
はっは
HA HA
Loke, here we go!!
At least wear underwear!
Go...
...report to HQ.

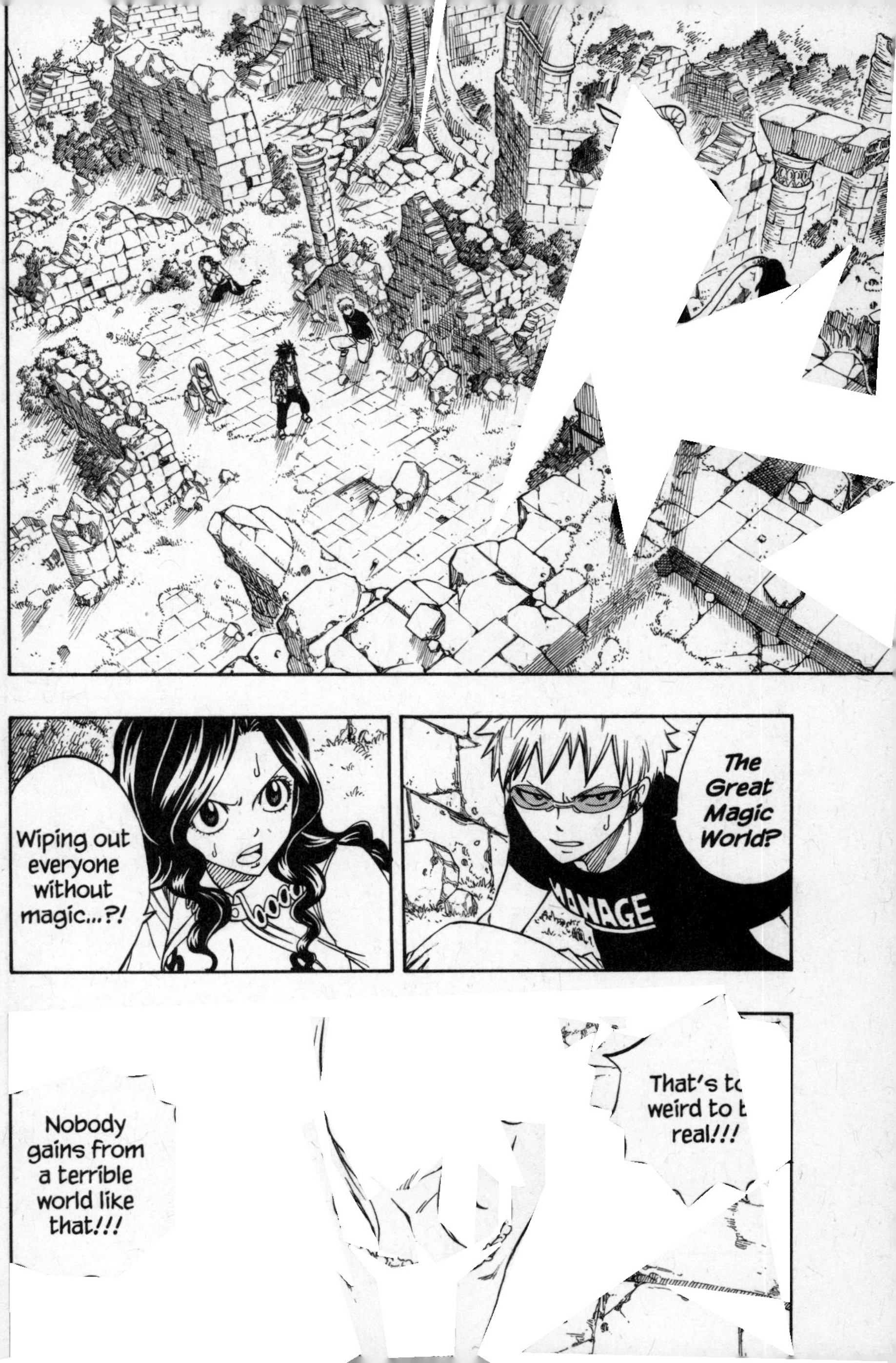
The Great Magic World?
Wiping out everyone without magic...?!
That's to weird to b real!!!
Nobody gains from a terrible world like that!!!

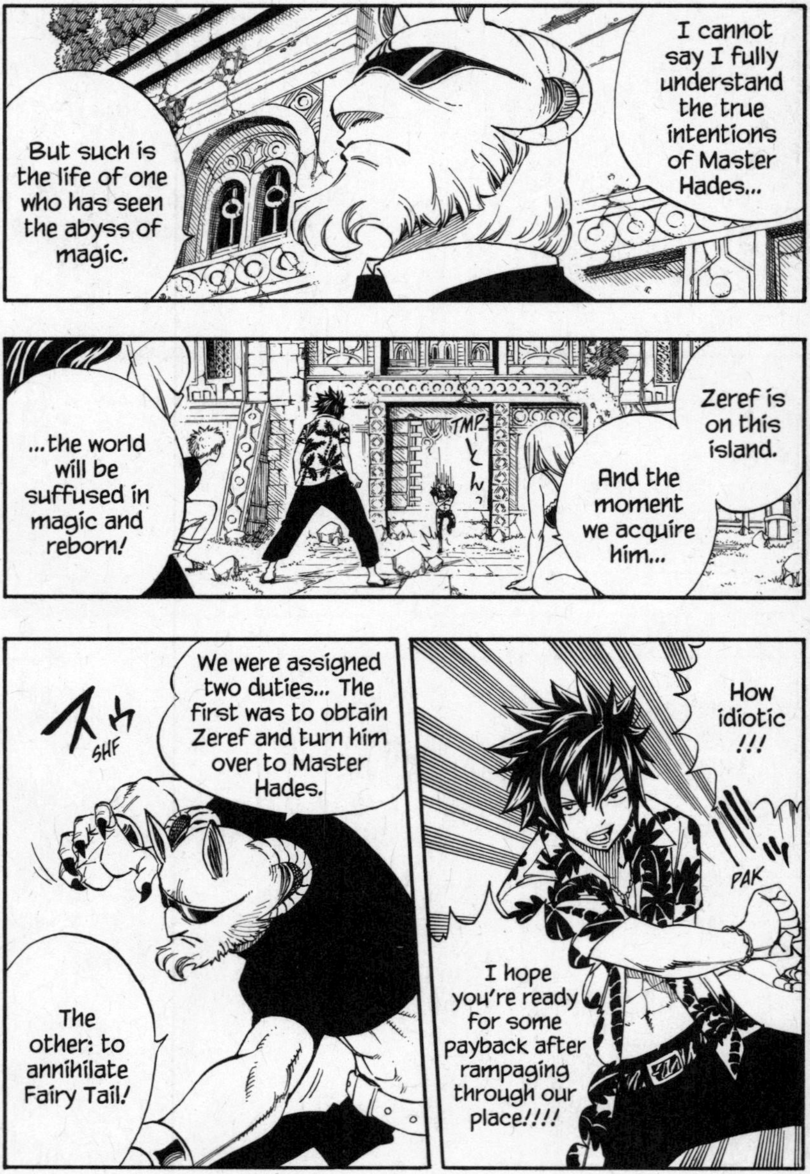
I cannot say I fully understand the true intentions of Master Hades...
But such is the life of one who has seen the abyss of magic.
Zeref is on this island.
And the moment we acquire him...
TMP
...the world will be suffused in magic and reborn!
How idiotic!!!
PAK
I hope you're ready for some payback after rampaging through our place!!!!
We were assigned two duties... The first was to obtain Zeref and turn him over to Master Hades.
SHF
The other: to annihilate Fairy Tail!

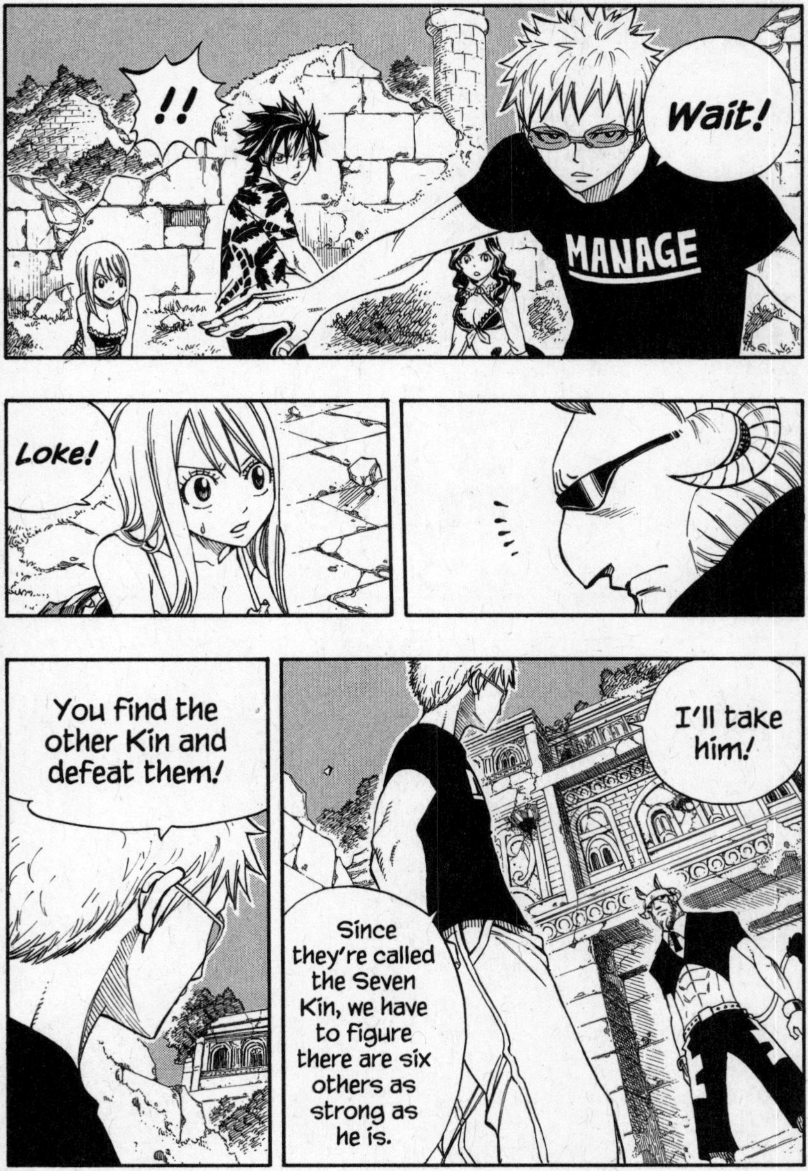
Wait!
!!
Loke!
I'll take him!
Since they're called the Seven Kin, we have to figure there are six others as strong as he is.
You find the other Kin and defeat them!

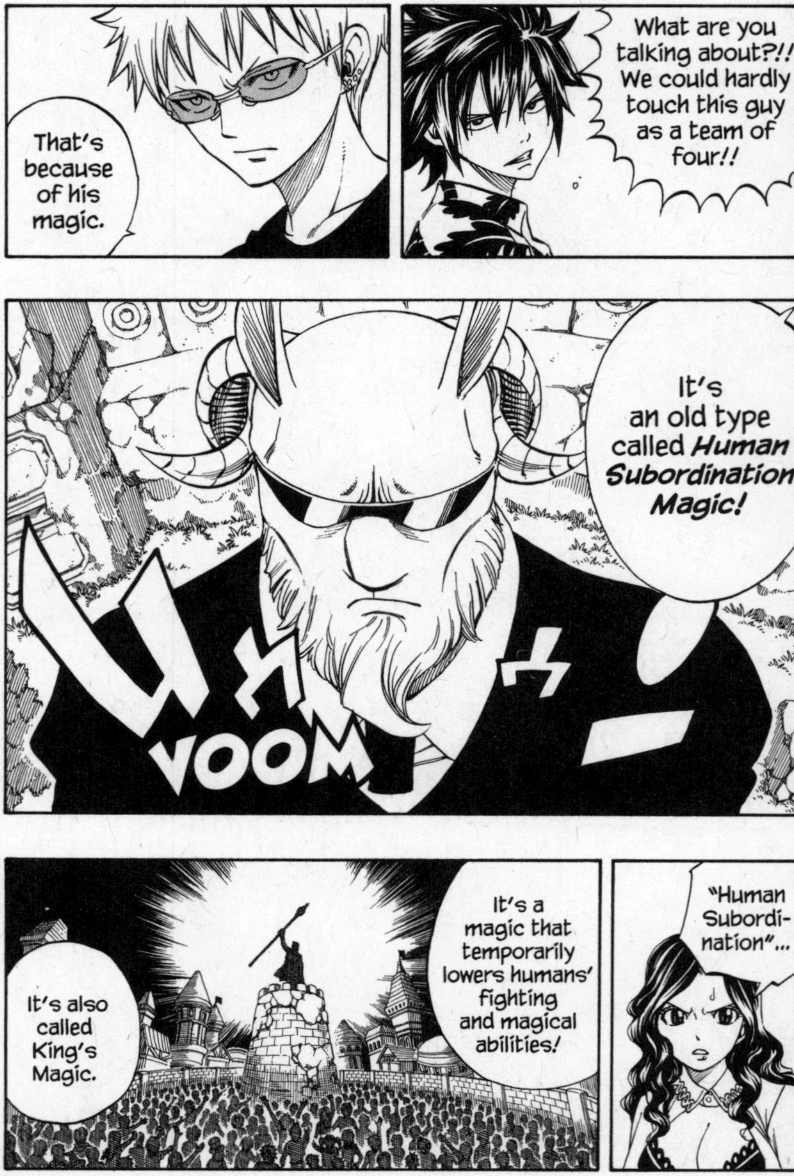
What are you talking about?!! We could hardly touch this guy as a team of four!!
That's because of his magic.
It's an old type called *Human Subordination Magic!*
VOOM
"Human Subordi-nation"...
It's a magic that temporarily lowers humans' fighting and magical abilities!
It's also called King's Magic.

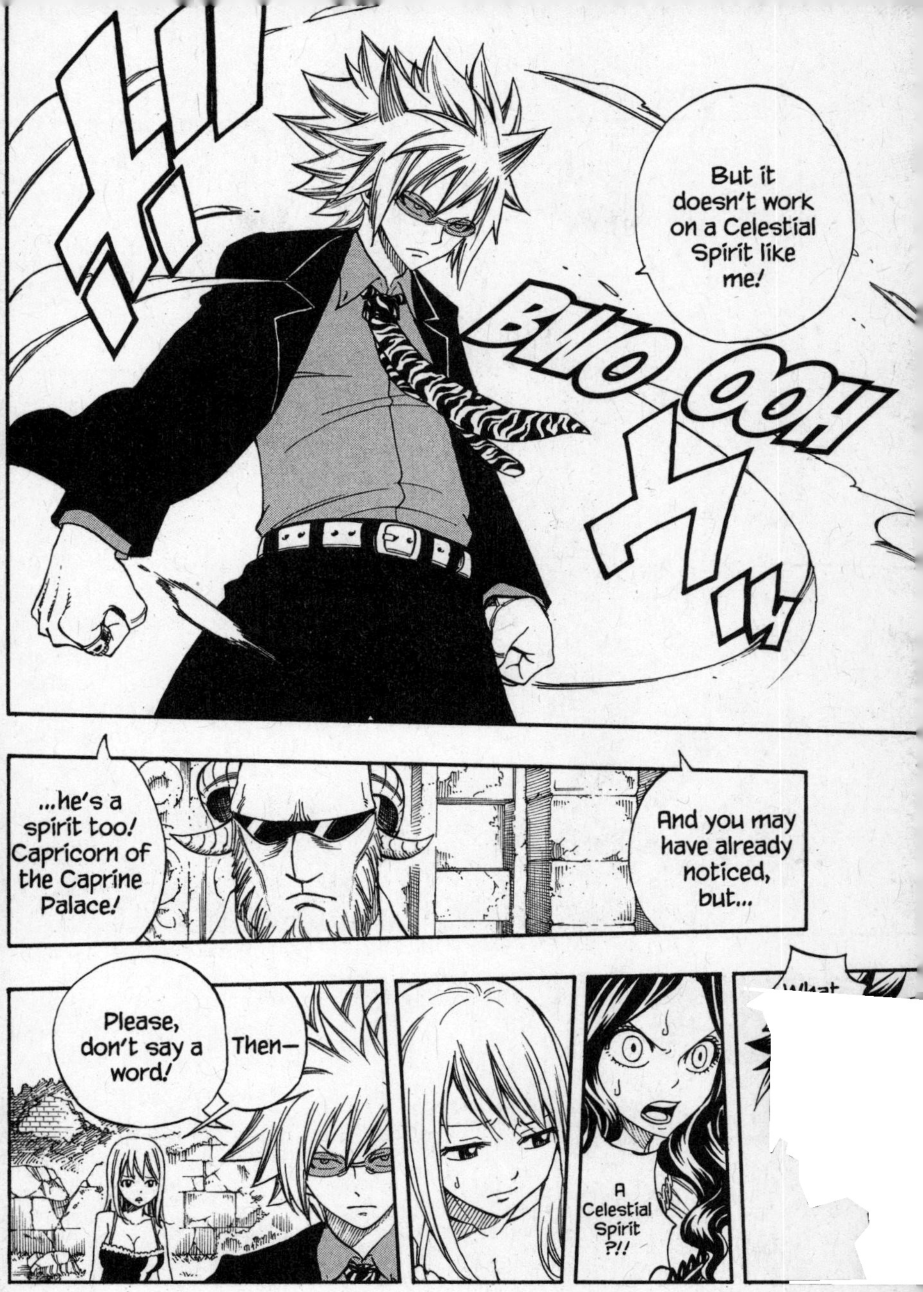
But it doesn't work on a Celestial Spirit like me!
BWOOOOH
And you may have already noticed, but...
...he's a spirit too! Capricorn of the Caprine Palace!
A Celestial Spirit ?!!
Then—
Please, don't say a word!

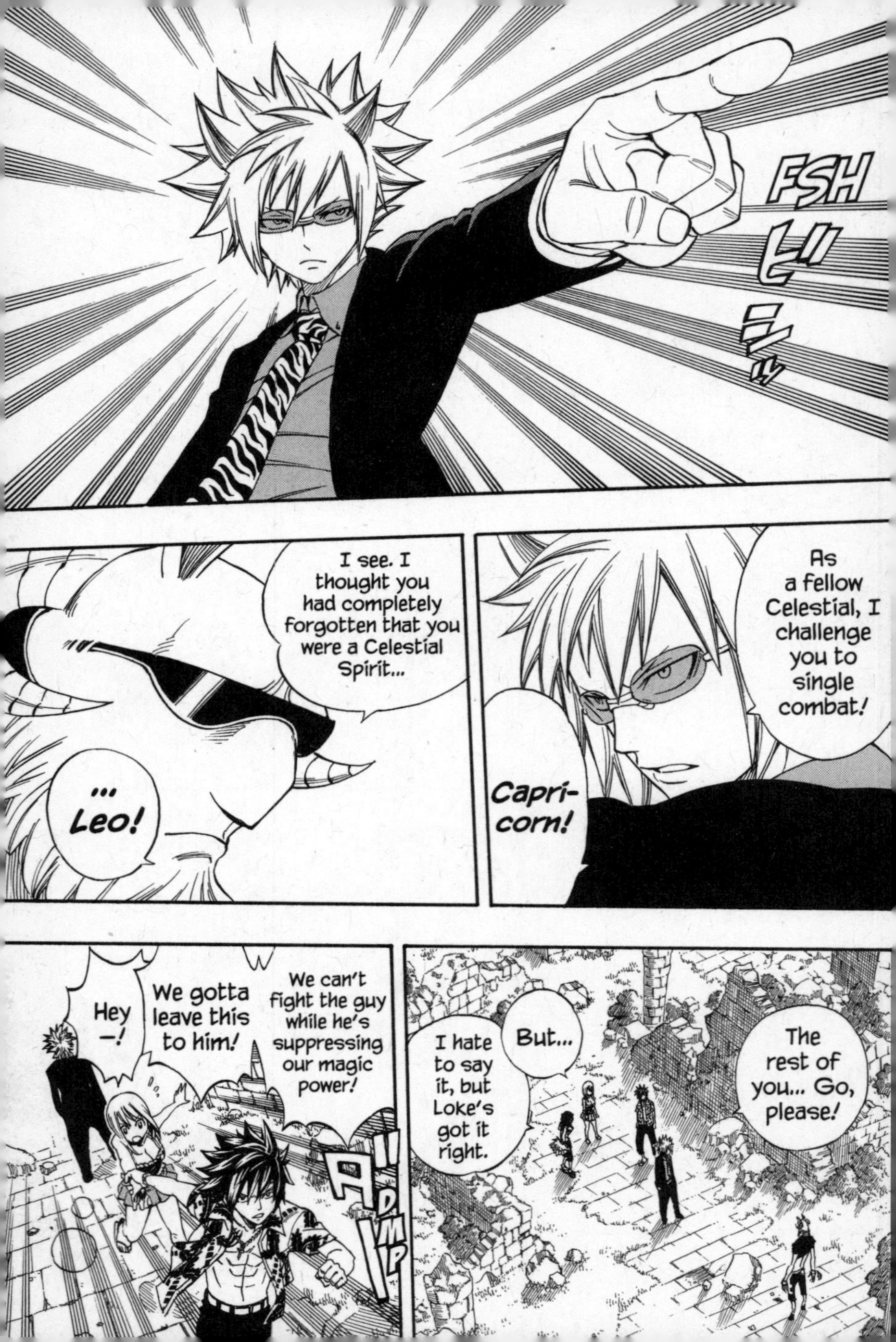
FSH
As a fellow Celestial, I challenge you to single combat!
Capri-corn!
I see. I thought you had completely forgotten that you were a Celestial Spirit...
...Leo!
The rest of you... Go, please!
But...
I hate to say it, but Loke's got it right.
We can't fight the guy while he's suppressing our magic power!
ADMP
We gotta leave this to him!
Hey—!

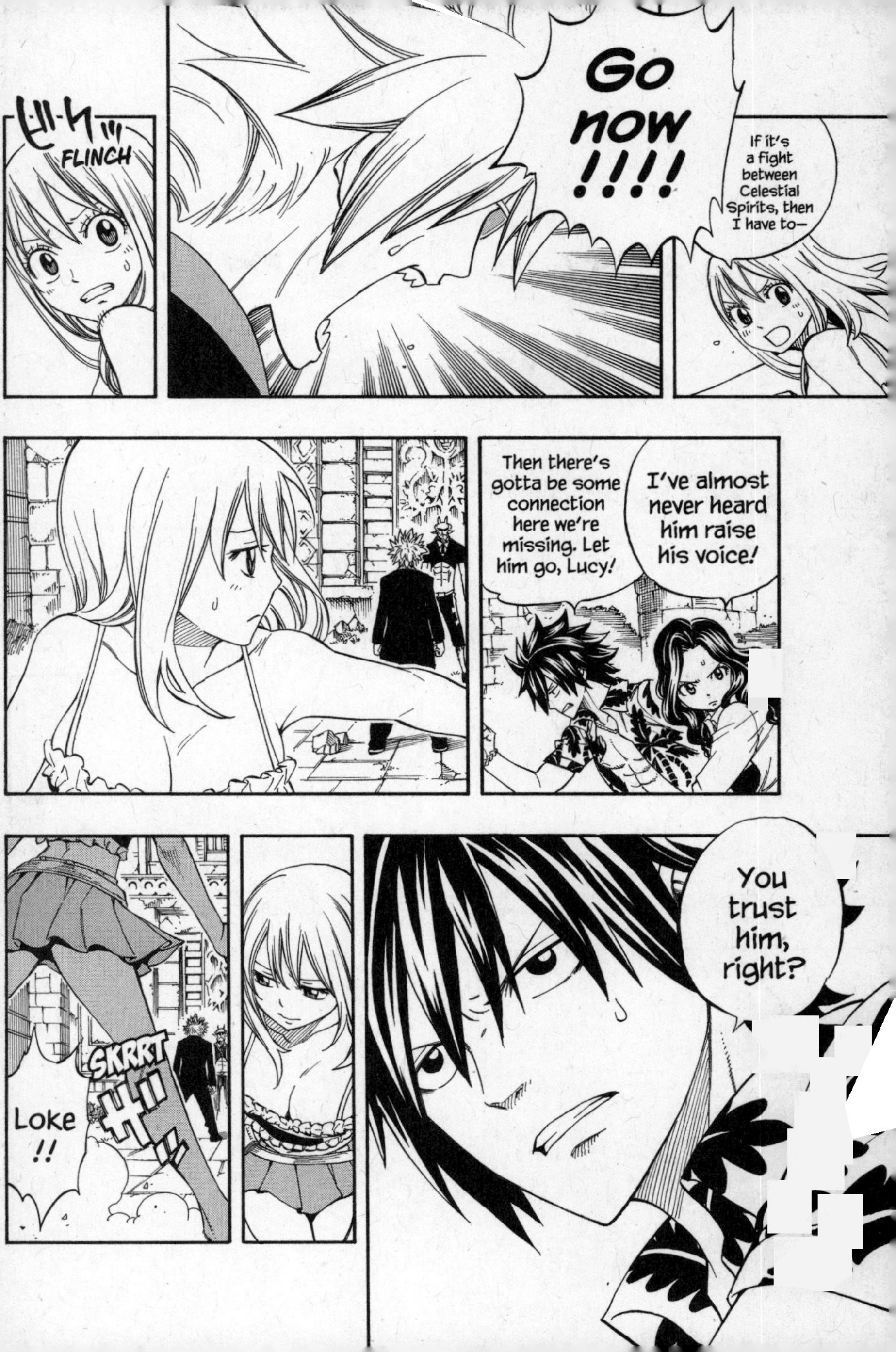
If it's a fight between Celestial Spirits, then I have to—
Go now!!!!
FLINCH
I've almost never heard him raise his voice!
Then there's gotta be some connection here we're missing. Let him go, Lucy!
You trust him, right?
SKRRT
Loke!!

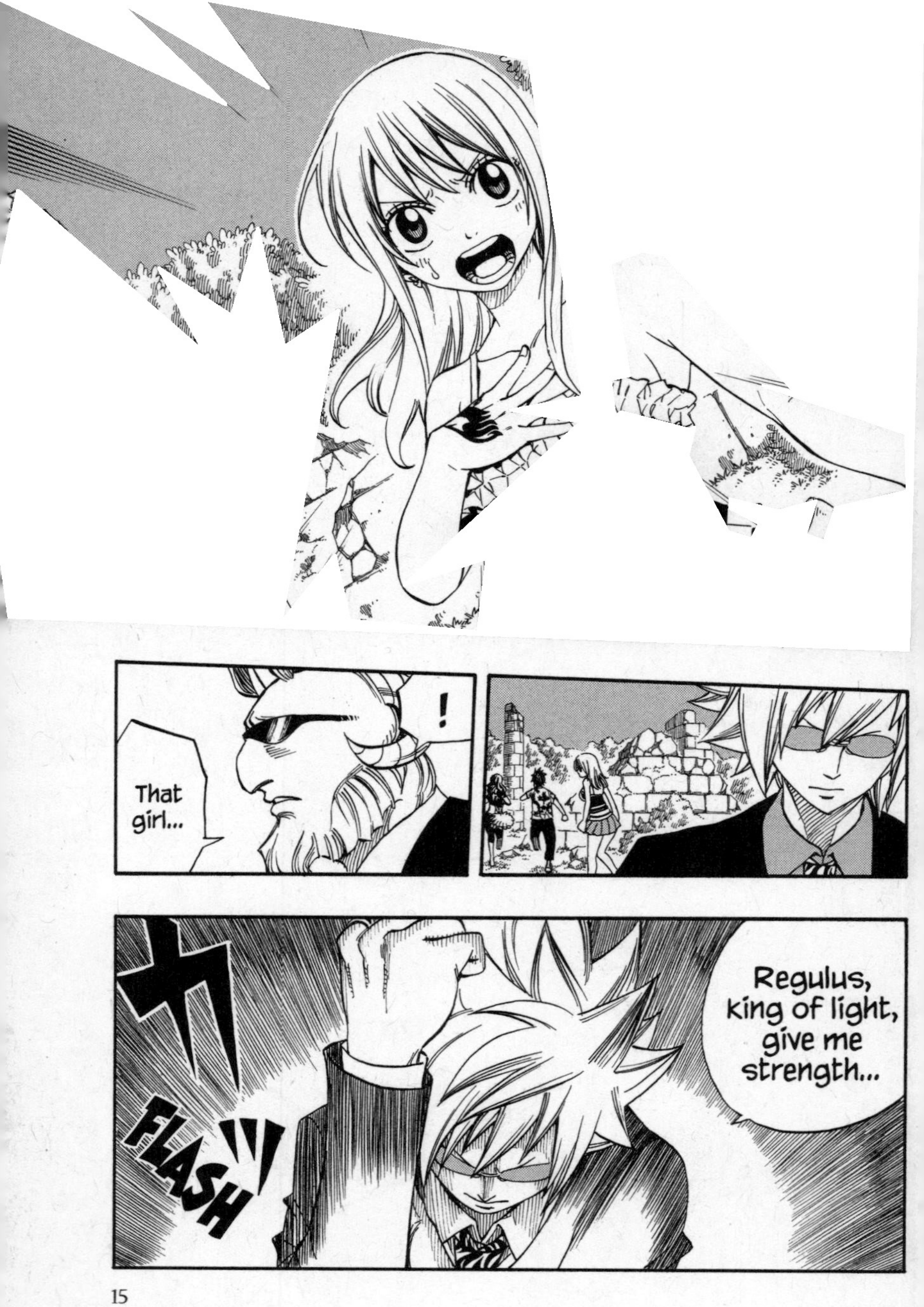
!
That girl...
Regulus, king of light, give me strength...
FLASH

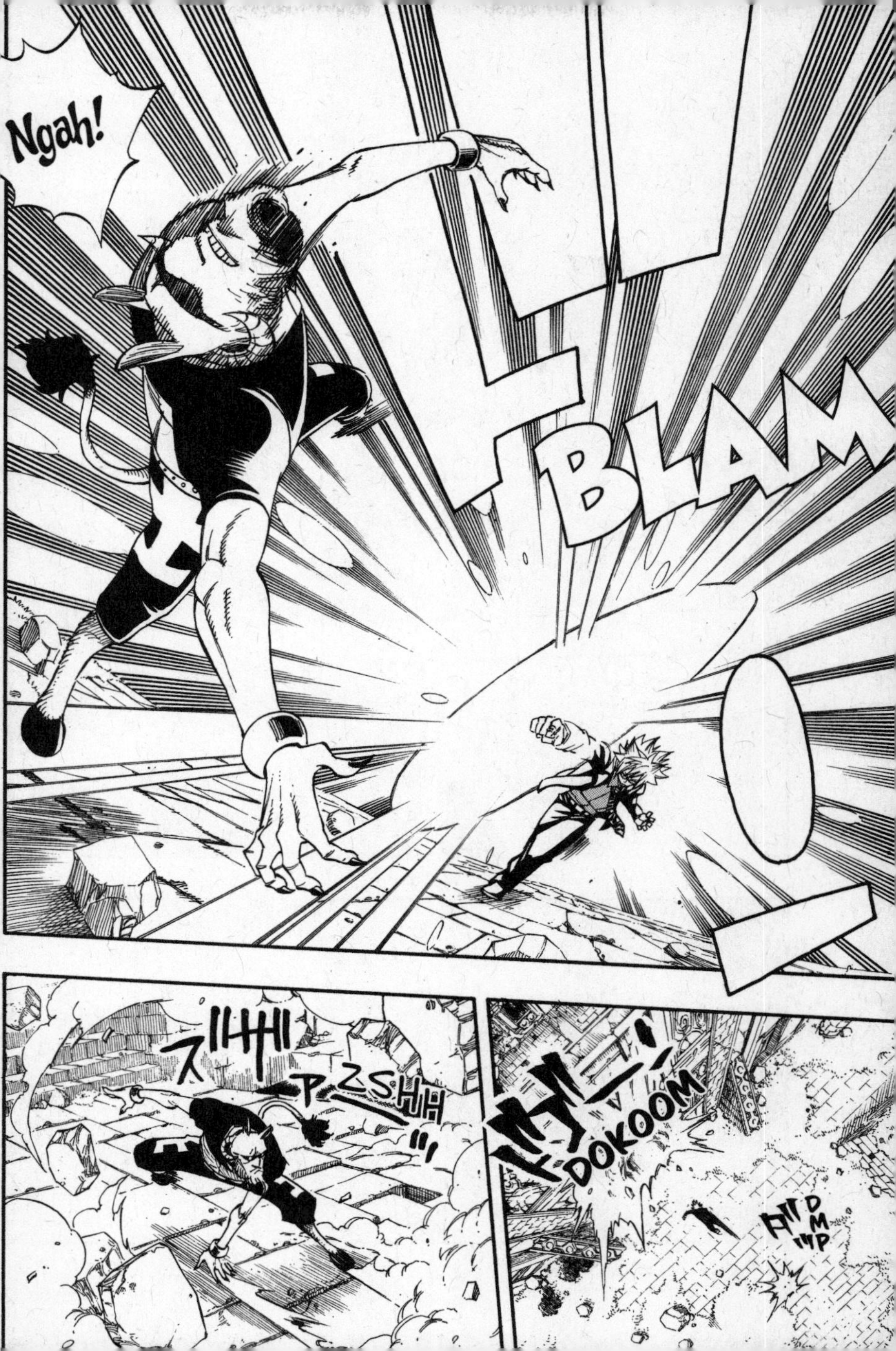
Ngah!
BLAM
DOKOOM
DMP
PZSHH

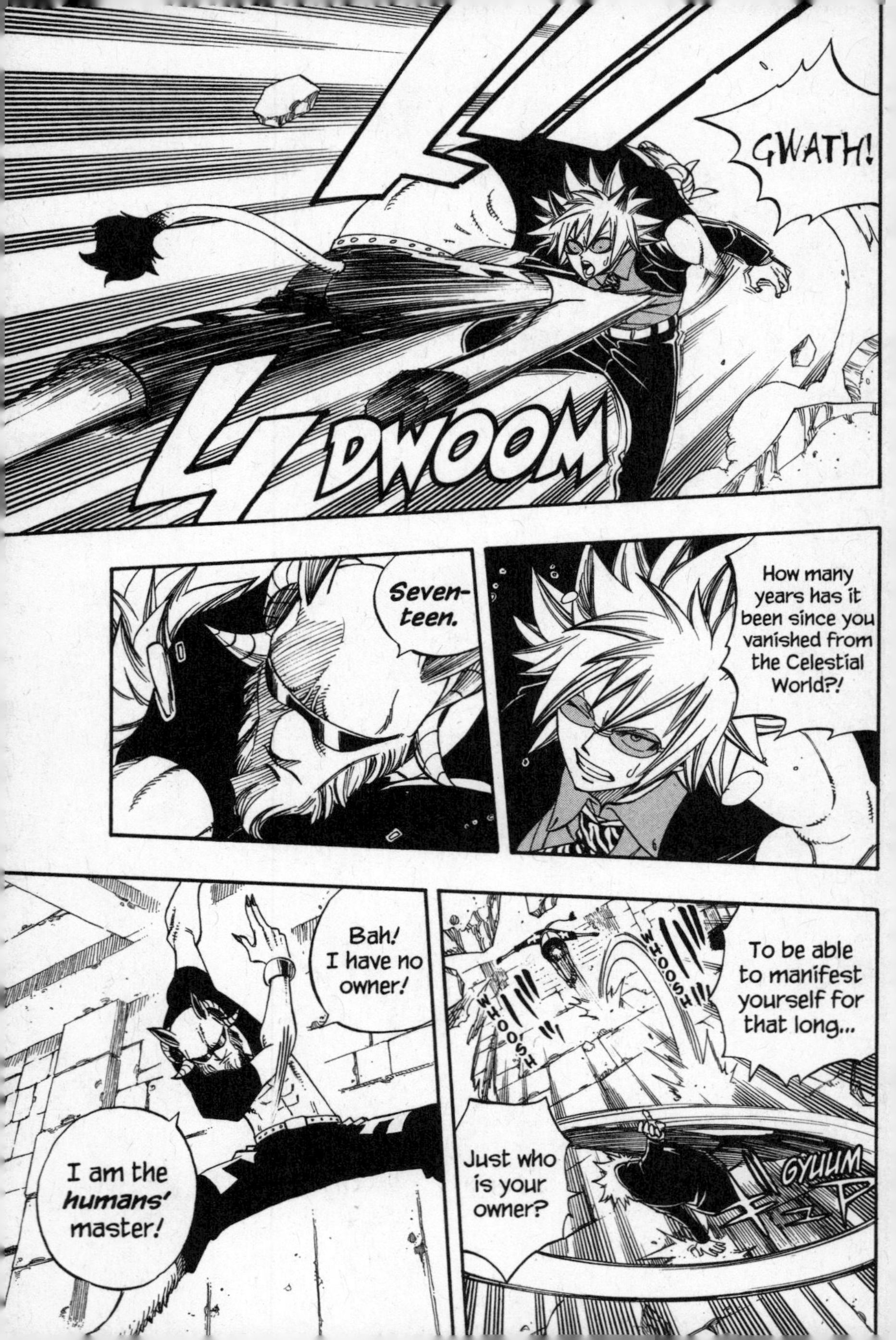
GWATH!
DWOOM
How many years has it been since you vanished from the Celestial World?!
Seventeen.
To be able to manifest yourself for that long...
WHOOSH
WHOOSH
Just who is your owner?
GYUUM
Bah! I have no owner!
I am the *humans'* master!

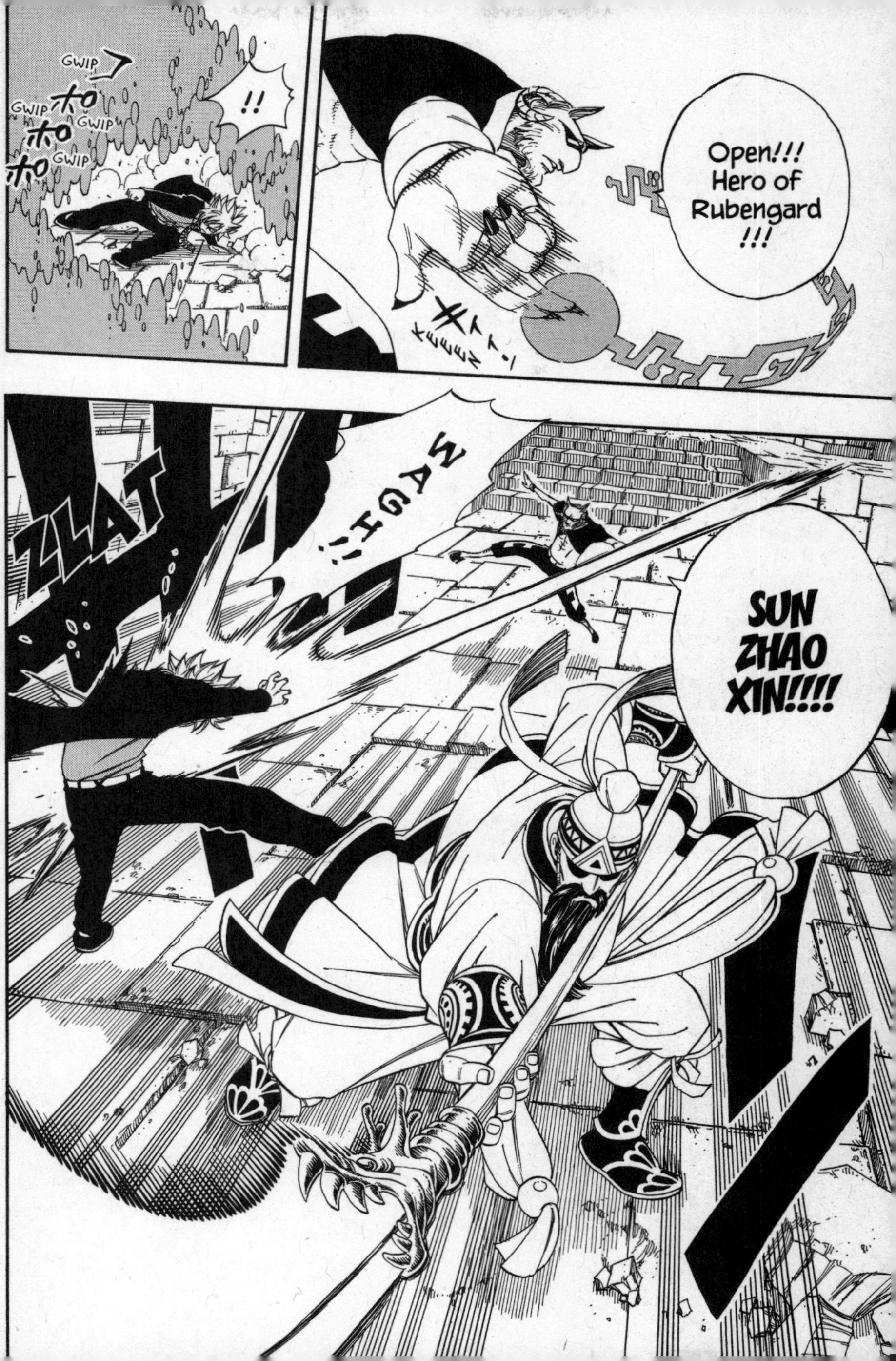
Open!!! Hero of Rubengard!!!
!!
GWIP
GWIP
GWIP
GWIP
WAGH!!
ZLAT
SUN ZHAO XIN!!!!!

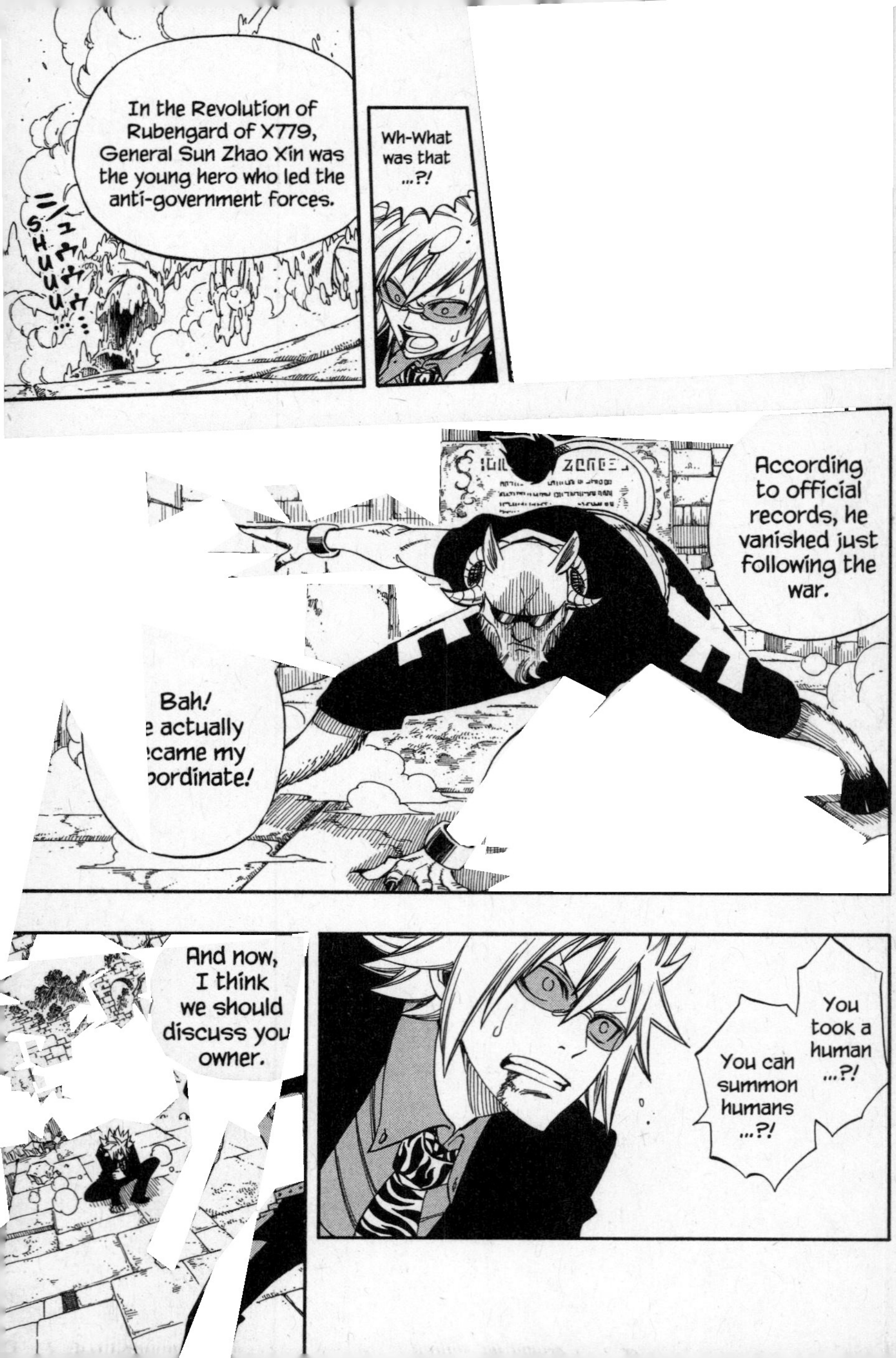
Wh-What was that ...?!
In the Revolution of Rubengard of X779, General Sun Zhao Xin was the young hero who led the anti-government forces.
SHUUUU...
According to official records, he vanished just following the war.
Bah!
e actually
ecame my
bordinate!
You took a human ...?!
You can summon humans ...?!
And now, I think we should discuss you owner.

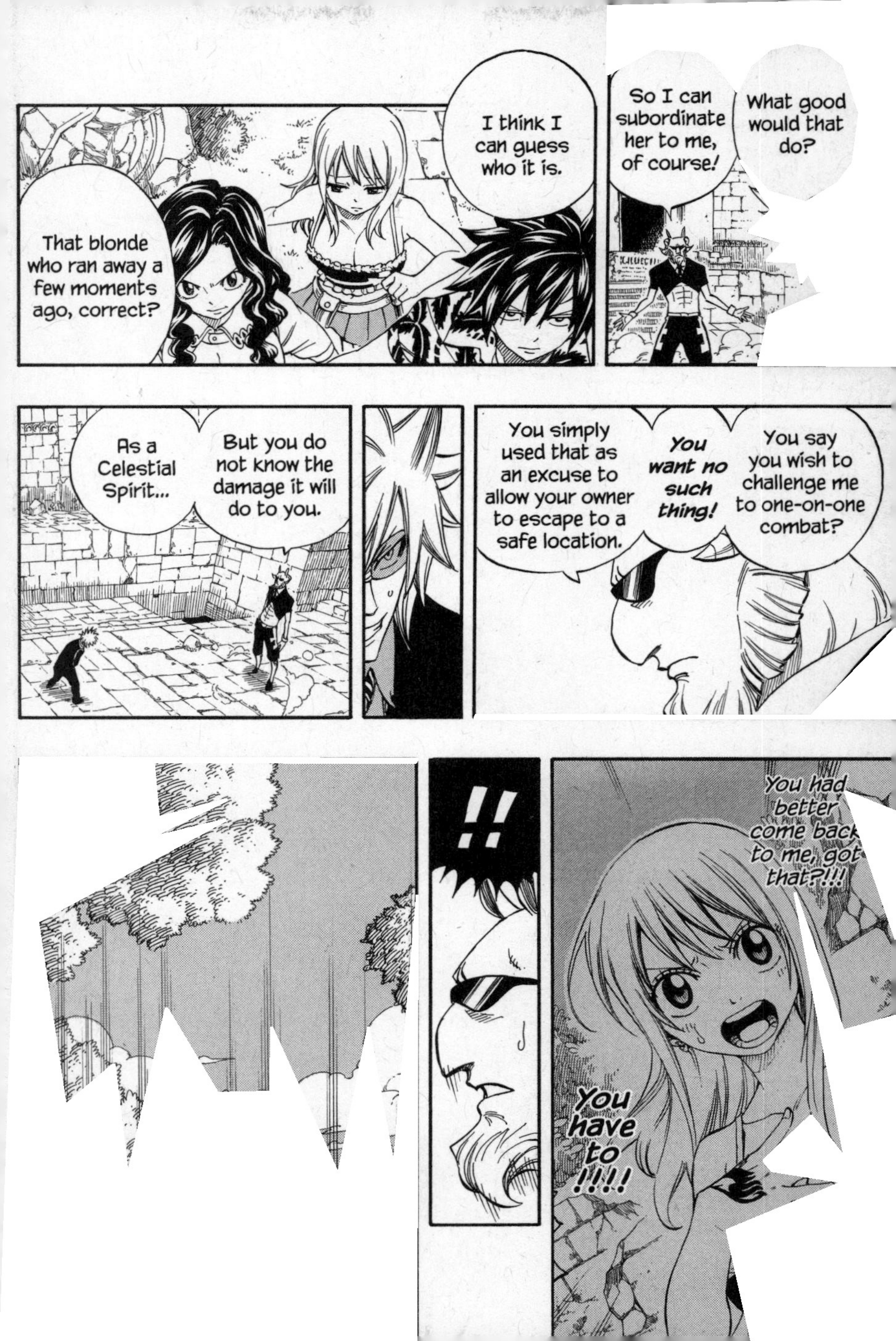
What good would that do?
So I can subordinate her to me, of course!
I think I can guess who it is.
That blonde who ran away a few moments ago, correct?
You say you wish to challenge me to one-on-one combat?
You want no such thing!
You simply used that as an excuse to allow your owner to escape to a safe location.
But you do not know the damage it will do to you.
As a Celestial Spirit...
You had better come back to me, got that?!!!
You have to !!!!
!!

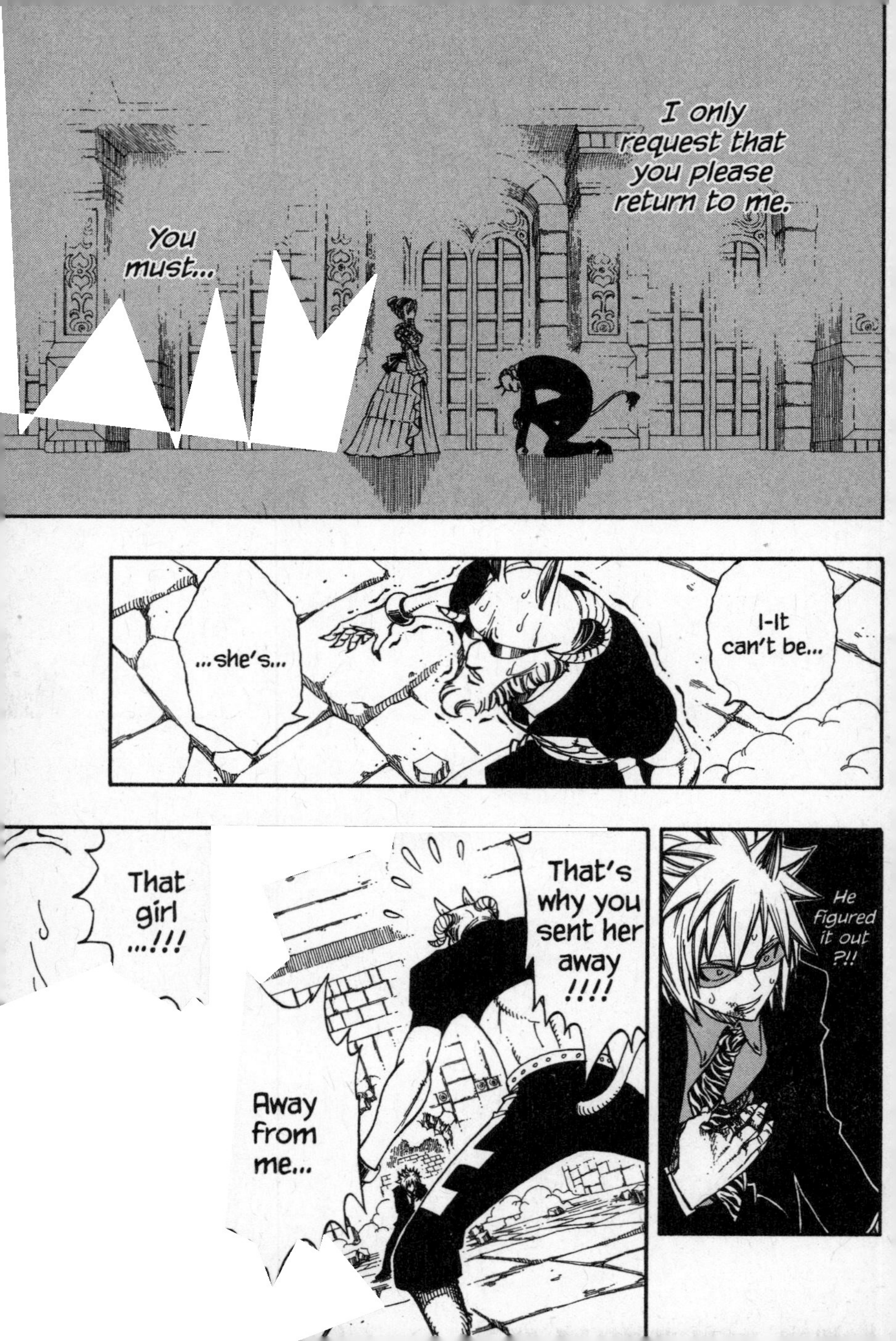
I only request that you please return to me.
You must...
I-It can't be...
...she's...
He figured it out?!!
That's why you sent her away!!!!
Away from me...
That girl...!!!

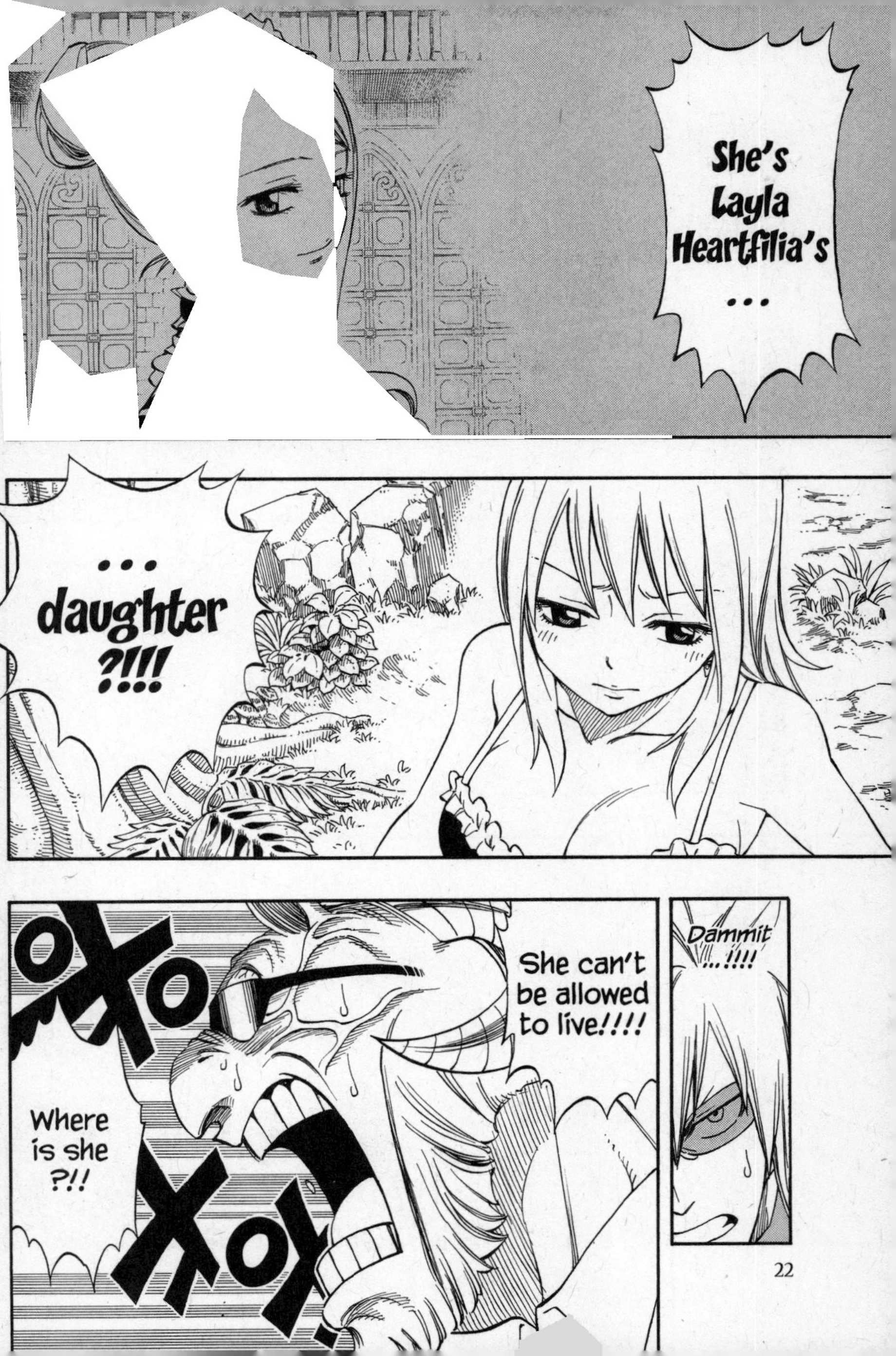
She's Layla Heartfilia's ...
... daughter ?!!!
Dammit ...!!!!
She can't be allowed to live!!!!
Where is she ?!!

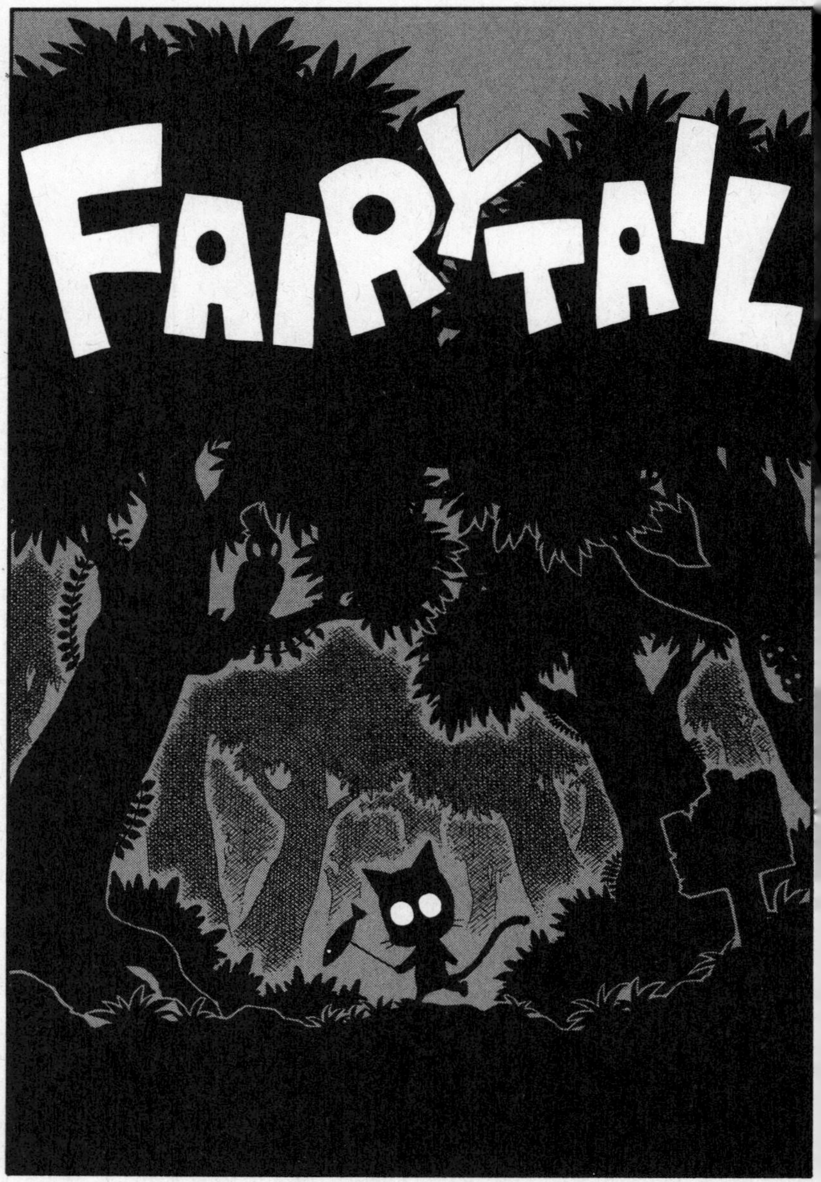
FAIRY TAIL

Chapter 224: The Ambition of Zoldio

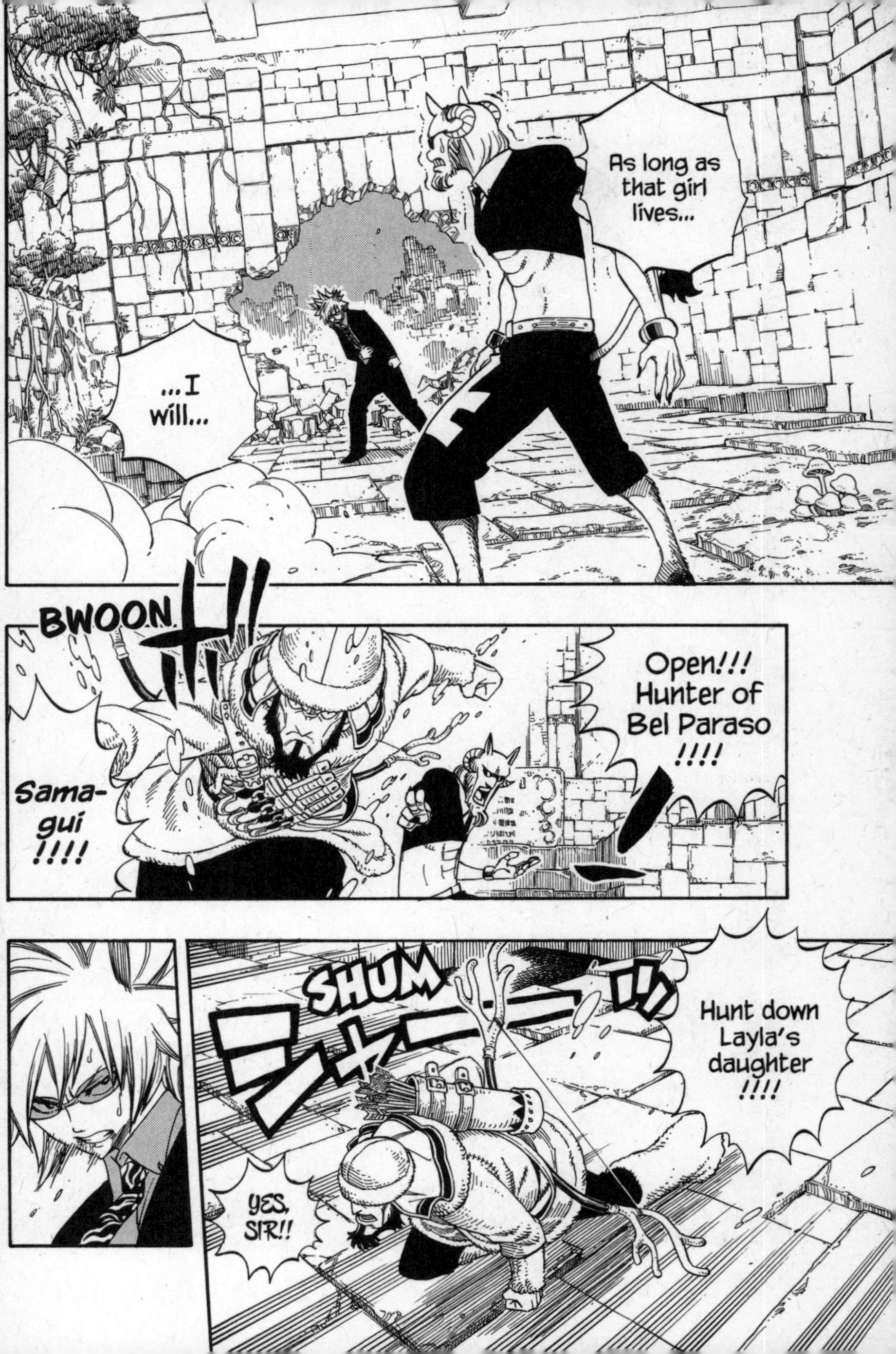
As long as that girl lives...
...I will...
Open!!! Hunter of Bel Paraso !!!!
BWOON
Sama-gui !!!!
Hunt down Layla's daughter !!!!
SHUM
YES, SIR!!

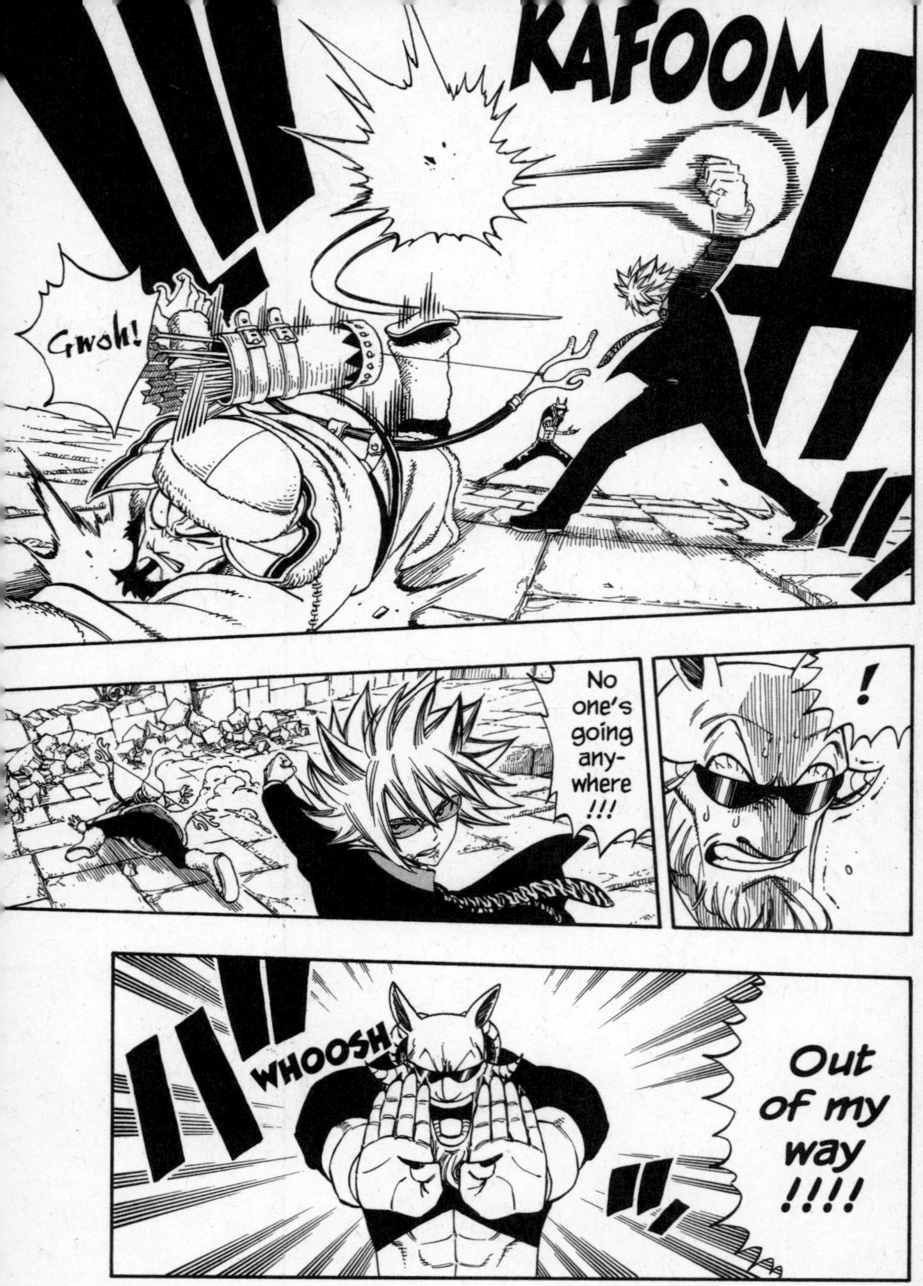
KAFOOM
Gwoh!
!
No one's going any-where !!!
WHOOSH
Out of my way !!!!

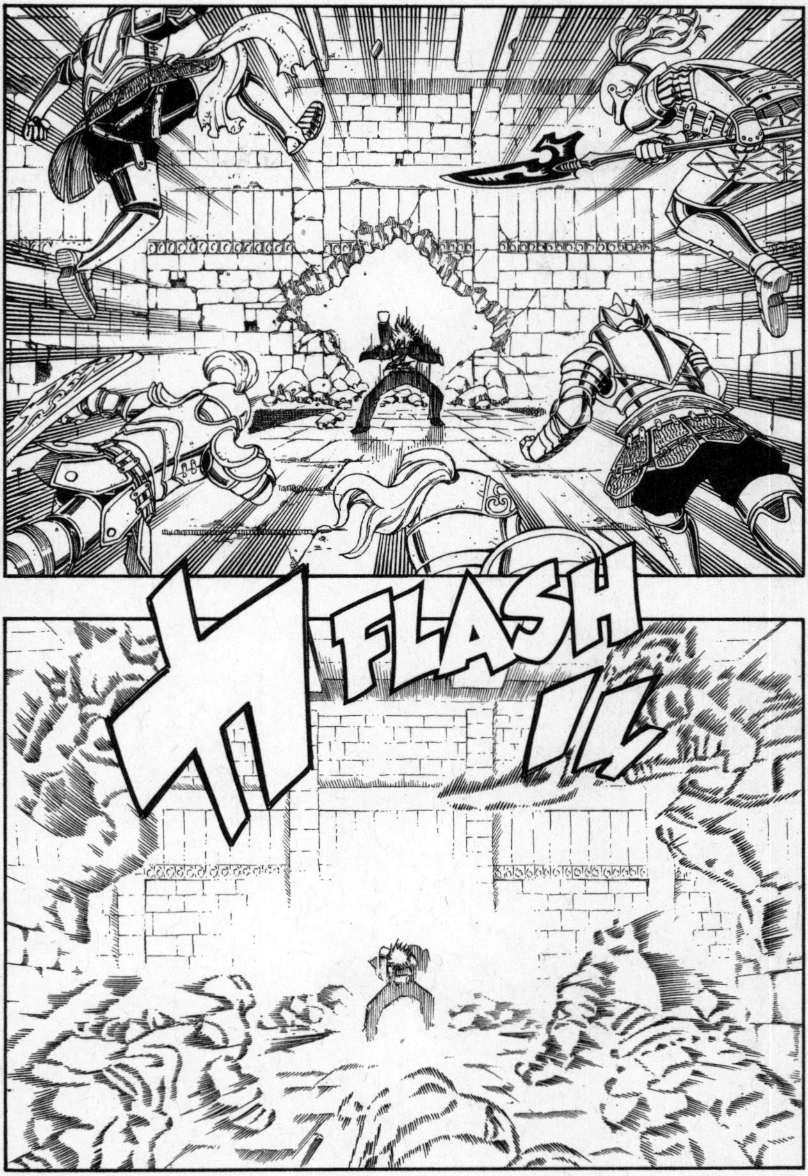
FLASH

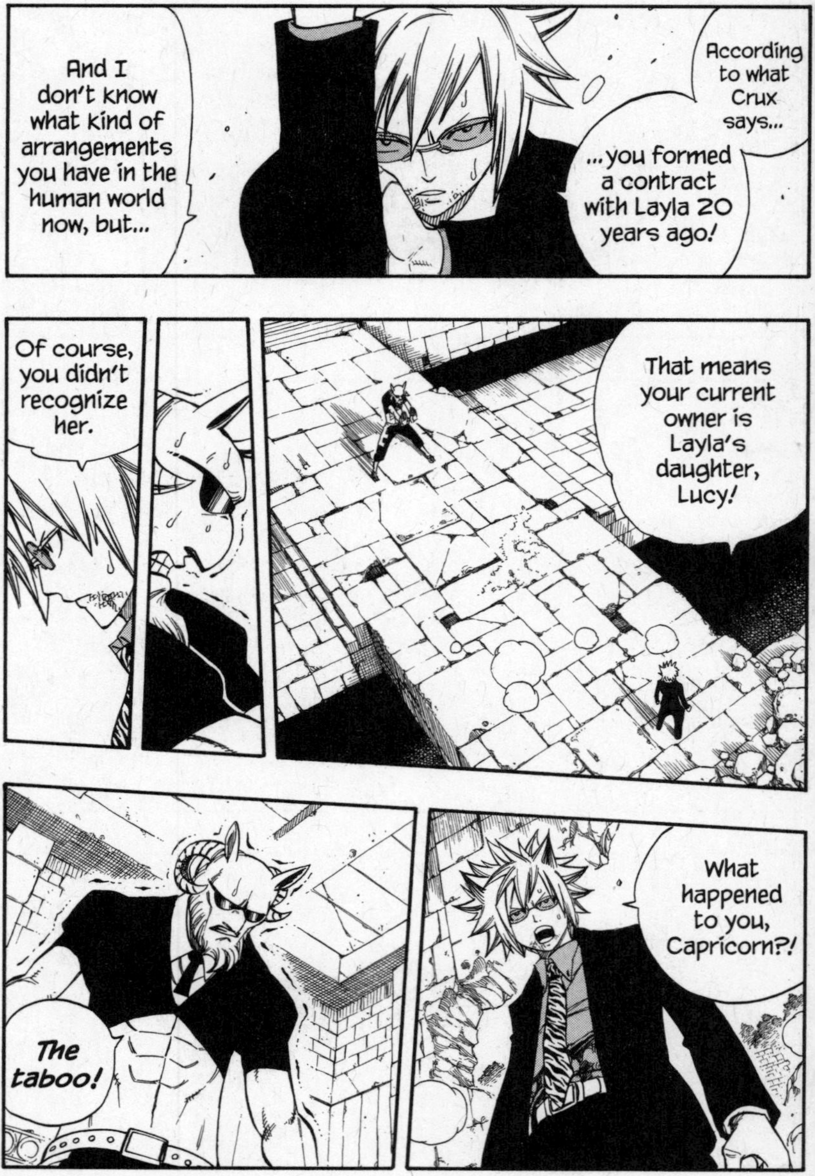
According to what Crux says...
...you formed a contract with Layla 20 years ago!
And I don't know what kind of arrangements you have in the human world now, but...
That means your current owner is Layla's daughter, Lucy!
Of course, you didn't recognize her.
What happened to you, Capricorn?!
The taboo!

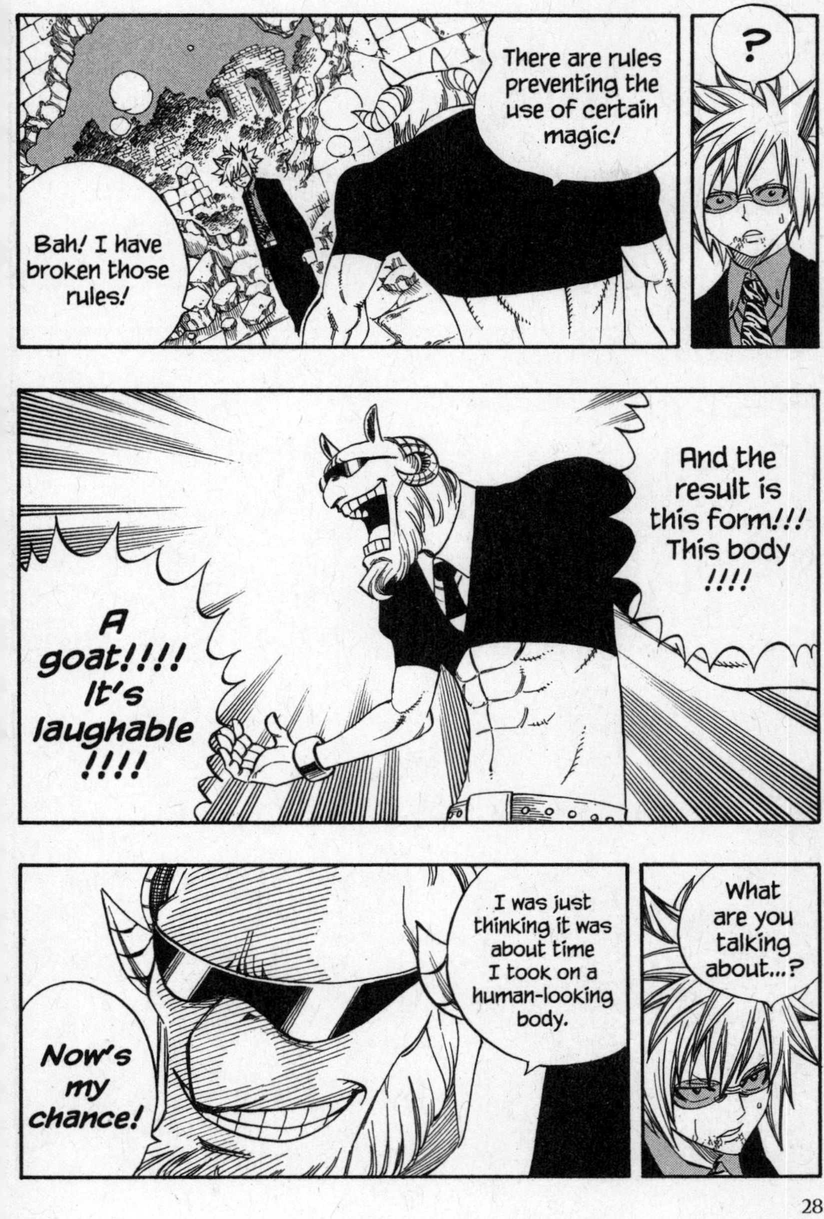
?
There are rules preventing the use of certain magic!
Bah! I have broken those rules!
And the result is this form!!! This body !!!!
A goat!!!! It's laughable !!!!
What are you talking about...?
I was just thinking it was about time I took on a human-looking body.
Now's my chance!

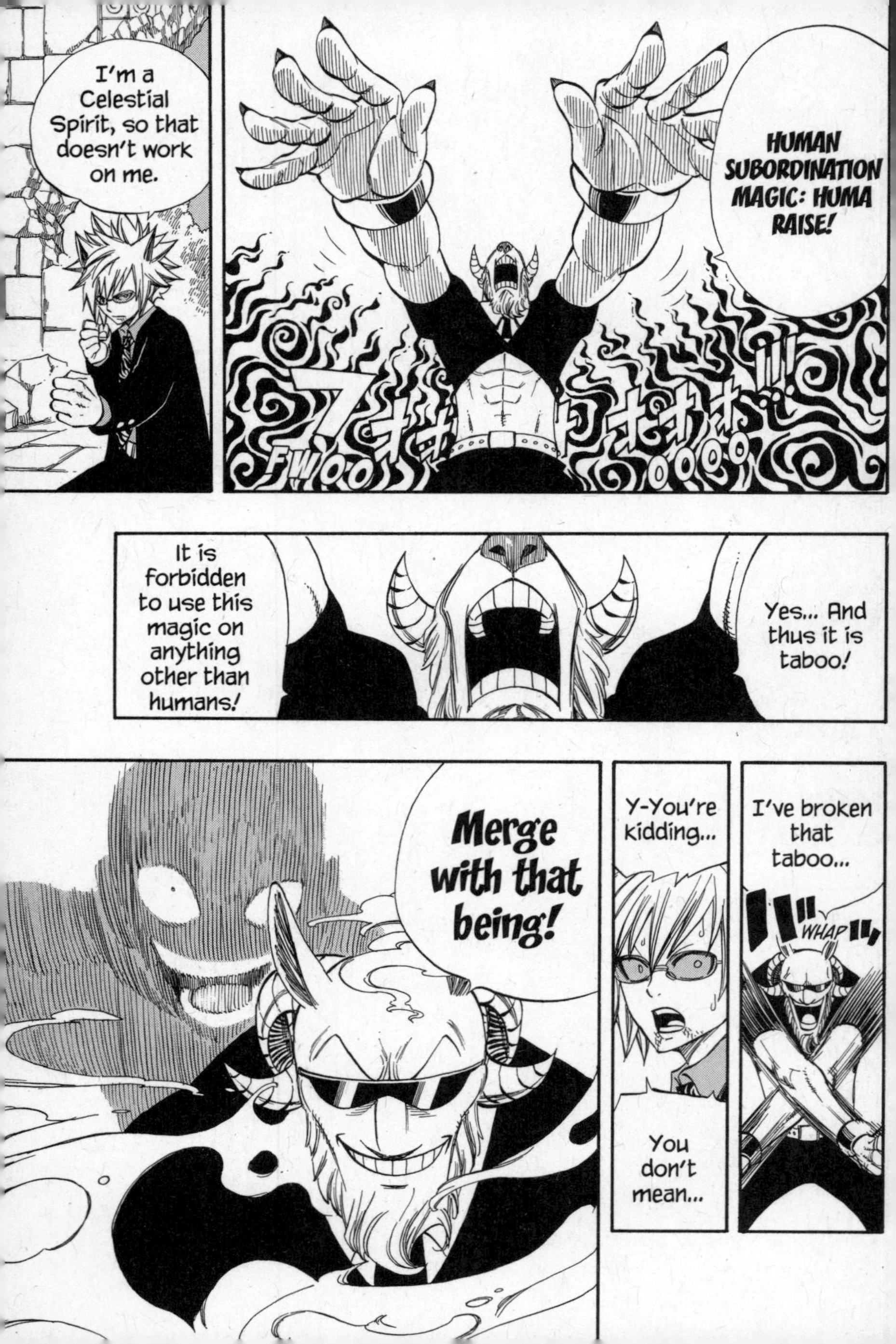
HUMAN SUBORDINATION MAGIC: HUMA RAISE!
FWOOOOOOO
I'm a Celestial Spirit, so that doesn't work on me.
Yes... And thus it is taboo!
It is forbidden to use this magic on anything other than humans!
I've broken that taboo...
WHAP
Y-You're kidding...
You don't mean...
Merge with that being!

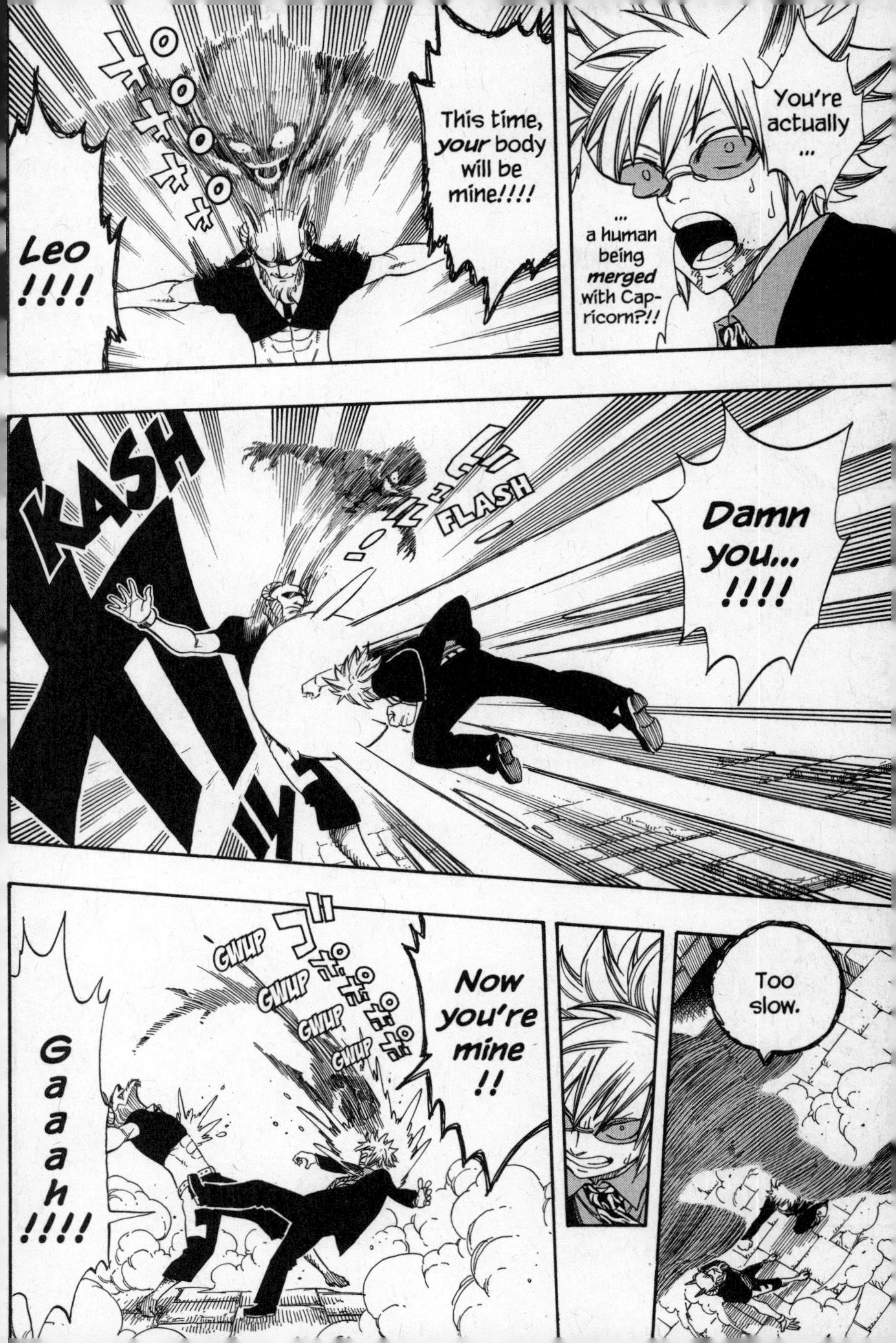
You're actually ...
... a human being merged with Capricorn?!!
This time, your body will be mine!!!!
Leo !!!!
Damn you... !!!!
FLASH
KASH
Too slow.
Now you're mine !!
GWUP
GWUP
GWUP
GWUP
Gaaah!!!!

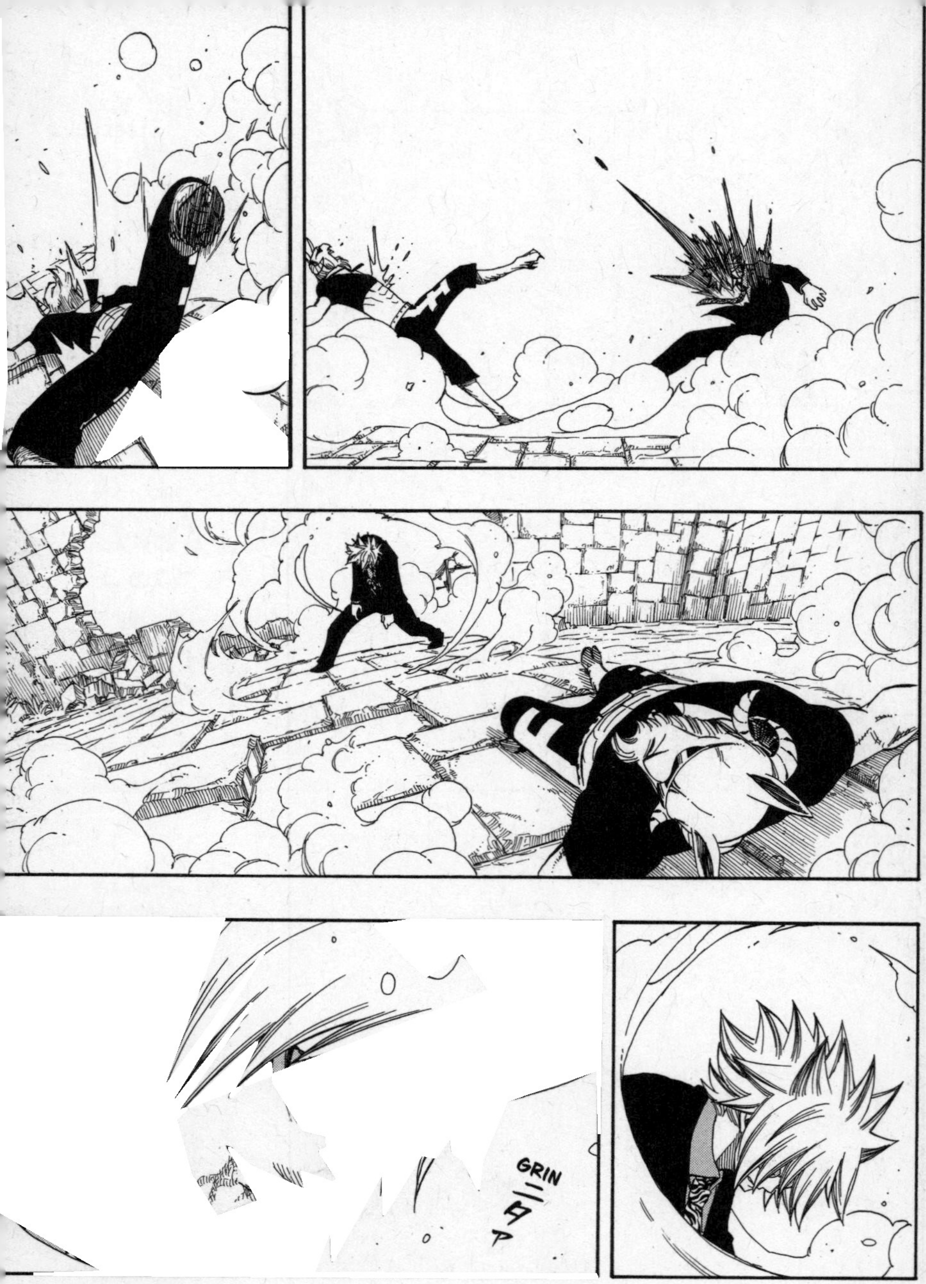
GRIN
ニタァ

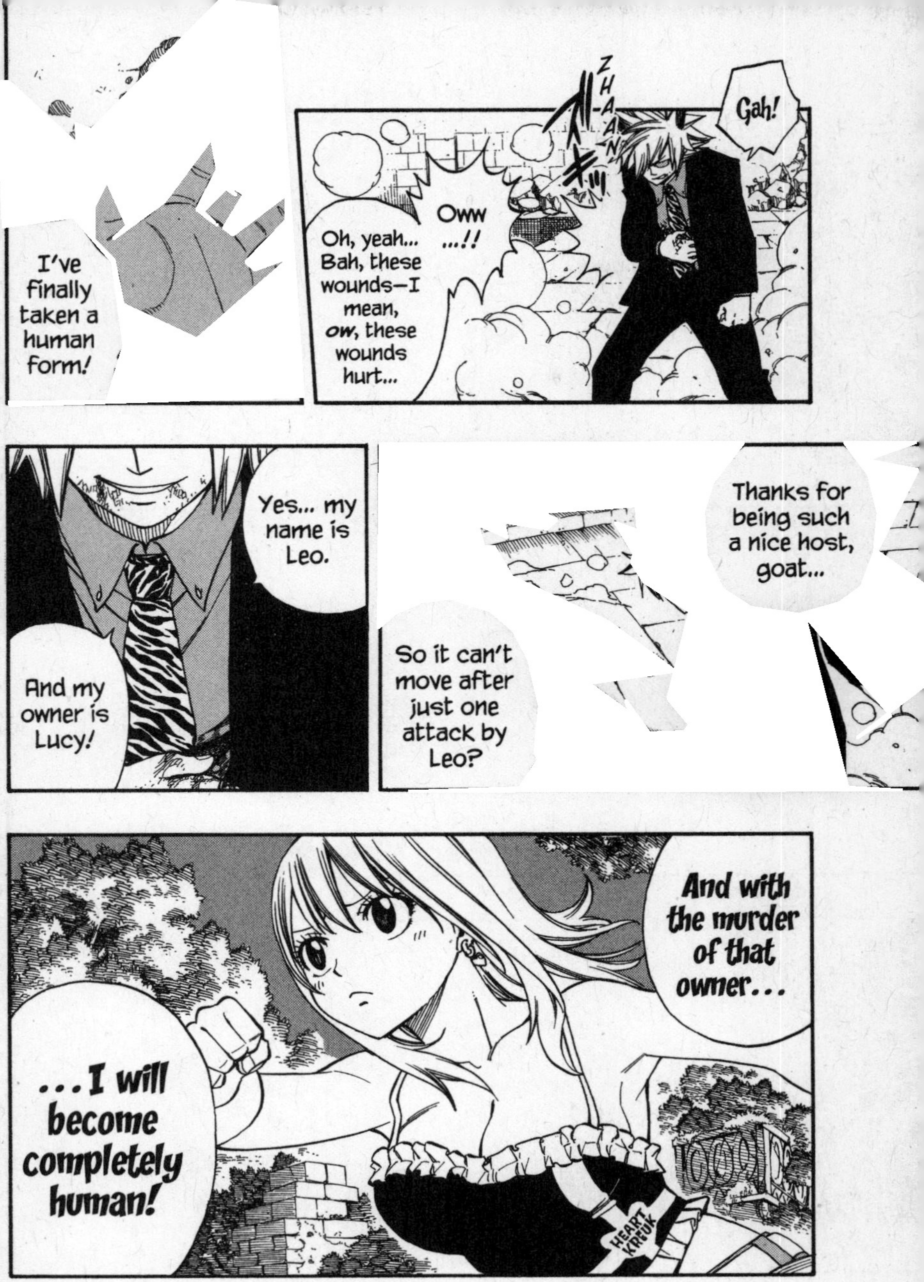
Gah!
ZHAAAN
Oww ...!!
Oh, yeah... Bah, these wounds—I mean, *ow*, these wounds hurt...
I've finally taken a human form!
Thanks for being such a nice host, goat...
So it can't move after just one attack by Leo?
Yes... my name is Leo.
And my owner is Lucy!
And with the murder of that owner...
...I will become completely human!
HEART KREUK

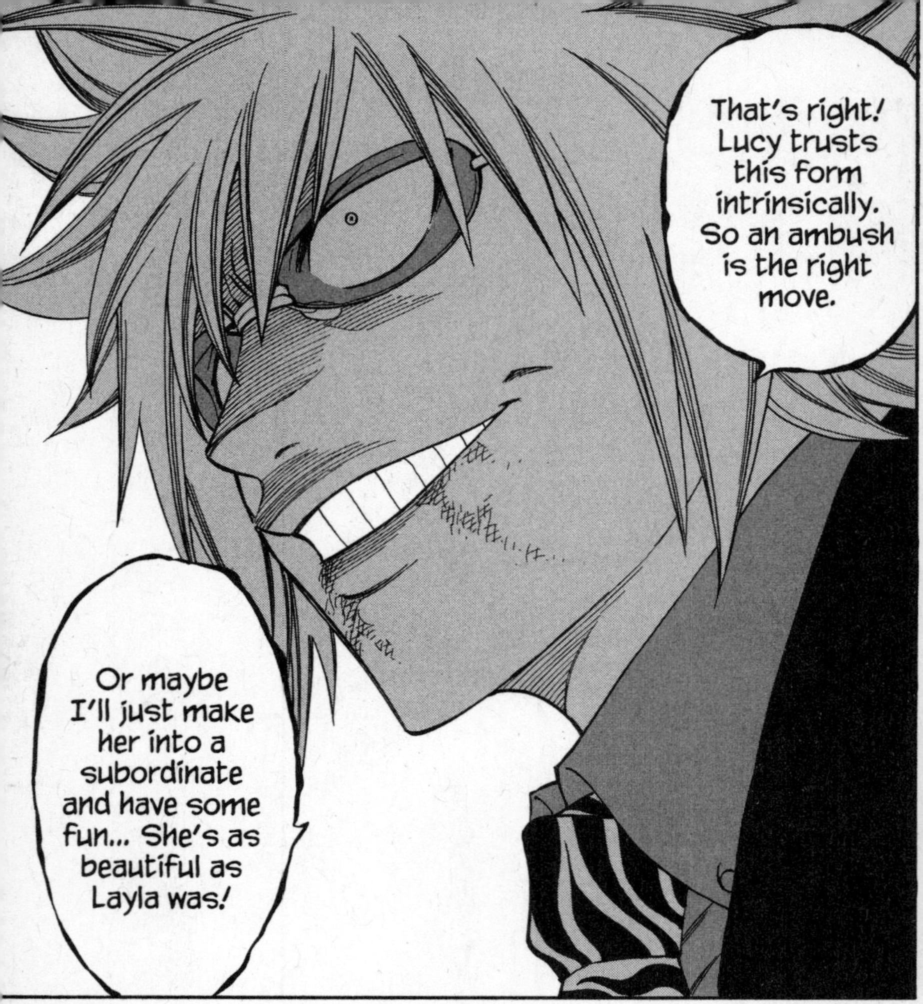
That's right! Lucy trusts this form intrinsically. So an ambush is the right move.
Or maybe I'll just make her into a subordinate and have some fun... She's as beautiful as Layla was!
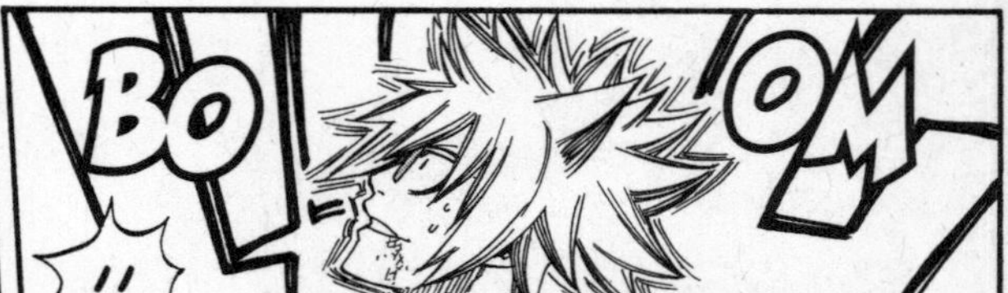
BOOM
!!
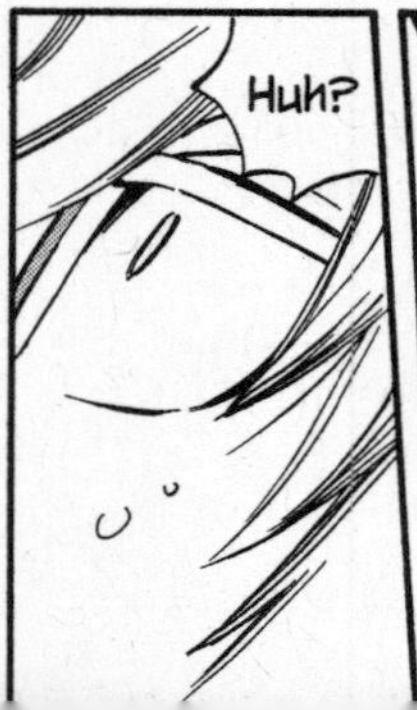
Huh?

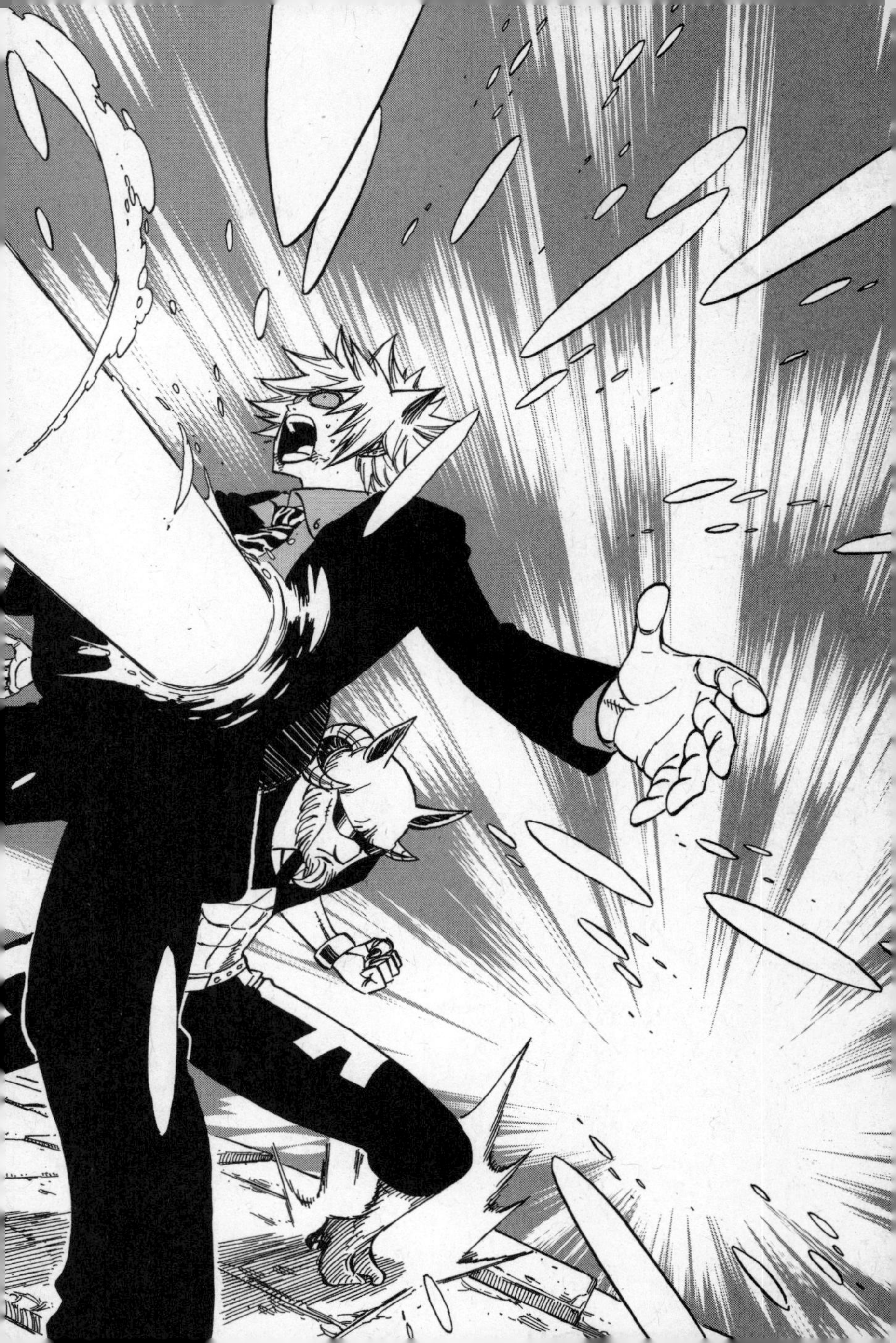

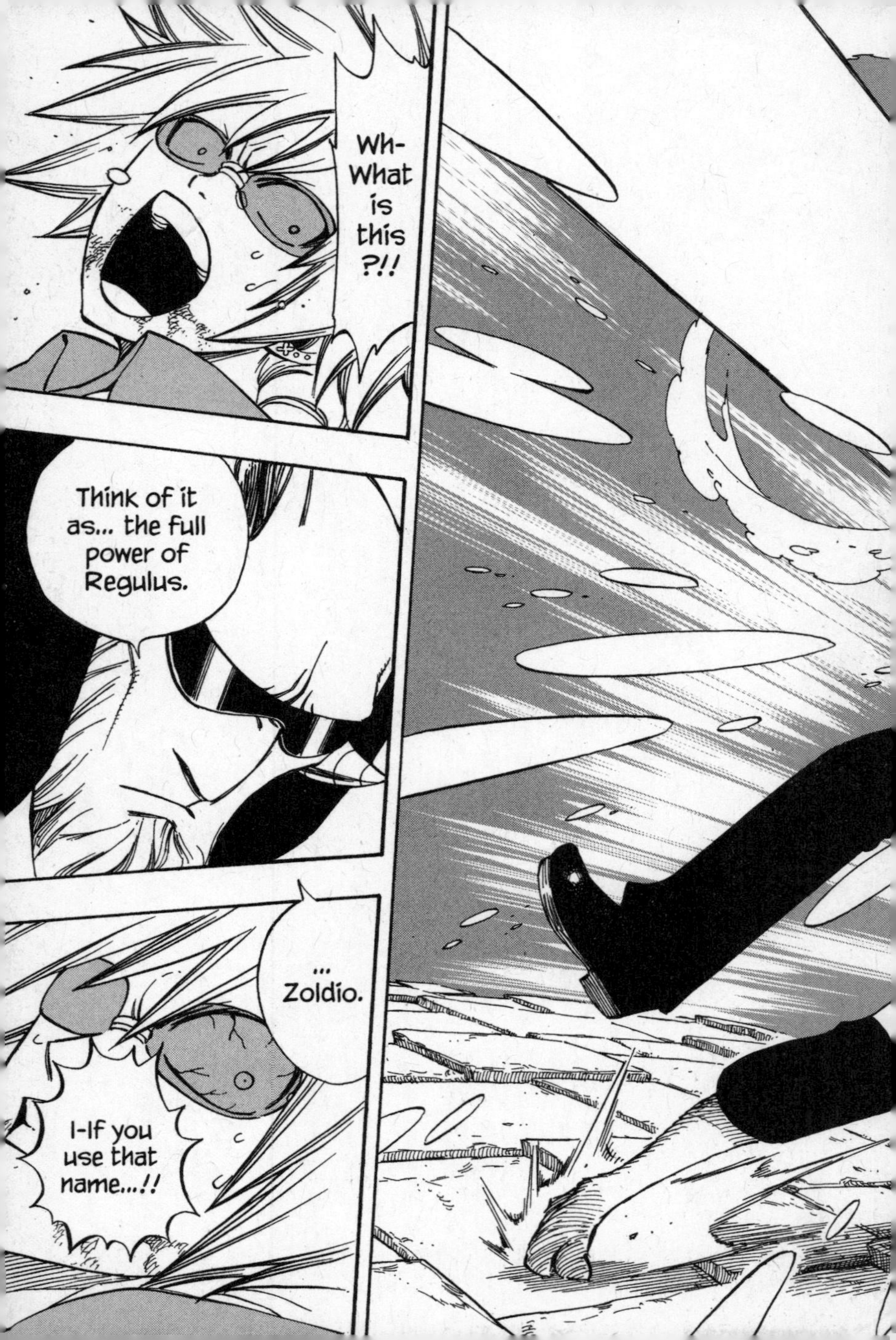
Wh-What is this?!!
Think of it as... the full power of Regulus.
...Zoldio.
I-If you use that name...!!

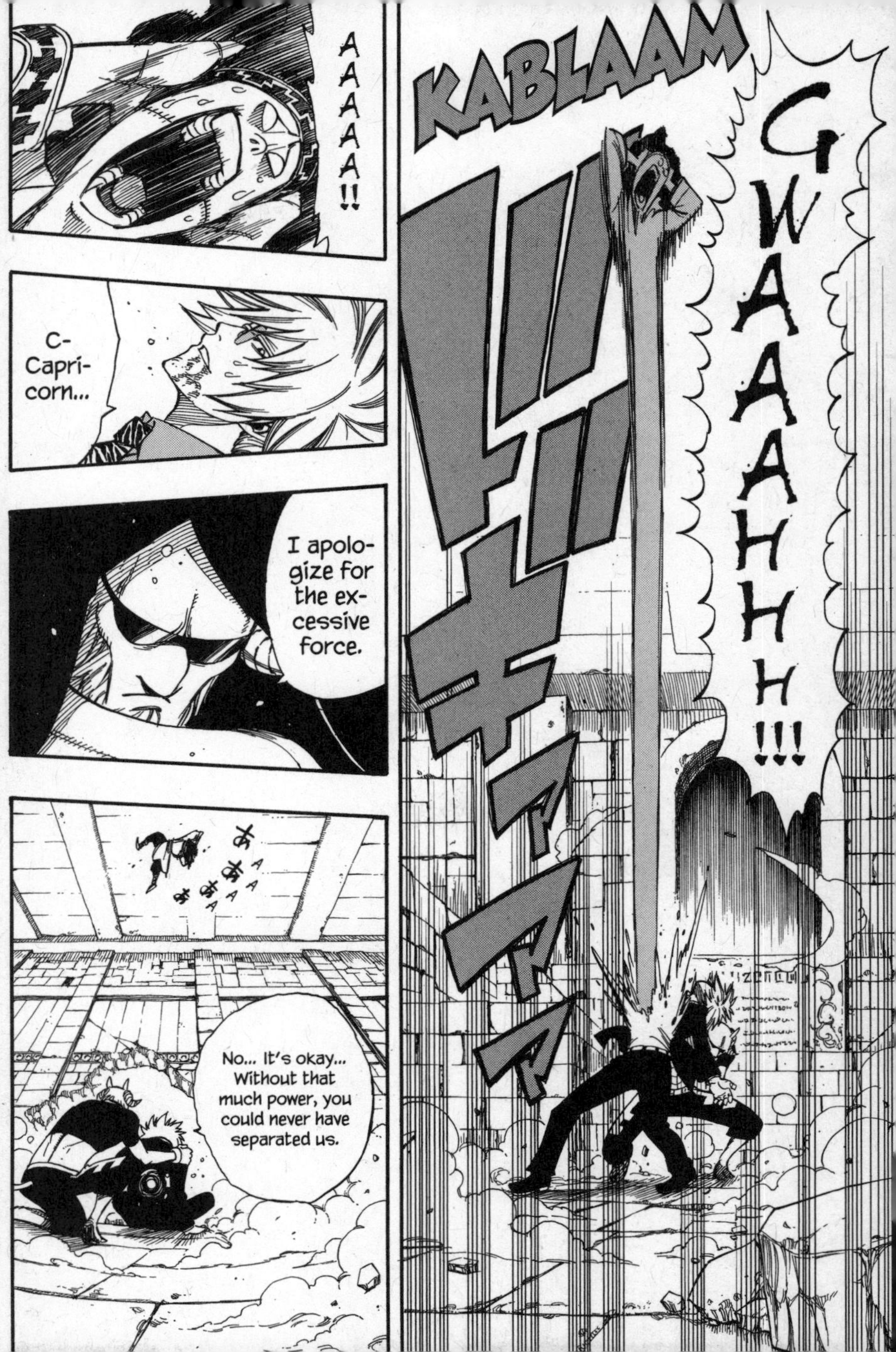
KABLAAM
GWAAAHHH!!!
AAAAAA!!
C-Capricorn...
I apologize for the excessive force.
No... It's okay... Without that much power, you could never have separated us.

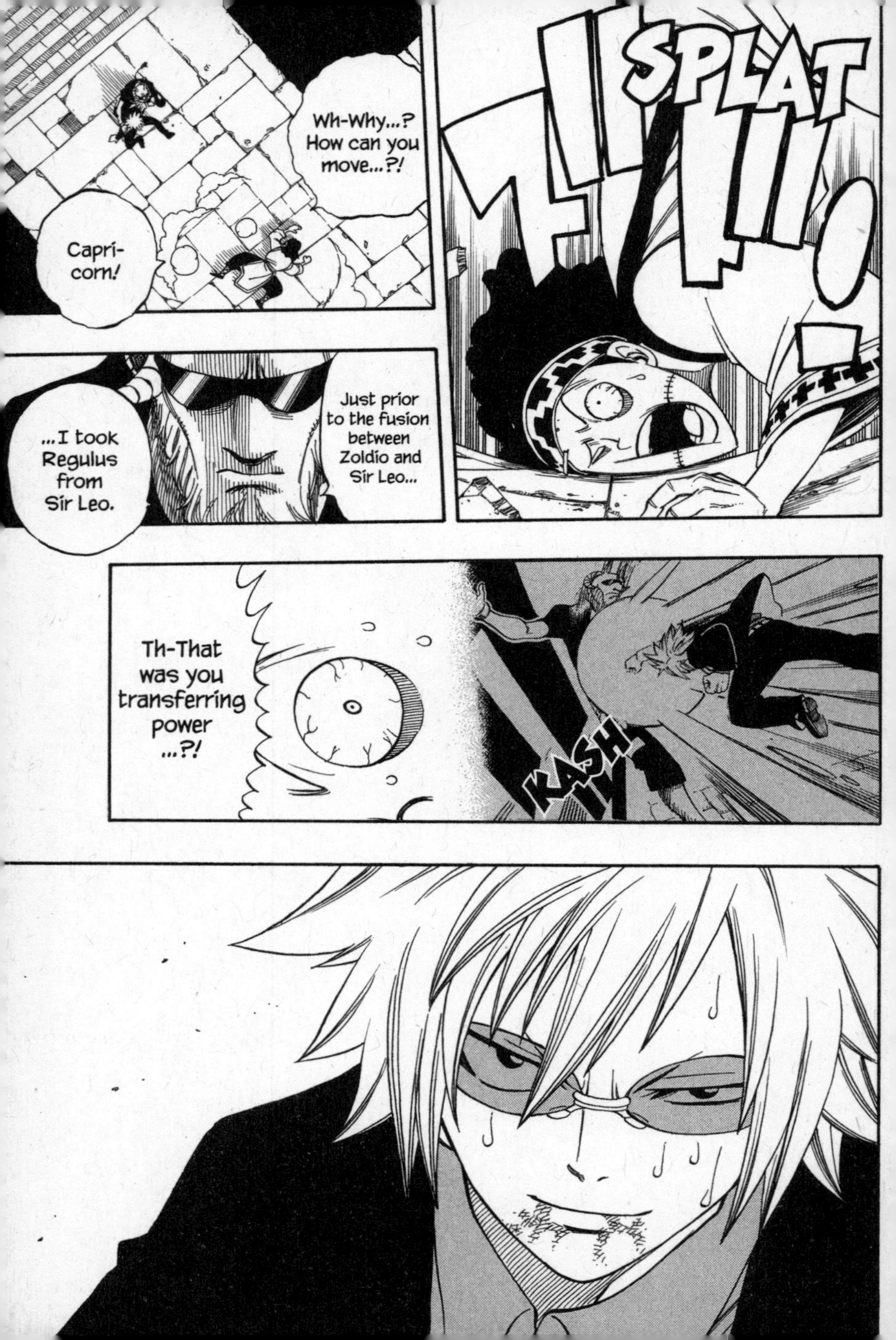
SPLAT
Wh-Why...? How can you move...?!
Capri-corn!
Just prior to the fusion between Zoldio and Sir Leo...
...I took Regulus from Sir Leo.
KASH
Th-That was you transferring power ...?!

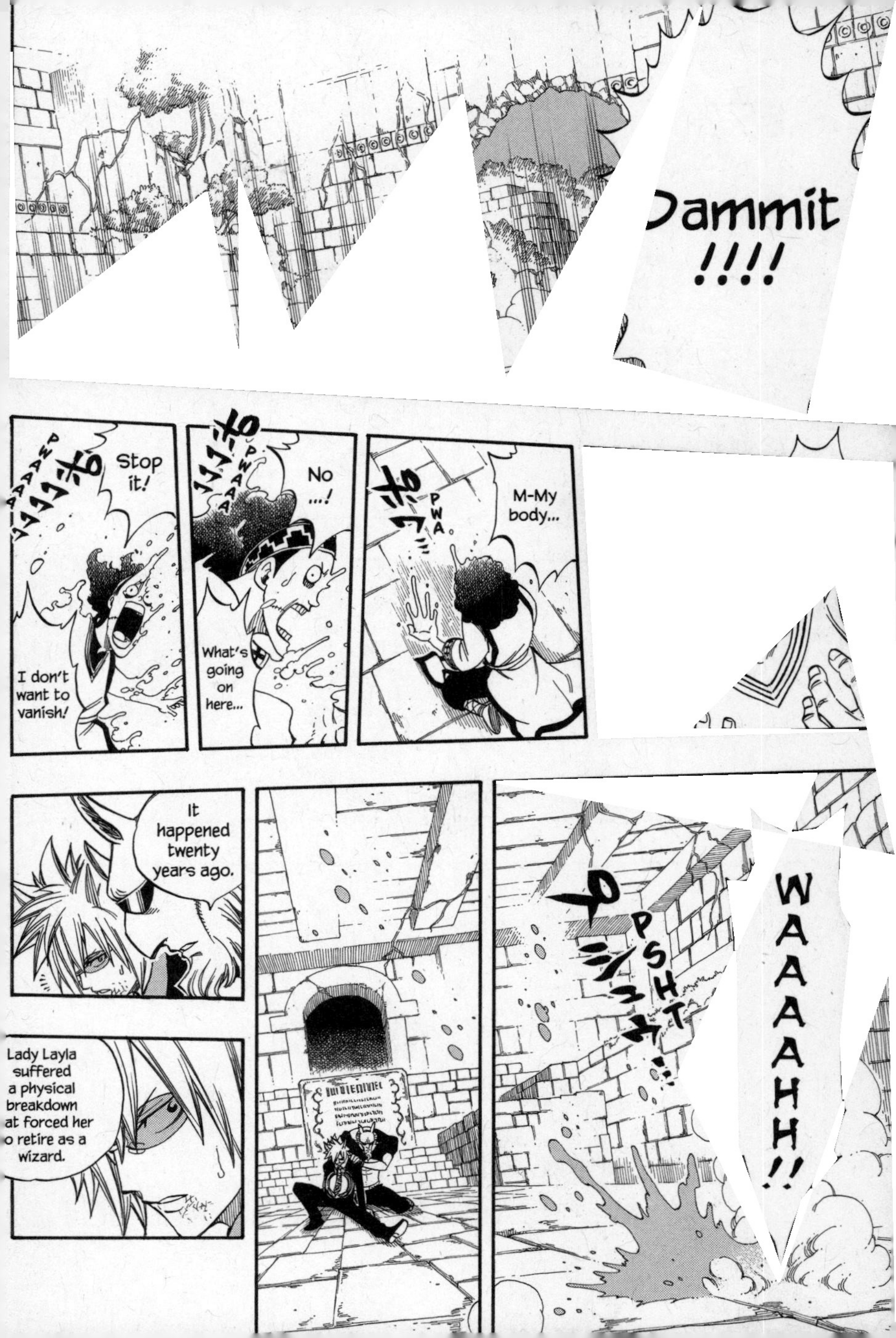
Dammit !!!!
M-My body...
PWA
No ...!
PWAAA
What's going on here...
Stop it!
PWAAAA
I don't want to vanish!
PSHT
WAAAAAHH!!
It happened twenty years ago.
Lady Layla suffered a physical breakdown at forced her o retire as a wizard.

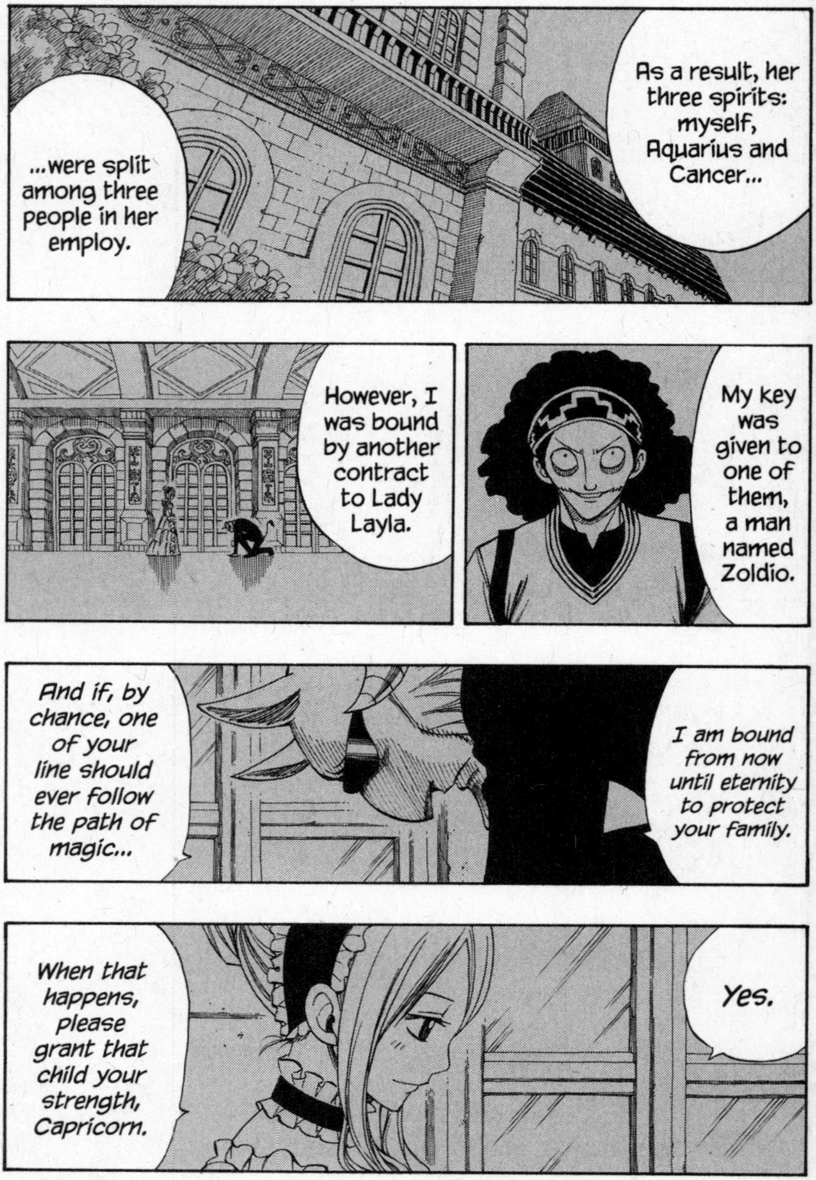
As a result, her three spirits: myself, Aquarius and Cancer...
...were split among three people in her employ.
My key was given to one of them, a man named Zoldio.
However, I was bound by another contract to Lady Layla.
I am bound from now until eternity to protect your family.
And if, by chance, one of your line should ever follow the path of magic...
Yes.
When that happens, please grant that child your strength, Capricorn.

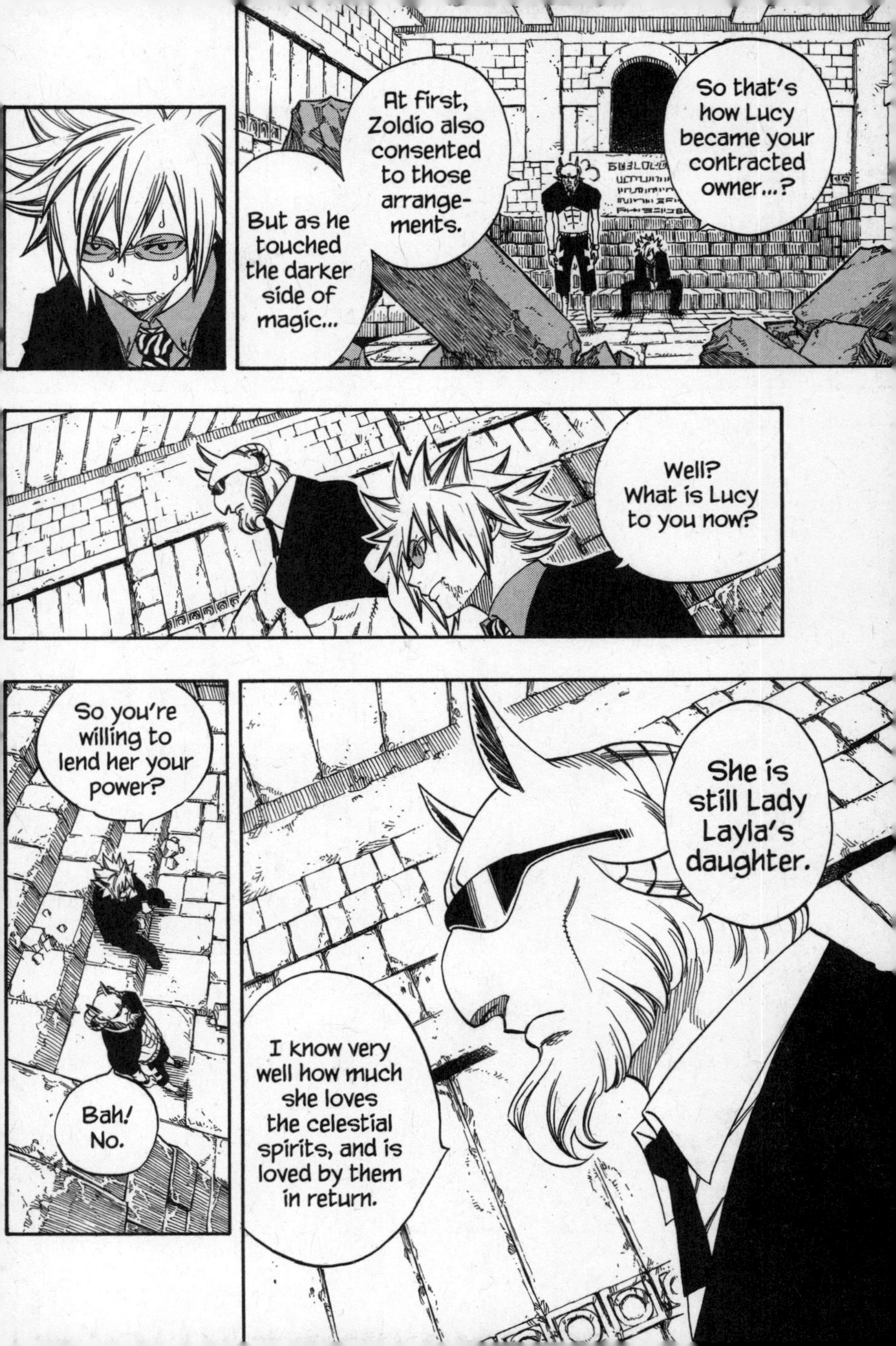
So that's how Lucy became your contracted owner...?
At first, Zoldio also consented to those arrange-ments.
But as he touched the darker side of magic...
Well? What is Lucy to you now?
She is still Lady Layla's daughter.
I know very well how much she loves the celestial spirits, and is loved by them in return.
So you're willing to lend her your power?
Bah! No.

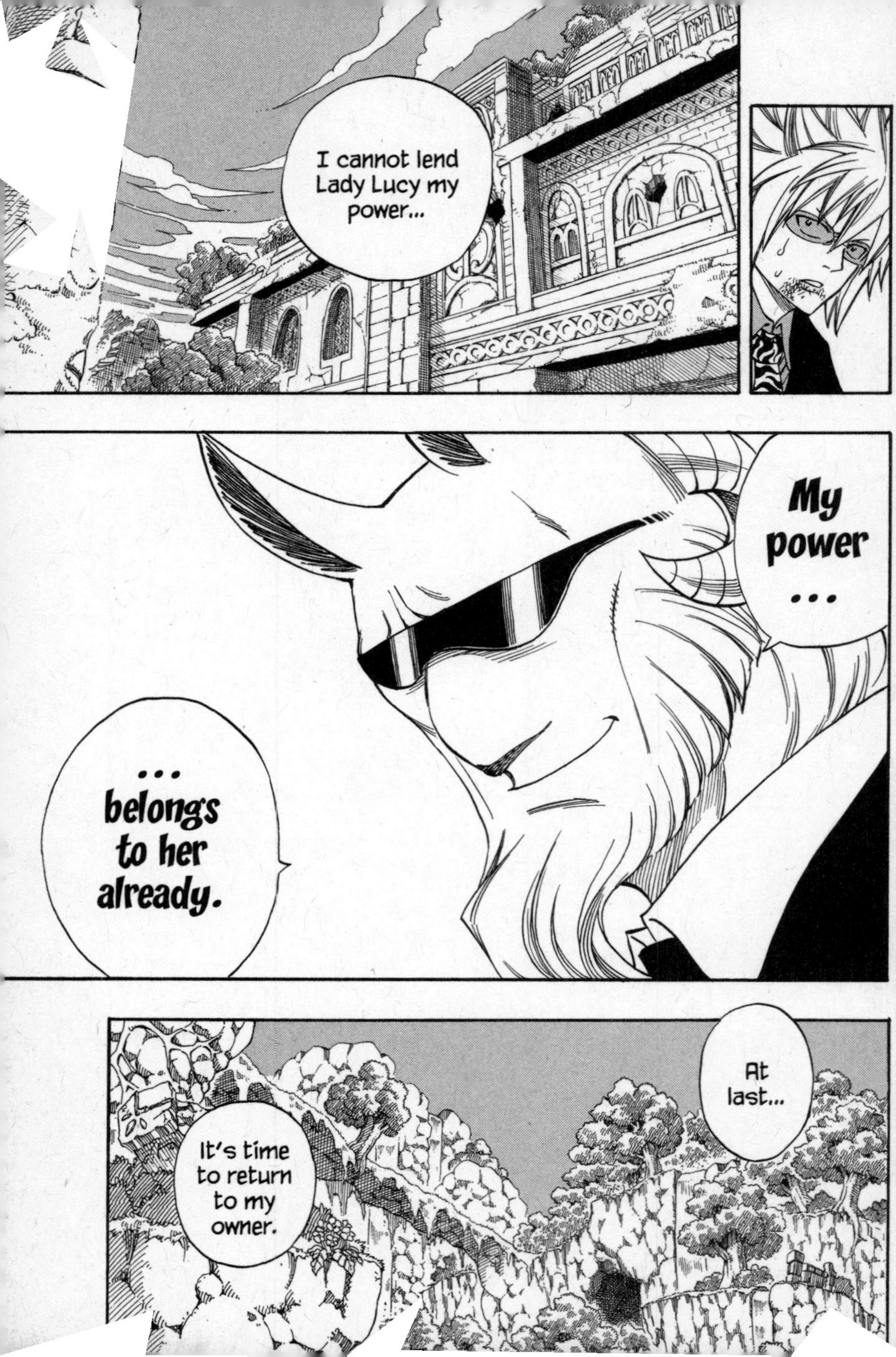
I cannot lend Lady Lucy my power...
My power ...
... belongs to her already.
At last...
It's time to return to my owner.

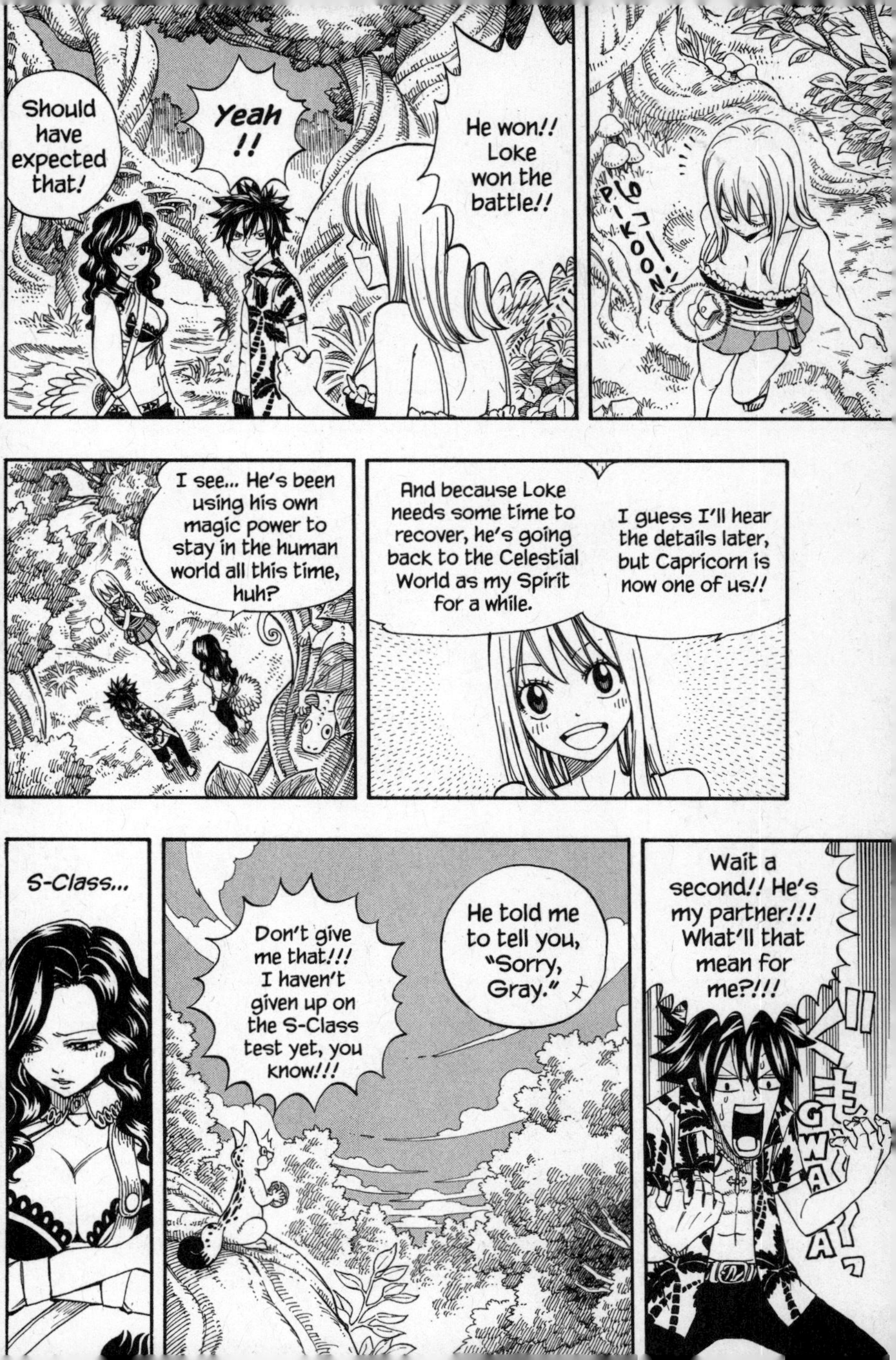
PIKOON!
He won!! Loke won the battle!!
Yeah!!
Should have expected that!
I guess I'll hear the details later, but Capricorn is now one of us!!
And because Loke needs some time to recover, he's going back to the Celestial World as my Spirit for a while.
I see... He's been using his own magic power to stay in the human world all this time, huh?
Wait a second!! He's my partner!!! What'll that mean for me?!!!
GWAA
He told me to tell you, "Sorry, Gray."
Don't give me that!!! I haven't given up on the S-Class test yet, you know!!!
S-Class...

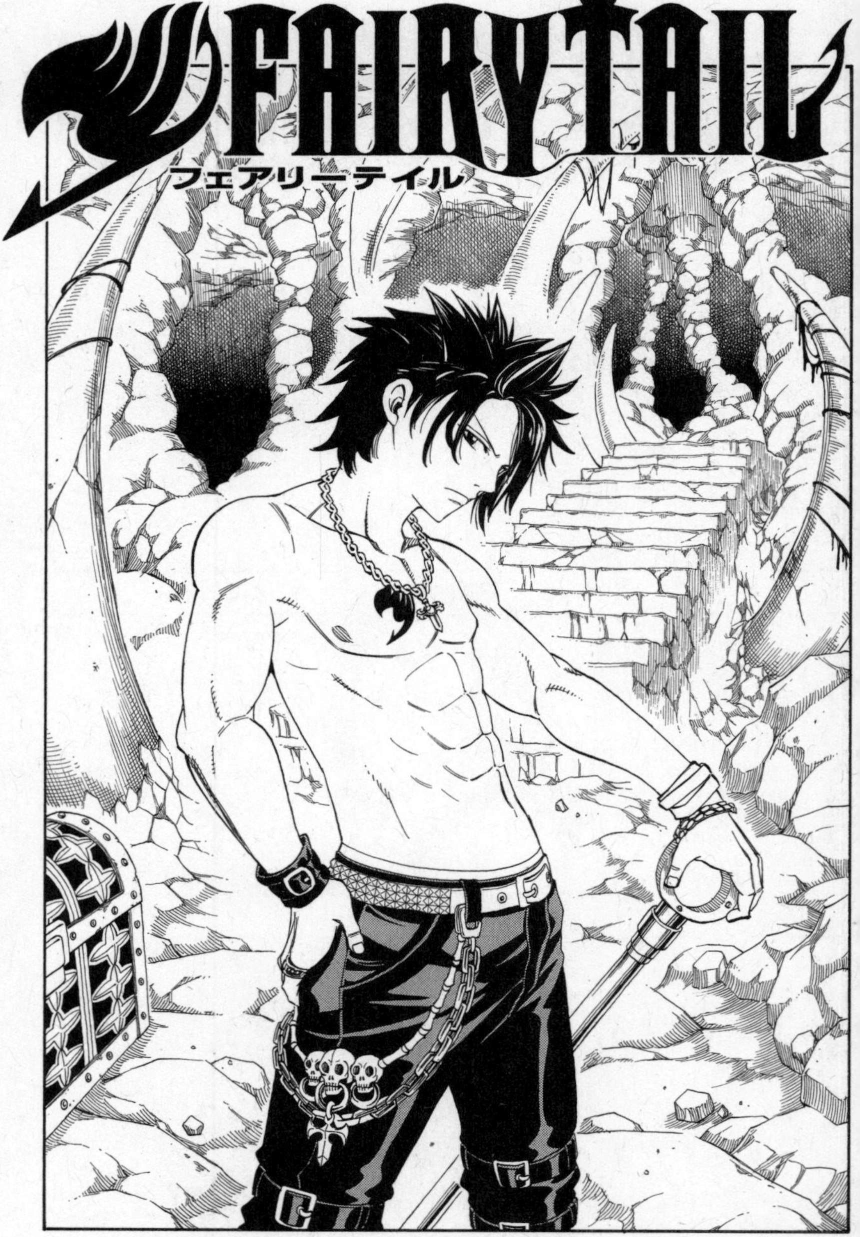
FAIRY TAIL
フェアリーテイル

Chapter 225: The Open Seam

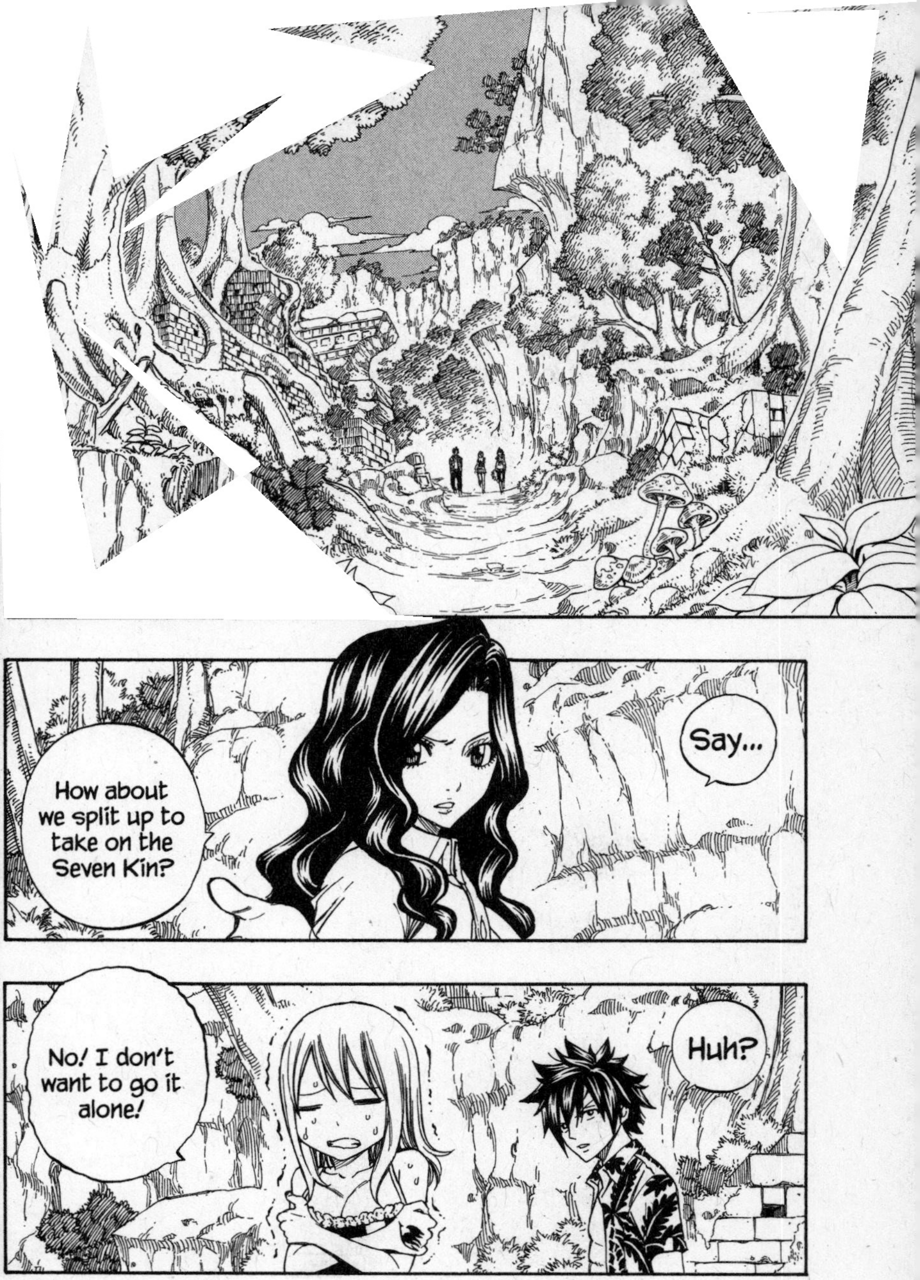
Say...
How about we split up to take on the Seven Kin?
Huh?
No! I don't want to go it alone!

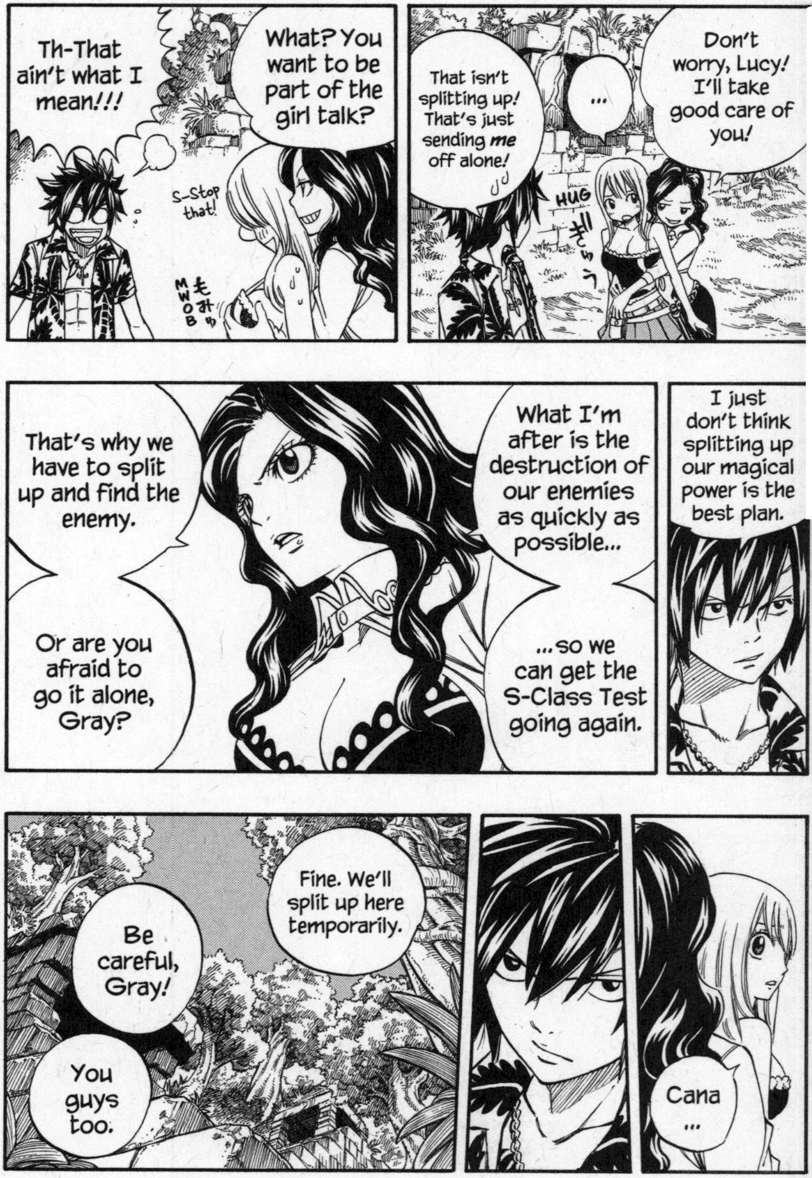
Don't worry, Lucy! I'll take good care of you!
...
That isn't splitting up! That's just sending *me* off alone!
HUG
What? You want to be part of the girl talk?
Th-That ain't what I mean!!!
S-Stop that!
MWOB
I just don't think splitting up our magical power is the best plan.
What I'm after is the destruction of our enemies as quickly as possible...
...so we can get the S-Class Test going again.
That's why we have to split up and find the enemy.
Or are you afraid to go it alone, Gray?
Cana ...
Fine. We'll split up here temporarily.
Be careful, Gray!
You guys too.

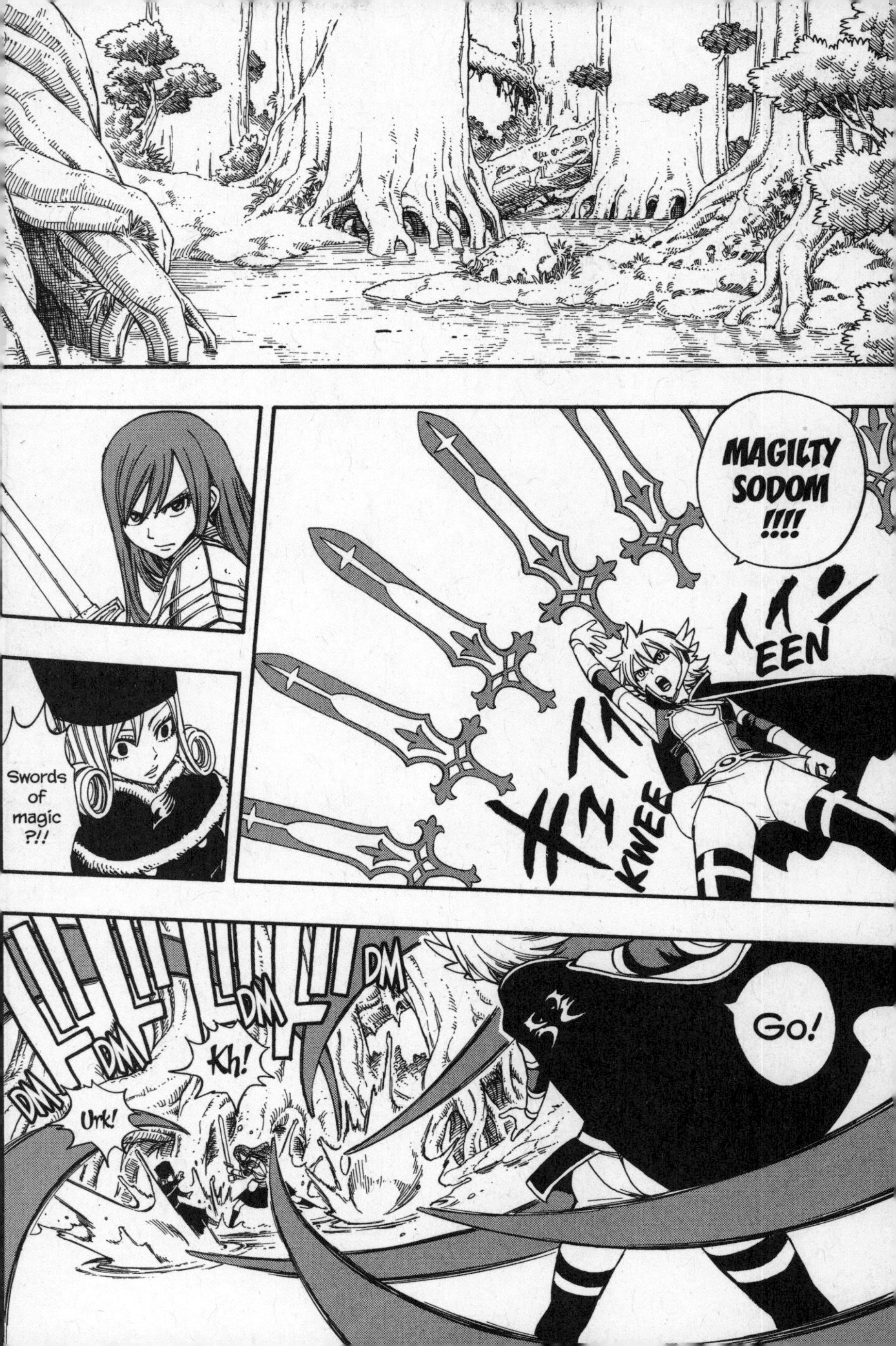
MAGILTY SODOM !!!!
EEN
KWEE
Swords of magic ?!!
Go!
DM
Kh!
DM
DM
DM
Urk!

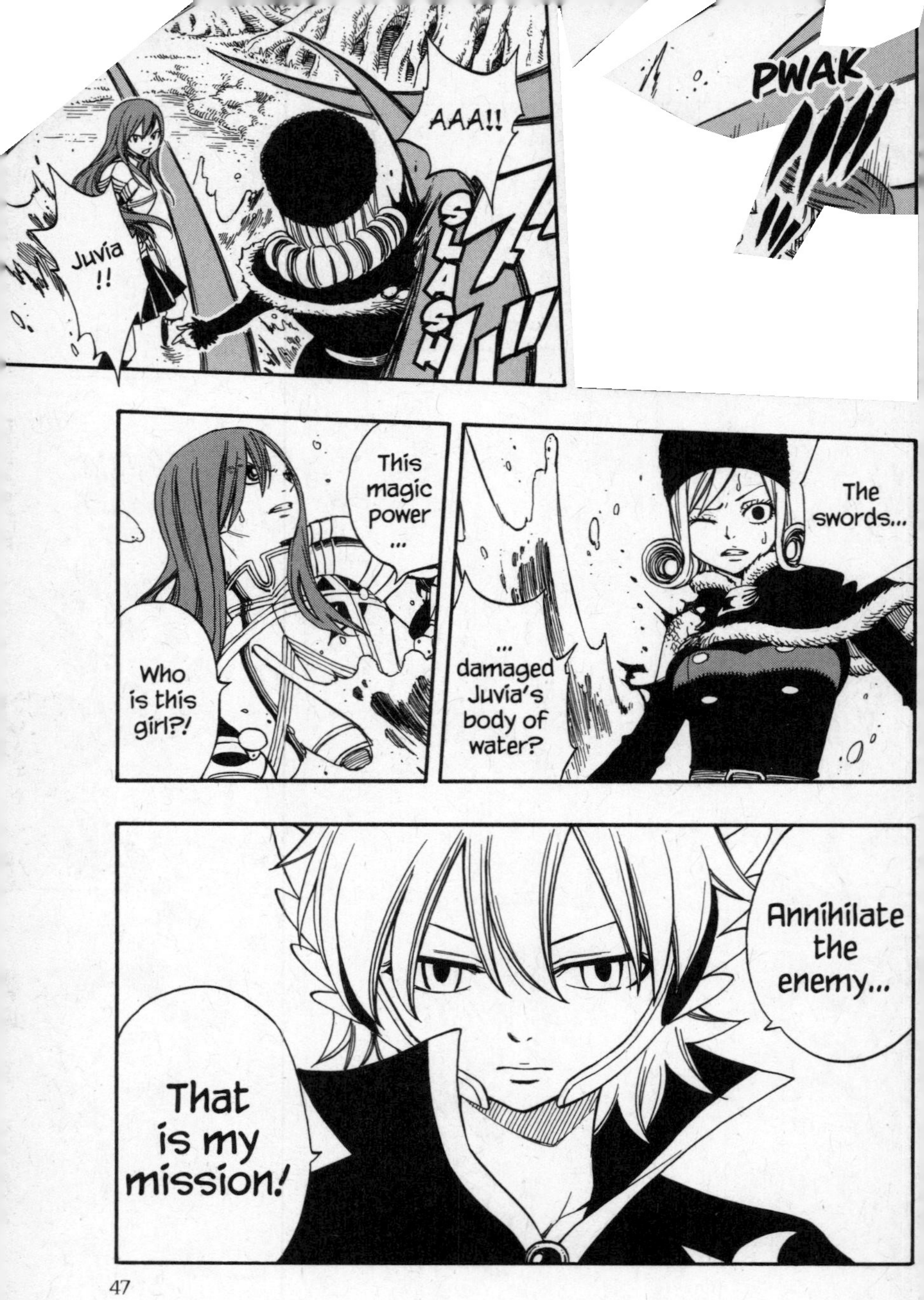

PWAK
AAA!!
SLASH
Juvia !!
The swords...
... damaged Juvia's body of water?
This magic power ...
Who is this girl?!
Annihilate the enemy...
That is my mission!

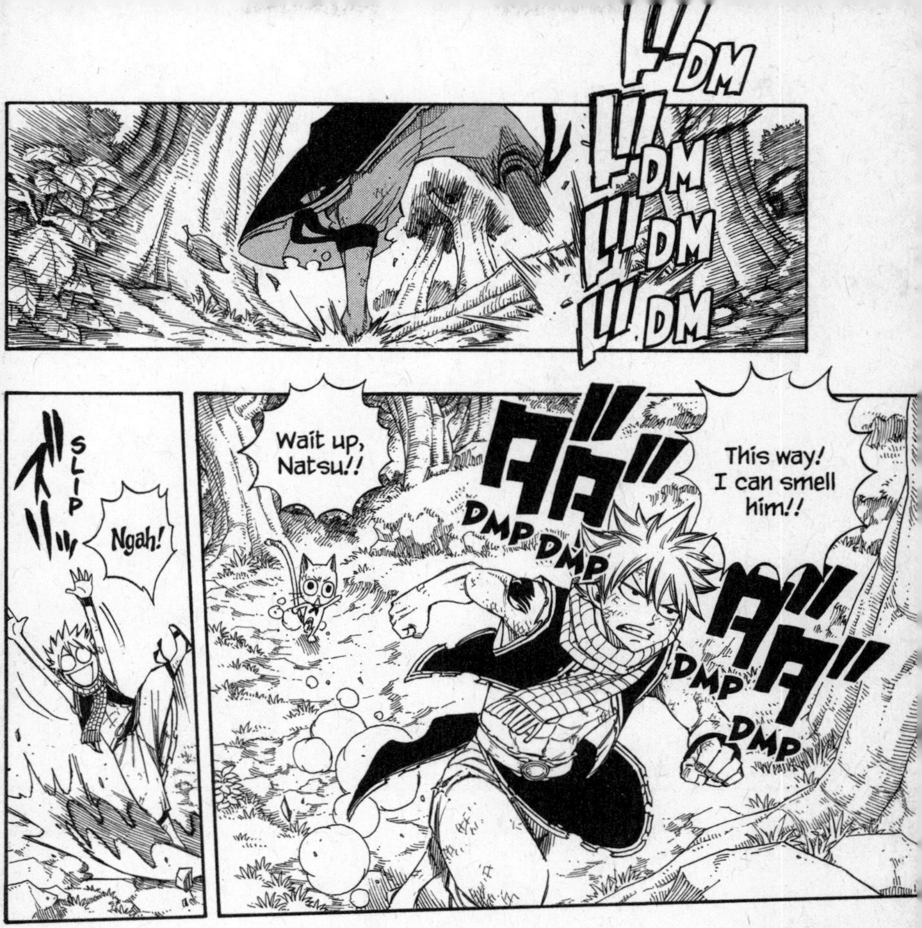
DM
DM
DM
DM
This way! I can smell him!!
DMP
DMP
DMP
DMP
Wait up, Natsu!!
DMP
DMP
SLIP
Ngah!

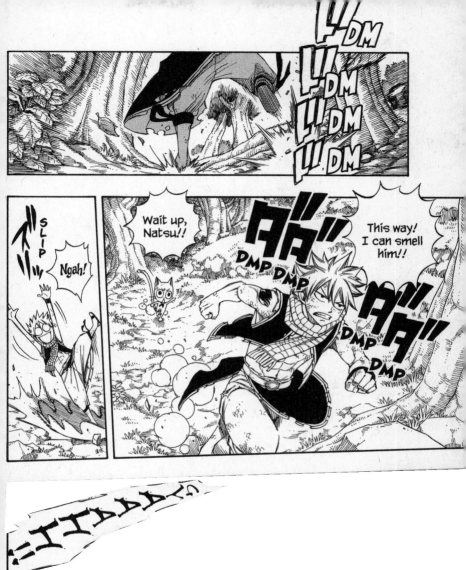

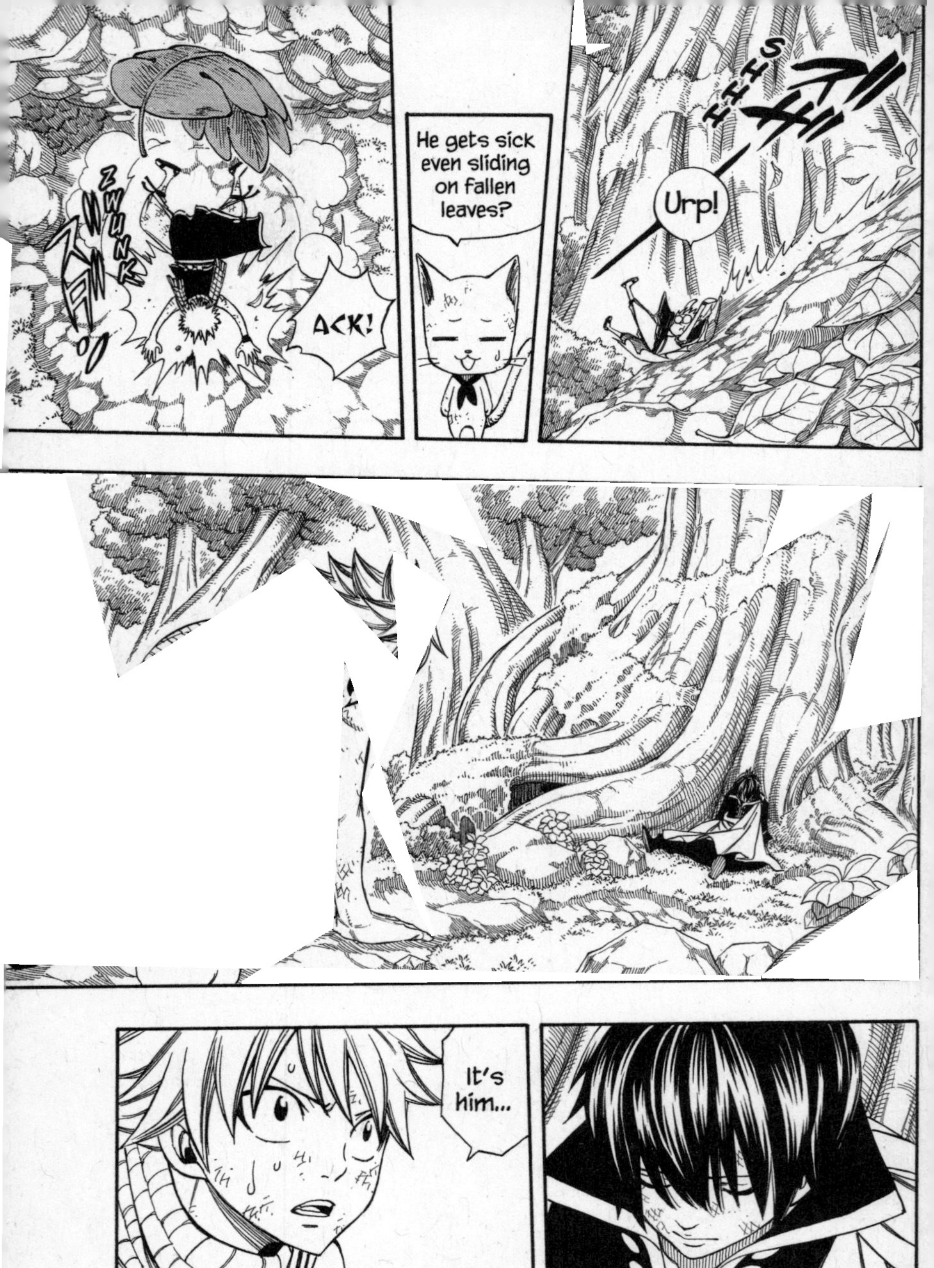
SHHHH
Urp!
He gets sick even sliding on fallen leaves?
ZWUNK
ACK!
It's him...

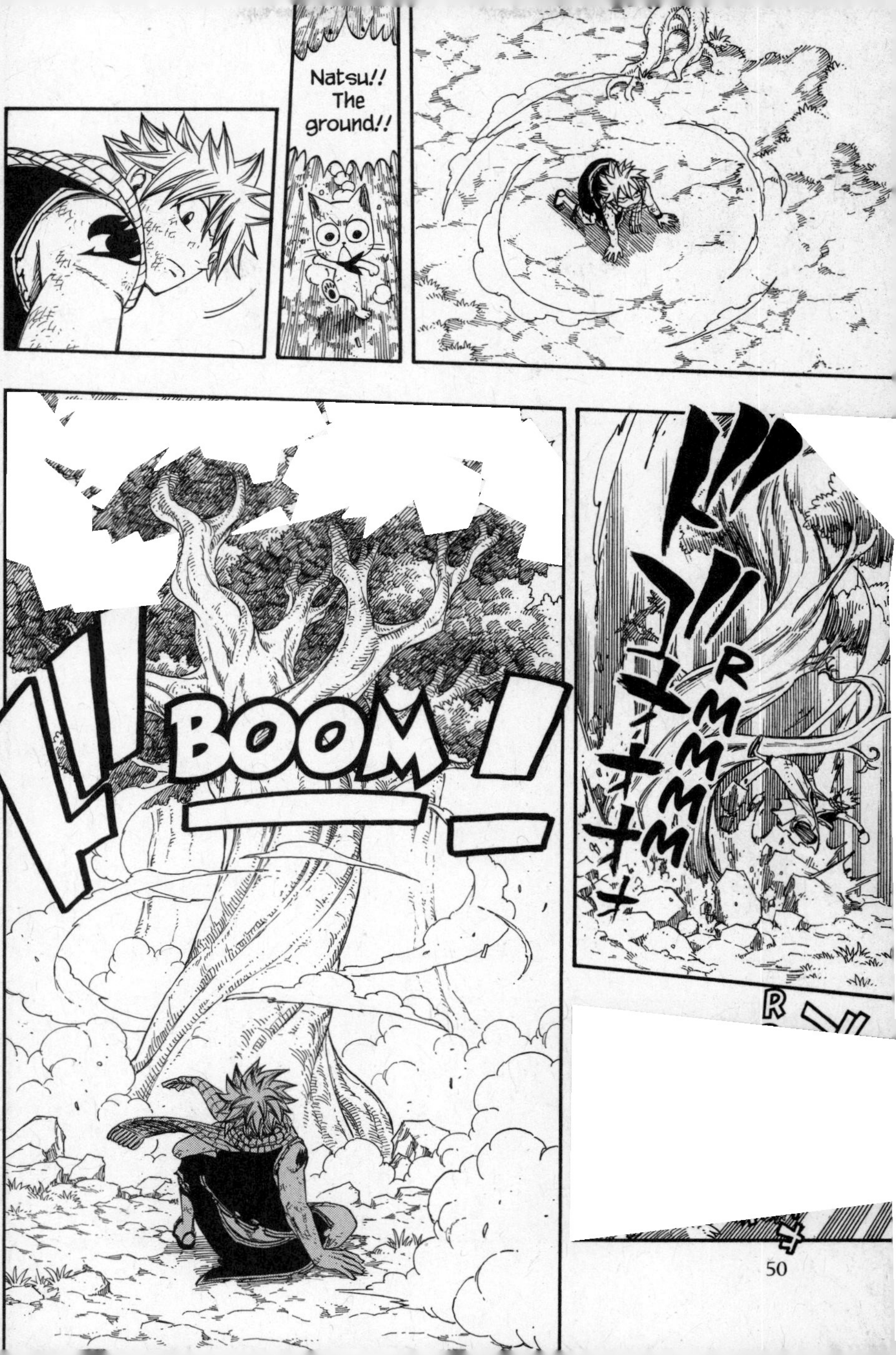
Natsu!! The ground!!
RMMMMM
BOOM
R

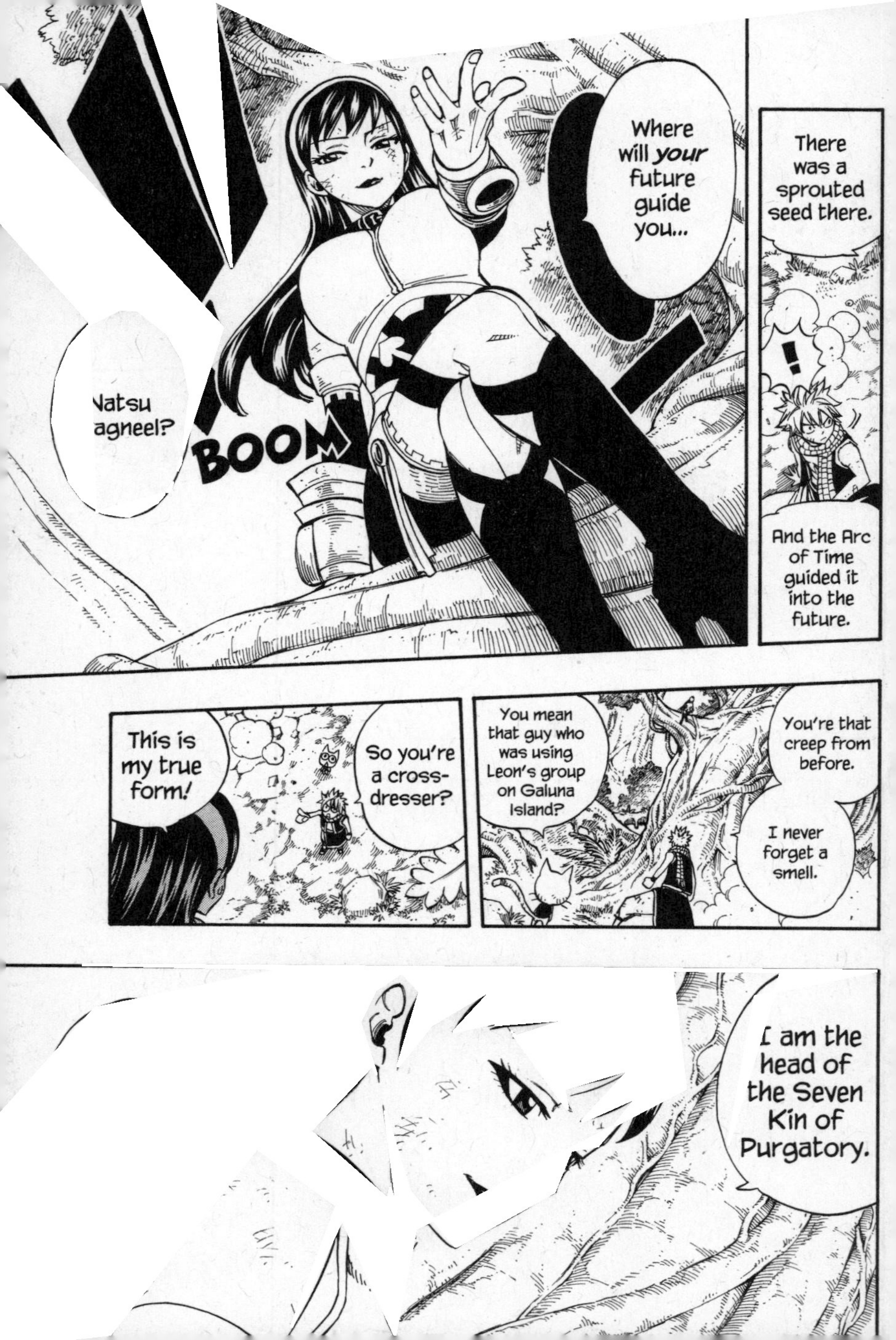

There was a sprouted seed there.
And the Arc of Time guided it into the future.
Where will *your* future guide you...
BOOM
Natsu agneel?
You're that creep from before.
I never forget a smell.
You mean that guy who was using Leon's group on Galuna Island?
So you're a cross-dresser?
This is my true form!
I am the head of the Seven Kin of Purgatory.

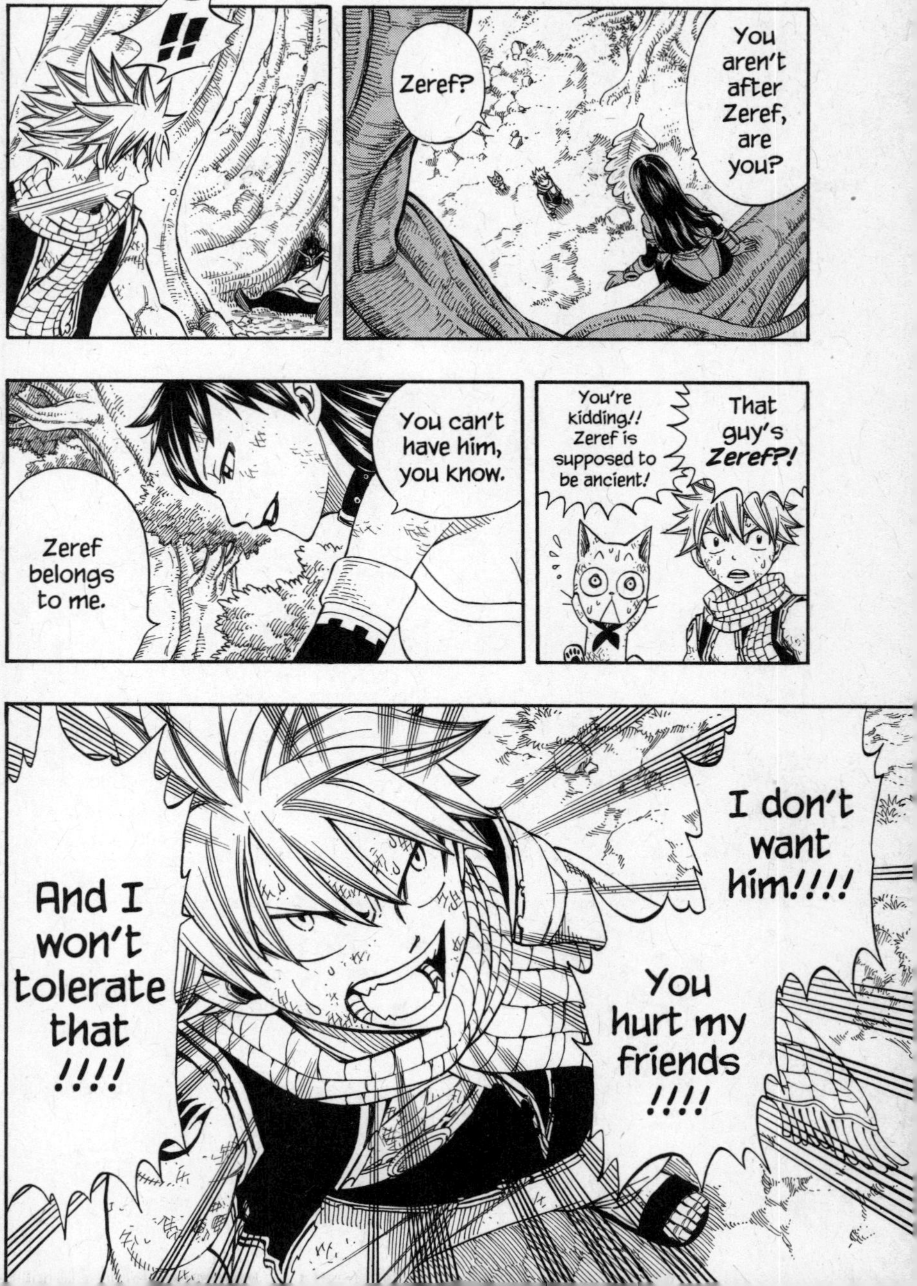
You aren't after Zeref, are you?
Zeref?
!!
That guy's *Zeref?!*
You're kidding!! Zeref is supposed to be ancient!
You can't have him, you know.
Zeref belongs to me.
I don't want him!!!!
You hurt my friends!!!!
And I won't tolerate that!!!!

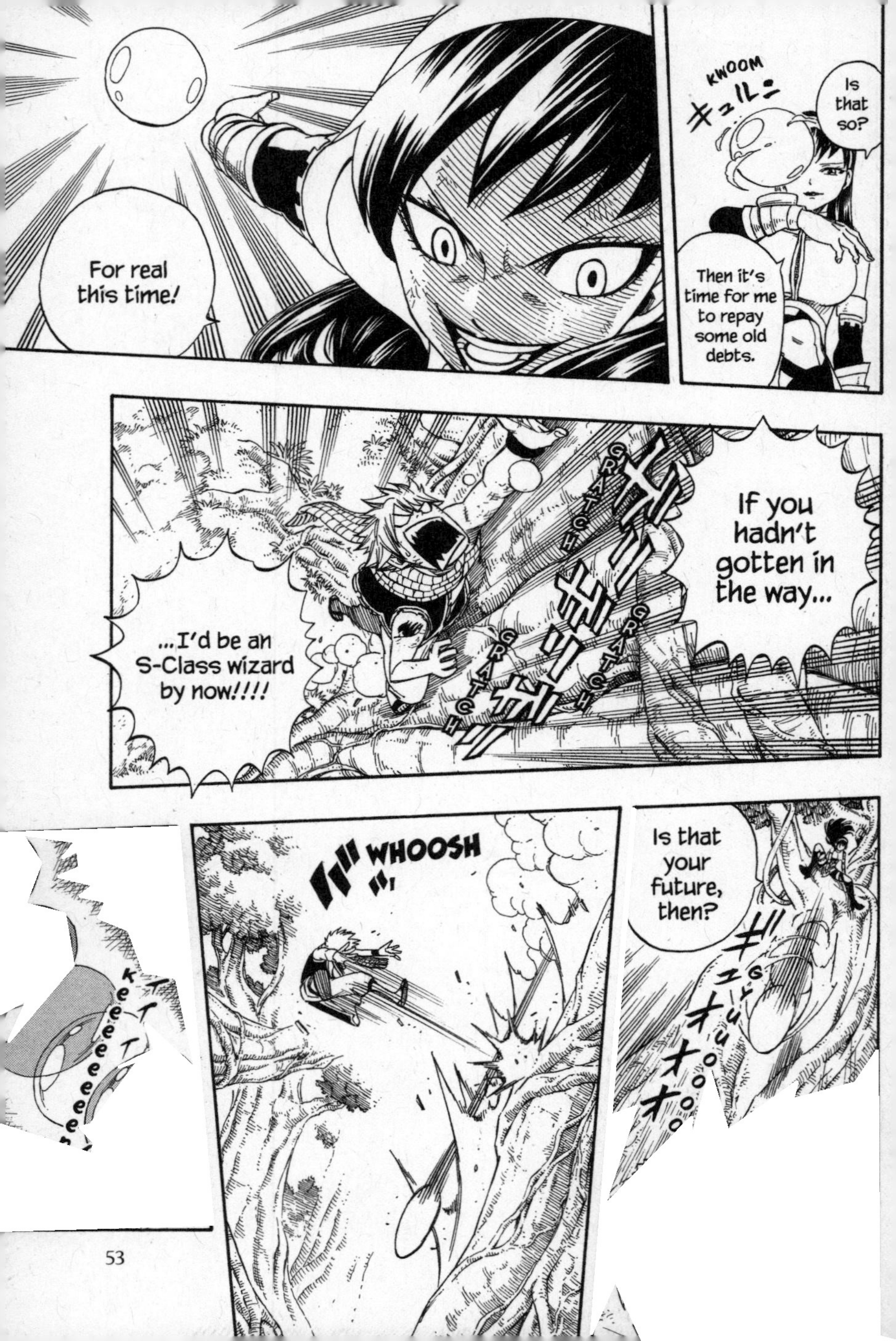
KWOOM
Is that so?
Then it's time for me to repay some old debts.
For real this time!
If you hadn't gotten in the way...
GRATCH
GRATCH
GRATCH
...I'd be an S-Class wizard by now!!!!
Is that your future, then?
WHOOSH

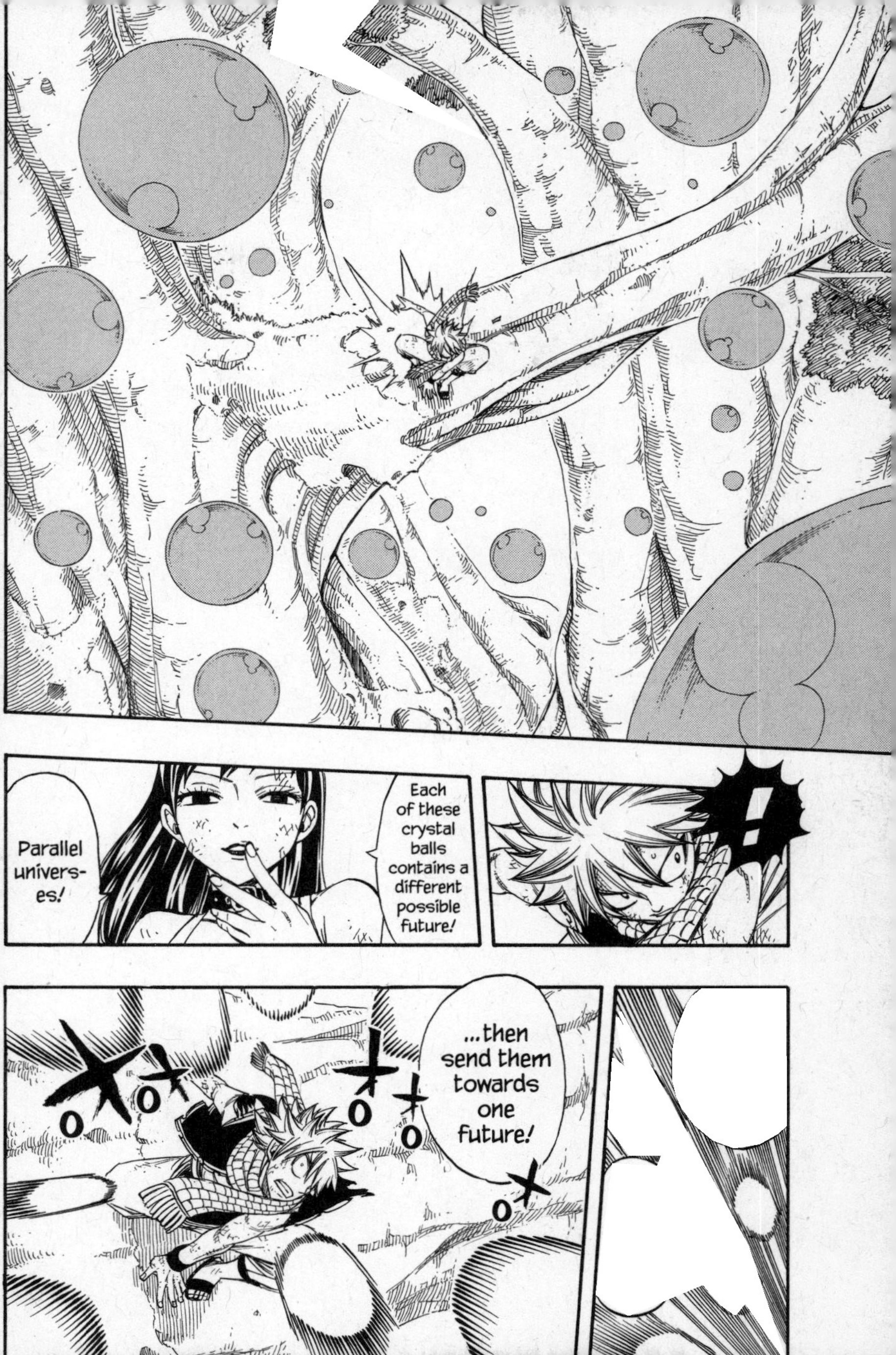
!
Each of these crystal balls contains a different possible future!
Parallel univers-es!
...then send them towards one future!

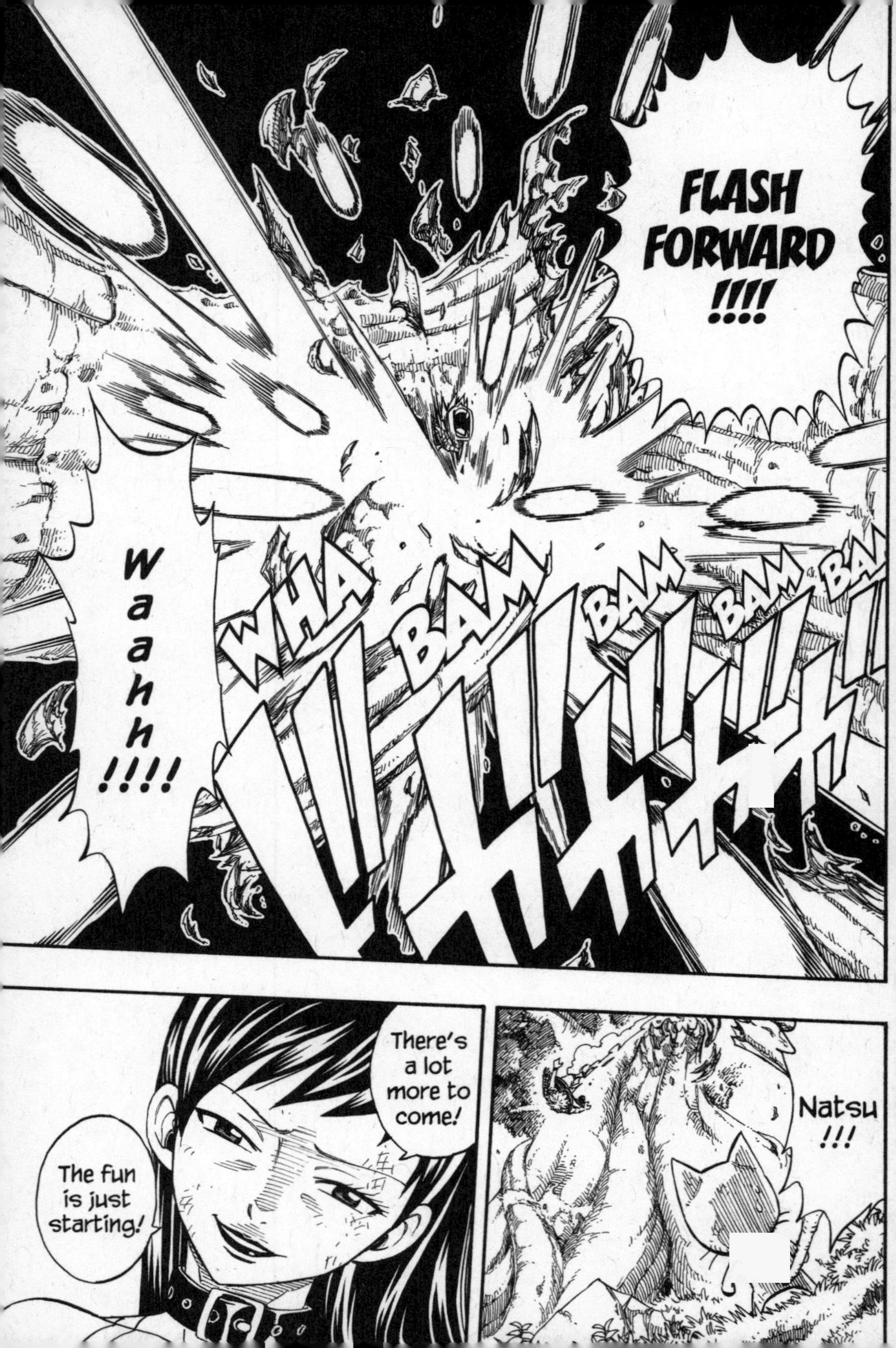
FLASH FORWARD !!!!
WHA
BAM BAM BAM
Waahh !!!!
Natsu !!!
There's a lot more to come!
The fun is just starting!

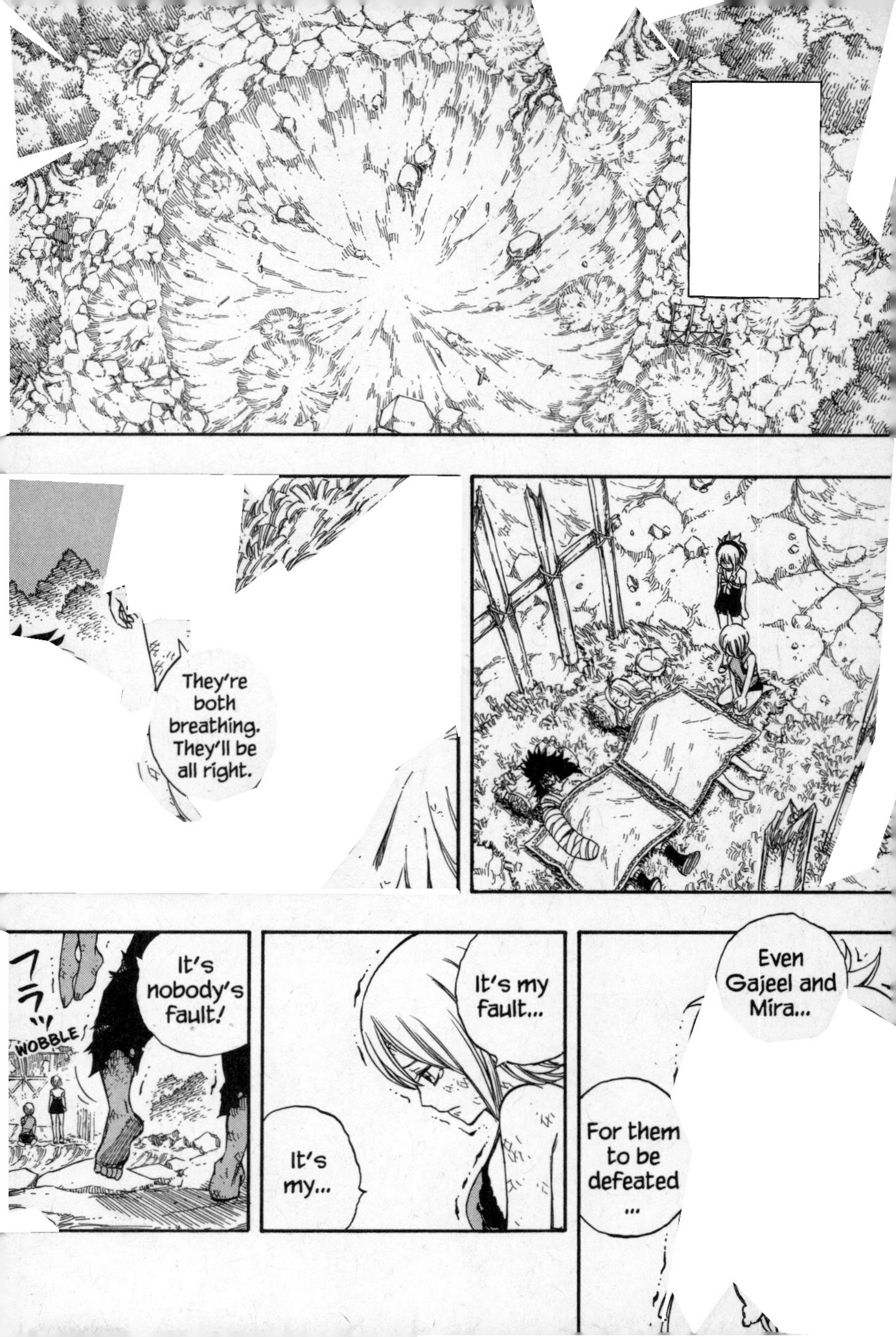
They're both breathing. They'll be all right.
Even Gajeel and Mira...
For them to be defeated ...
It's my fault...
It's my...
It's nobody's fault!
フラッ
WOBBLE

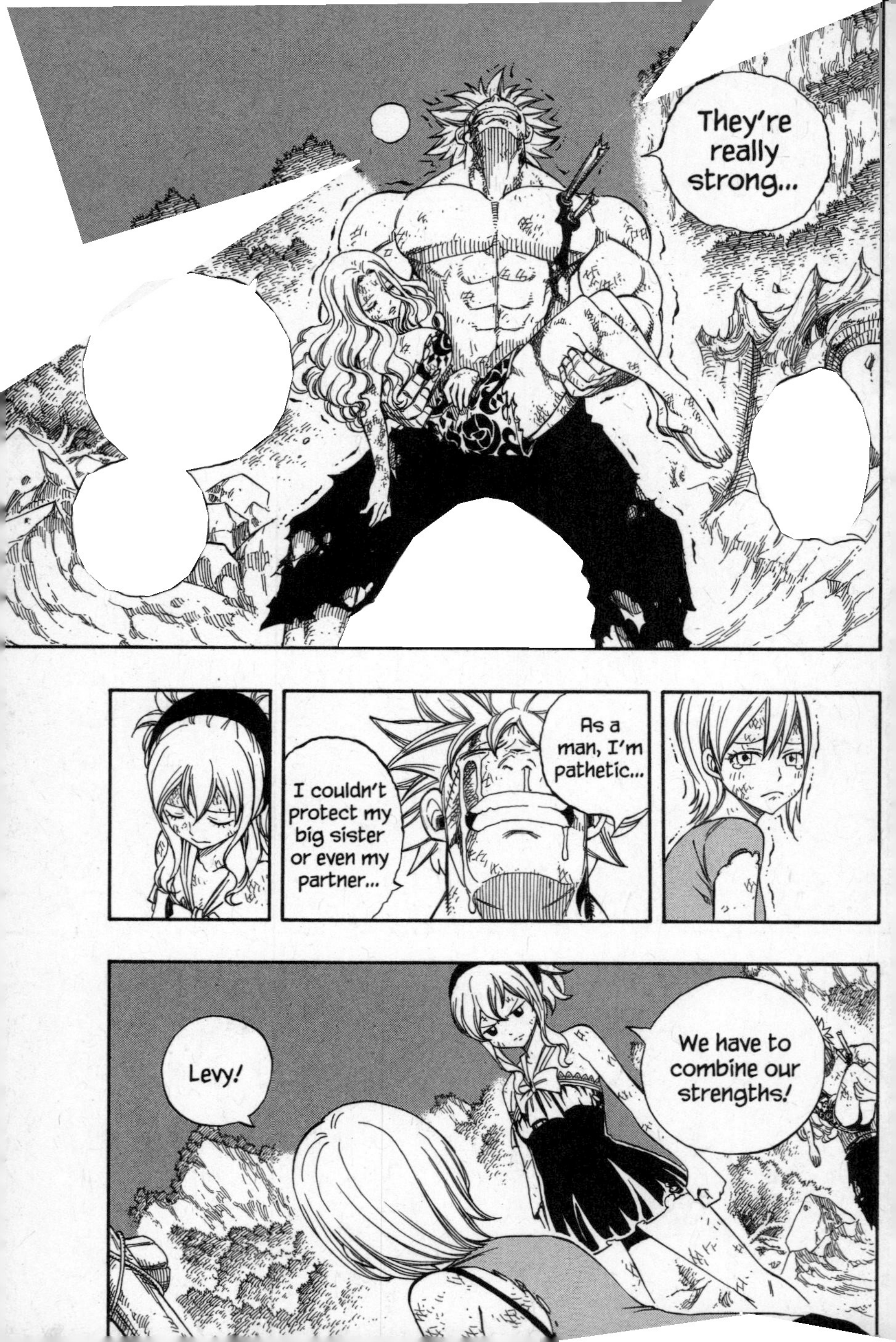
They're really strong...
As a man, I'm pathetic...
I couldn't protect my big sister or even my partner...
We have to combine our strengths!
Levy!

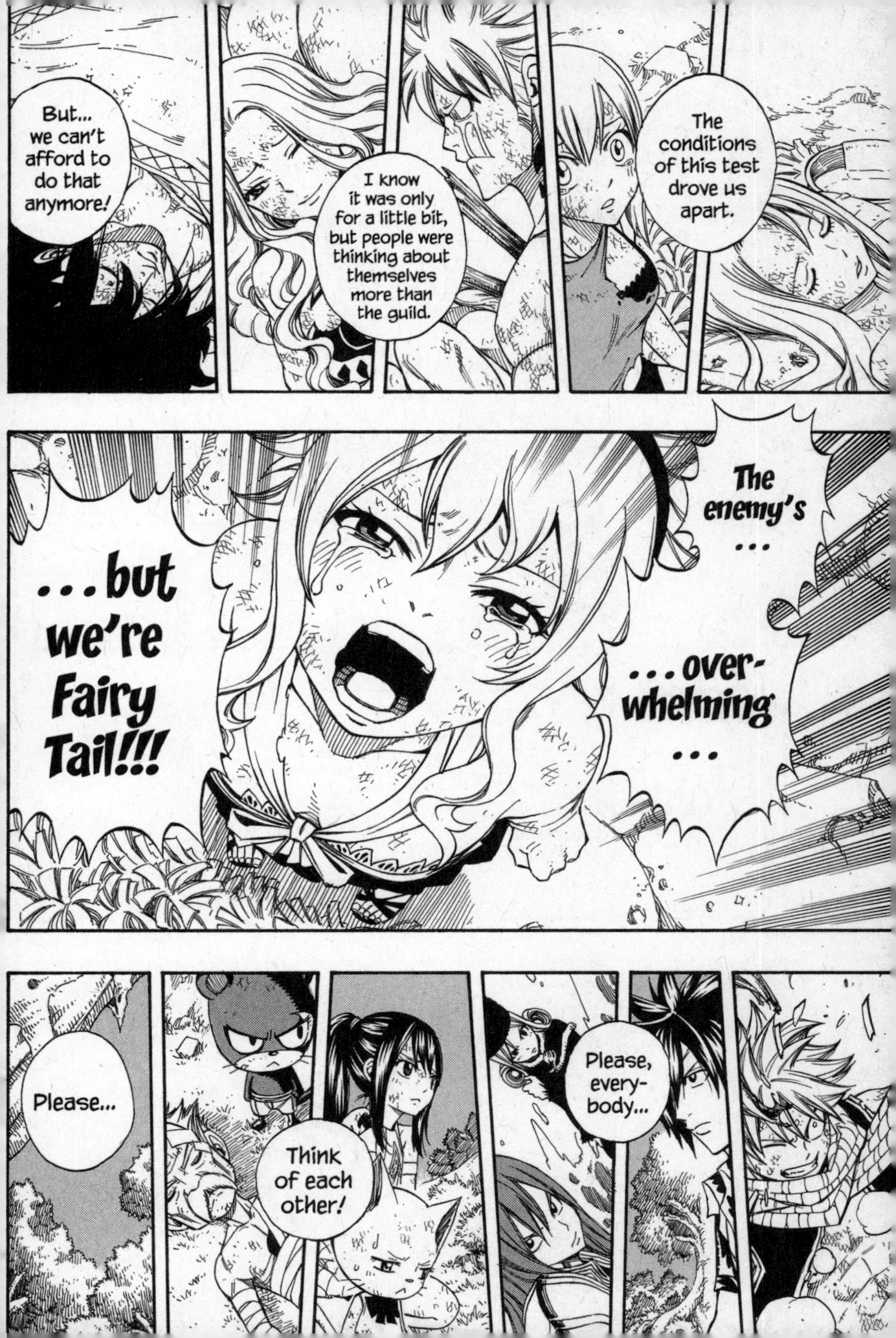
The conditions of this test drove us apart.
I know it was only for a little bit, but people were thinking about themselves more than the guild.
But... we can't afford to do that anymore!
The enemy's ...
...over-whelming ...
...but we're Fairy Tail!!!
Please, every-body...
Think of each other!
Please...

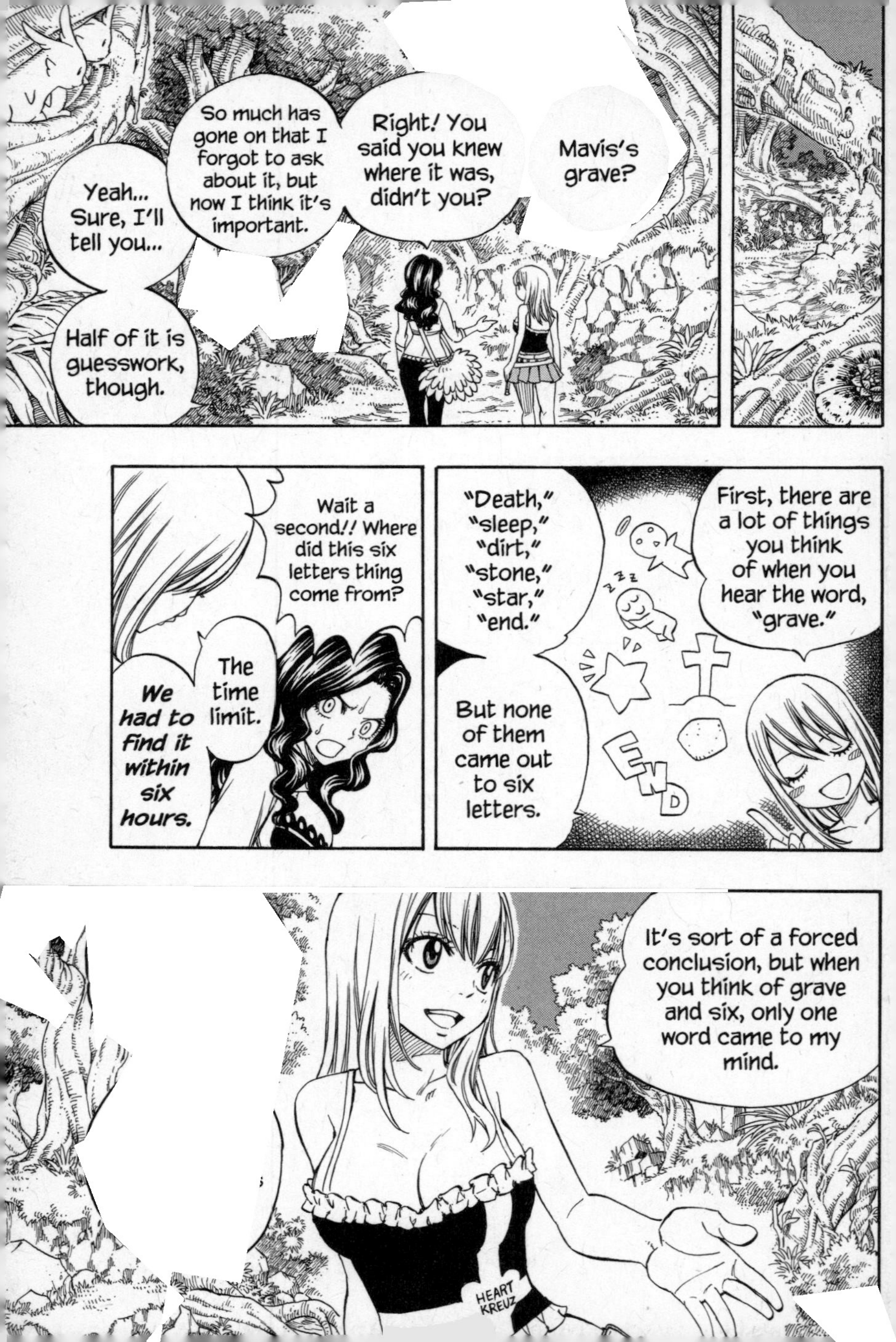
Mavis's grave?
Right! You said you knew where it was, didn't you?
So much has gone on that I forgot to ask about it, but now I think it's important.
Yeah... Sure, I'll tell you...
Half of it is guesswork, though.
First, there are a lot of things you think of when you hear the word, "grave."
"Death," "sleep," "dirt," "stone," "star," "end."
END
But none of them came out to six letters.
Wait a second!! Where did this six letters thing come from?
The time limit.
We had to find it within six hours.
It's sort of a forced conclusion, but when you think of grave and six, only one word came to my mind.
HEART KREUZ

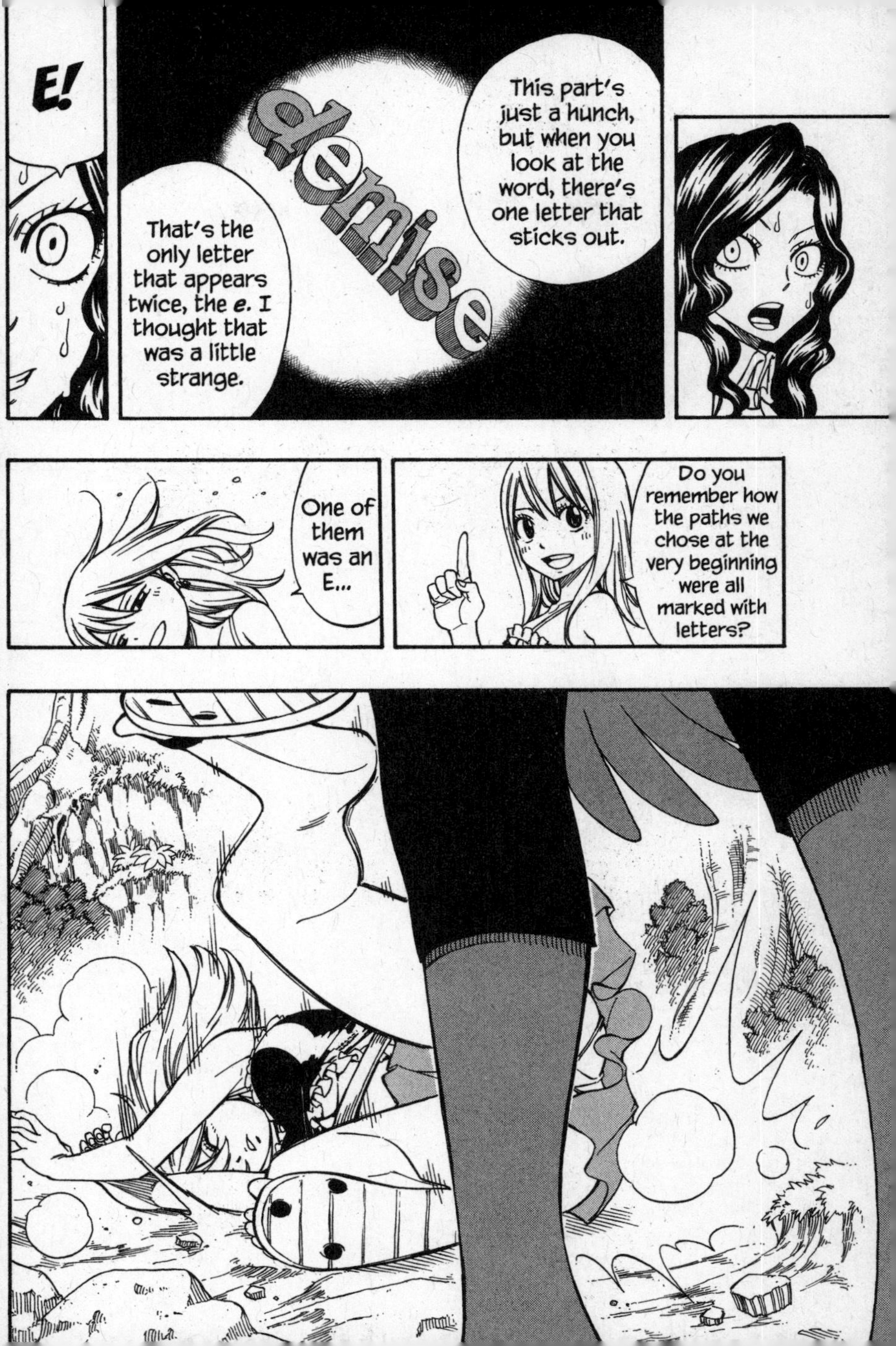
This part's just a hunch, but when you look at the word, there's one letter that sticks out.
demise
That's the only letter that appears twice, the *e*. I thought that was a little strange.
E!
Do you remember how the paths we chose at the very beginning were all marked with letters?
One of them was an E...

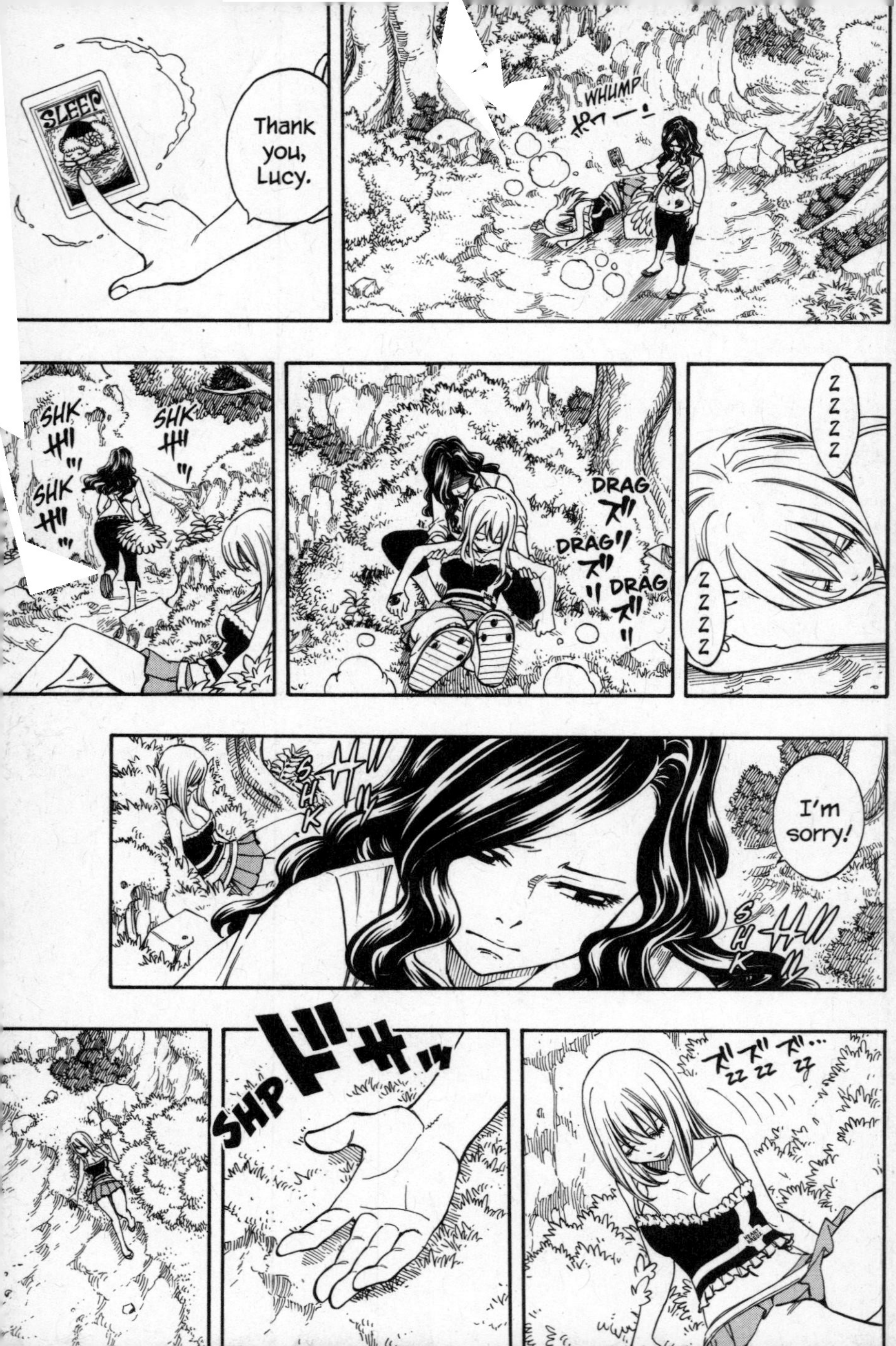
WHUMP
Thank you, Lucy.
ZZZZ
ZZZZ
DRAG
DRAG
DRAG
SHK
SHK
SHK
I'm sorry!
SHK
SHK
SHP

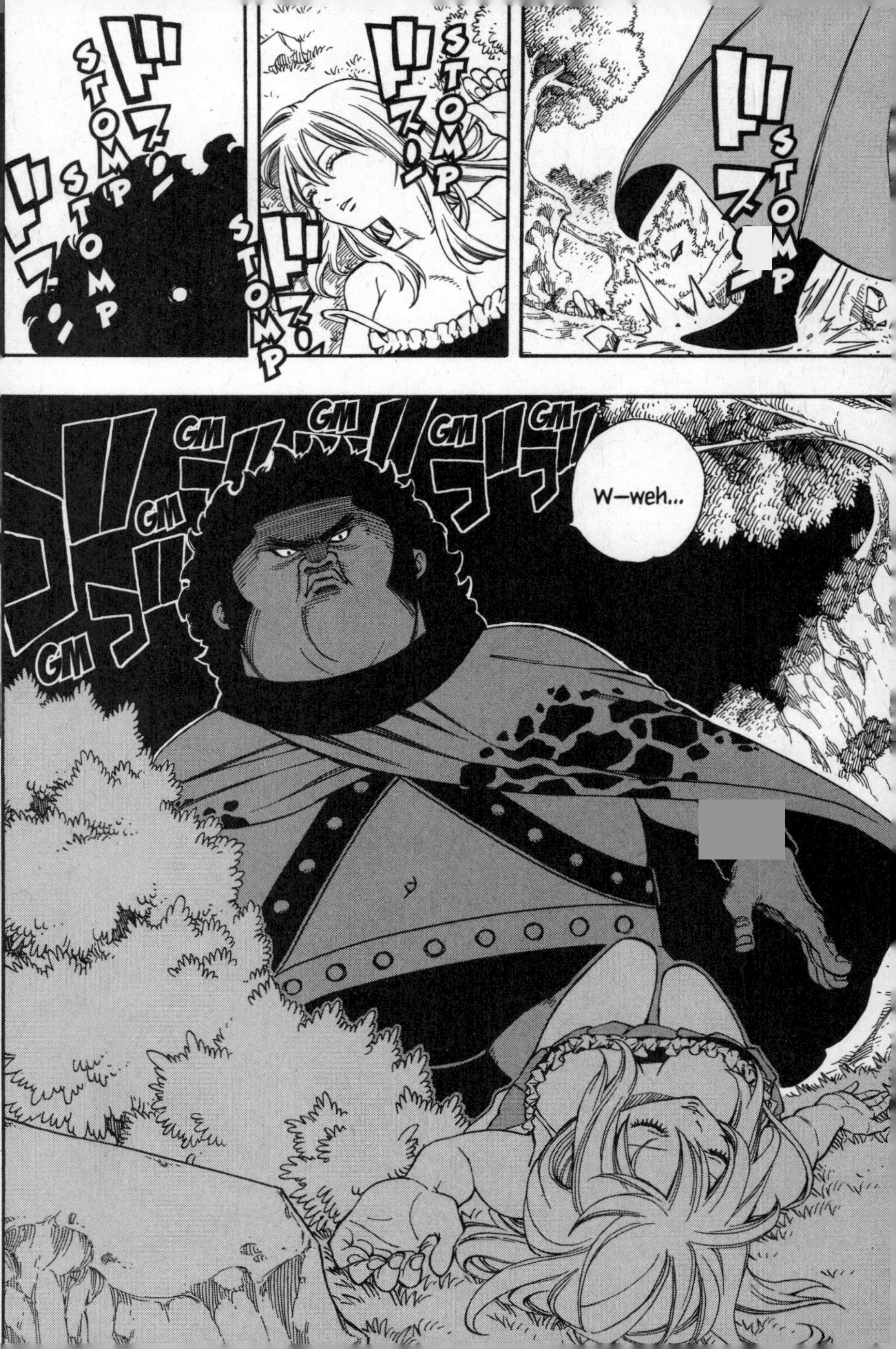
STOMP
STOMP
STOMP
STOMP
STOMP
W—weh...
GM
GM
GM
GM
GM
GM

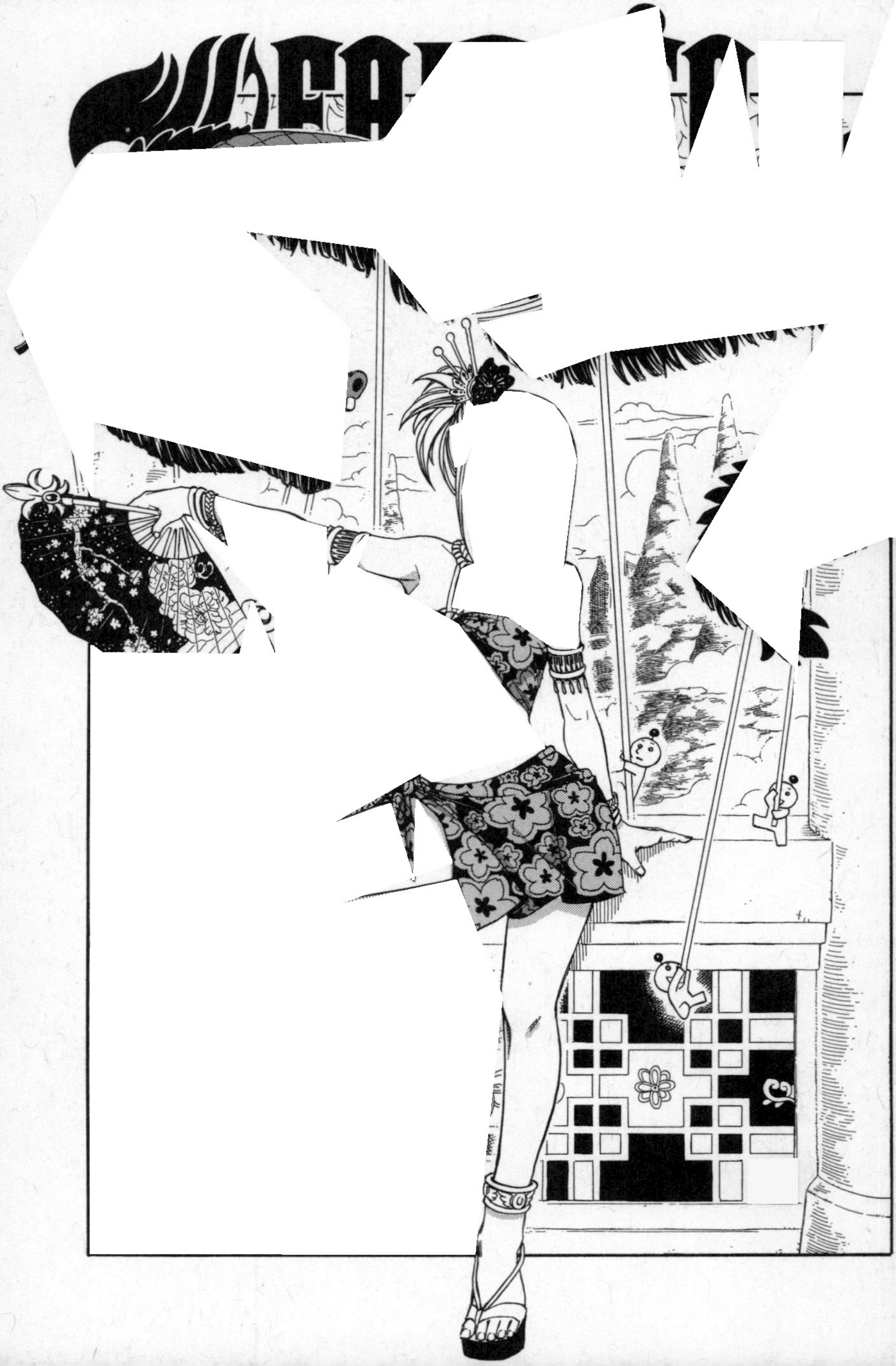

Chapter 226: A Curse of Vengeance

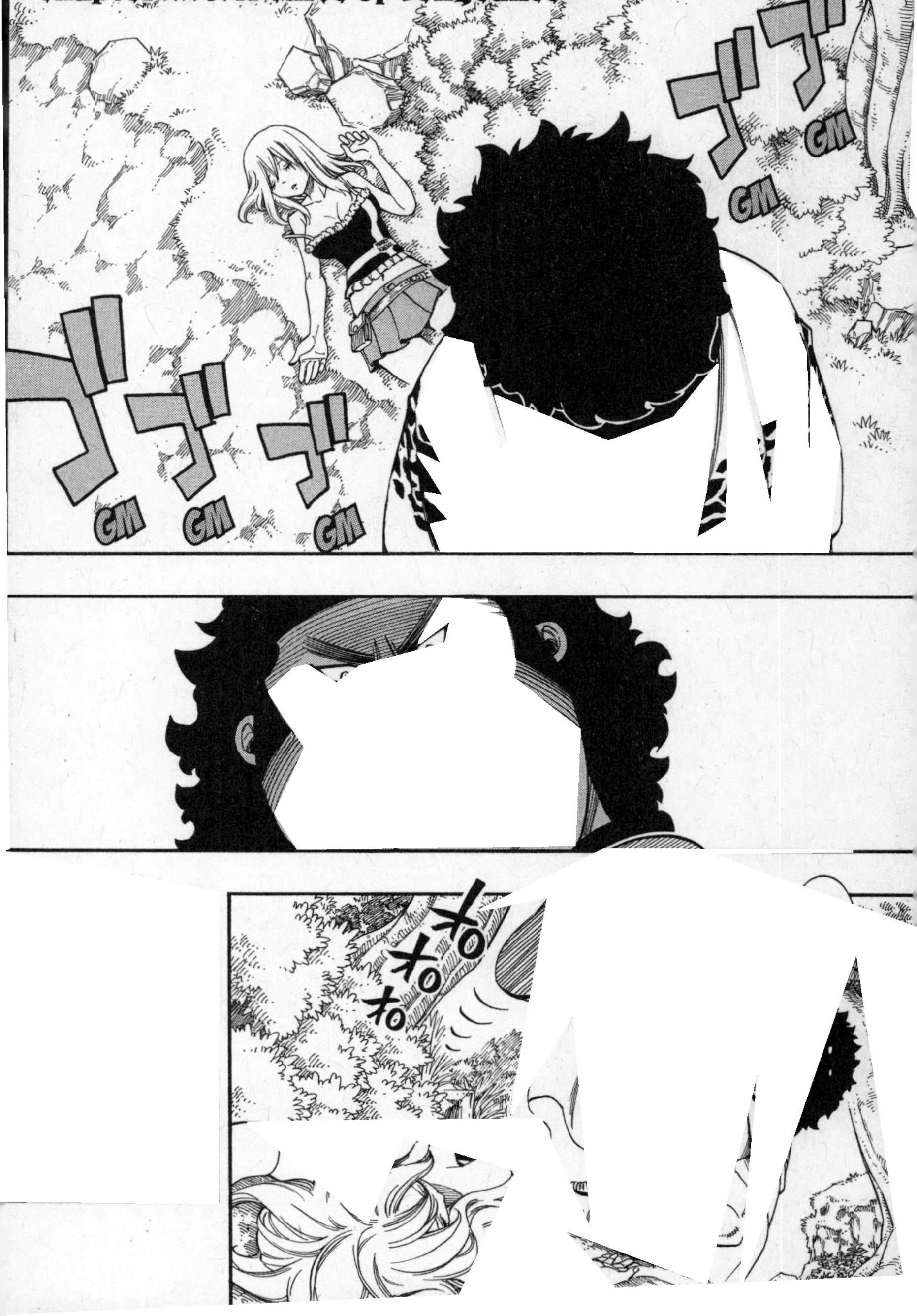
GM GM GM
GM GM GM
XO XO XO

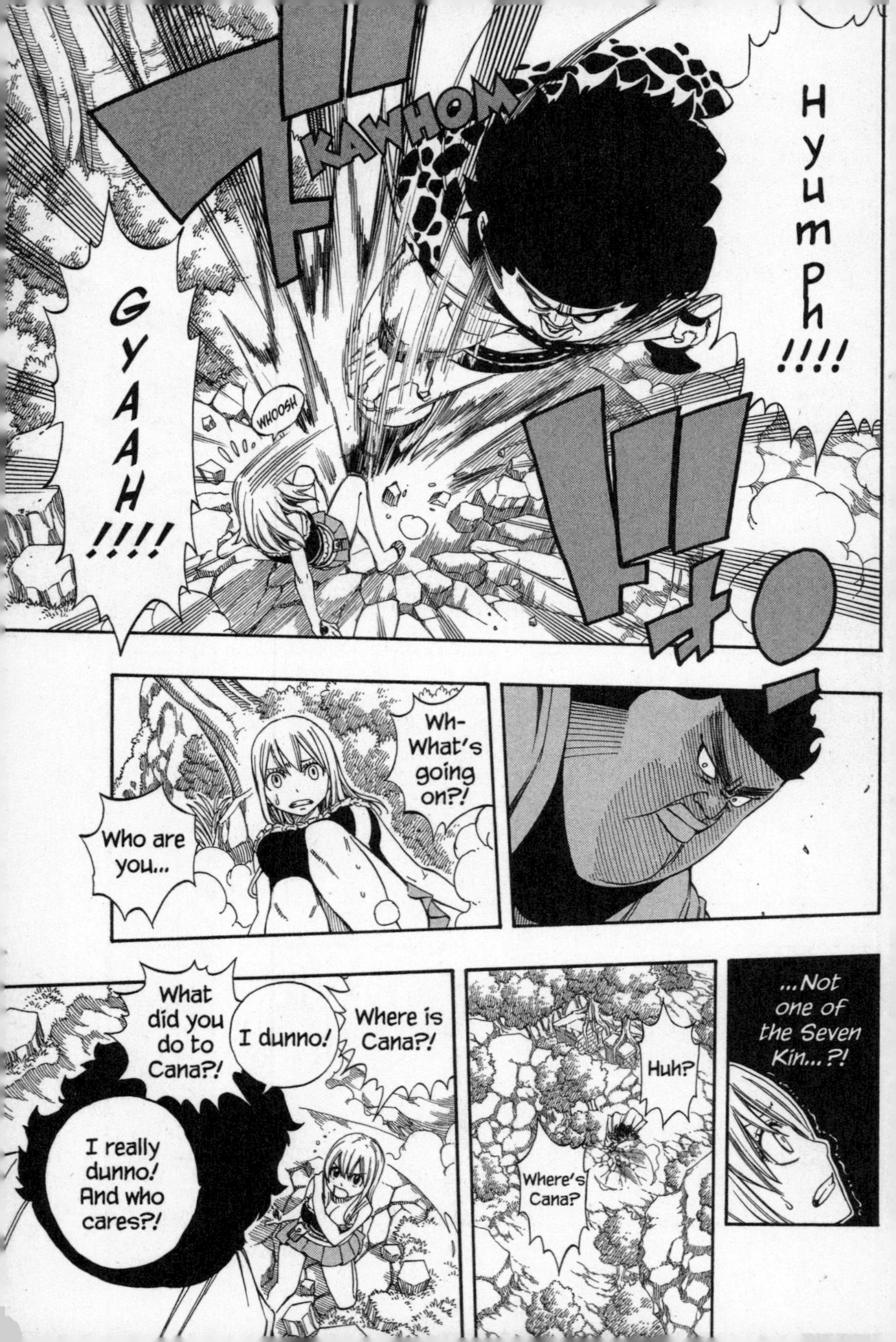
Hyumph!!!!
KAWHOM
WHOOSH
GYAAH!!!!
Wh- What's going on?!
Who are you...
...Not one of the Seven Kin...?!
Huh?
Where's Cana?
Where is Cana?!
I dunno!
What did you do to Cana?!
I really dunno! And who cares?!

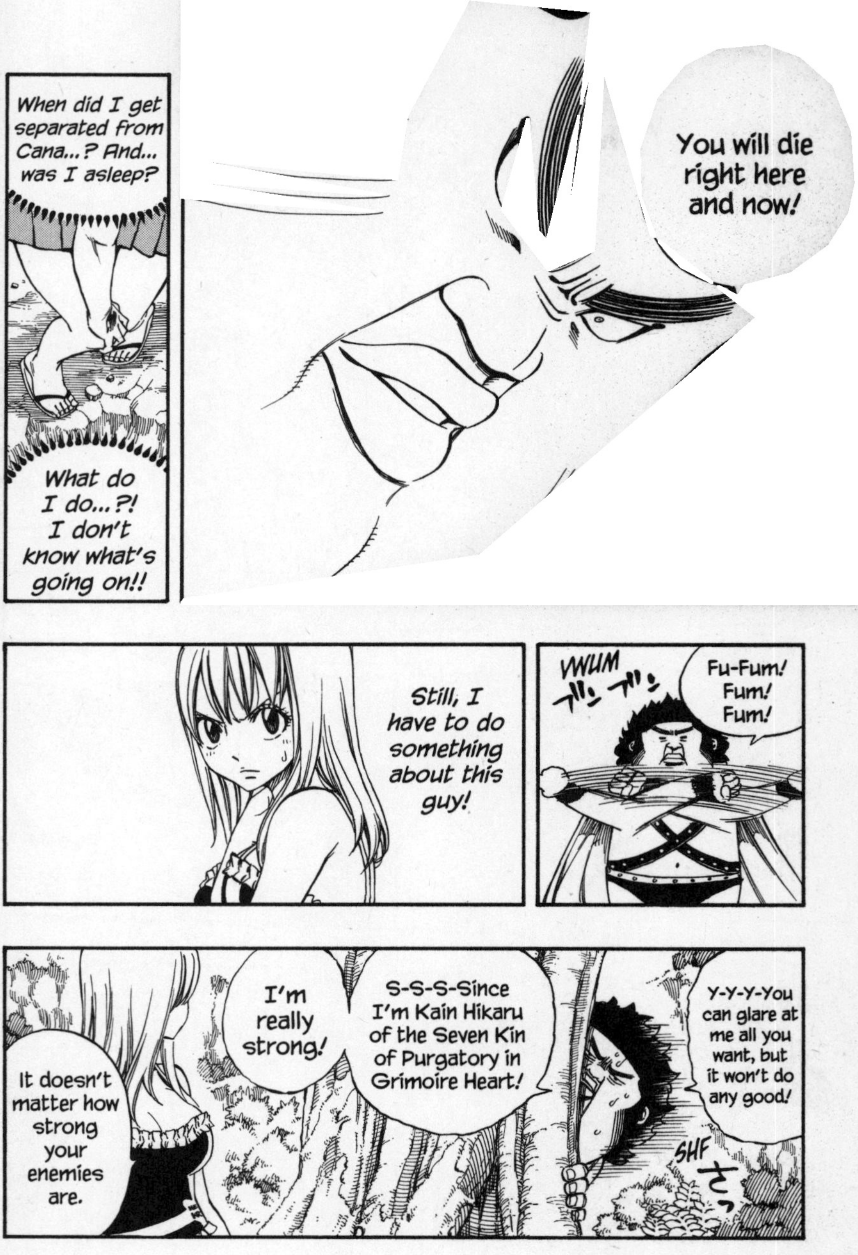
You will die right here and now!
When did I get separated from Cana...? And... was I asleep?
What do I do...?! I don't know what's going on!!
VWUM
Fu-Fum! Fum! Fum!
Still, I have to do something about this guy!
Y-Y-Y-You can glare at me all you want, but it won't do any good!
SHF
S-S-S-Since I'm Kain Hikaru of the Seven Kin of Purgatory in Grimoire Heart!
I'm really strong!
It doesn't matter how strong your enemies are.

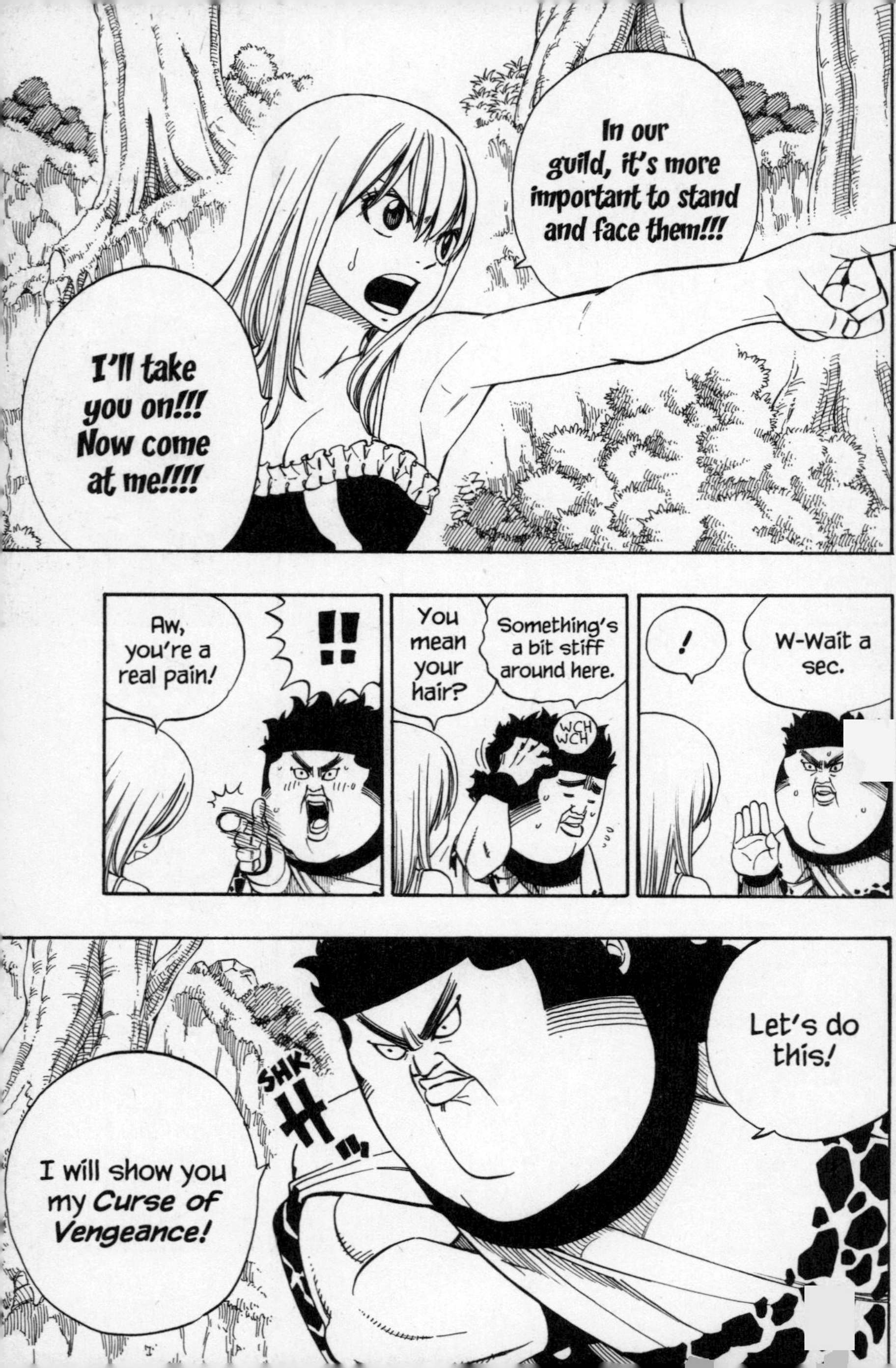
In our guild, it's more important to stand and face them!!!
I'll take you on!!! Now come at me!!!!
W-Wait a sec.
!
Something's a bit stiff around here.
WCH WCH
You mean your hair?
!!
Aw, you're a real pain!
Let's do this!
SHK
I will show you my *Curse of Vengeance!*

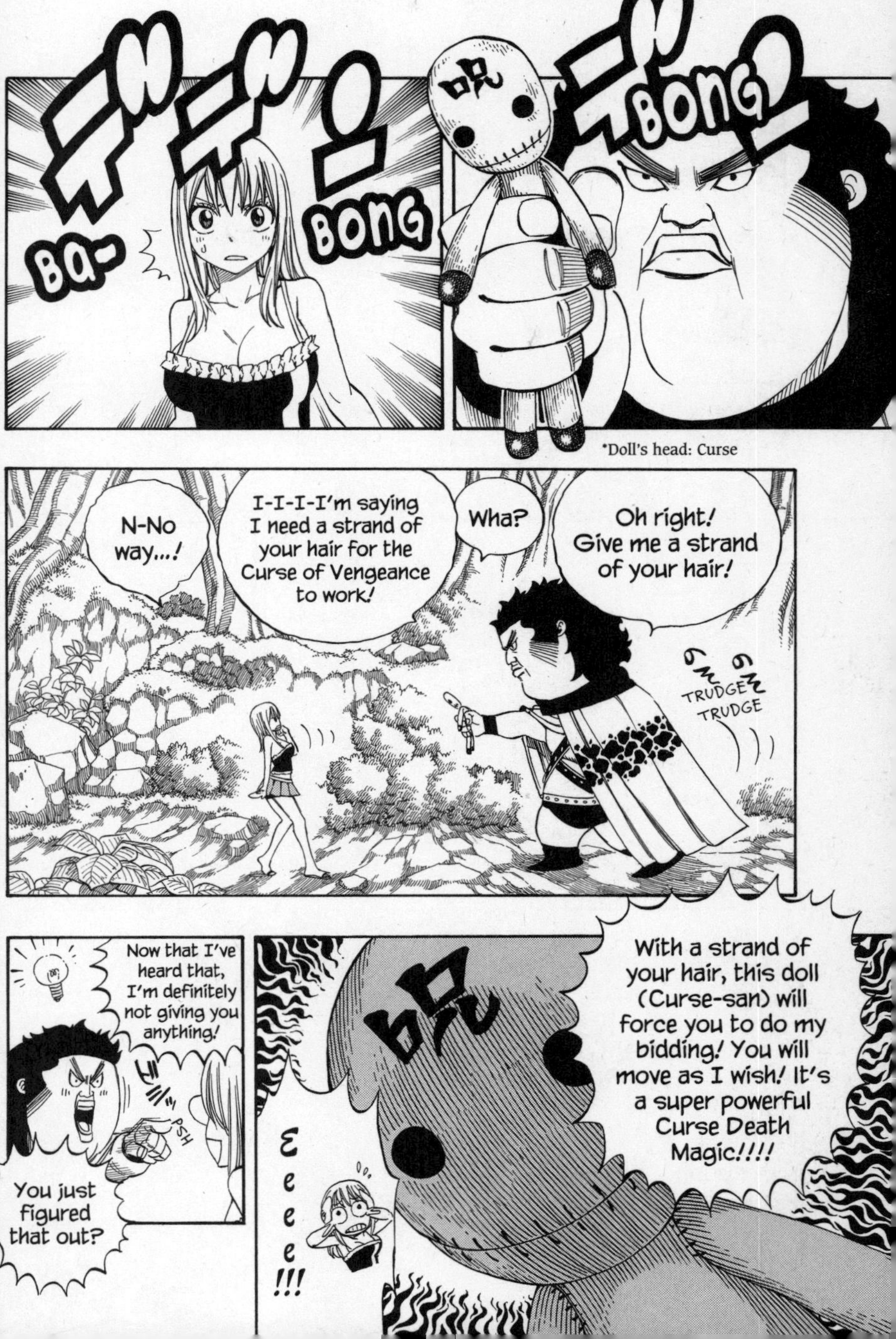
BONG
BA-
BONG
Oh right! Give me a strand of your hair!
Wha?
I-I-I-I'm saying I need a strand of your hair for the Curse of Vengeance to work!
N-No way...!
TRUDGE TRUDGE
With a strand of your hair, this doll (Curse-san) will force you to do my bidding! You will move as I wish! It's a super powerful Curse Death Magic!!!!
Eeee!!!
Now that I've heard that, I'm definitely not giving you anything!
PSH
You just figured that out?

*Doll's head: Curse

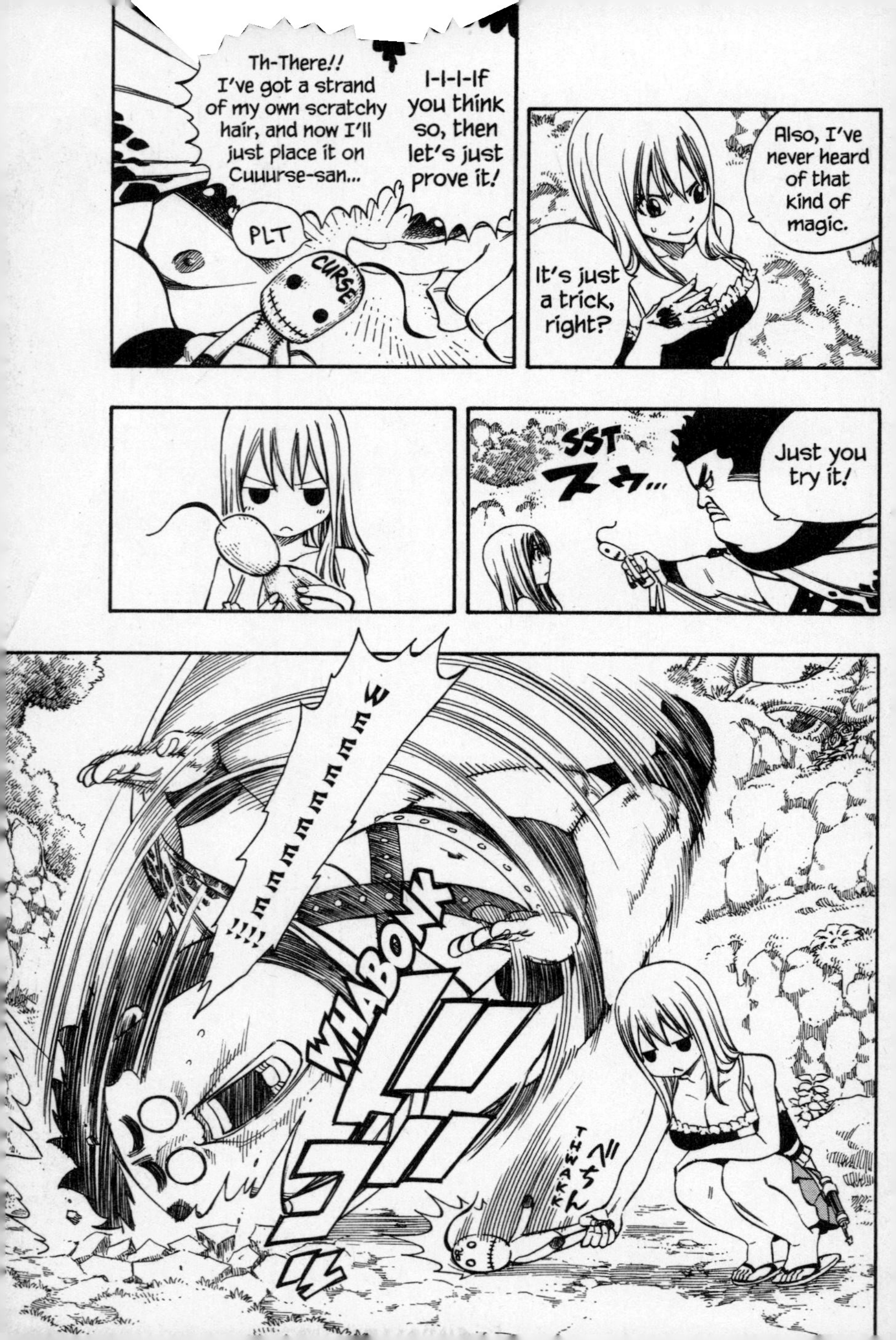
Also, I've never heard of that kind of magic.
It's just a trick, right?
I-I-I-If you think so, then let's just prove it!
Th-There!! I've got a strand of my own scratchy hair, and now I'll just place it on Cuuurse-san...
PLT
CURSE
SST
Just you try it!
WHABONK
Wmmmmmmmmmmm!!!!
THWAKK

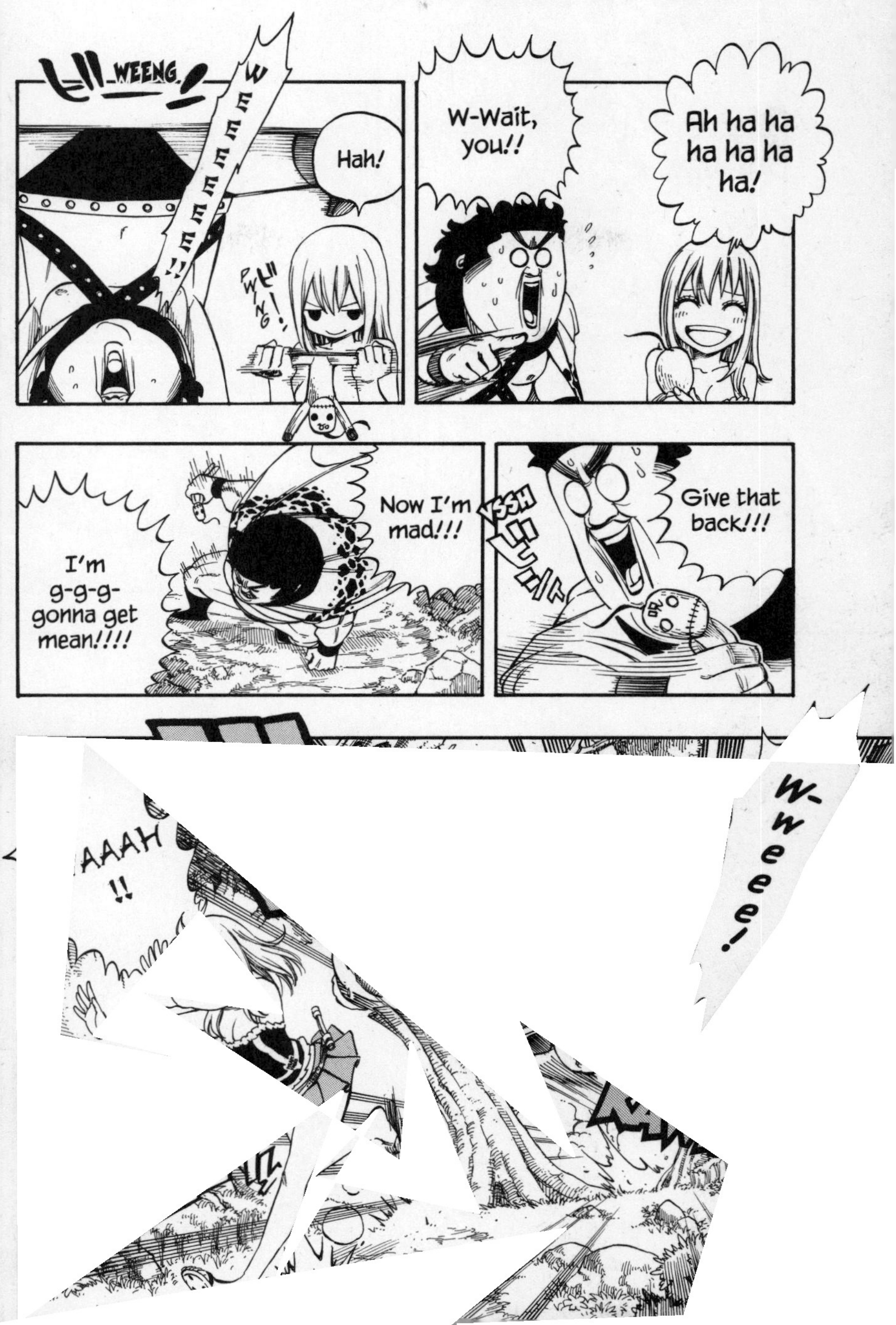
Ah ha ha ha ha ha ha!
W-Wait, you!!
WEENG
WEEEEEEEE!!
Hah!
PWING
Give that back!!!
VSSH
Now I'm mad!!!
I'm g-g-g-gonna get mean!!!!
W-weeee!
AAAH!!

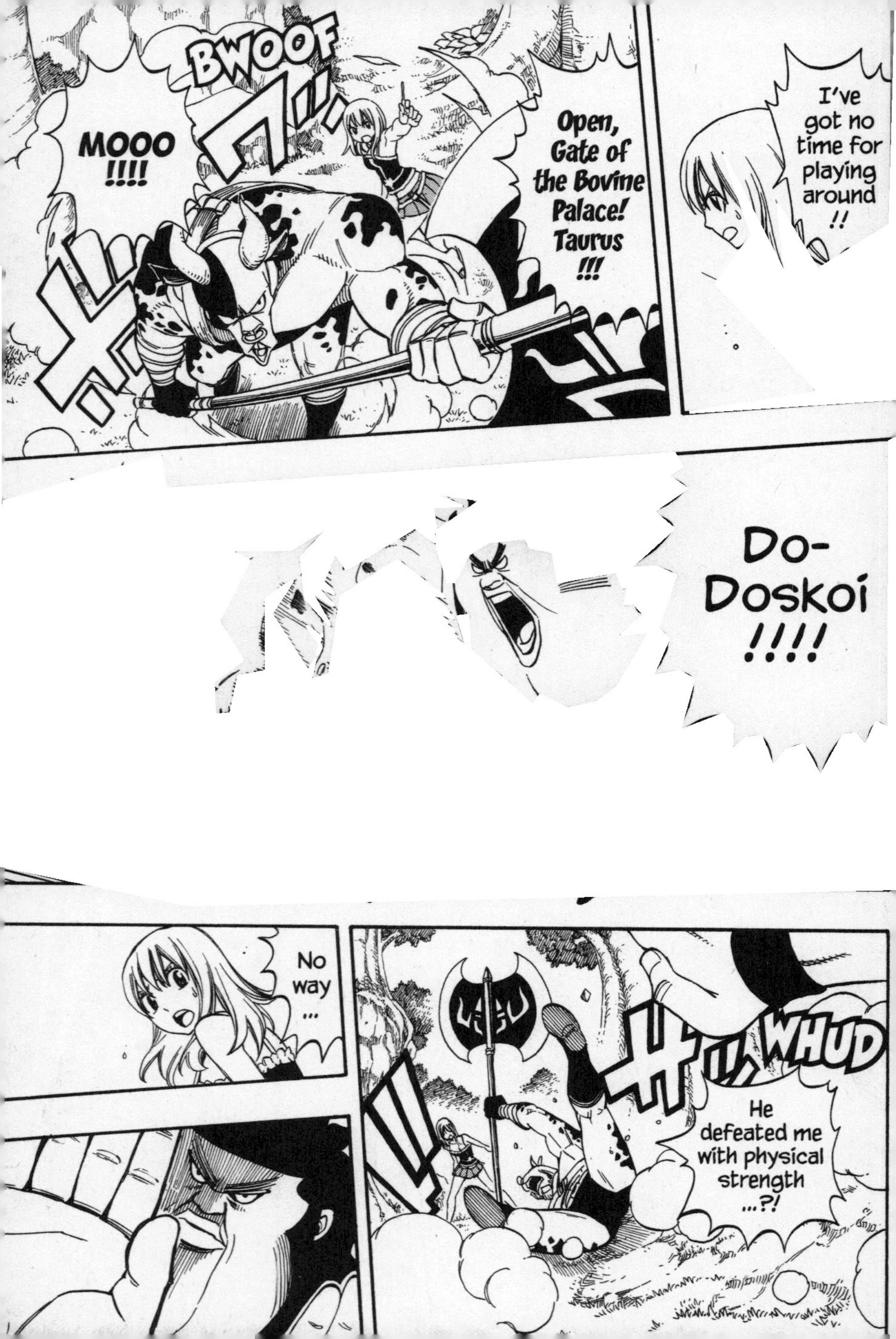
I've got no time for playing around !!
Open, Gate of the Bovine Palace! Taurus !!!
BWOOF
MOOO !!!!
Do-Doskoi !!!!
WHUD
He defeated me with physical strength ...?!
No way ...

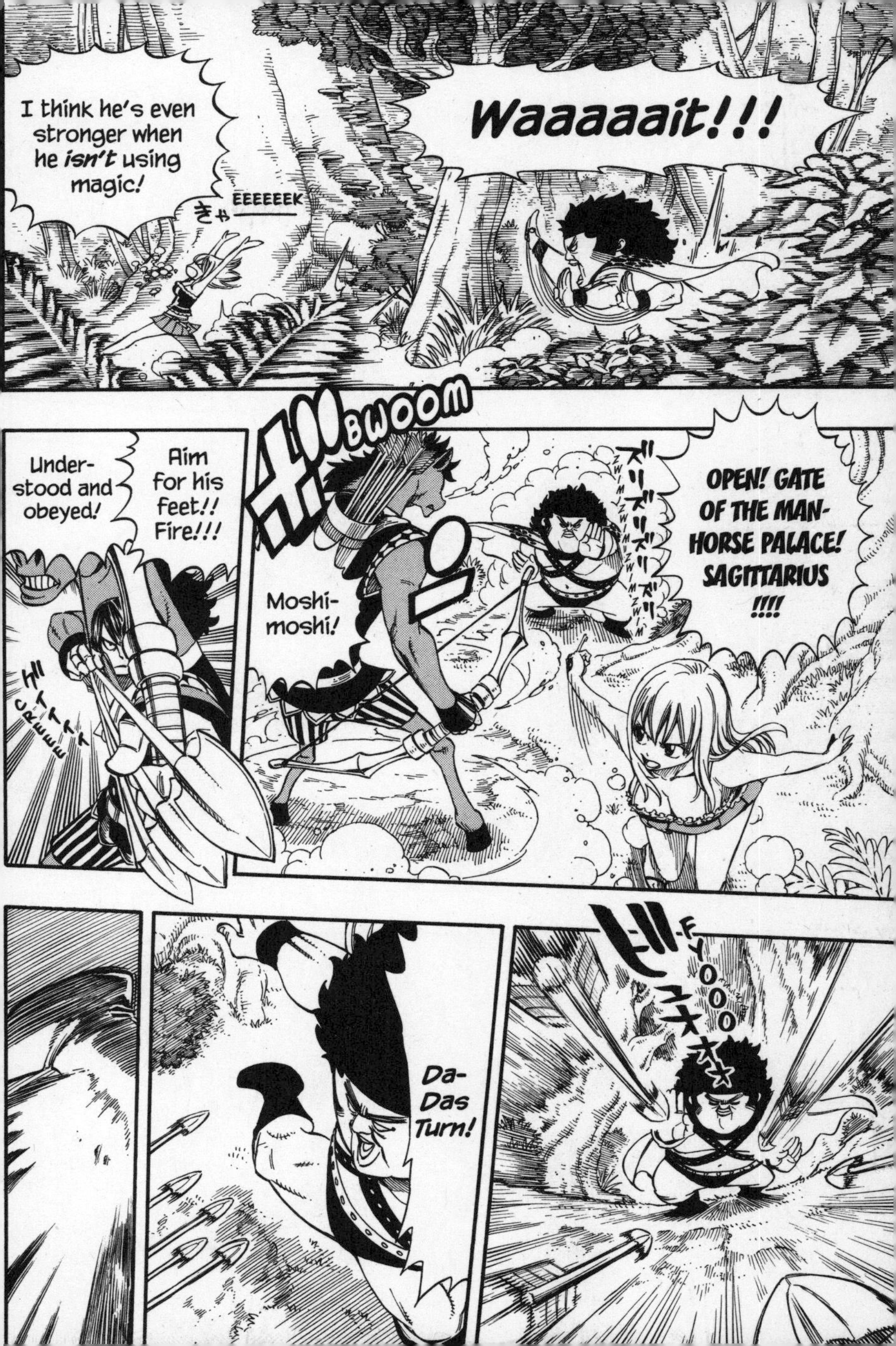
Waaaaaait!!!
きゃー EEEEEEK
I think he's even stronger when he *isn't* using magic!
OPEN! GATE OF THE MAN-HORSE PALACE! SAGITTARIUS!!!!
ZWIM ZWIM ZWIM ZWIM
Moshi-moshi!
BWOOM
Aim for his feet!! Fire!!!
Understood and obeyed!
CREEEE
FYOOOO
Da-Das Turn!

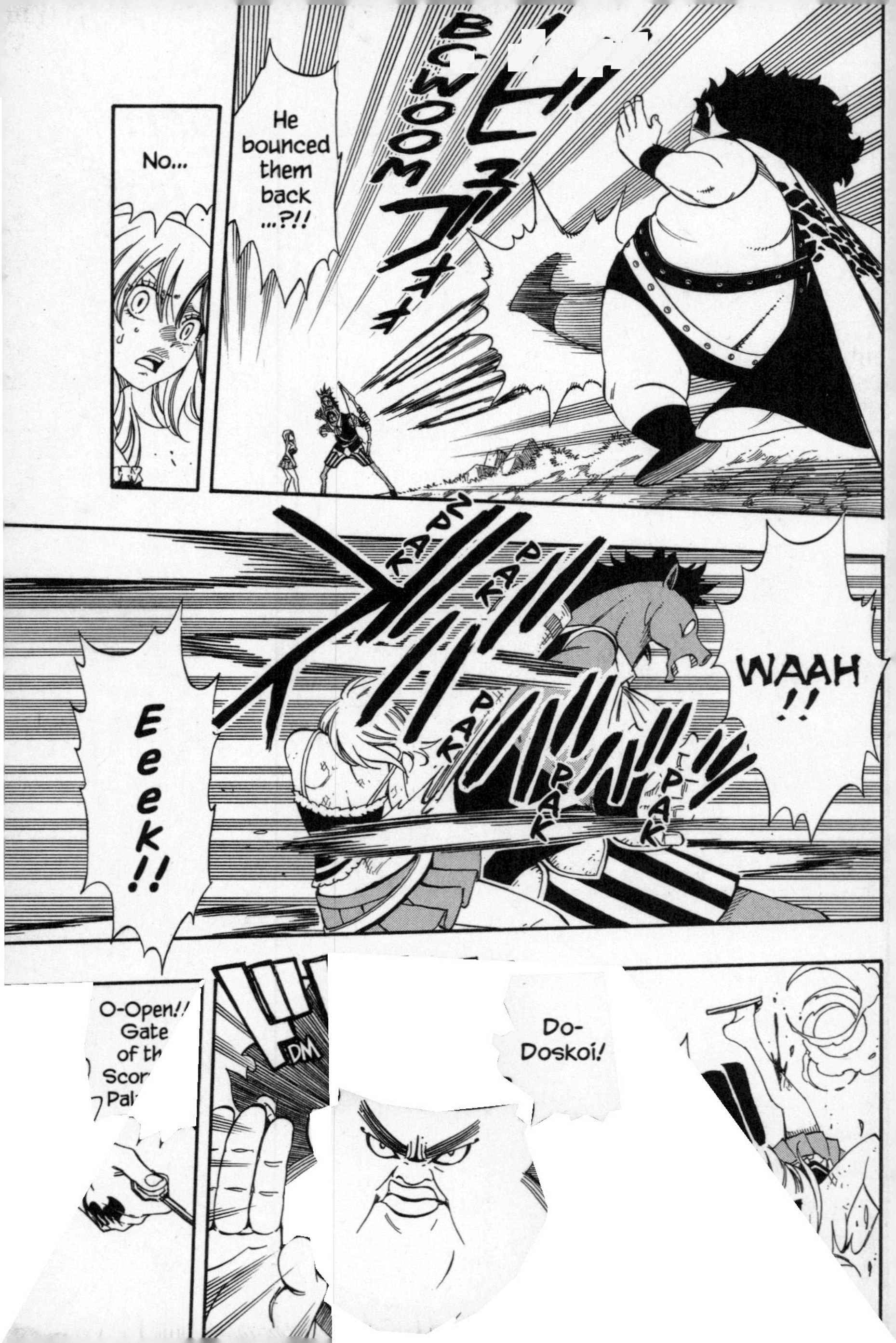

BCWOOM
He bounced them back ...?!!
No...
WAAH!!
PAK
PAK
ZPAK
PAK
PAK
PAK
PAK
Eeek!!
Do-Doskoi!
DM
O-Open!! Gate of th Scor Pal

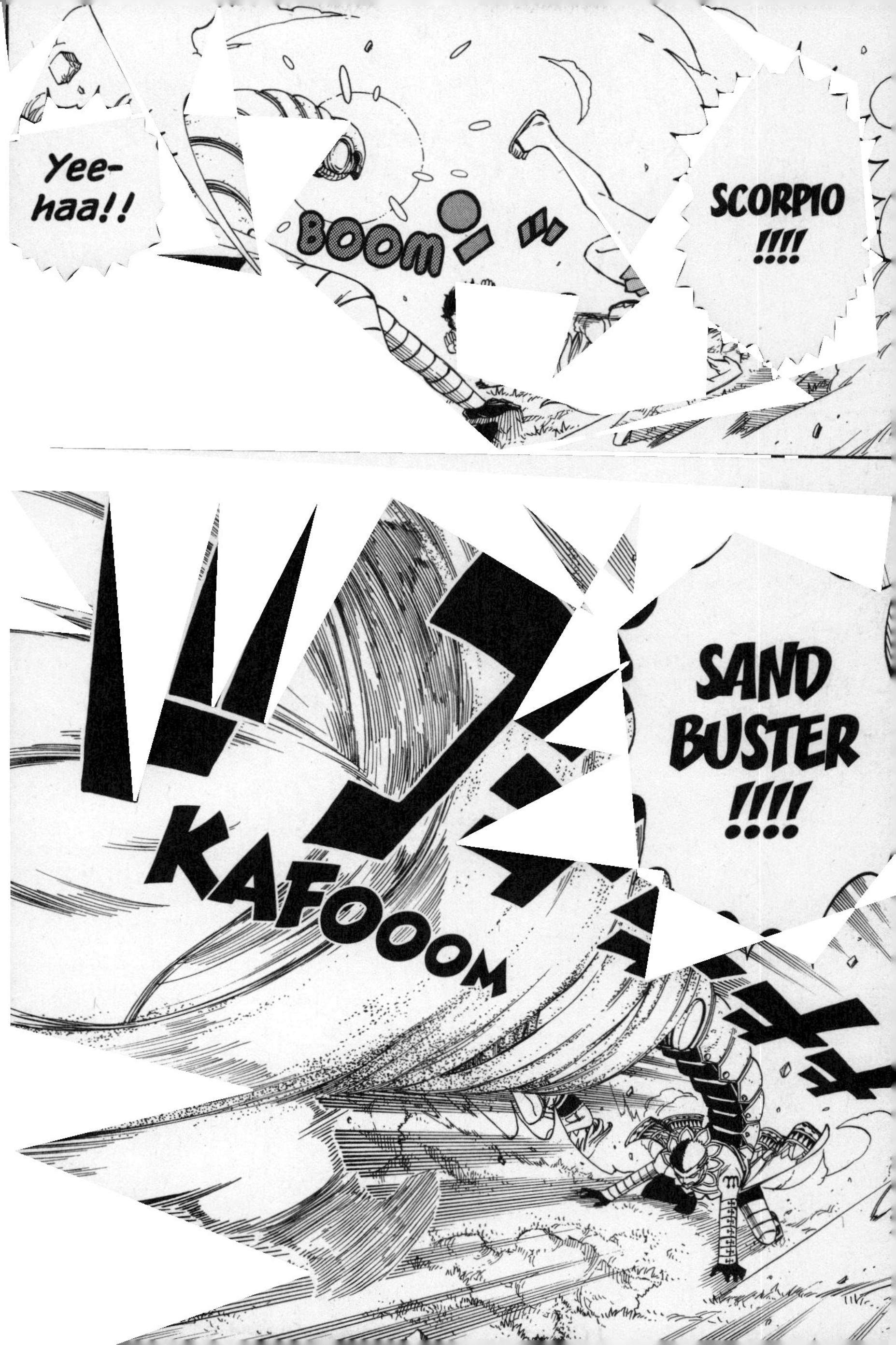
SCORPIO !!!!
BOOM
Yee-haa!!
SAND BUSTER !!!!
KAFOOOM

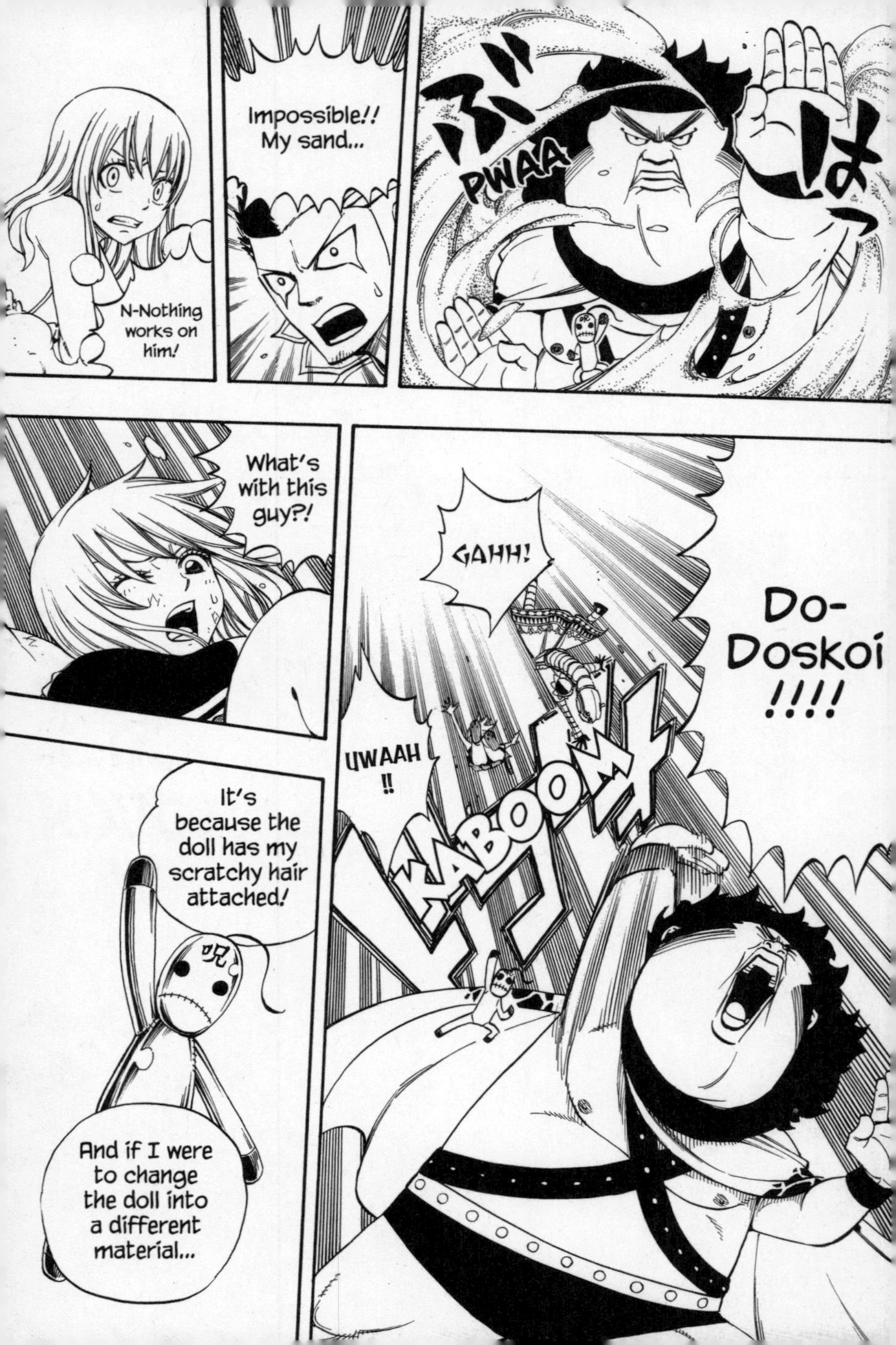
ぶはっ
PWAA
Impossible!! My sand...
N-Nothing works on him!
GAHH!
Do-Doskoi!!!!
UWAAH!!
KABOOM
What's with this guy?!
It's because the doll has my scratchy hair attached!
呪
And if I were to change the doll into a different material...

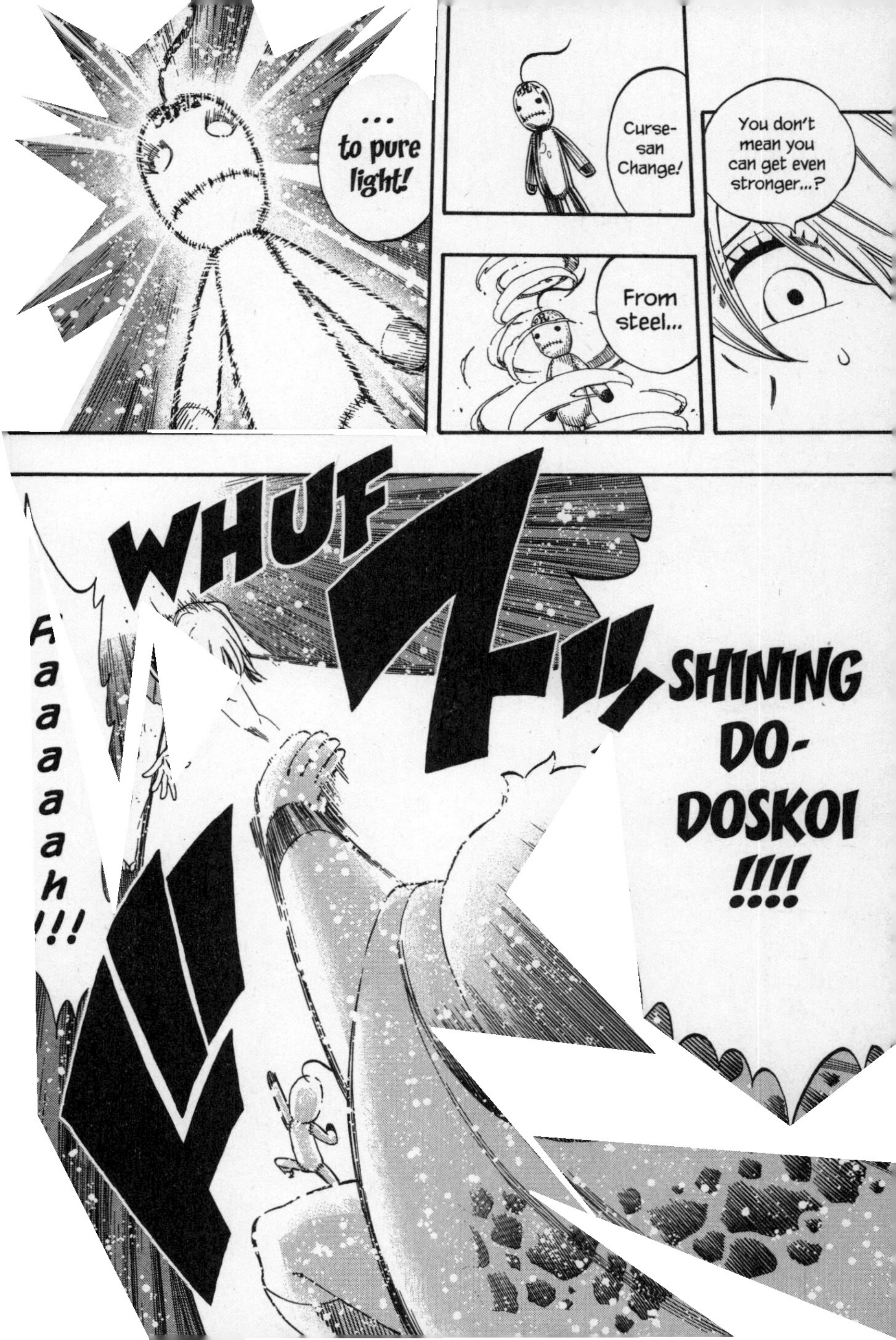

You don't mean you can get even stronger...?
Curse-san Change!
From steel...
... to pure light!
SHINING DO-DOSKOI!!!!
WHUF
Aaaaaah!!!

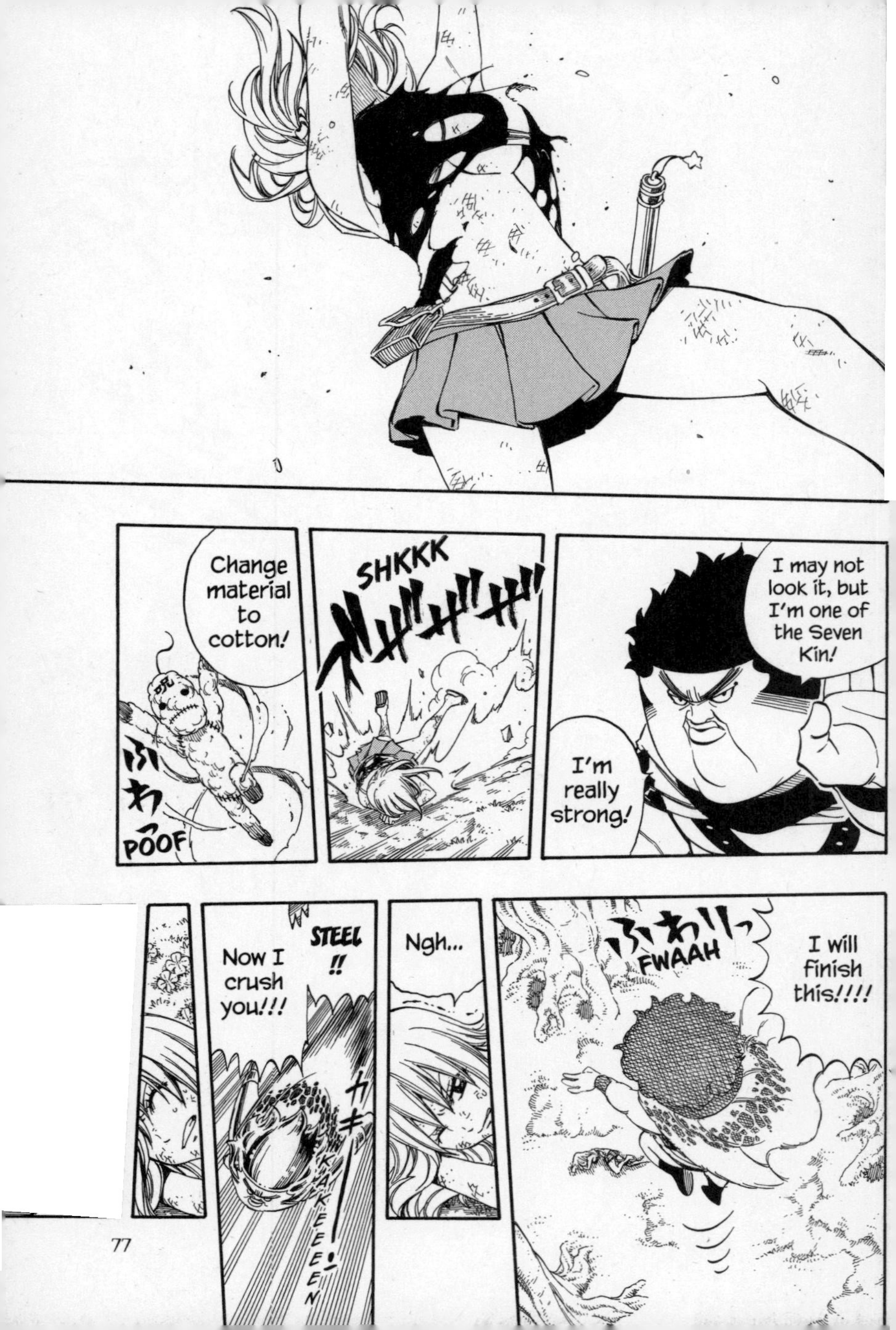
I may not look it, but I'm one of the Seven Kin!
I'm really strong!
SHKKK
Change material to cotton!
ふわ
POOF
ふわ!!っ
FWAAH
I will finish this!!!!
Ngh...
STEEL!!
Now I crush you!!!
カキ
KAKEEEEN!

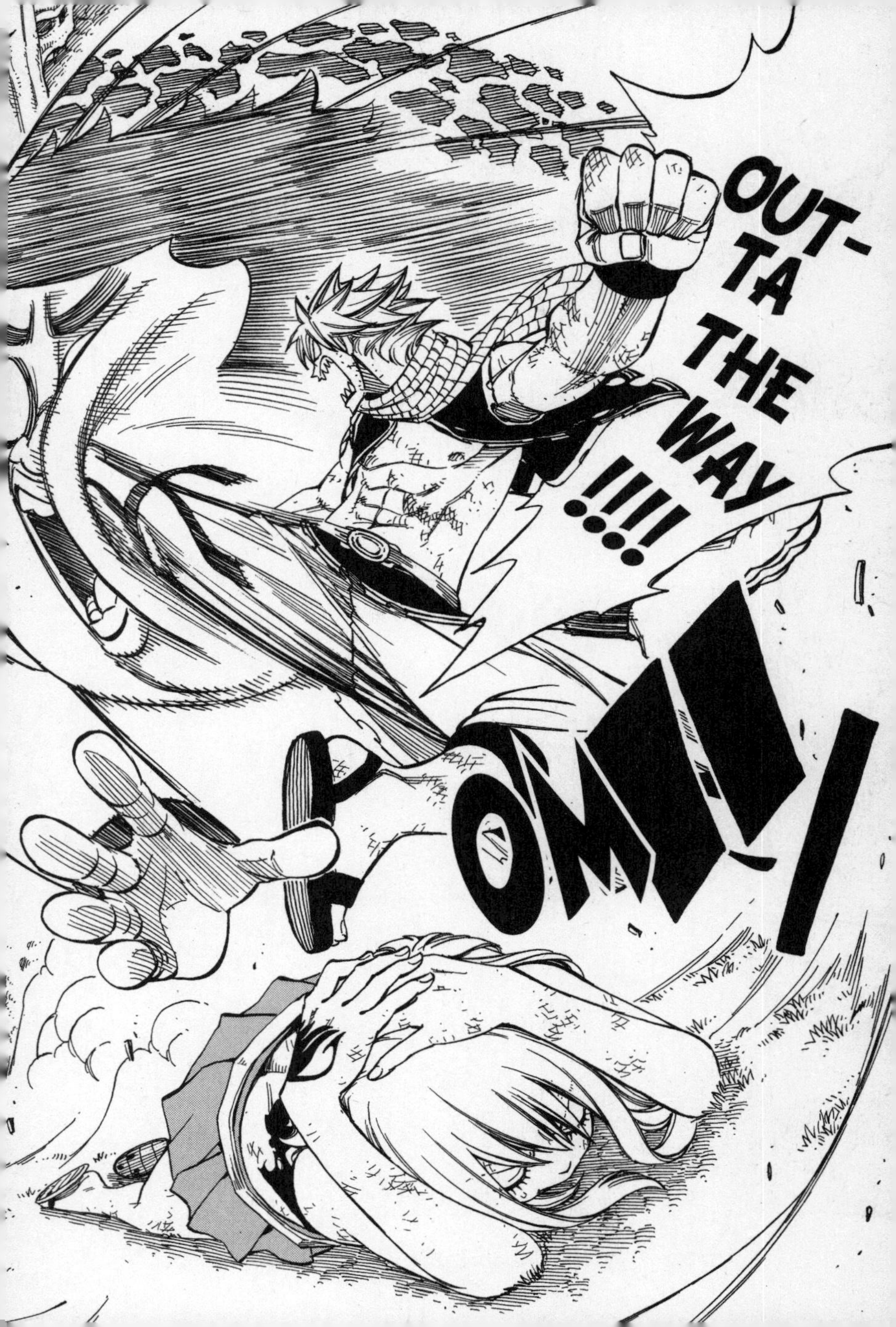
OUT-TA THE WAY!!!!!
POW!!

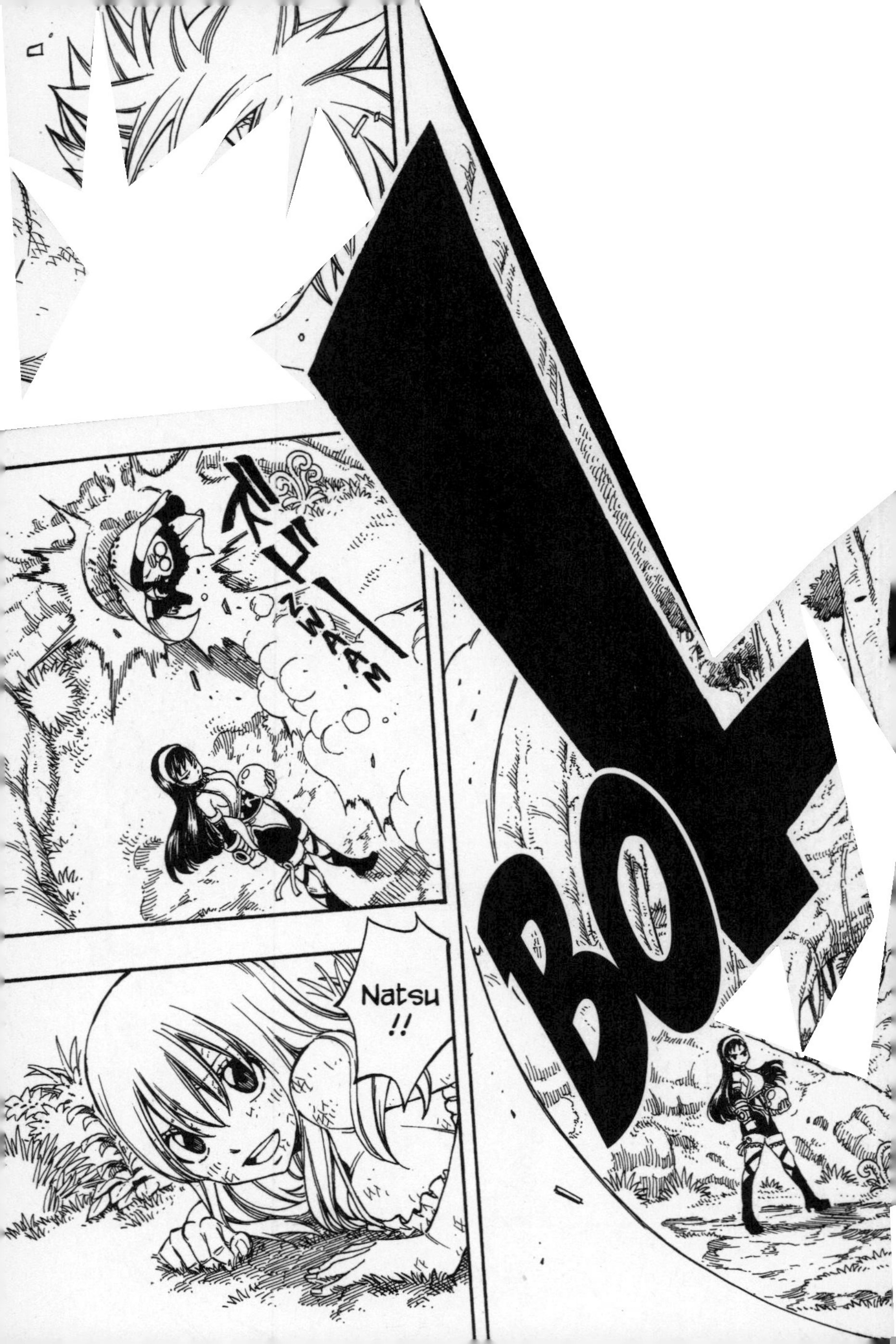
BOOM
NWAAM
Natsu !!

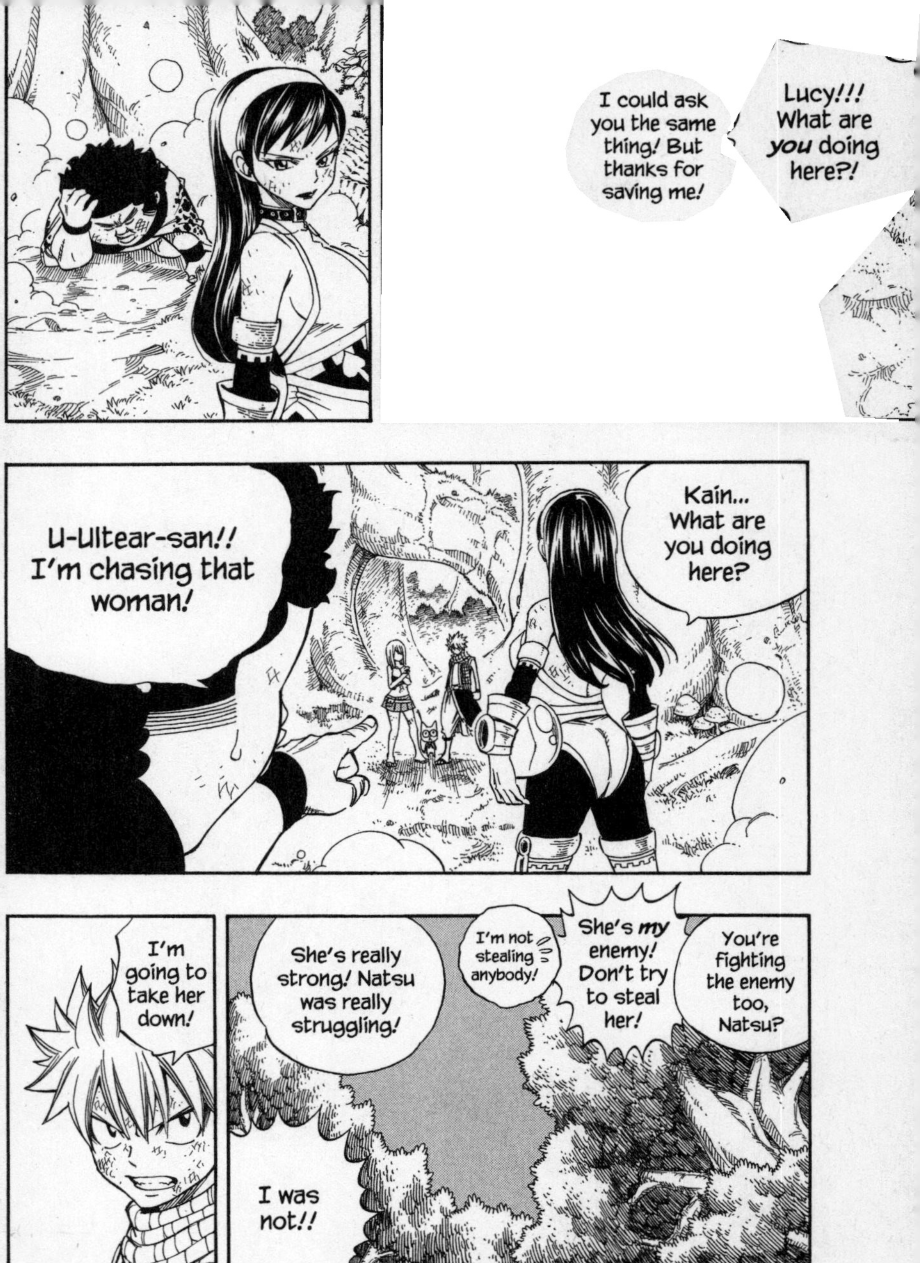

Lucy!!! What are *you* doing here?!
I could ask you the same thing! But thanks for saving me!
Kain... What are you doing here?
U-Ultear-san!! I'm chasing that woman!
You're fighting the enemy too, Natsu?
She's *my* enemy! Don't try to steal her!
I'm not stealing anybody!
She's really strong! Natsu was really struggling!
I was not!!
I'm going to take her down!

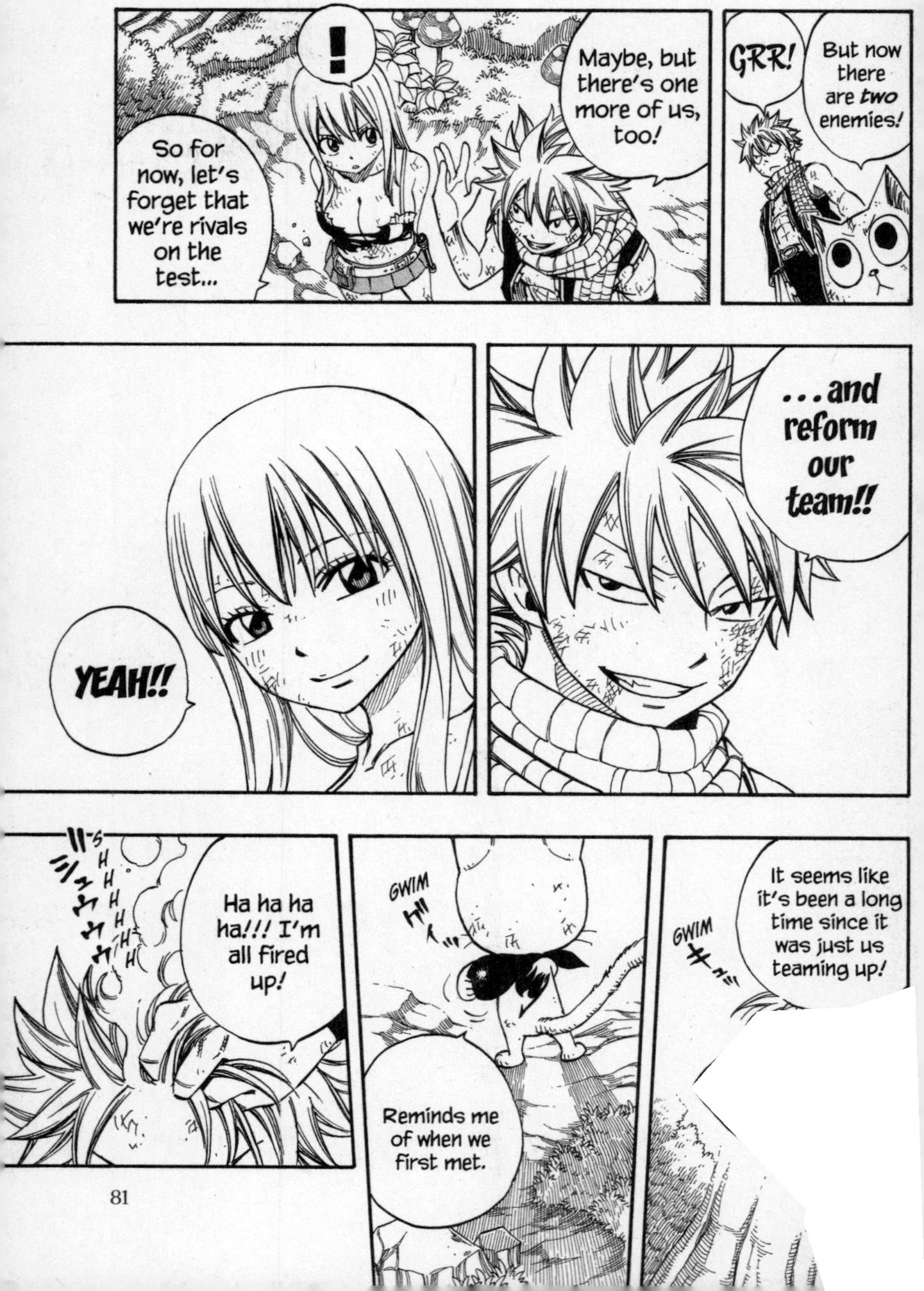
But now there are *two* enemies!
GRR!
Maybe, but there's one more of us, too!
!
So for now, let's forget that we're rivals on the test...
...and reform our team!!
YEAH!!
GWIM
It seems like it's been a long time since it was just us teaming up!
GWIM
Reminds me of when we first met.
Ha ha ha ha!!! I'm all fired up!
SHHHHHHH

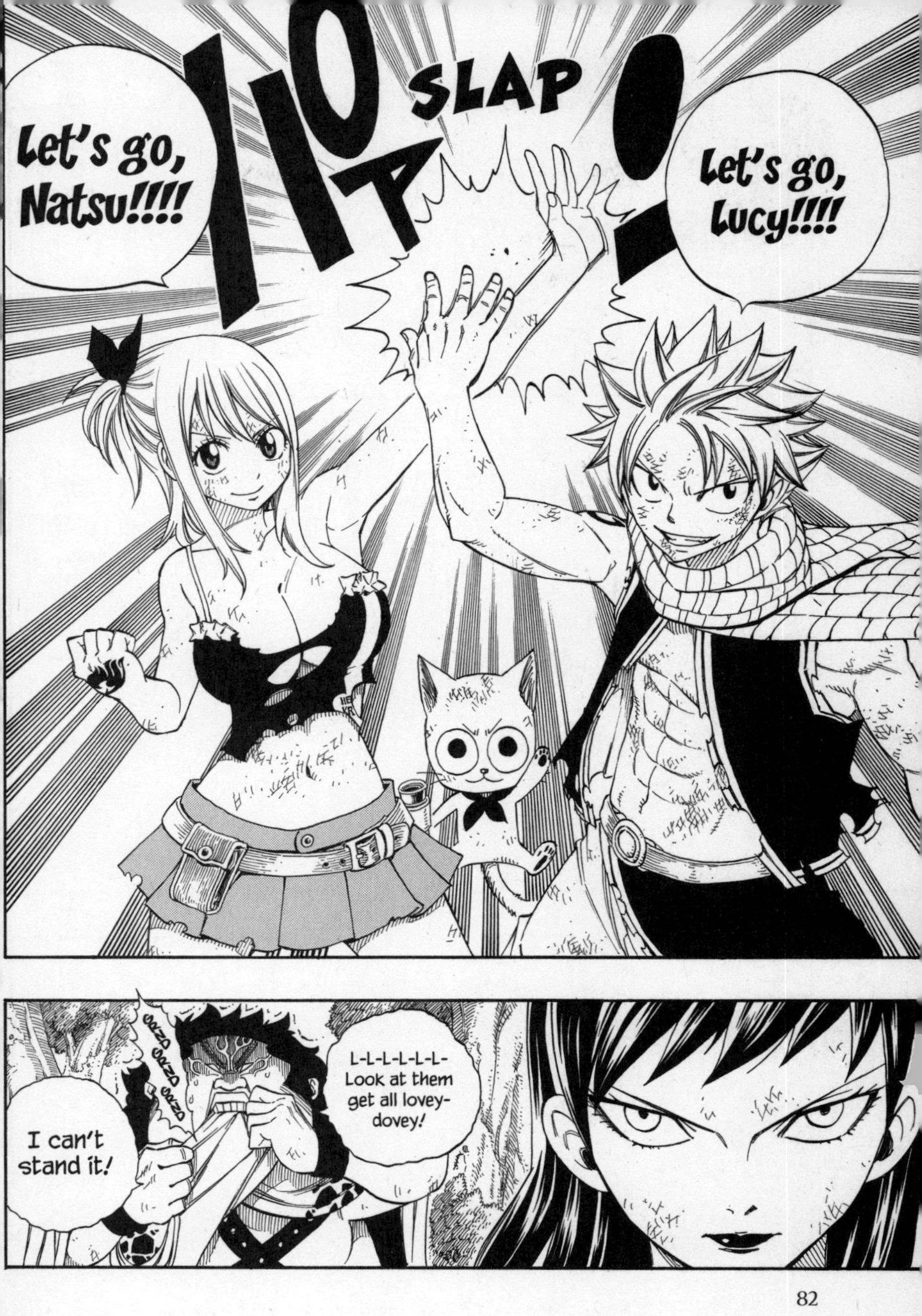
Let's go, Lucy!!!!
SLAP
Let's go, Natsu!!!!
L-L-L-L-L-L-Look at them get all lovey-dovey!
I can't stand it!

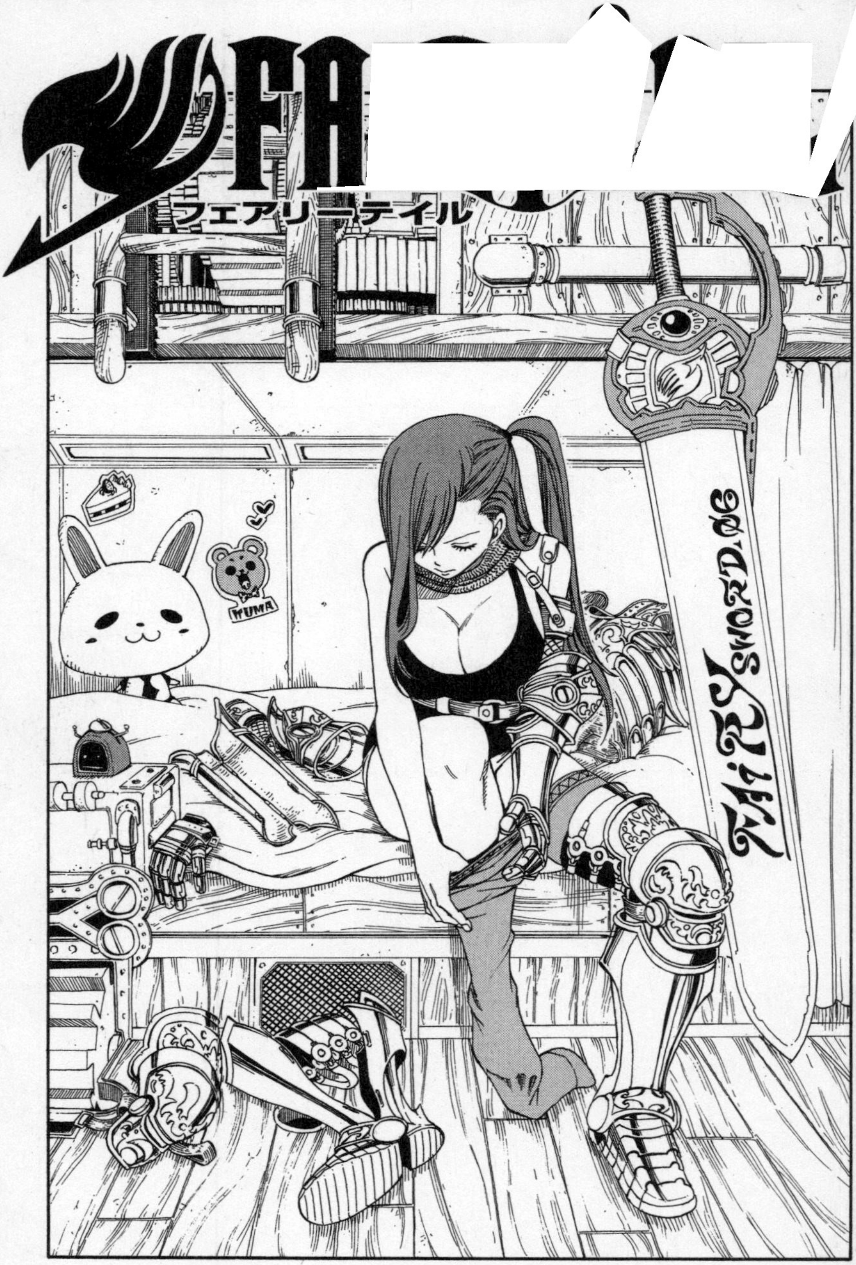
フェアリーテイル

Chapter 227: Lucy Fire

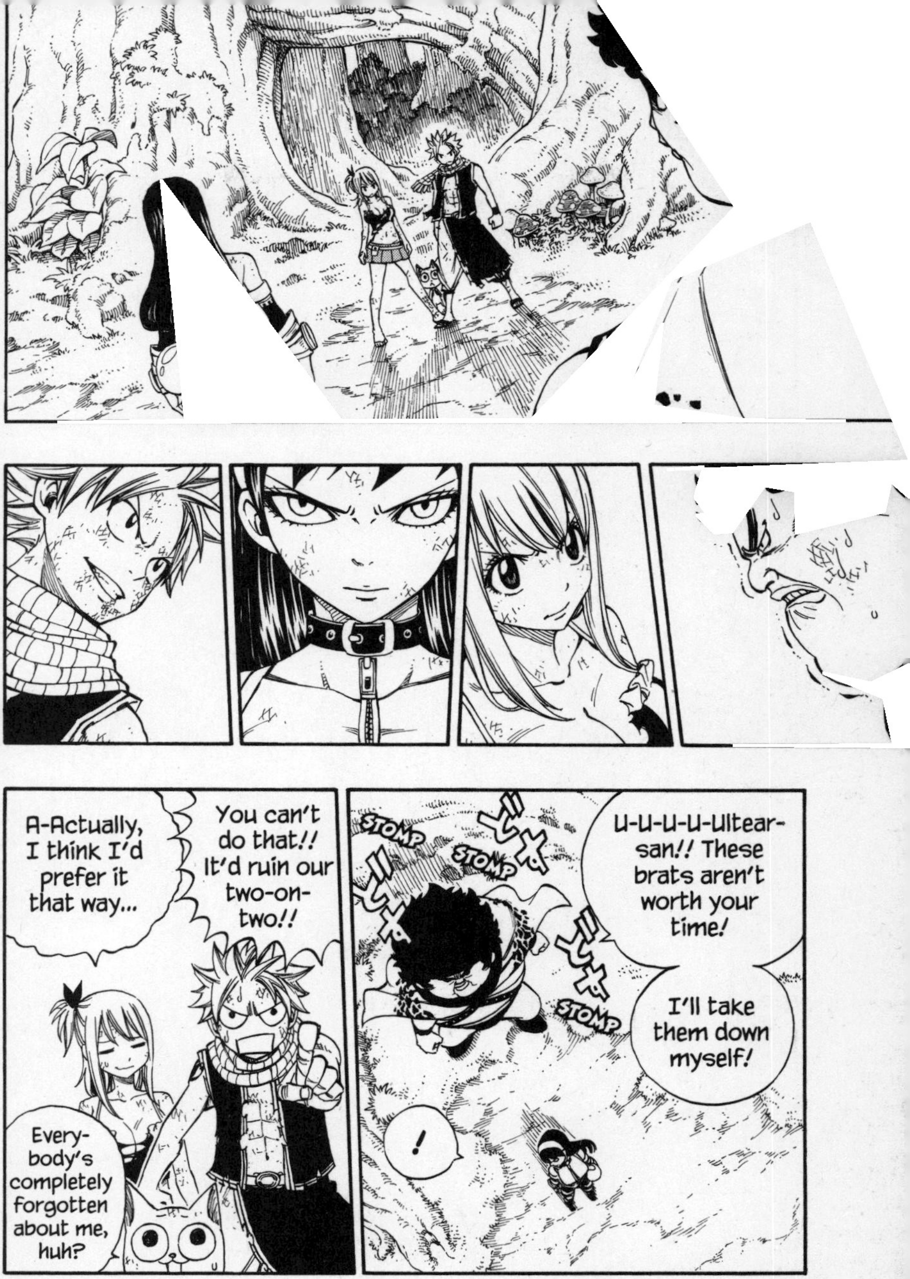
STOMP
STOMP
U-U-U-U-Ultear-san!! These brats aren't worth your time!
STOMP
I'll take them down myself!
!
You can't do that!! It'd ruin our two-on-two!!
A-Actually, I think I'd prefer it that way...
Every-body's completely forgotten about me, huh?

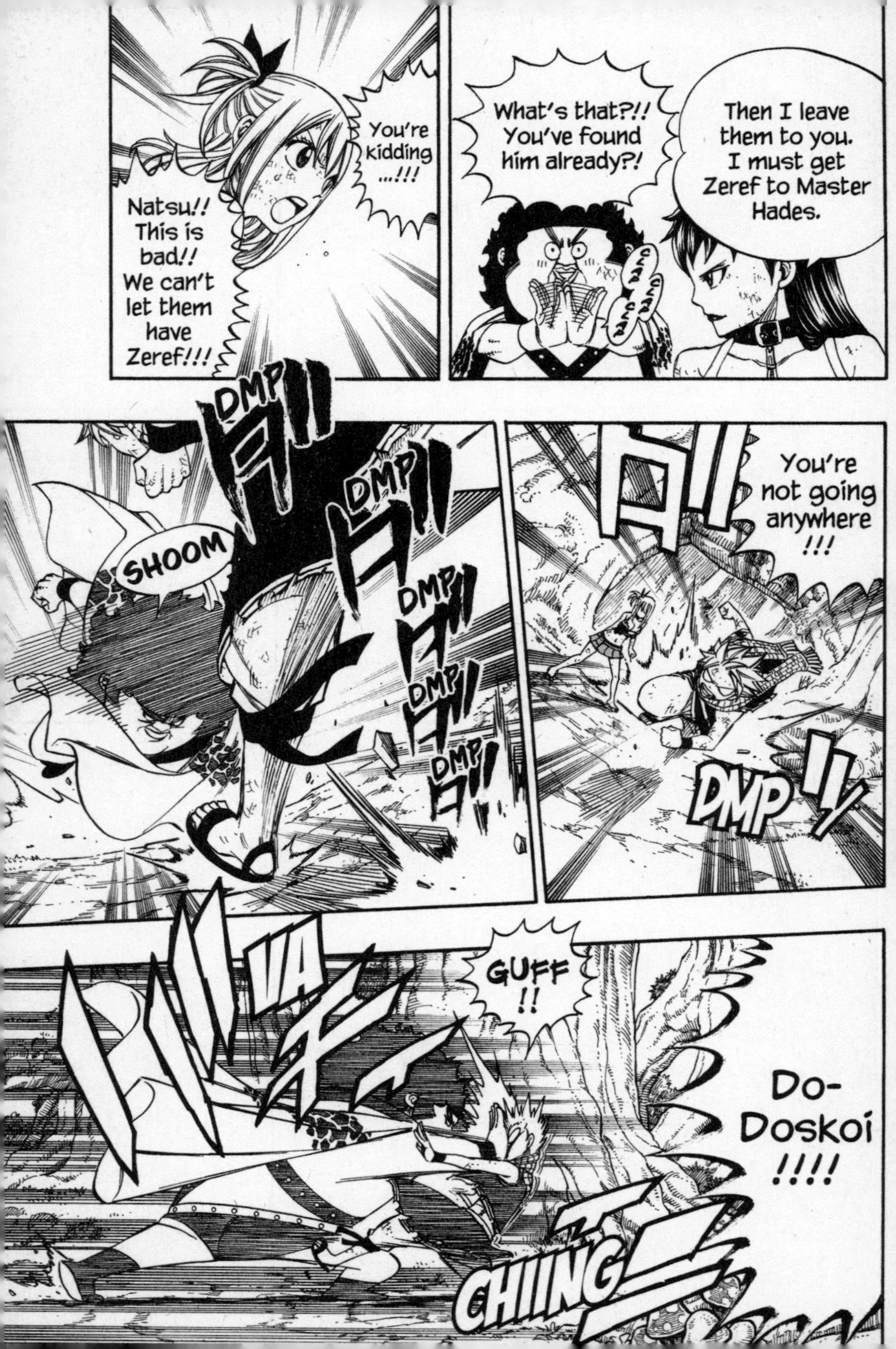
Then I leave them to you. I must get Zeref to Master Hades.
What's that?!! You've found him already?!
CLAP CLAP CLAP CLAP
You're kidding ...!!!
Natsu!! This is bad!! We can't let them have Zeref!!!
You're not going anywhere !!!
DMP
DMP
DMP
DMP
DMP
DMP
SHOOM
Do-Doskoi !!!!
GUFF !!
CHIING

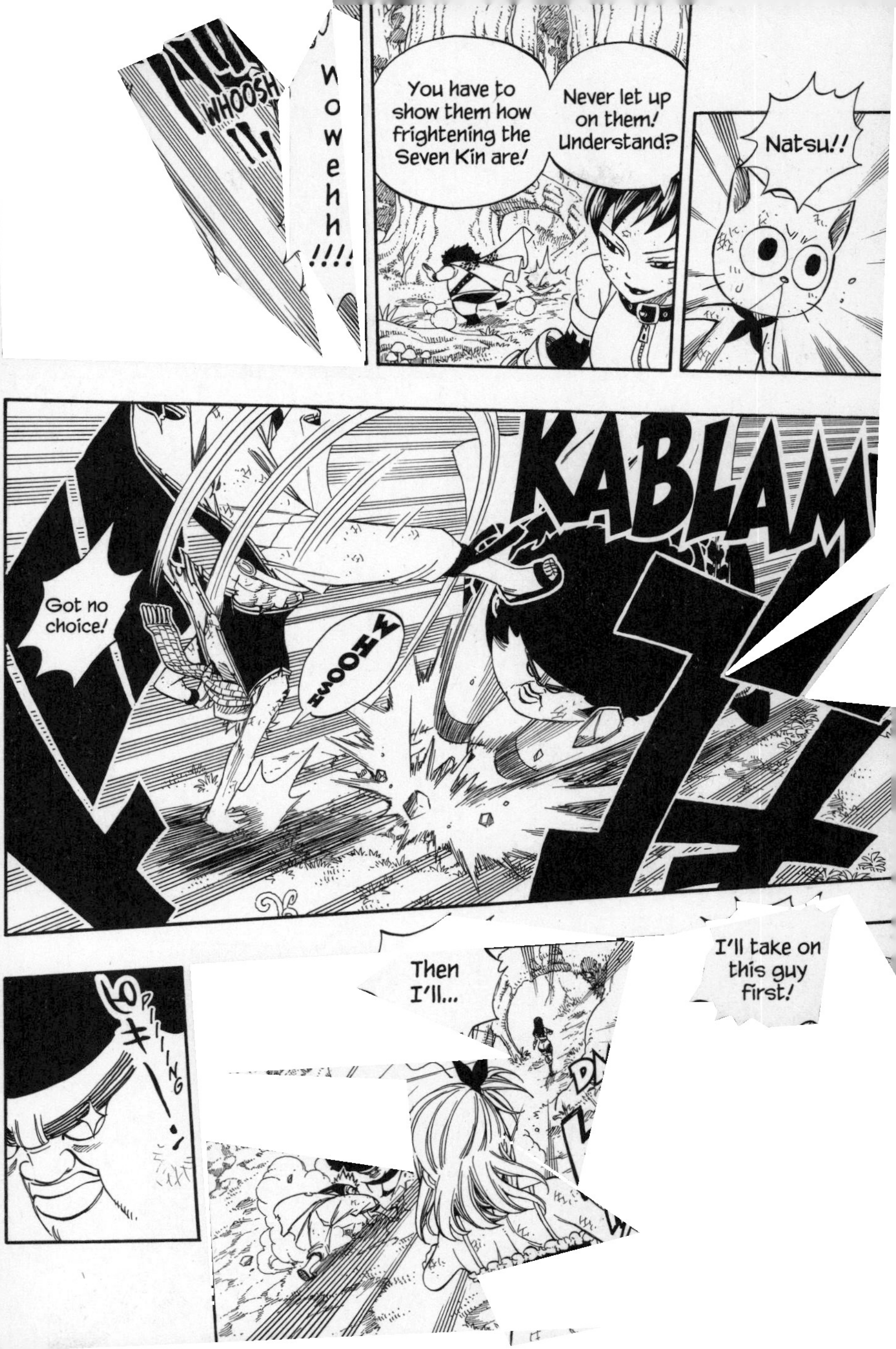
Natsu!!
Never let up on them! Understand?
You have to show them how frightening the Seven Kin are!
WHOOSH
KABLAM
WHOOSH
Got no choice!
I'll take on this guy first!
Then I'll...

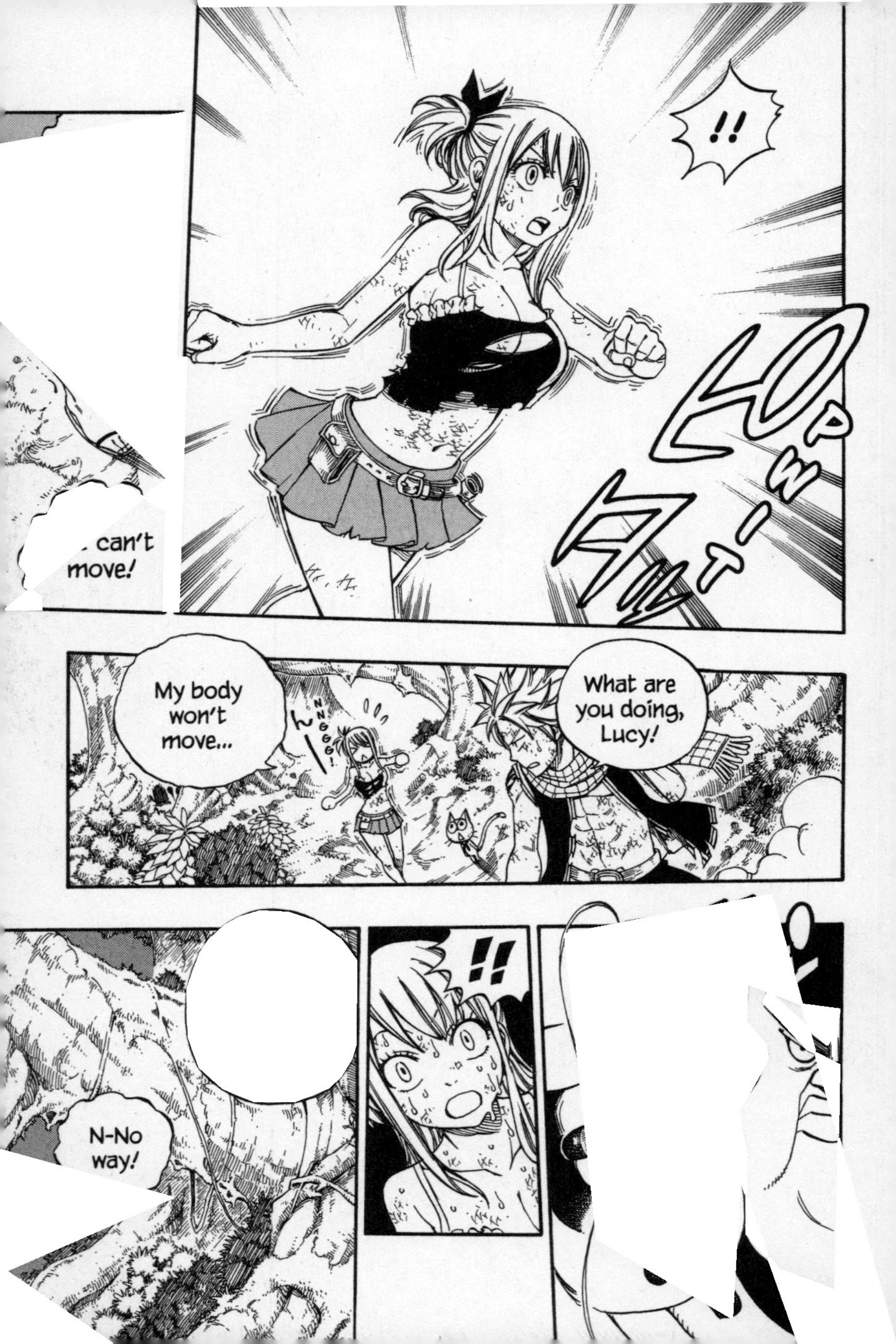
!!
PWIT
can't move!
What are you doing, Lucy!
NNGGG!
My body won't move...
!!
N-No way!

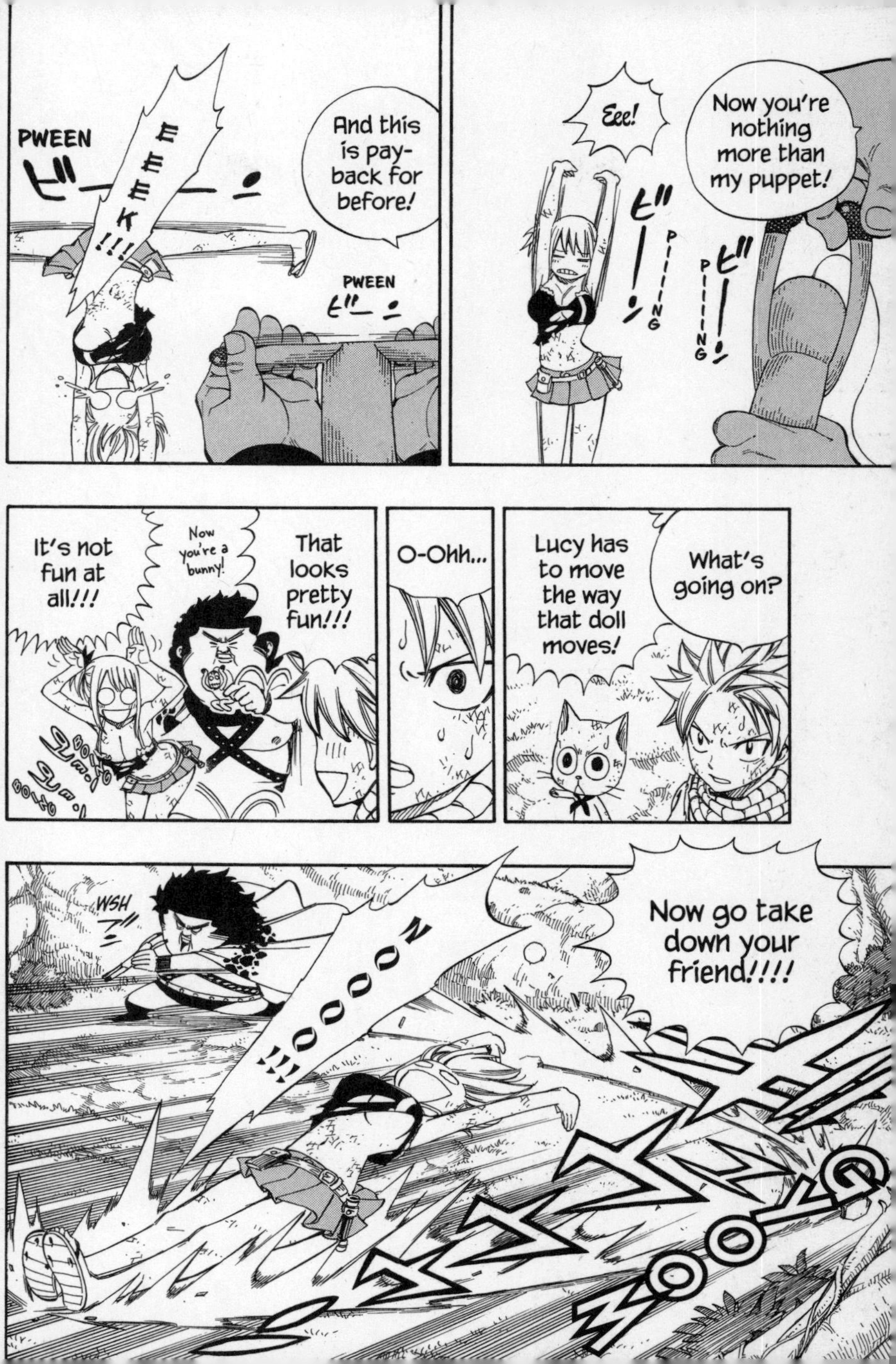
Now you're nothing more than my puppet!
Eee!
PIIIING
PIIIING
And this is pay-back for before!
PWEEN
EEEEK!!!
PWEEN
What's going on?
Lucy has to move the way that doll moves!
O-Ohh...
That looks pretty fun!!!
Now you're a bunny!
It's not fun at all!!!
BOING
BOING
Now go take down your friend!!!!
NOOOOO!!!
WSH

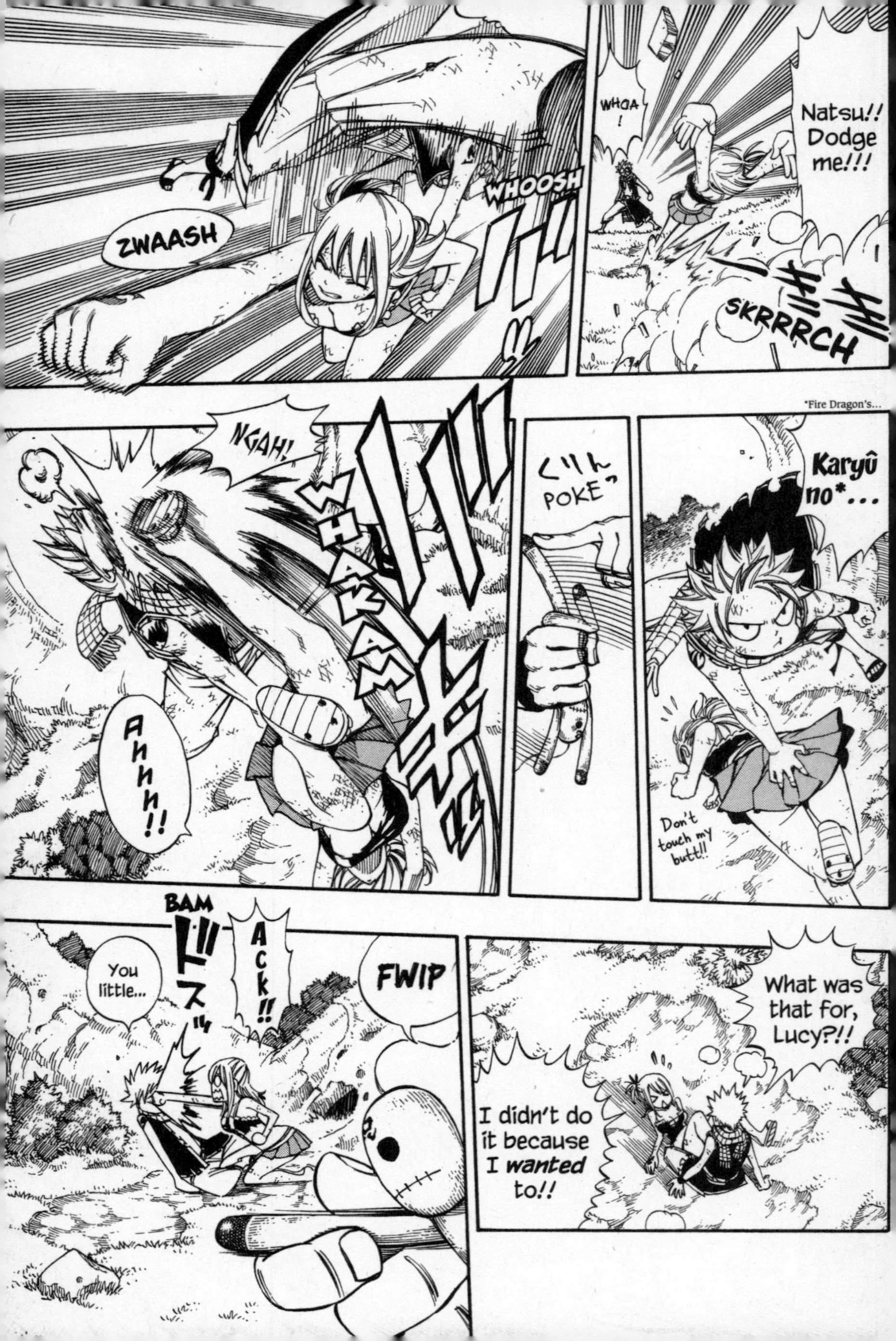
Natsu!! Dodge me!!!
WHOA!
SKRRRCH
WHOOSH
ZWAASH
Karyû no*...
Don't touch my butt!!
くりん
POKE
NGAH!
WHAKAM
Annn!!
What was that for, Lucy?!!
I didn't do it because I *wanted* to!!
FWIP
Ack!!
BAM
You little...

*Fire Dragon's...

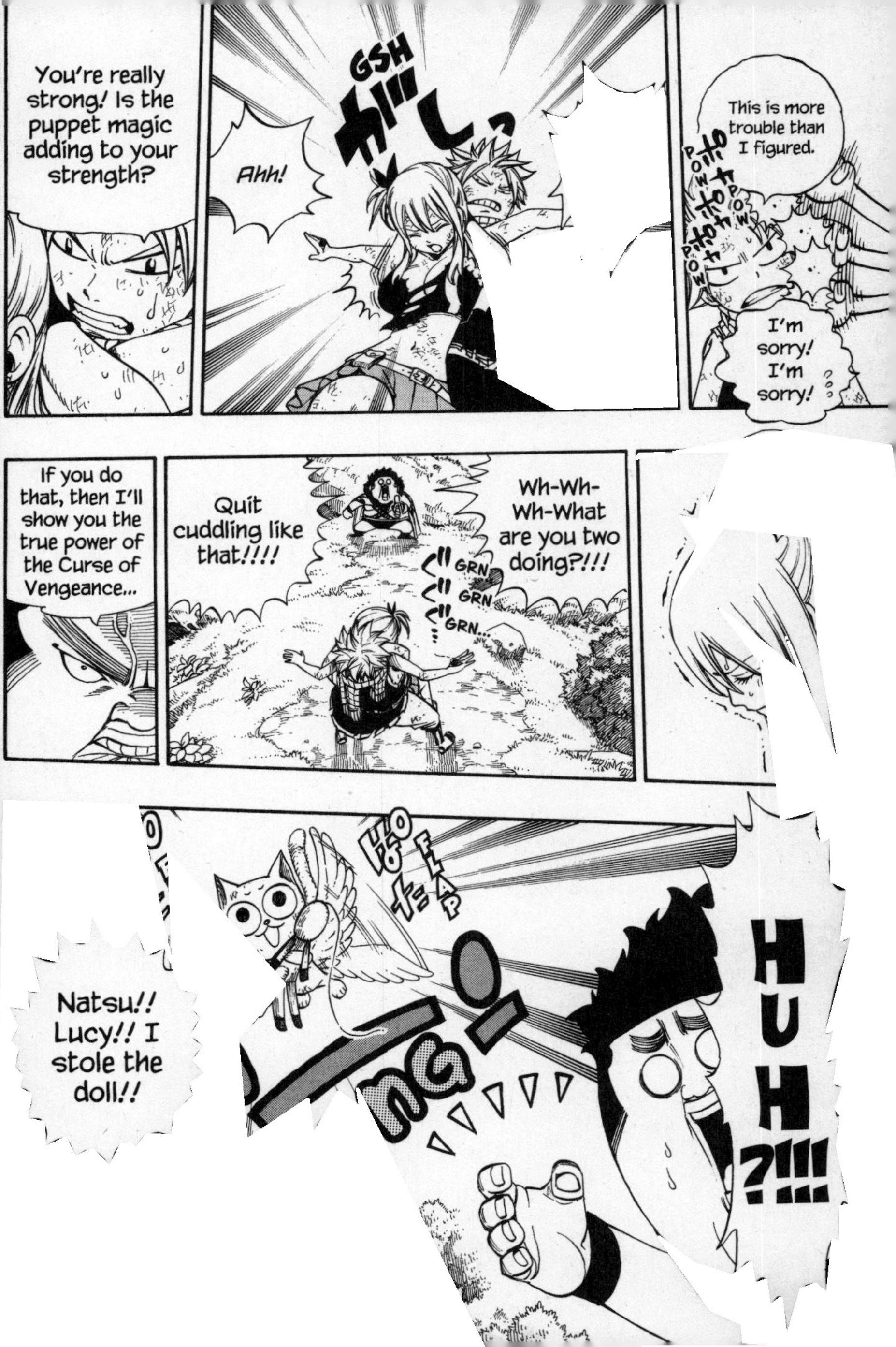
This is more trouble than I figured.
POW POW POW POW
I'm sorry! I'm sorry!
GSH
Ahh!
You're really strong! Is the puppet magic adding to your strength?
Wh-Wh-Wh-What are you two doing?!!!
GRN GRN GRN...
Quit cuddling like that!!!!
If you do that, then I'll show you the true power of the Curse of Vengeance...
HUH?!!!
FLAP
Natsu!! Lucy!! I stole the doll!!

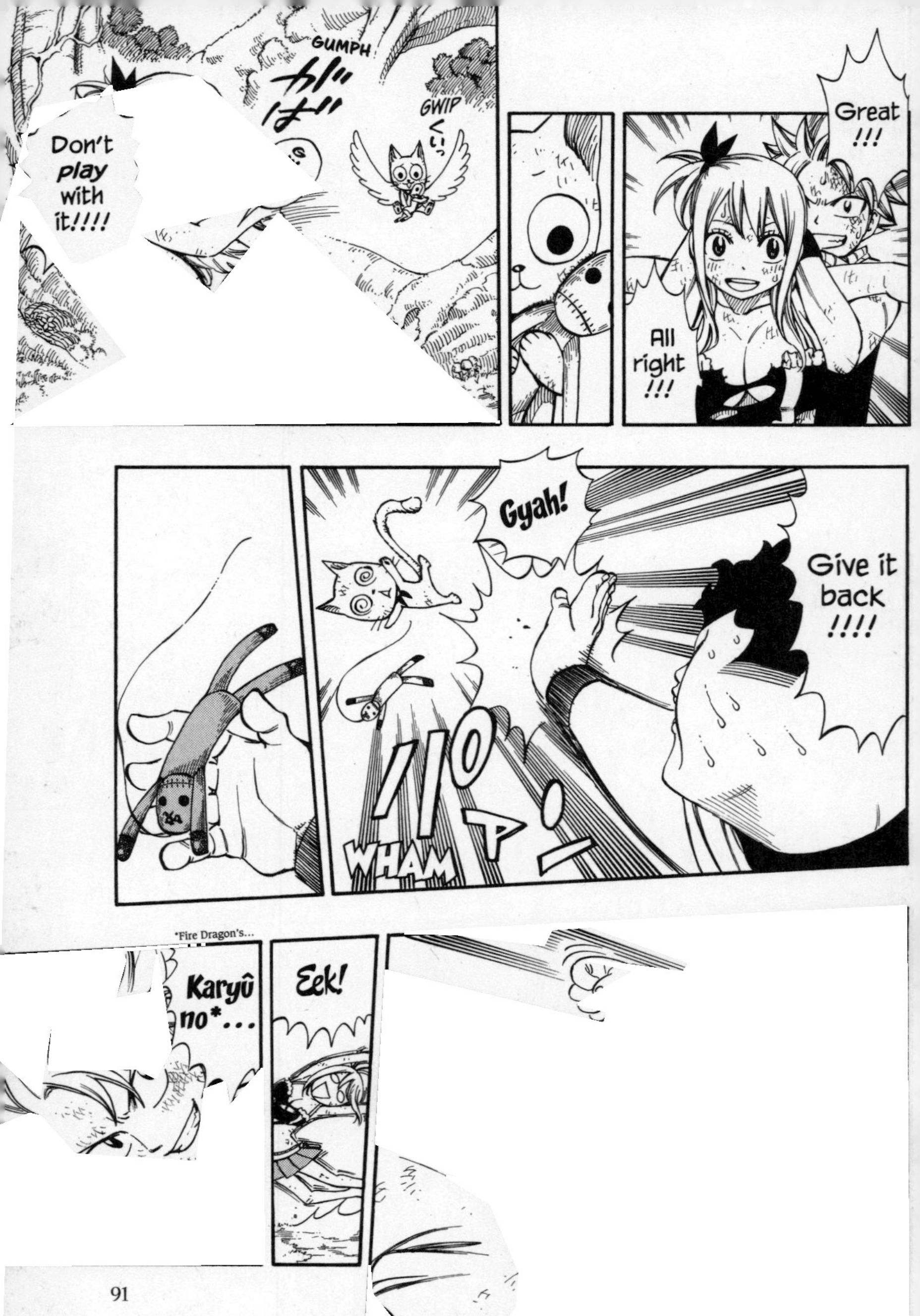
Great!!!
All right!!!
GUMPH
GWIP
Don't play with it!!!!
Gyah!
Give it back!!!!
WHAM
Eek!
Karyû no*...
*Fire Dragon's...

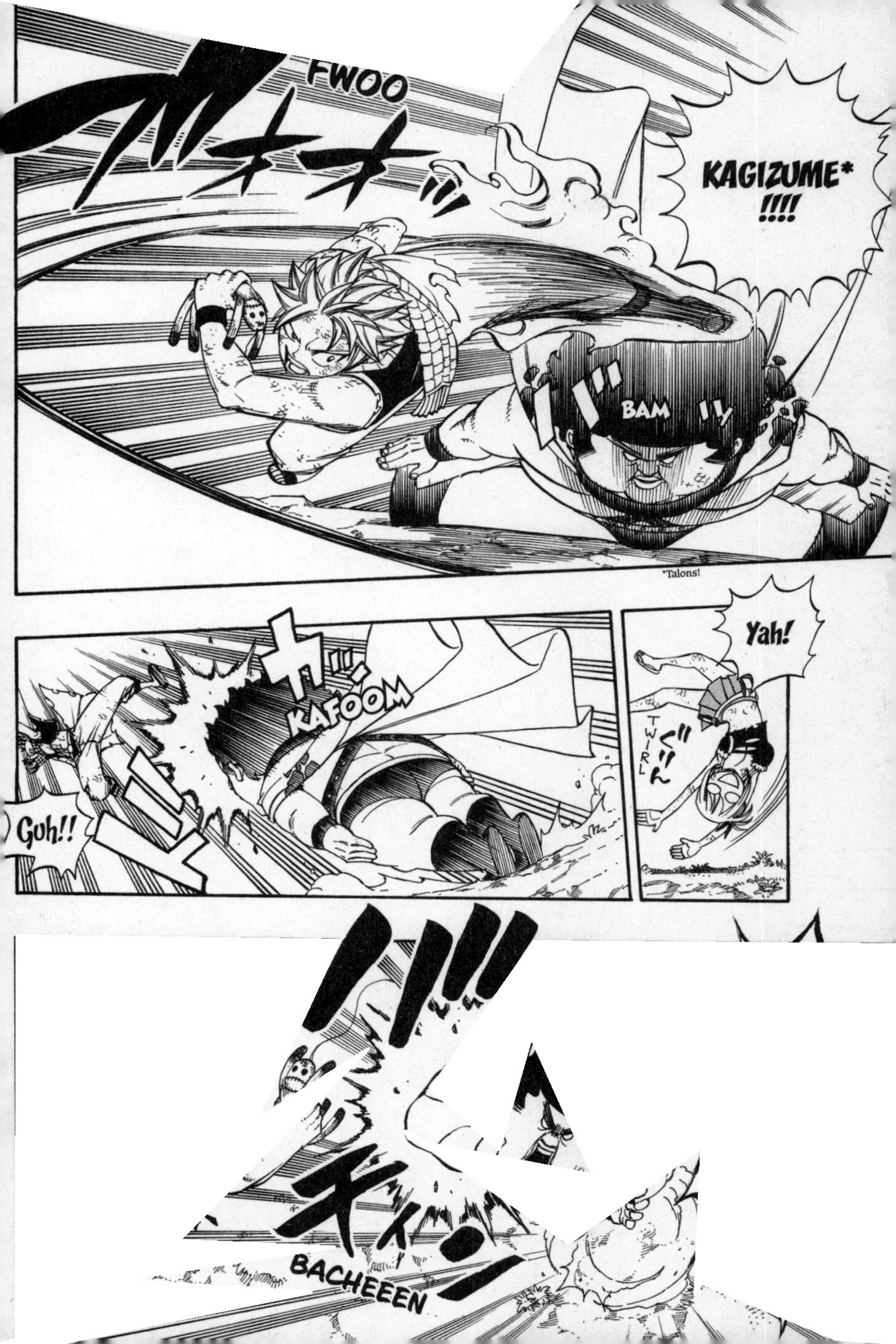

FWOO
KAGIZUME* !!!!
BAM
Yah!
TWIRL
KAFOOM
Guh!!
BACHEEEN

*Talons!

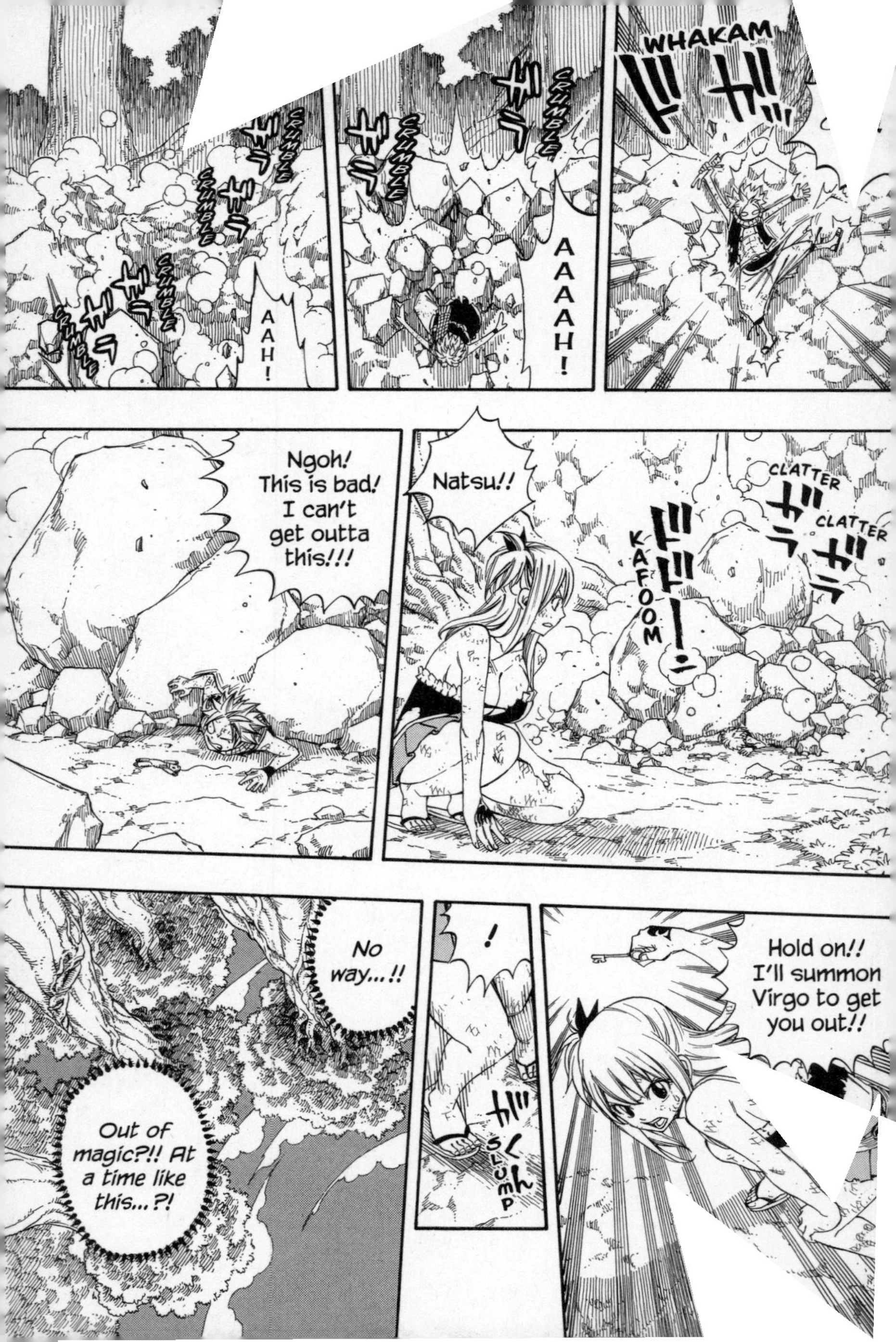
WHAKAM
CRUMBLE
CRUMBLE
AAAAAH!
CRUMBLE
CRUMBLE
CRUMBLE
CRUMBLE
AAH!
CLATTER
CLATTER
KAFOOM
Natsu!!
Ngoh! This is bad! I can't get outta this!!!
Hold on!! I'll summon Virgo to get you out!!
!
SLUMP
No way...!!
Out of magic?!! At a time like this...?!

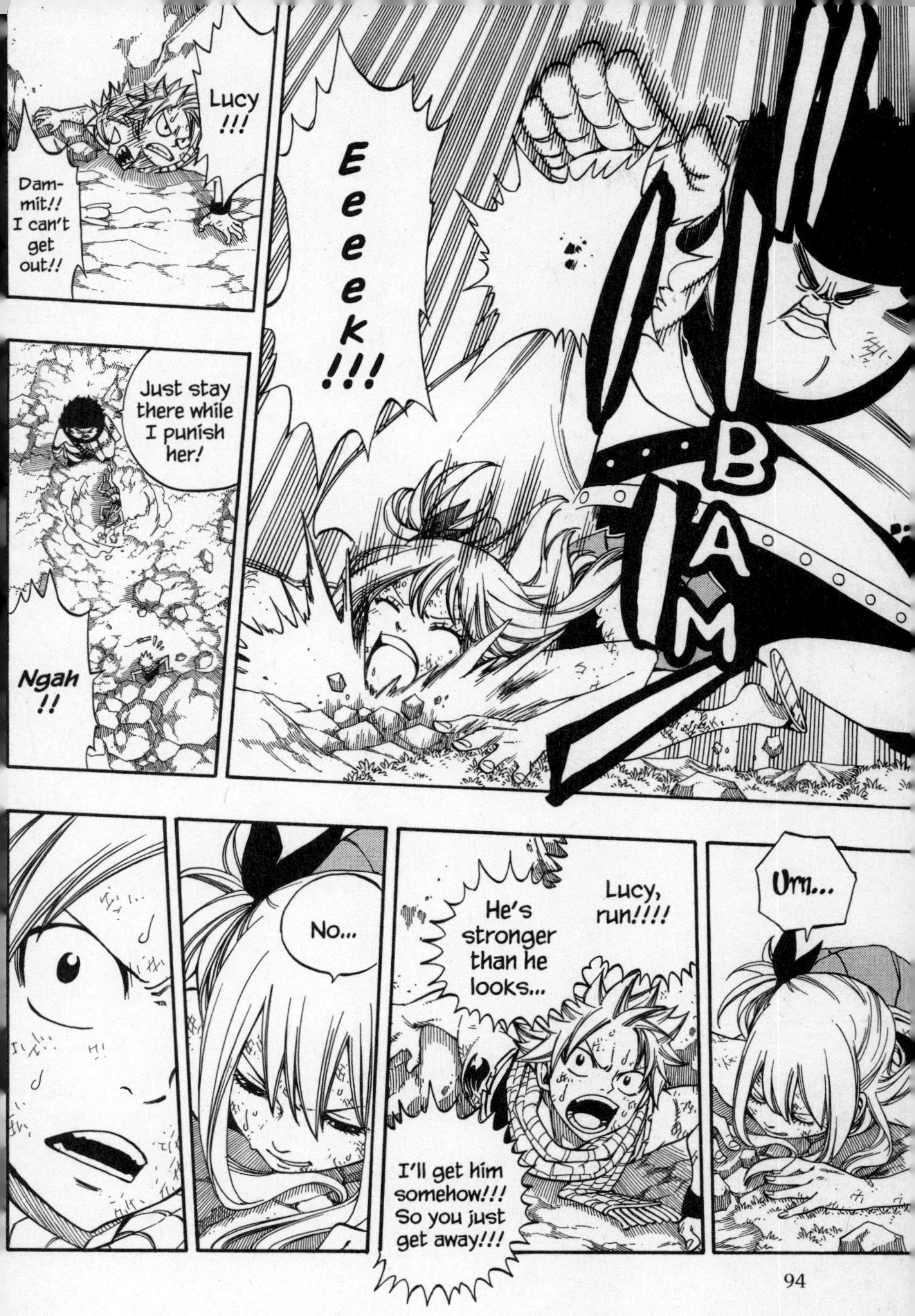

Eeeek!!!
BAM
Lucy!!!
Dammit!! I can't get out!!
Just stay there while I punish her!
Ngah!!
Urn...
Lucy, run!!!!
He's stronger than he looks...
I'll get him somehow!!! So you just get away!!!
No...

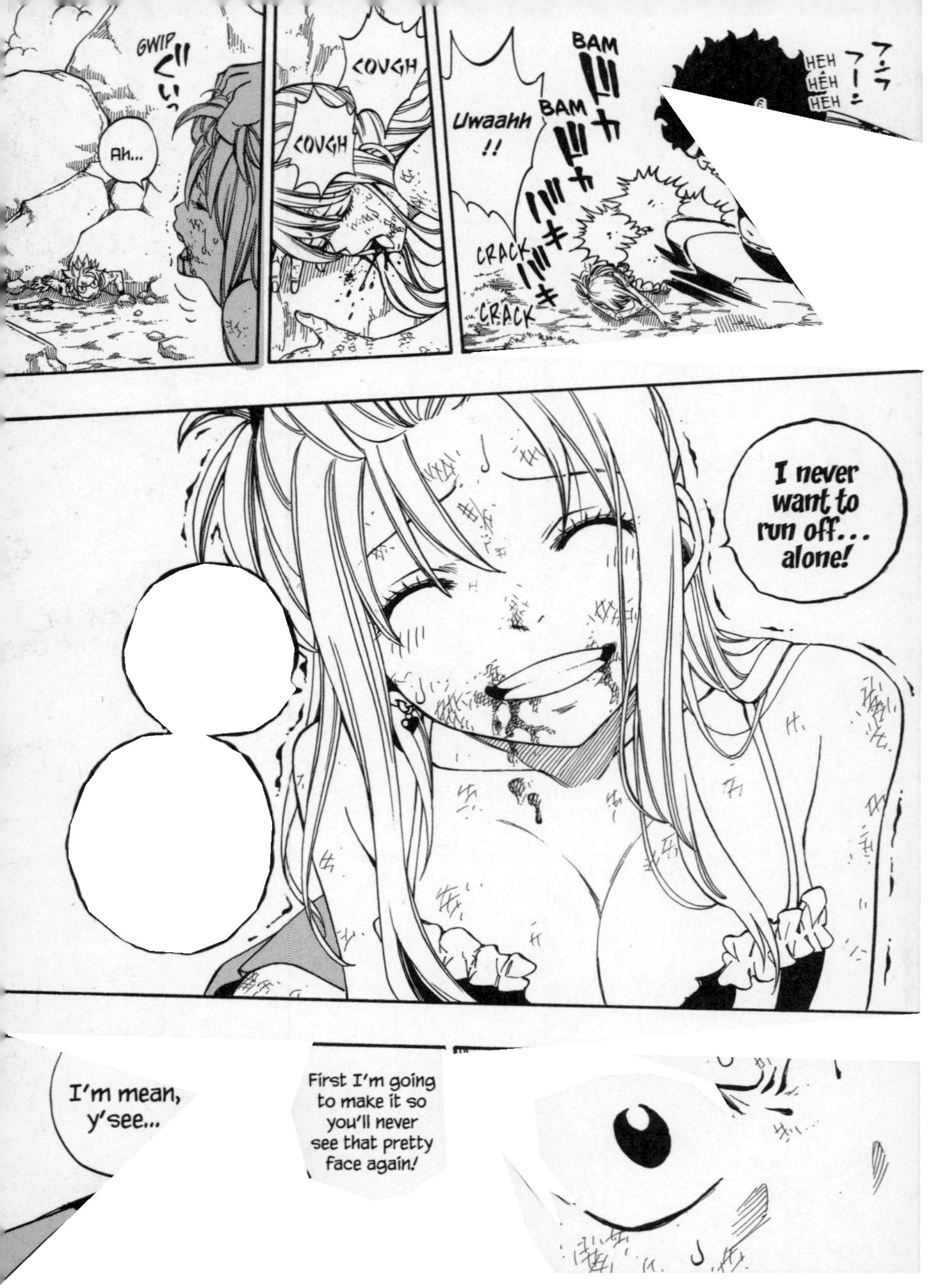
HEH
HEH
HEH
BAM
BAM
Uwaahh !!
CRACK
CRACK
COUGH
COUGH
GWIP
ぐいっ
Ah...
I never want to run off... alone!
First I'm going to make it so you'll never see that pretty face again!
I'm mean, y'see...

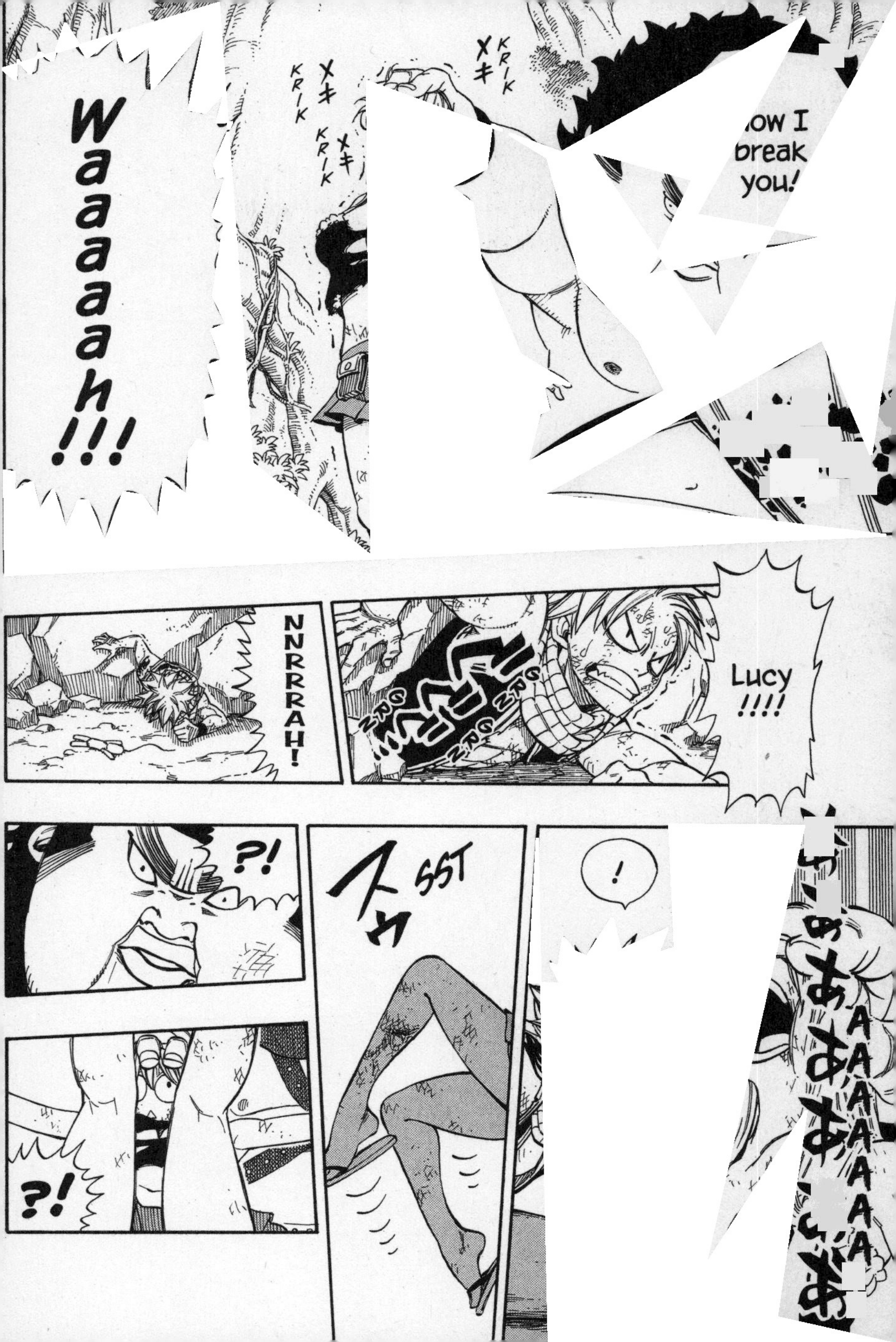
ow I break you!
メキ KRIK
メキ KRIK
Waaaaaah!!!
Lucy!!!!
GRRR
NNRRRAH!
あああ AAAAAAA
!
スッ SST
?!
?!

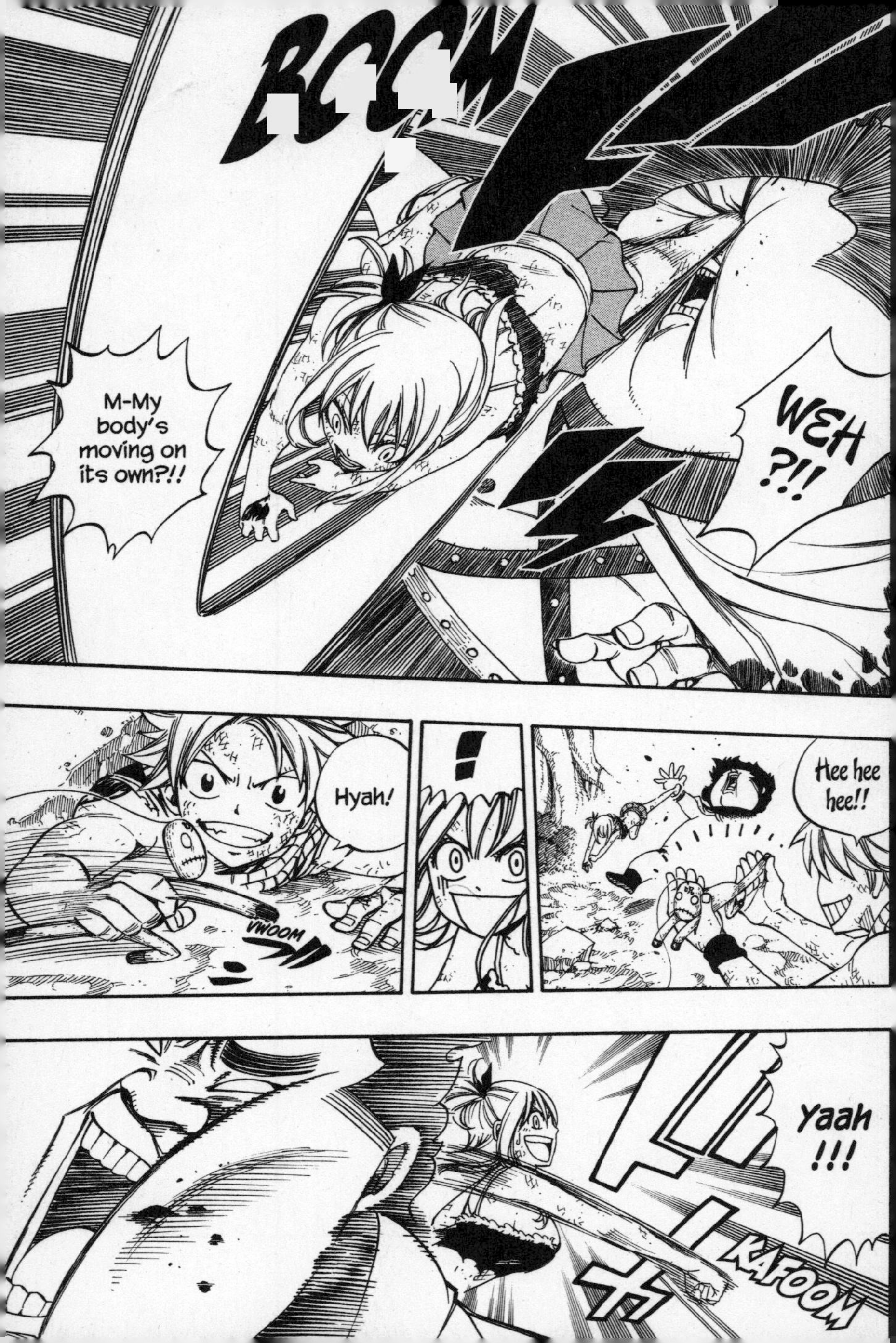
BOOM
WEH ?!!
M-My body's moving on its own?!!
Hee hee hee!!
!
Hyah!
VWOOM
Yaah !!!
KAFOOM

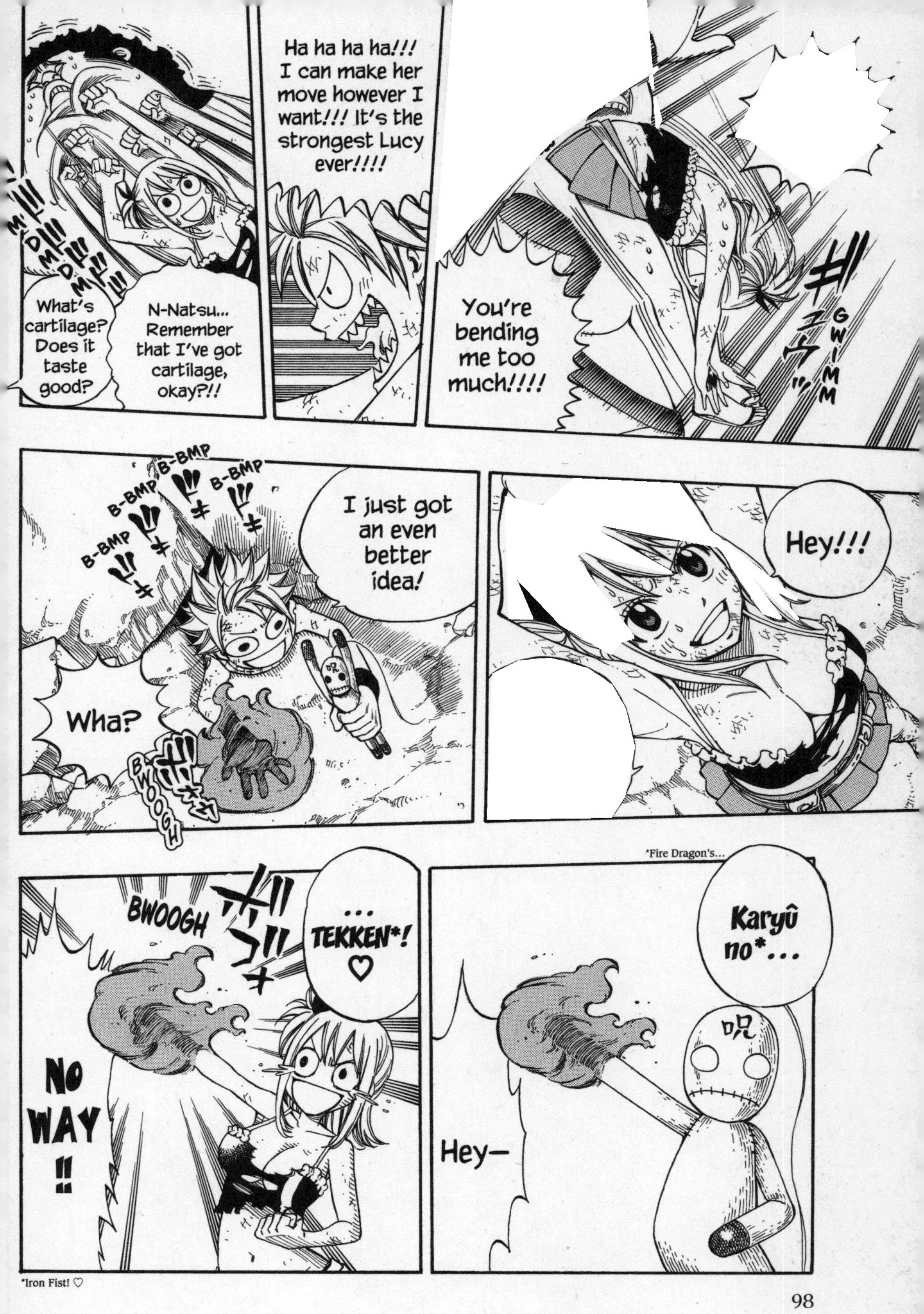
You're bending me too much!!!!
GWIMM
Ha ha ha ha!!! I can make her move however I want!!! It's the strongest Lucy ever!!!!
N-Natsu... Remember that I've got cartilage, okay?!!
What's cartilage? Does it taste good?
D-M D-M
Hey!!!
I just got an even better idea!
B-BMP B-BMP B-BMP B-BMP
Wha?
BWOOGH
Karyû no*...
Hey—
...TEKKEN*! ♡
BWOOGH
NO WAY!!

*Fire Dragon's...

*Iron Fist! ♡

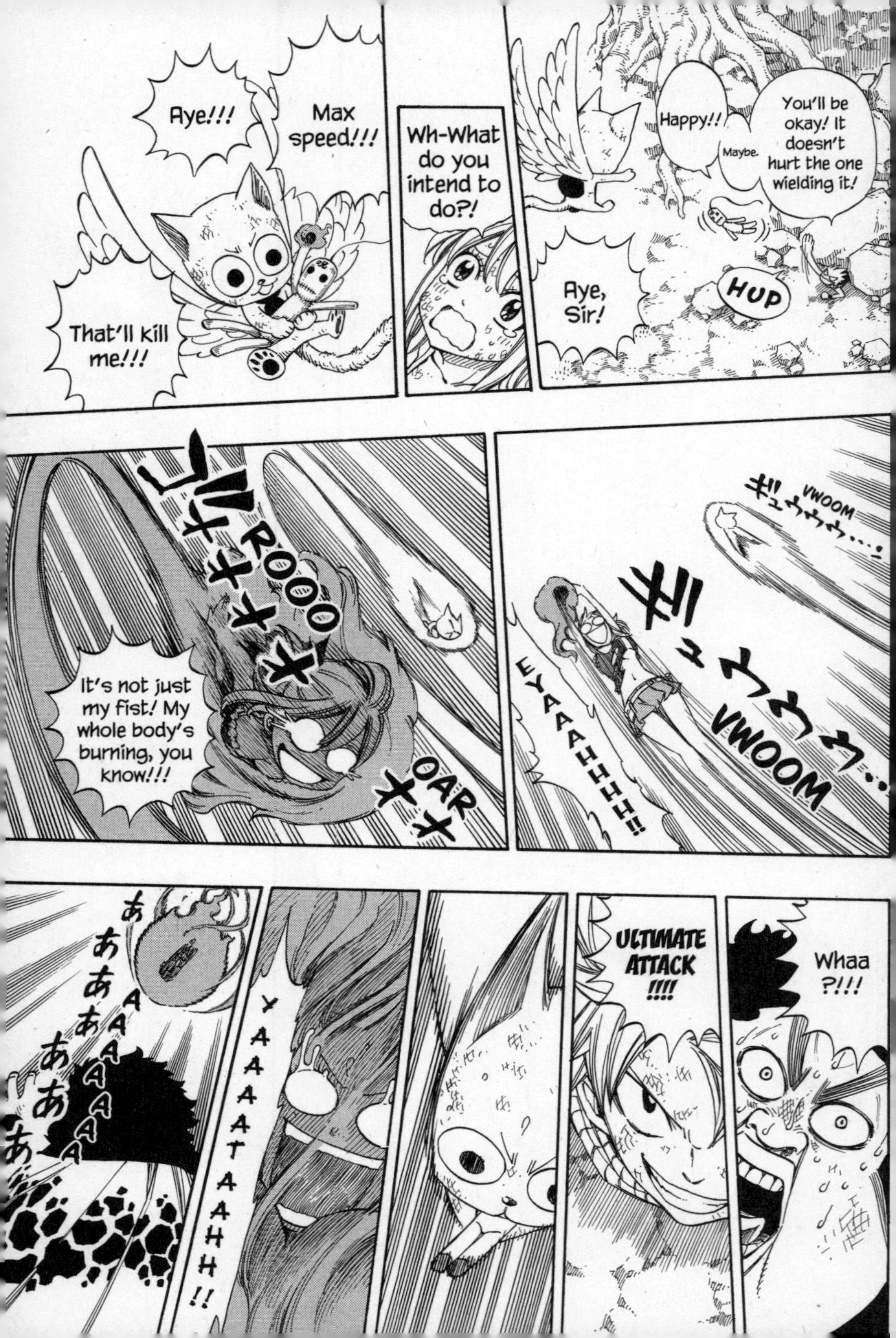
Happy!!
You'll be okay! It doesn't hurt the one wielding it!
Maybe.
Aye, Sir!
HUP
Wh-What do you intend to do?!
Max speed!!!
Aye!!!
That'll kill me!!!
VWOOM
VWOOM
EYAAAAHHHH!!
ROOOO
It's not just my fist! My whole body's burning, you know!!!
OAR
Whaa?!!!
ULTIMATE ATTACK!!!!
YAAAAATAAAHH!!
AAAAAAA

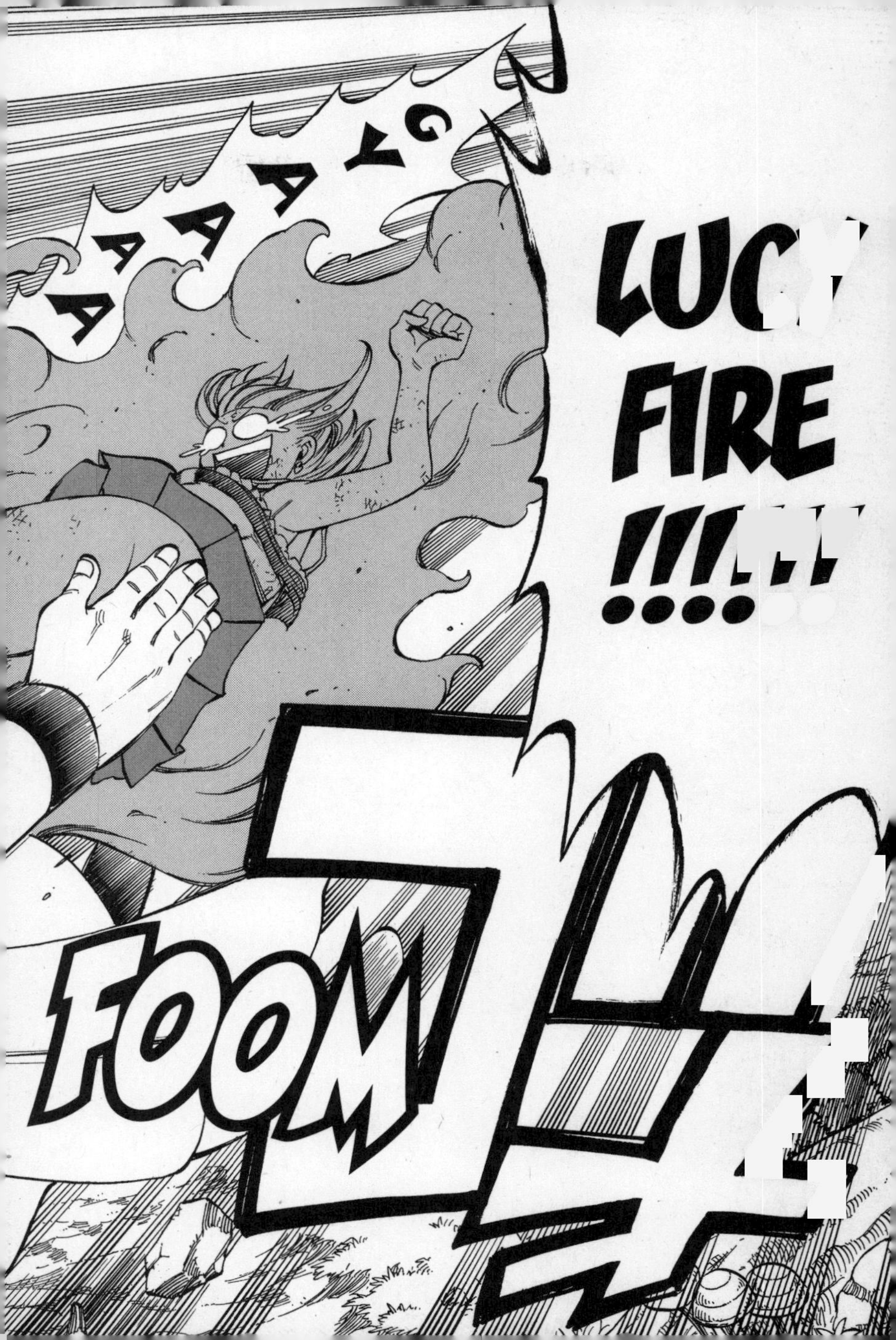
AAAAAYG
LUCY FIRE!!!!!
FOOM

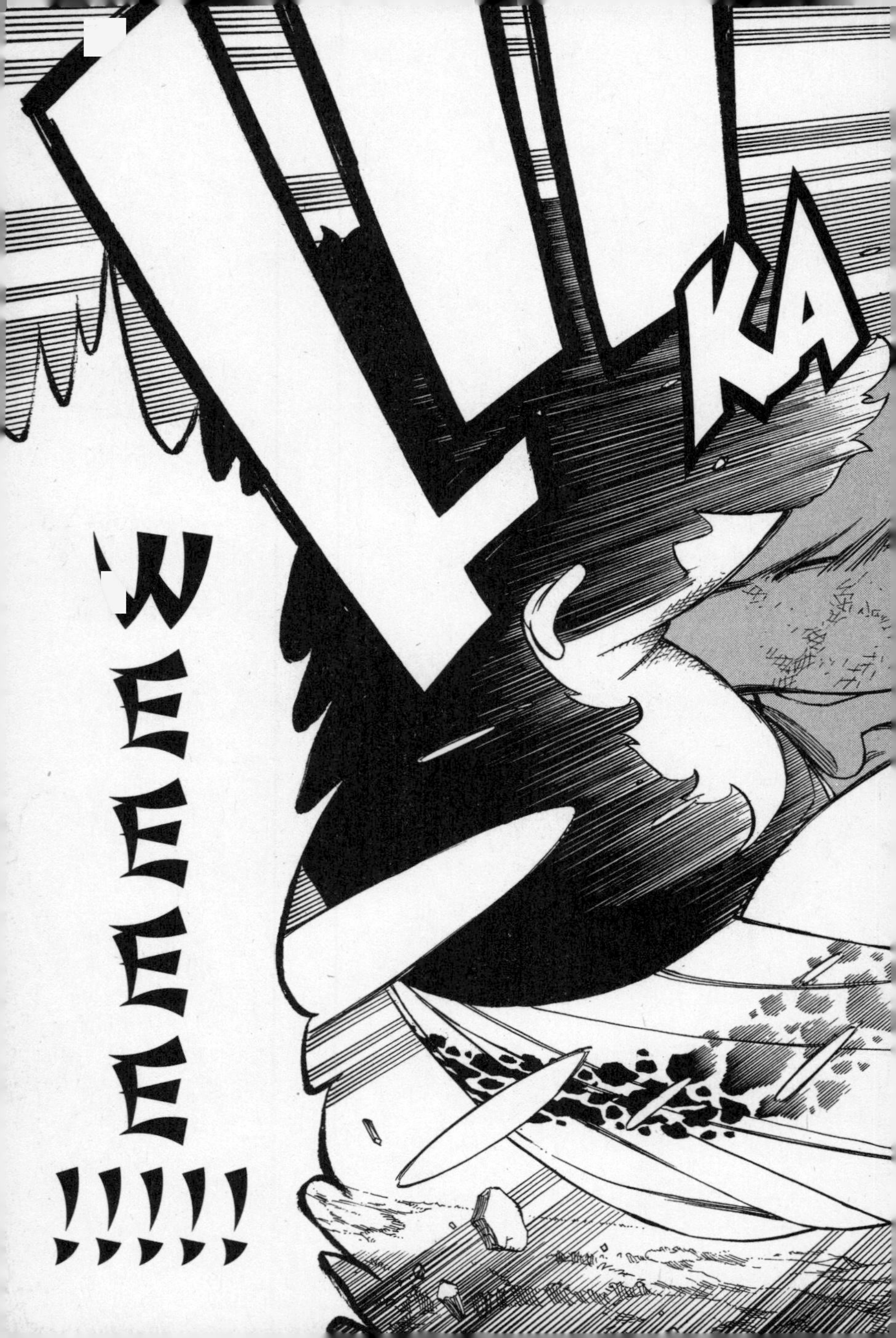
KA
WEEEE!!!!!

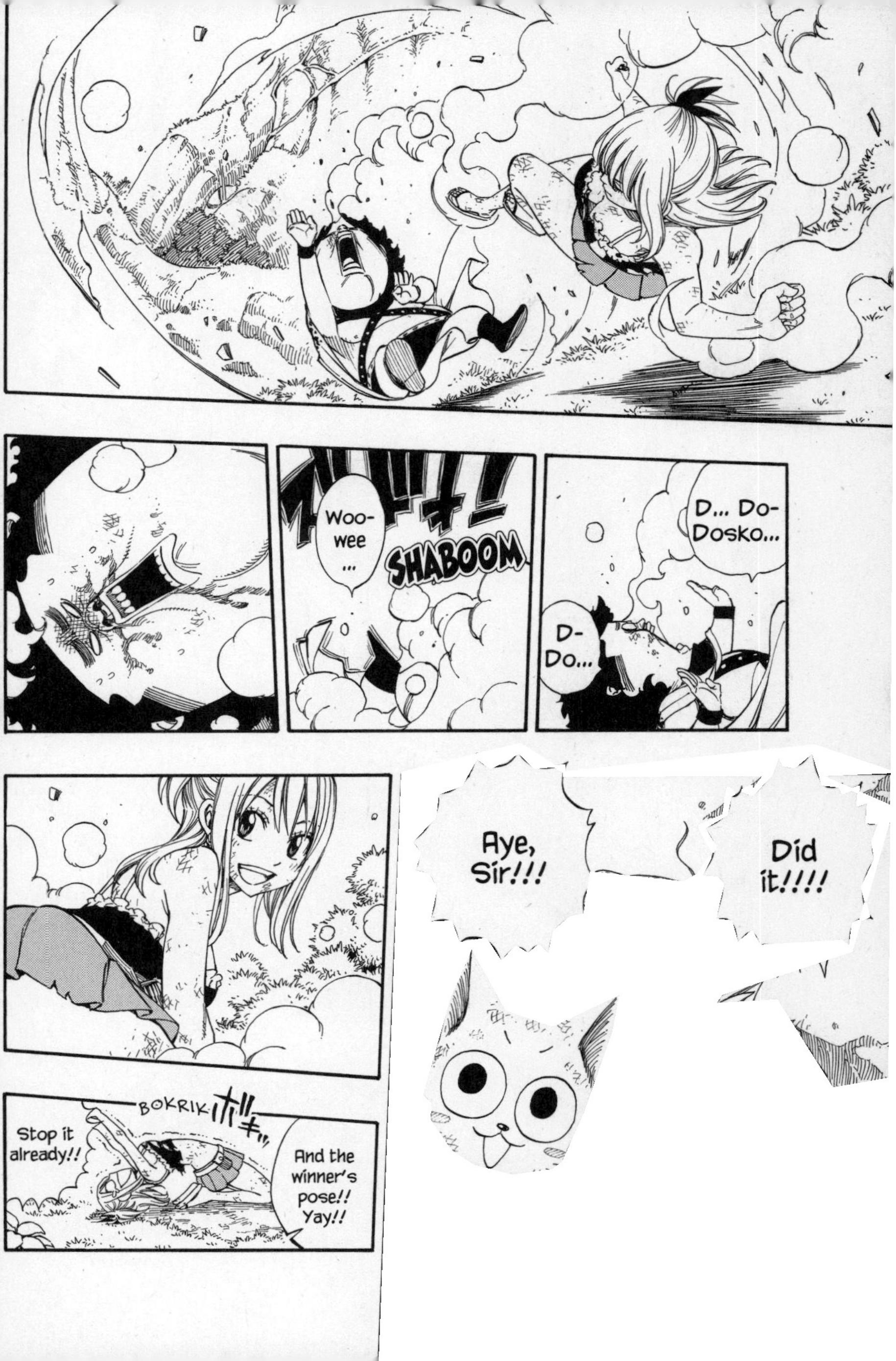
D... Do-Dosko...
D-Do...
SHABOOM
Woo-wee ...
Did it!!!!
Aye, Sir!!!
BOKRIK
And the winner's pose!! Yay!!
Stop it already!!

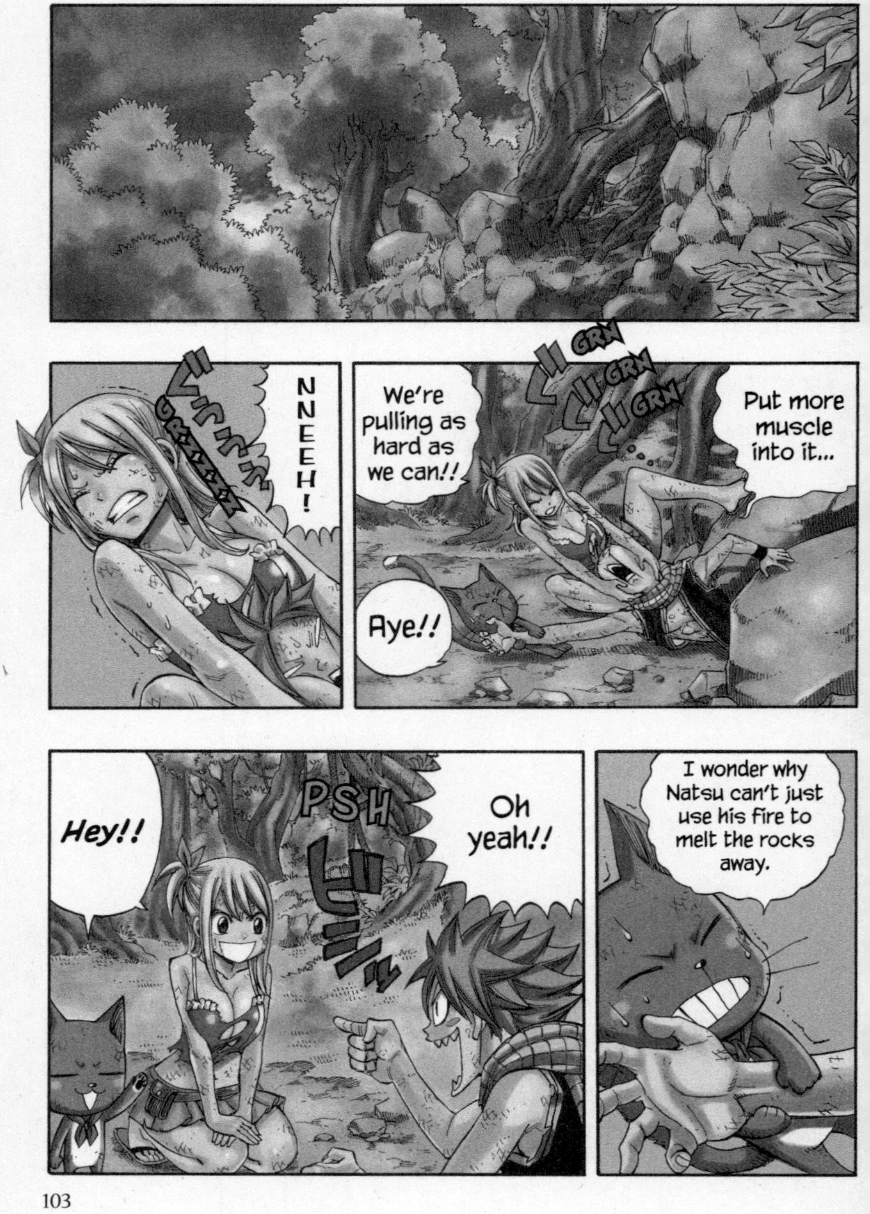
Put more muscle into it...
GRN
GRN
GRN
We're pulling as hard as we can!!
Aye!!
NNEEEH!
I wonder why Natsu can't just use his fire to melt the rocks away.
Oh yeah!!
PSH
Hey!!

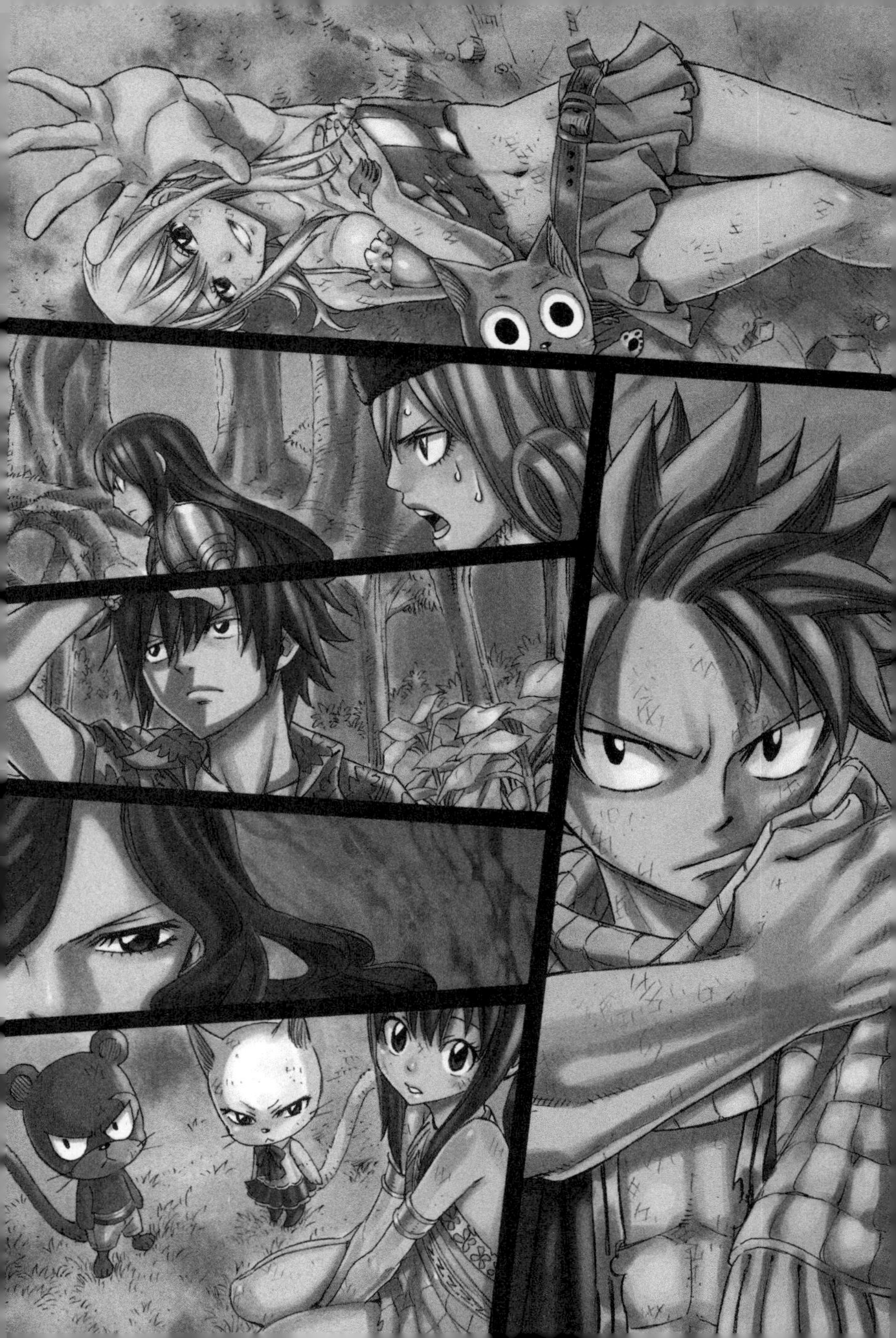

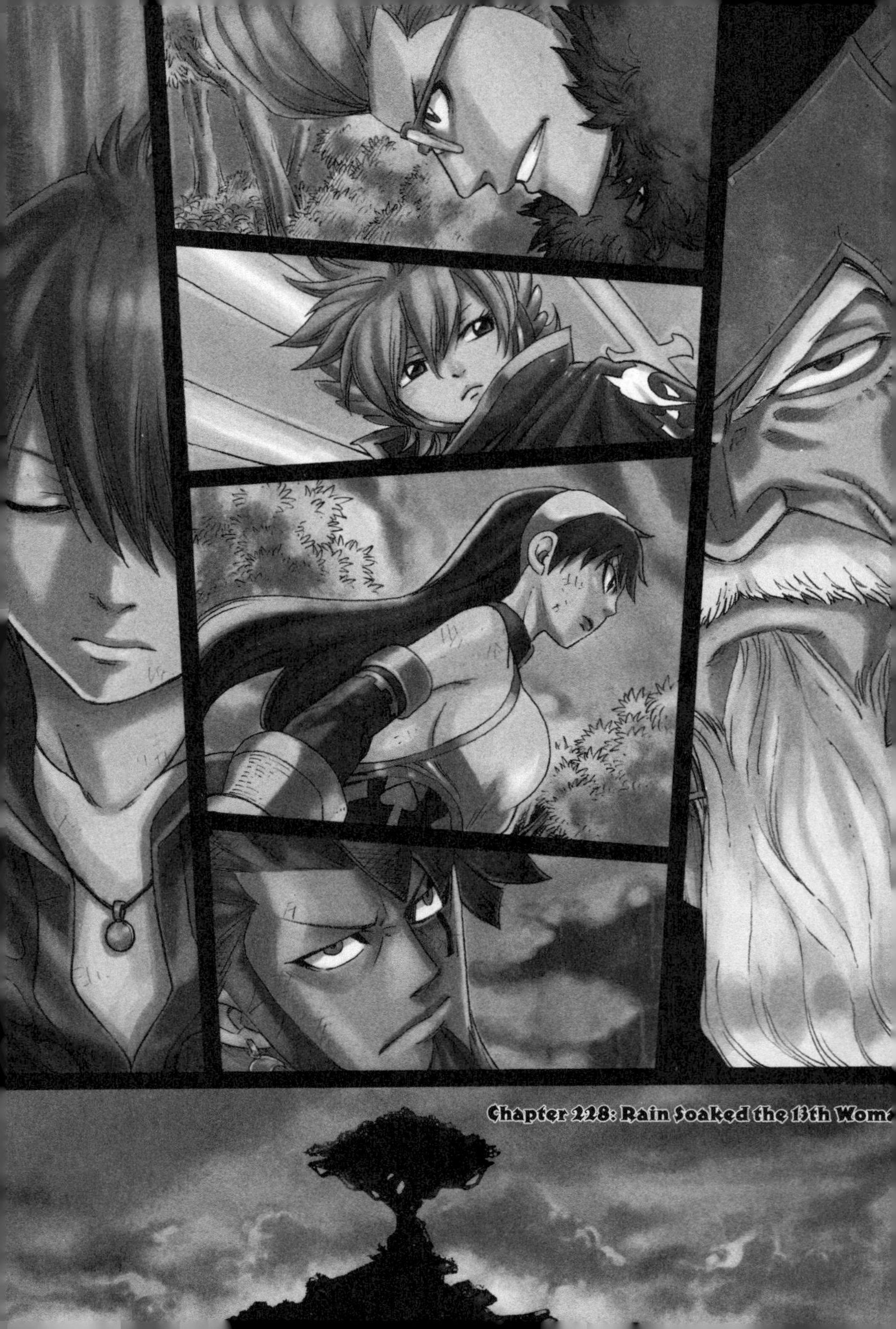
Chapter 228: Rain Soaked the 13th Wom

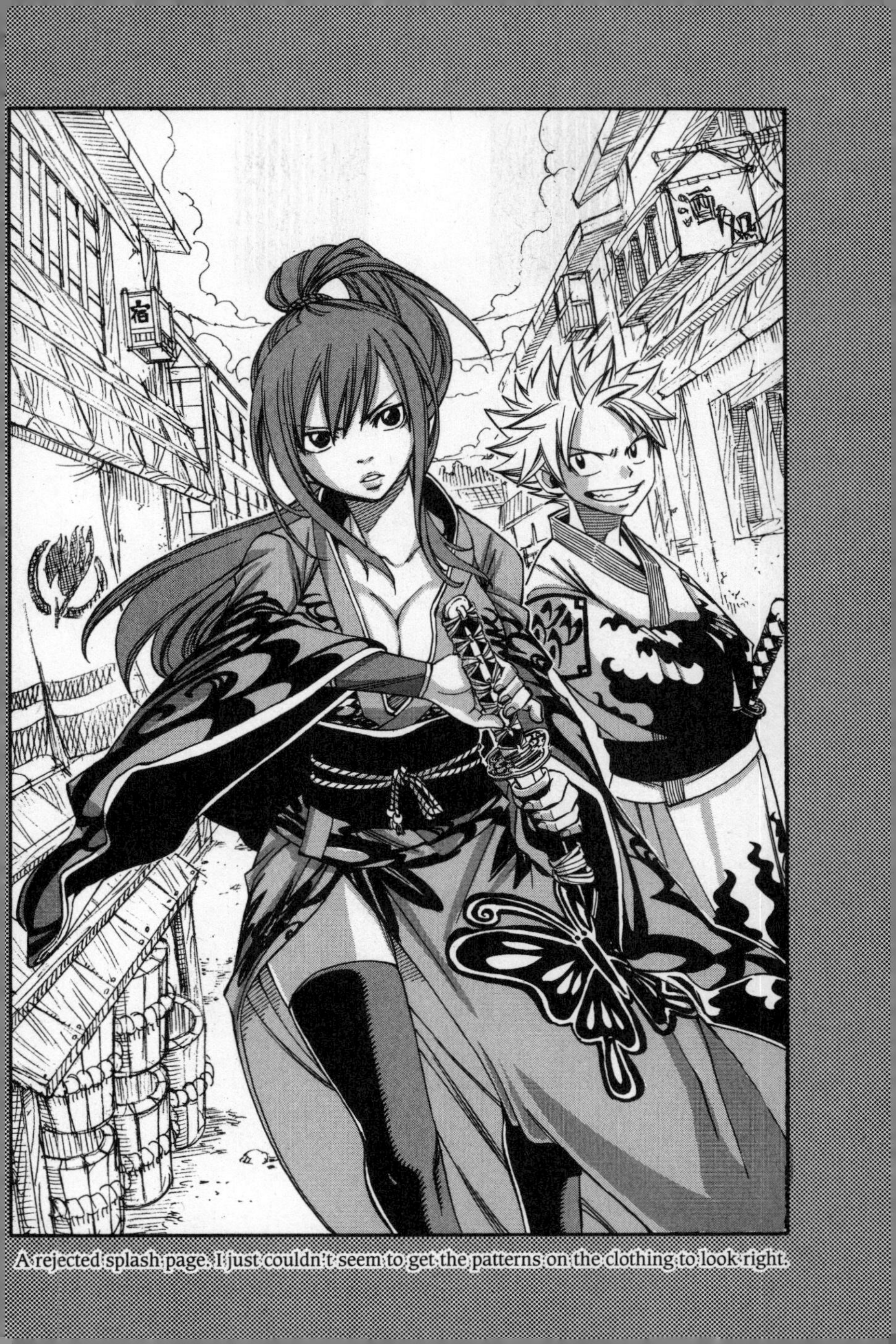
宿

A rejected splash page. I just couldn't seem to get the patterns on the clothing to look right.

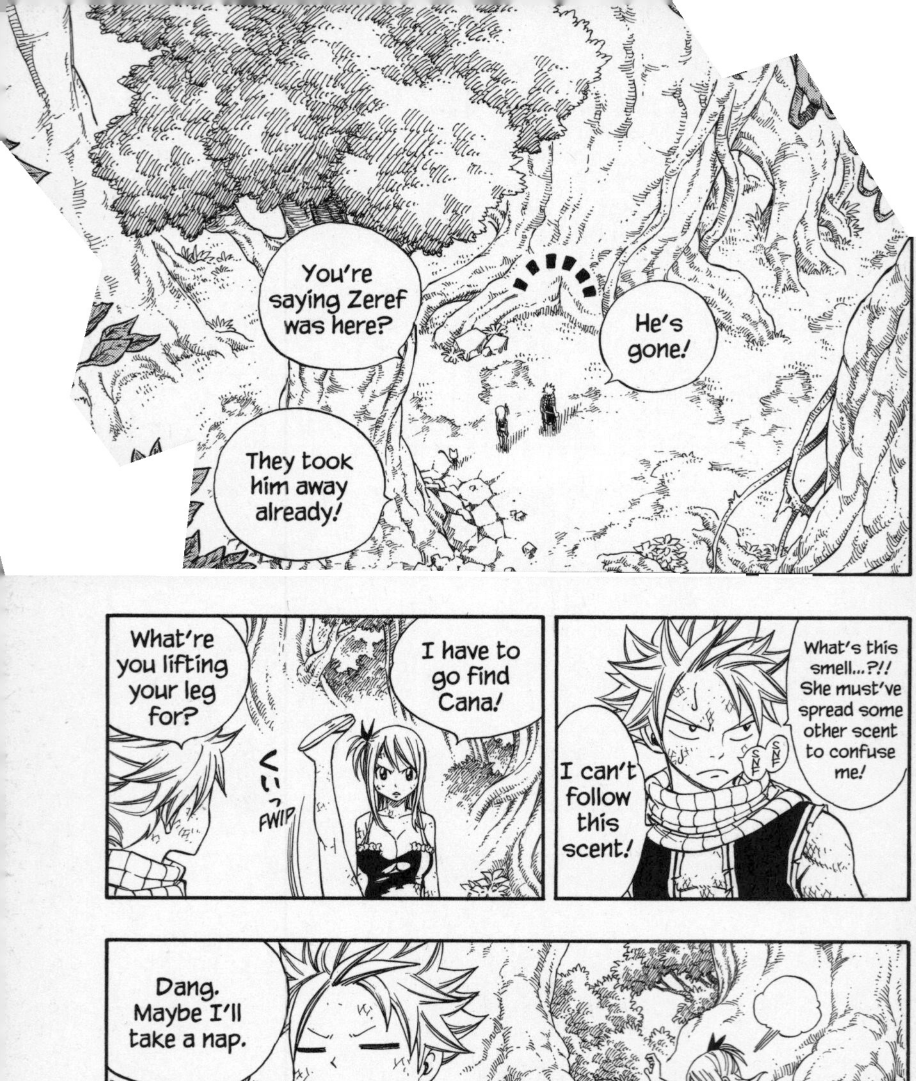
......
He's gone!
You're saying Zeref was here?
They took him away already!
What's this smell...?!! She must've spread some other scent to confuse me!
SNF SNF
I can't follow this scent!
I have to go find Cana!
くいっ FWIP
What're you lifting your leg for?
Dang. Maybe I'll take a nap.

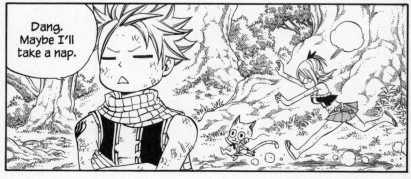

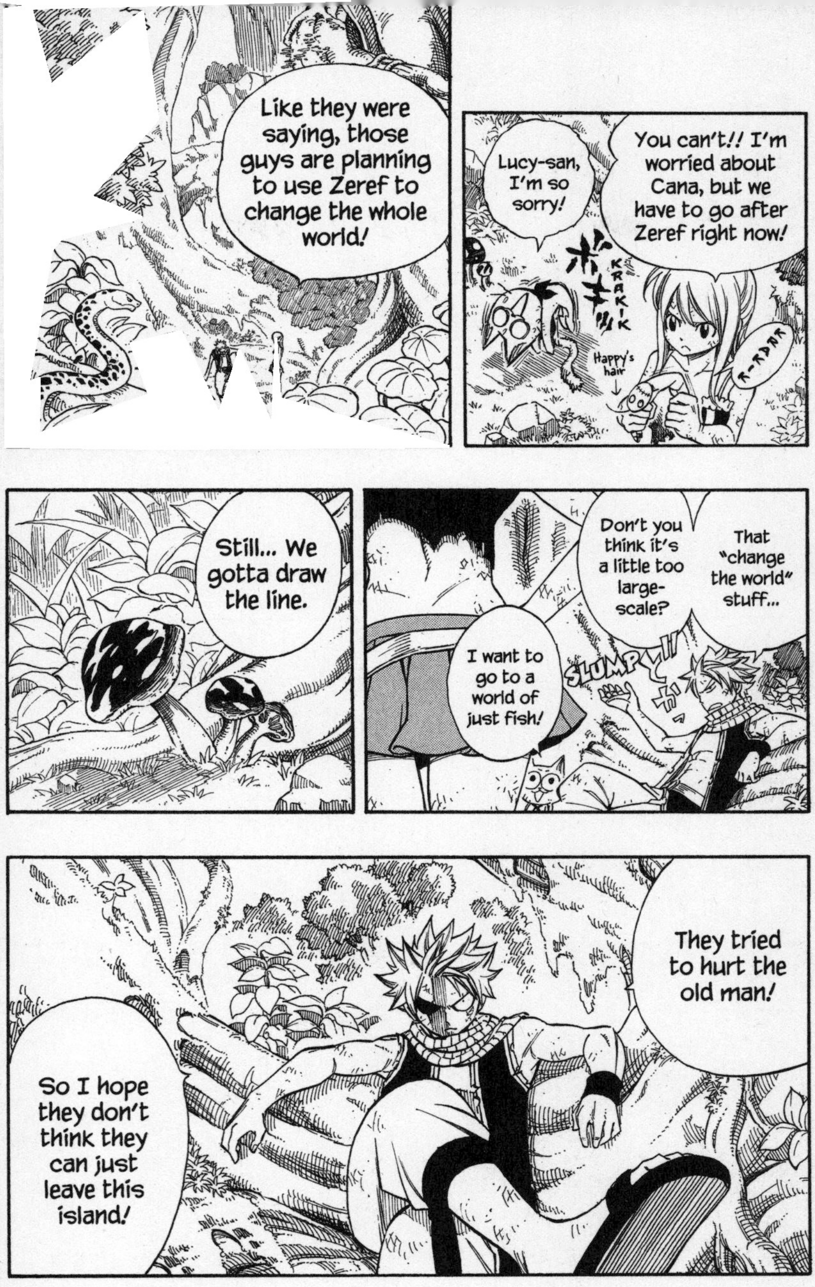
You can't!! I'm worried about Cana, but we have to go after Zeref right now!
Lucy-san, I'm so sorry!
KRAKIK
Happy's hair
Like they were saying, those guys are planning to use Zeref to change the whole world!
That "change the world" stuff...
Don't you think it's a little too large-scale?
SLUMP
I want to go to a world of just fish!
Still... We gotta draw the line.
They tried to hurt the old man!
So I hope they don't think they can just leave this island!

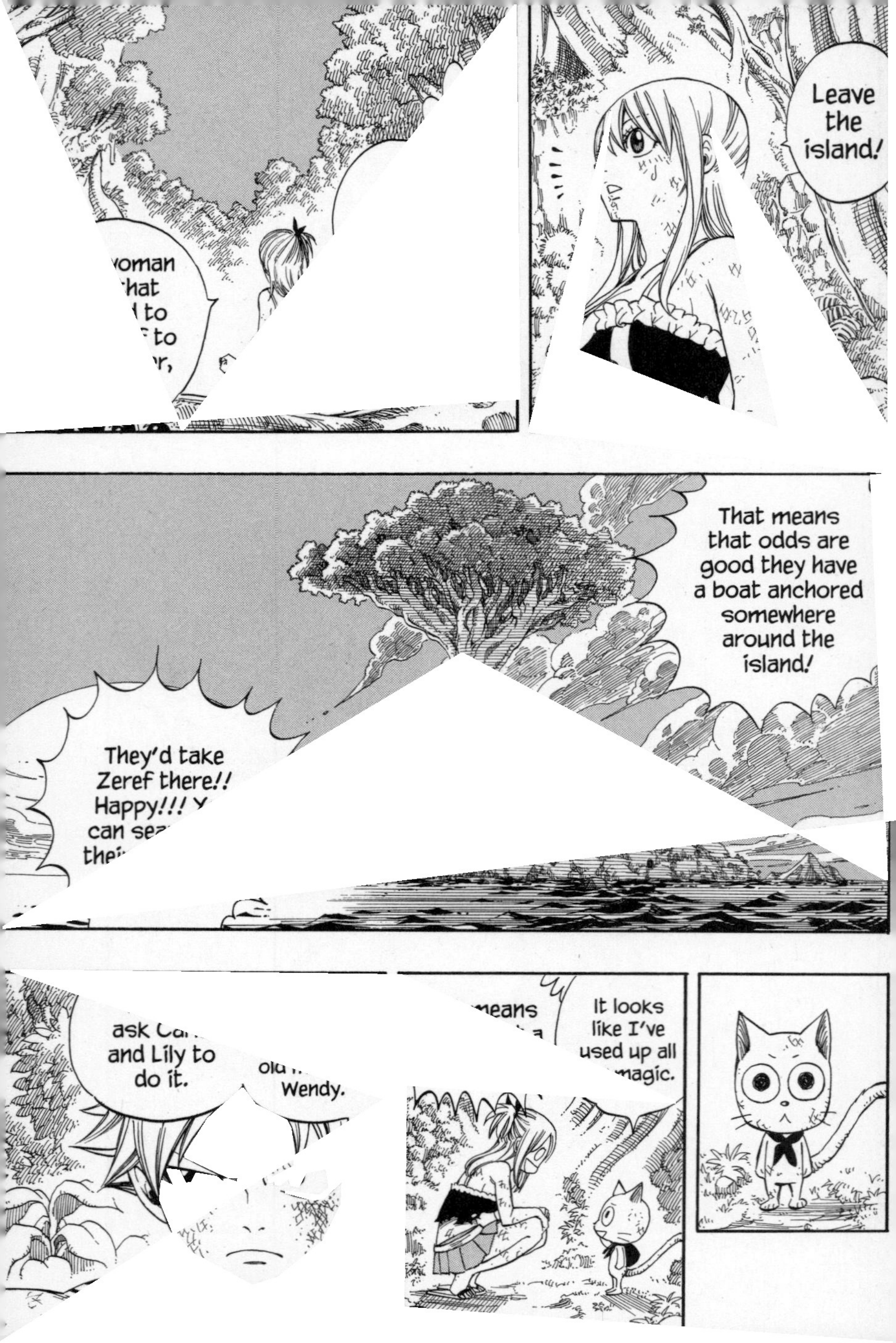

Leave the island!
woman hat d to to er,
That means that odds are good they have a boat anchored somewhere around the island!
They'd take Zeref there!! Happy!!!
It looks like I've used up all magic.
means a Wendy.
ask and Lily to do it.

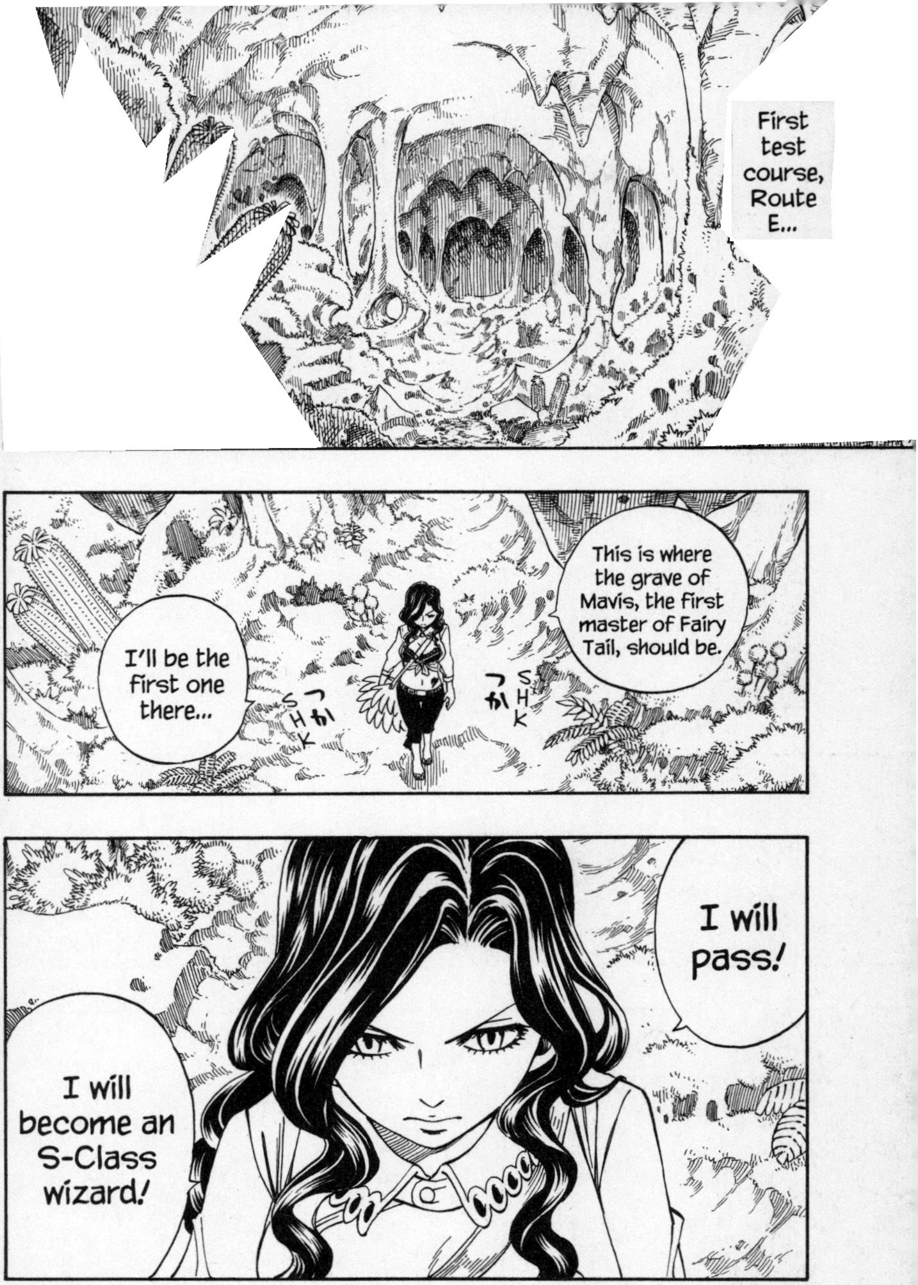
First test course, Route E...
This is where the grave of Mavis, the first master of Fairy Tail, should be.
つか SHK
つか SHK
I'll be the first one there...
I will pass!
I will become an S-Class wizard!

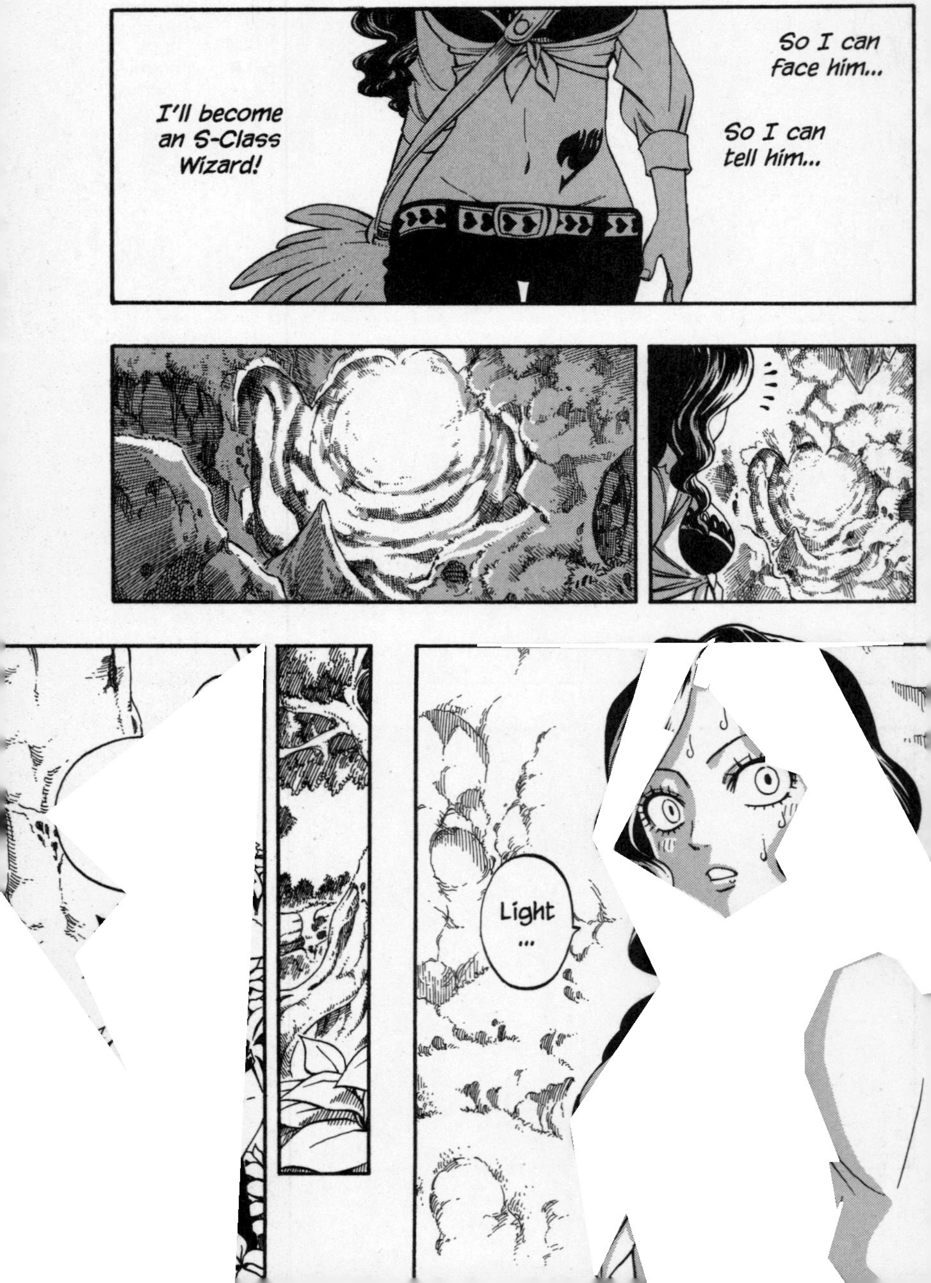
So I can face him...
So I can tell him...
I'll become an S-Class Wizard!
Light ...

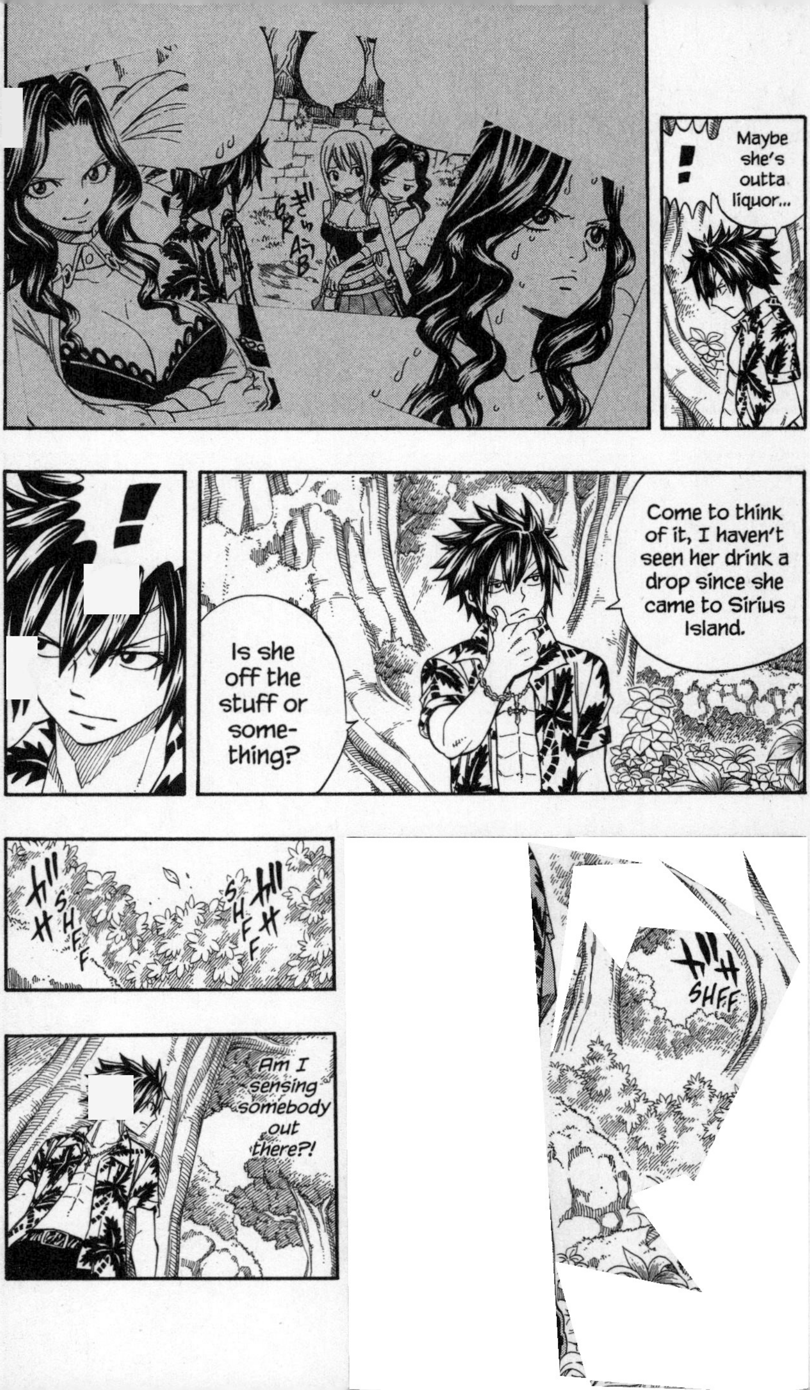
!
Maybe she's outta liquor...
Come to think of it, I haven't seen her drink a drop since she came to Sirius Island.
Is she off the stuff or something?
!
SHFF
SHFF
SHFF
Am I sensing somebody out there?!

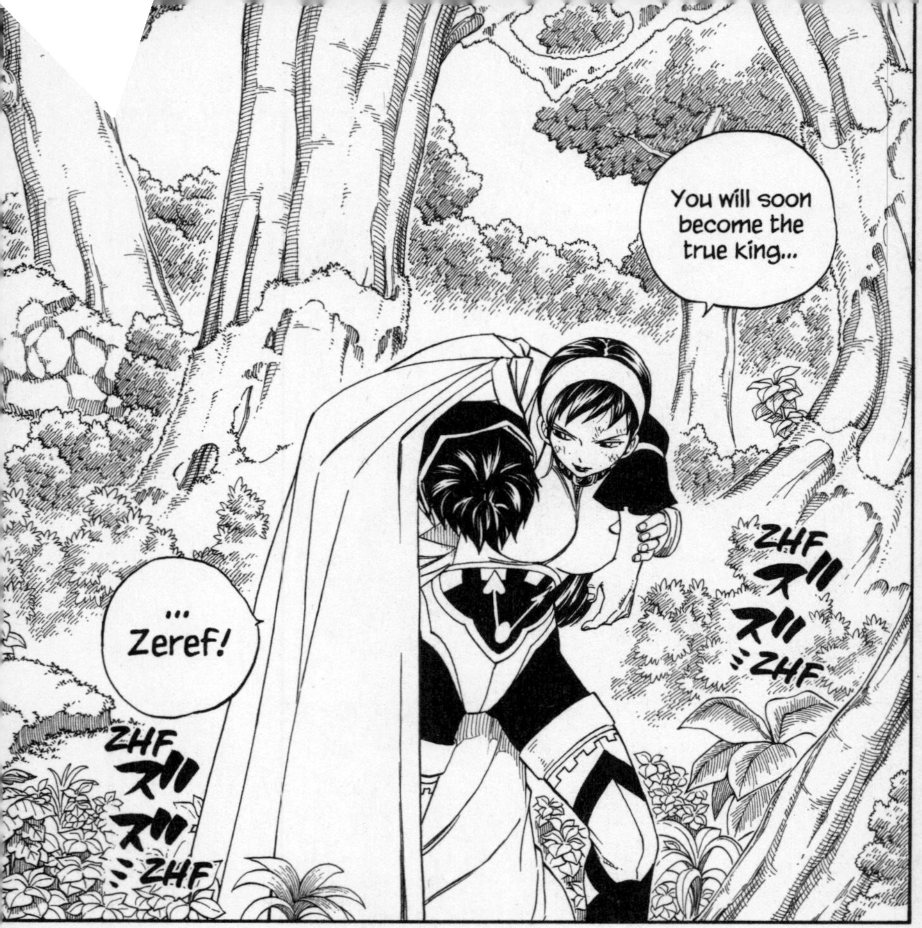
You will soon become the true king...
ZHF
ZHF
... Zeref!
ZHF
ZHF

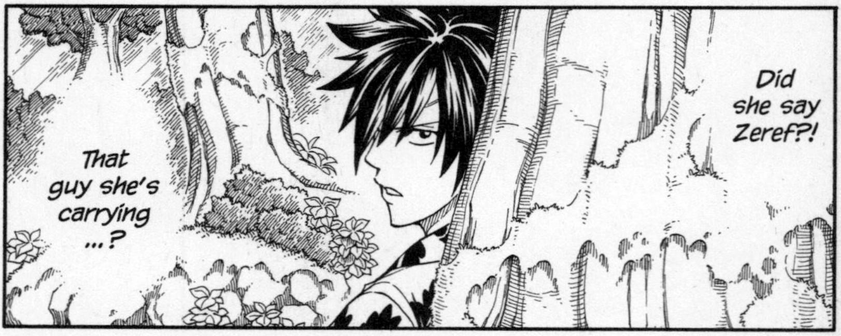
Did she say Zeref?!
That guy she's carrying ...?

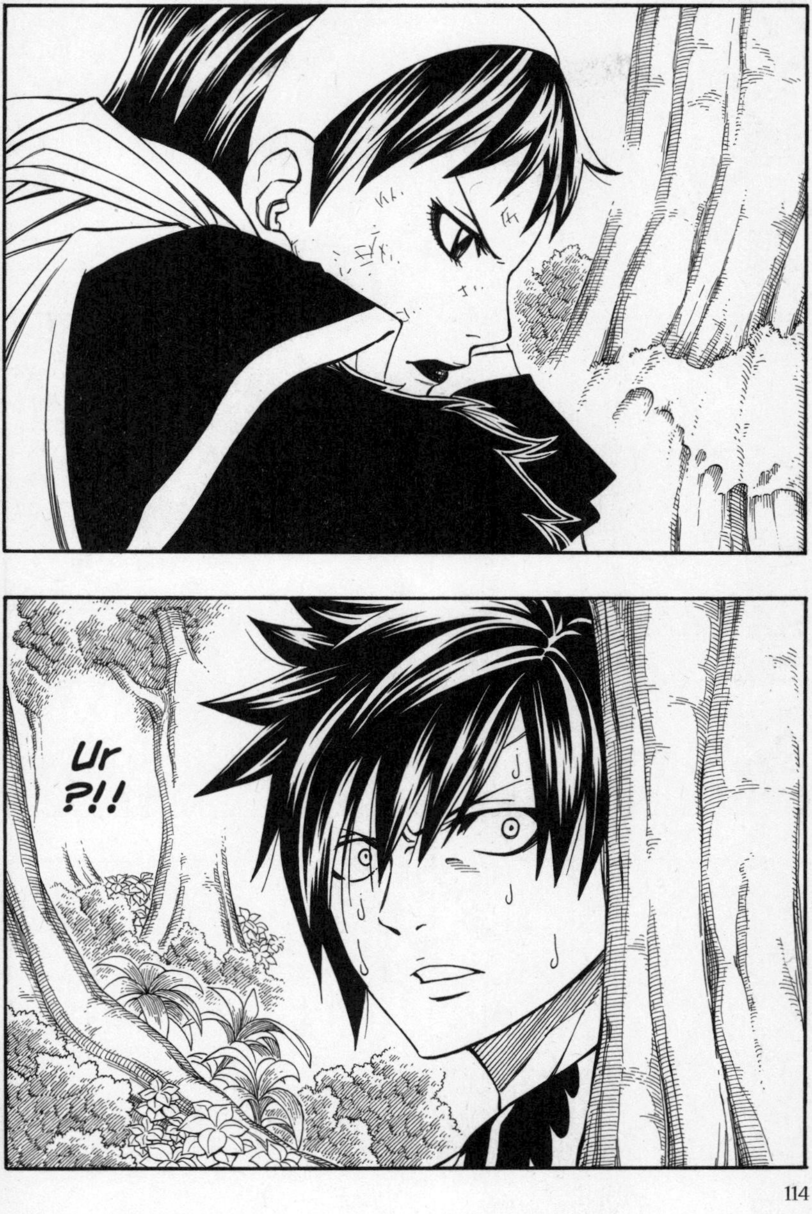
Ur
?!!

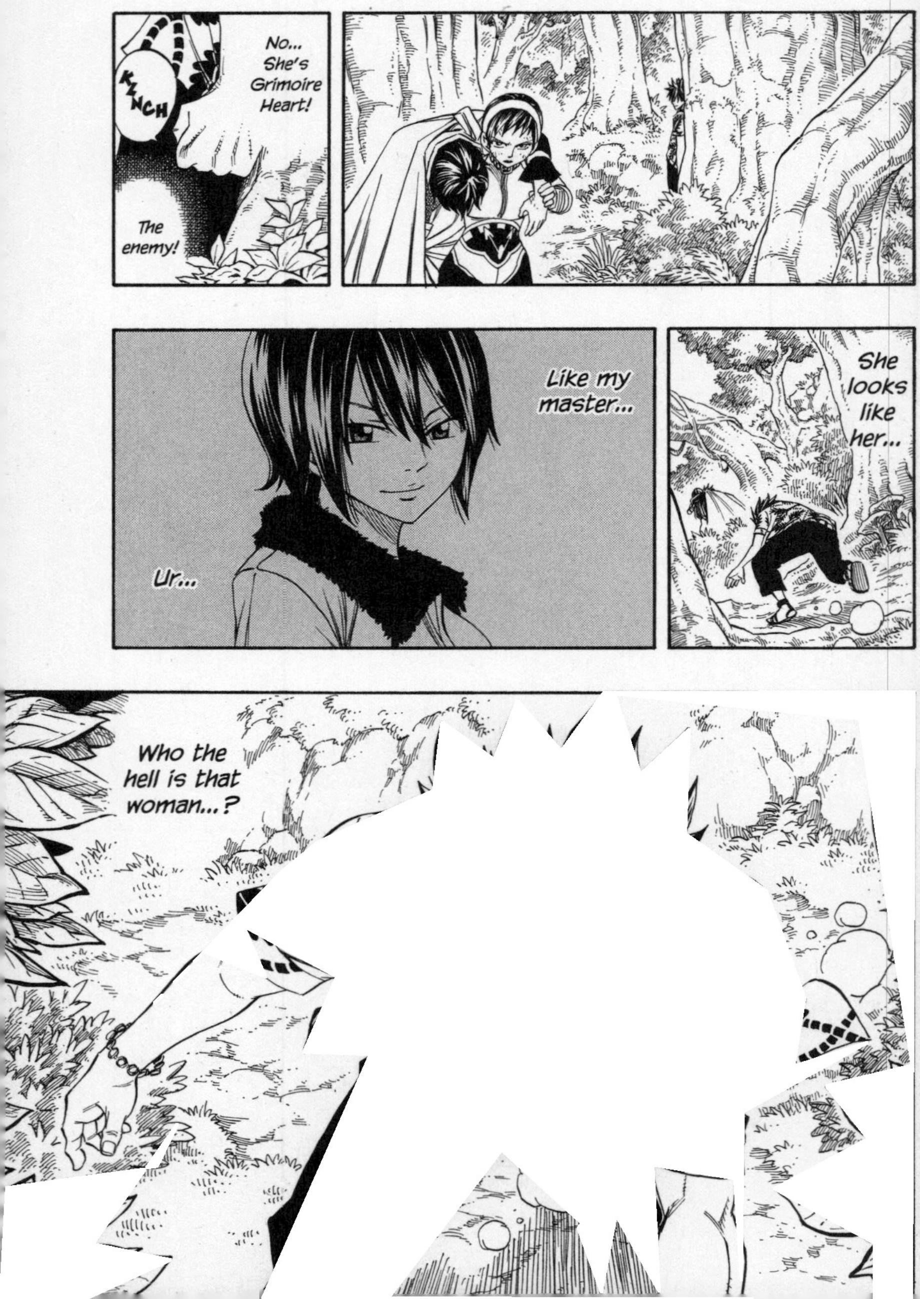
KENCH
No... She's Grimoire Heart!
The enemy!
She looks like her...
Like my master...
Ur...
Who the hell is that woman...?

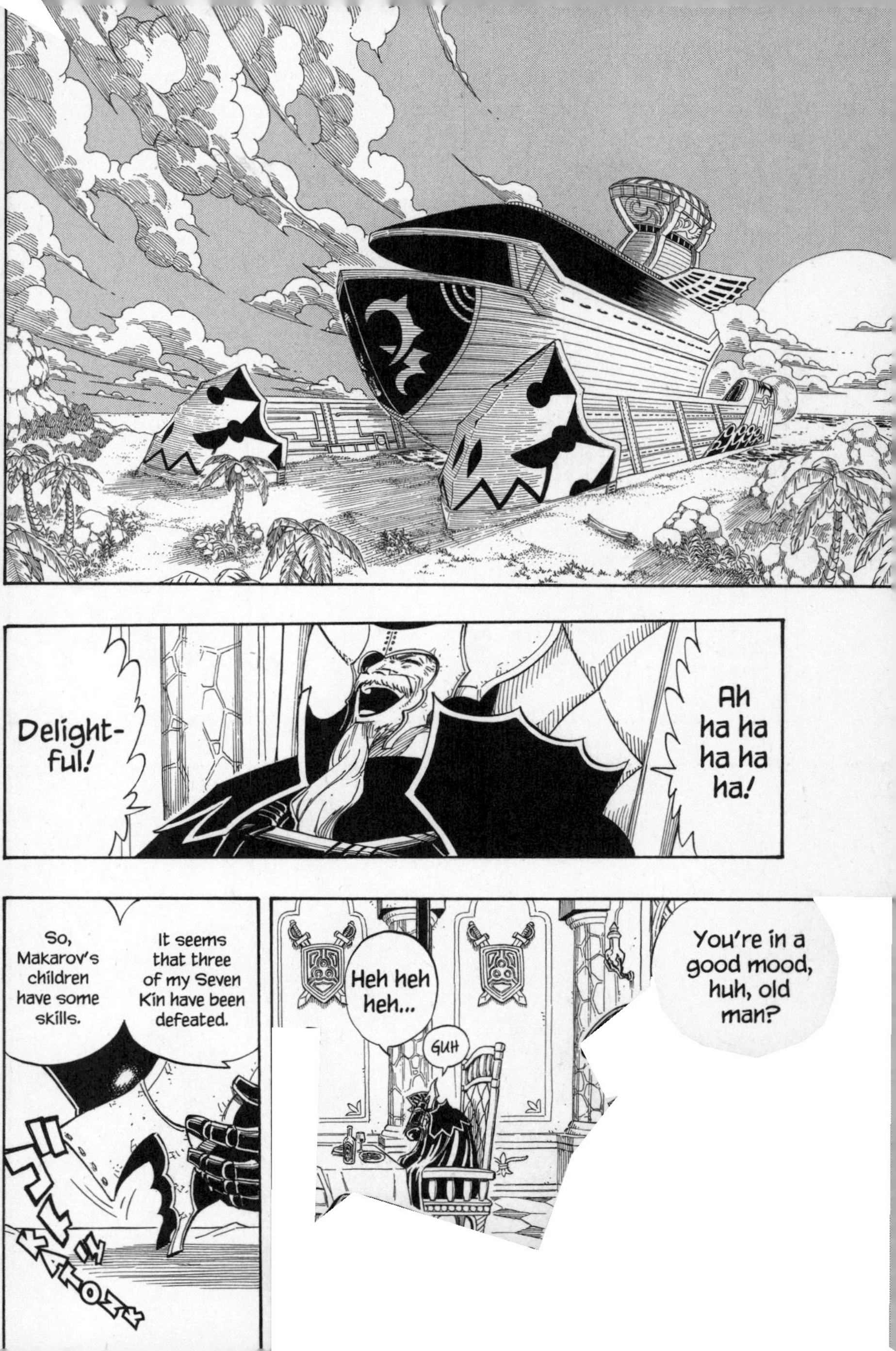
Ah ha ha ha ha ha!
Delight-ful!
You're in a good mood, huh, old man?
Heh heh heh...
GUH
It seems that three of my Seven Kin have been defeated.
So, Makarov's children have some skills.

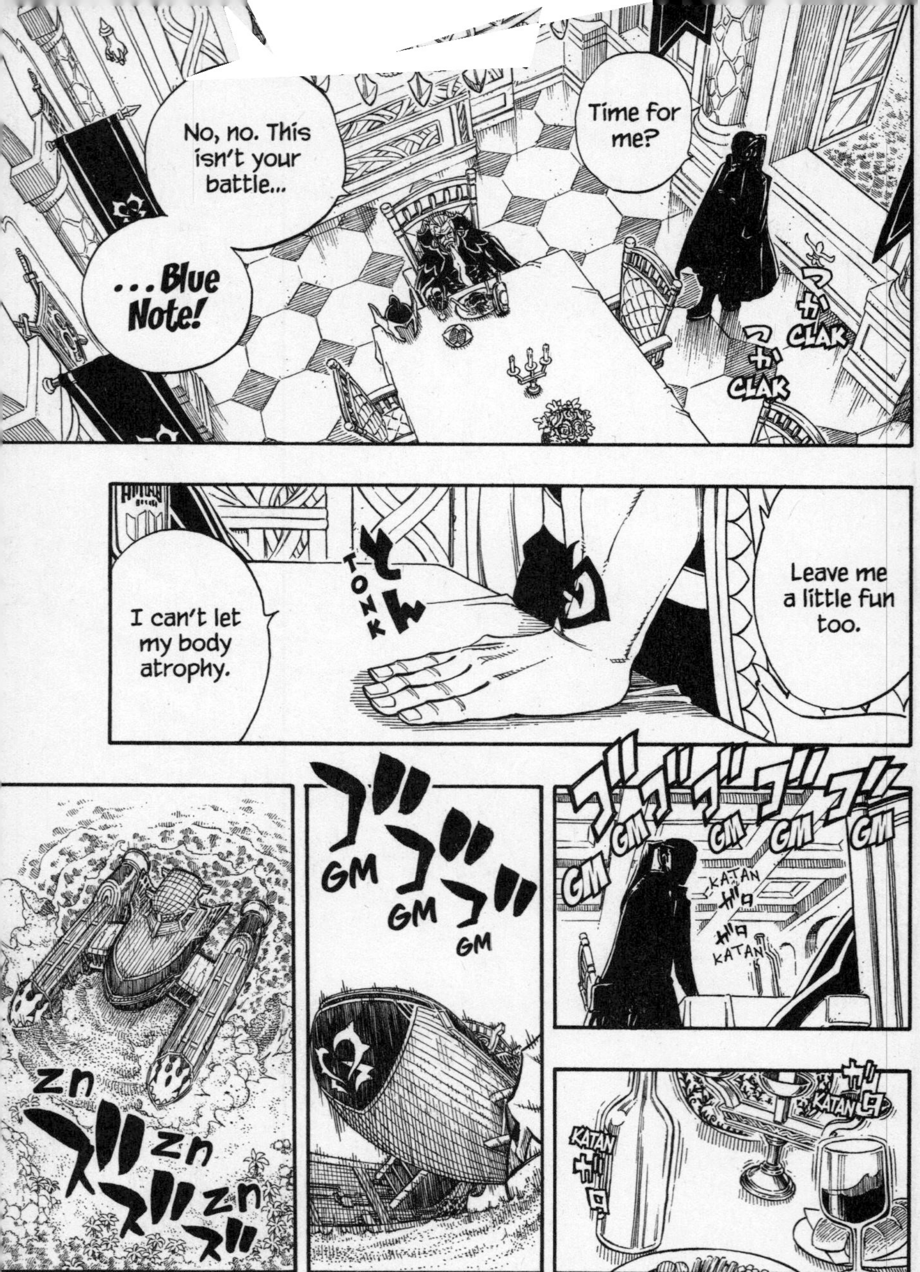
Time for me?
CLAK
CLAK
No, no. This isn't your battle...
...Blue Note!
Leave me a little fun too.
TONK
I can't let my body atrophy.
GM GM GM GM GM GM
KATAN
KATAN
KATAN
KATAN
GM
GM
GM
zn
zn
zn

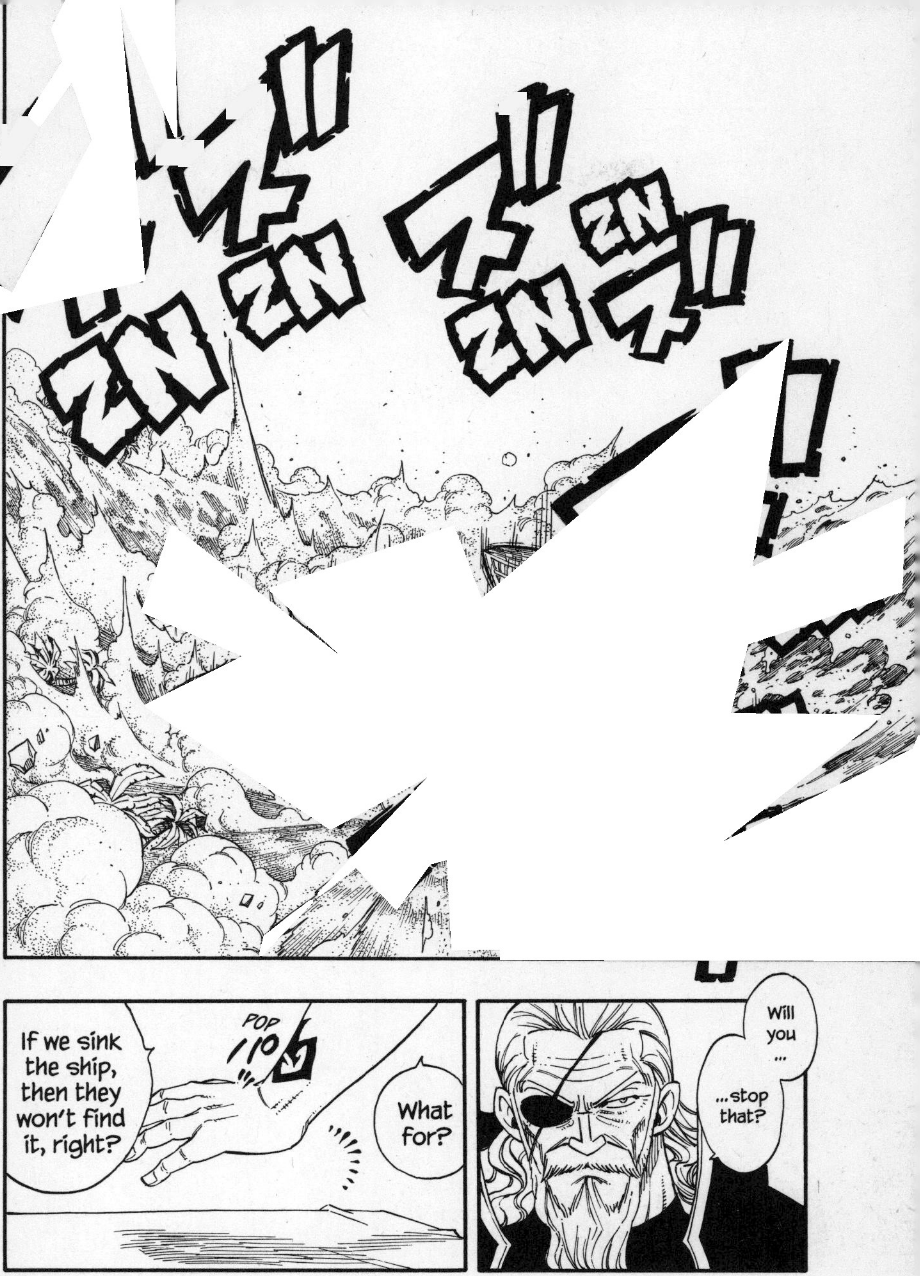
ZN
ZN
ZN
ZN
ZN
Will you ...
...stop that?
POP
What for?
If we sink the ship, then they won't find it, right?

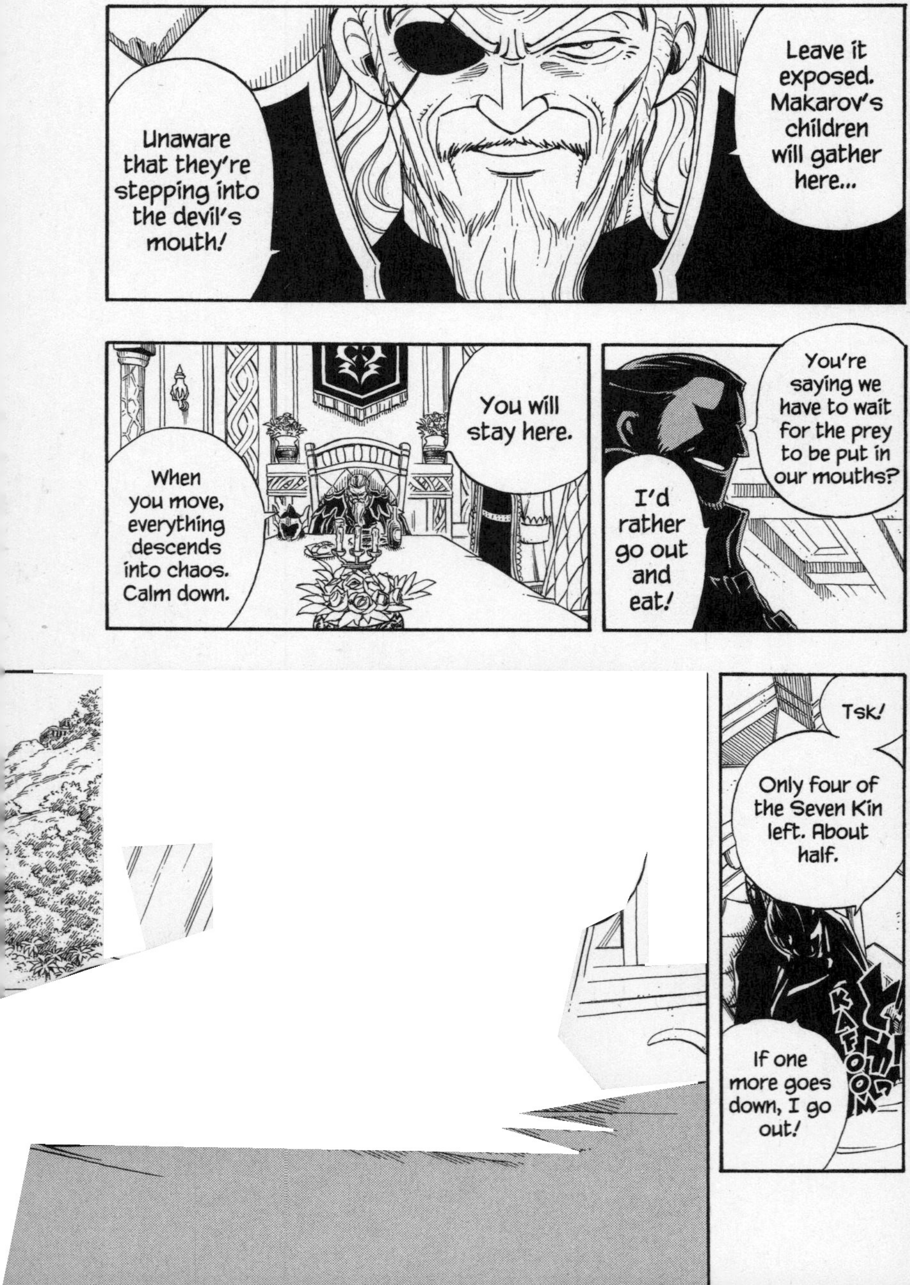
Leave it exposed. Makarov's children will gather here...
Unaware that they're stepping into the devil's mouth!
You're saying we have to wait for the prey to be put in our mouths?
I'd rather go out and eat!
You will stay here.
When you move, everything descends into chaos. Calm down.
Tsk!
Only four of the Seven Kin left. About half.
If one more goes down, I go out!

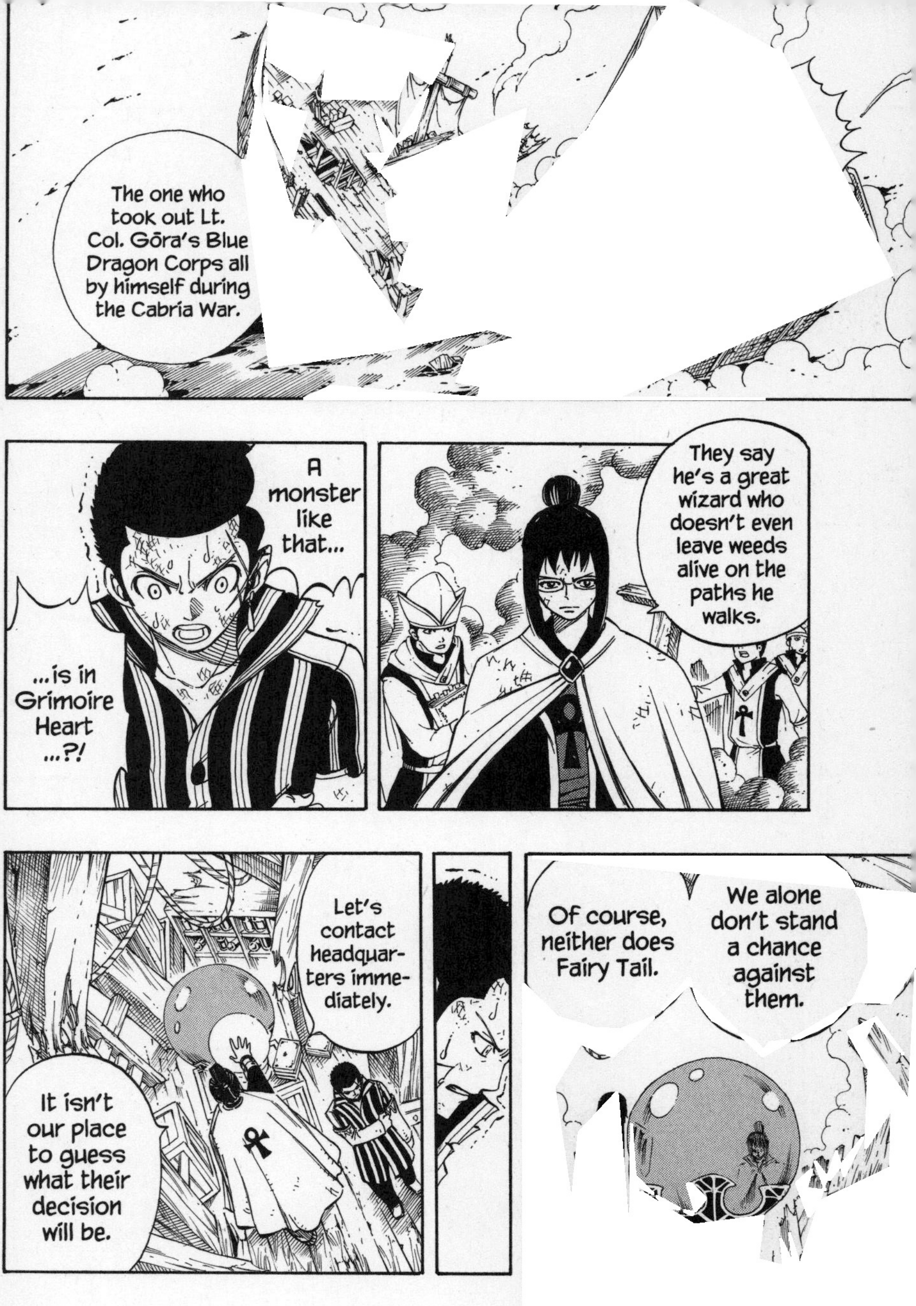
The one who took out Lt. Col. Gōra's Blue Dragon Corps all by himself during the Cabria War.
They say he's a great wizard who doesn't even leave weeds alive on the paths he walks.
A monster like that...
...is in Grimoire Heart ...?!
We alone don't stand a chance against them.
Of course, neither does Fairy Tail.
Let's contact headquar-ters imme-diately.
It isn't our place to guess what their decision will be.

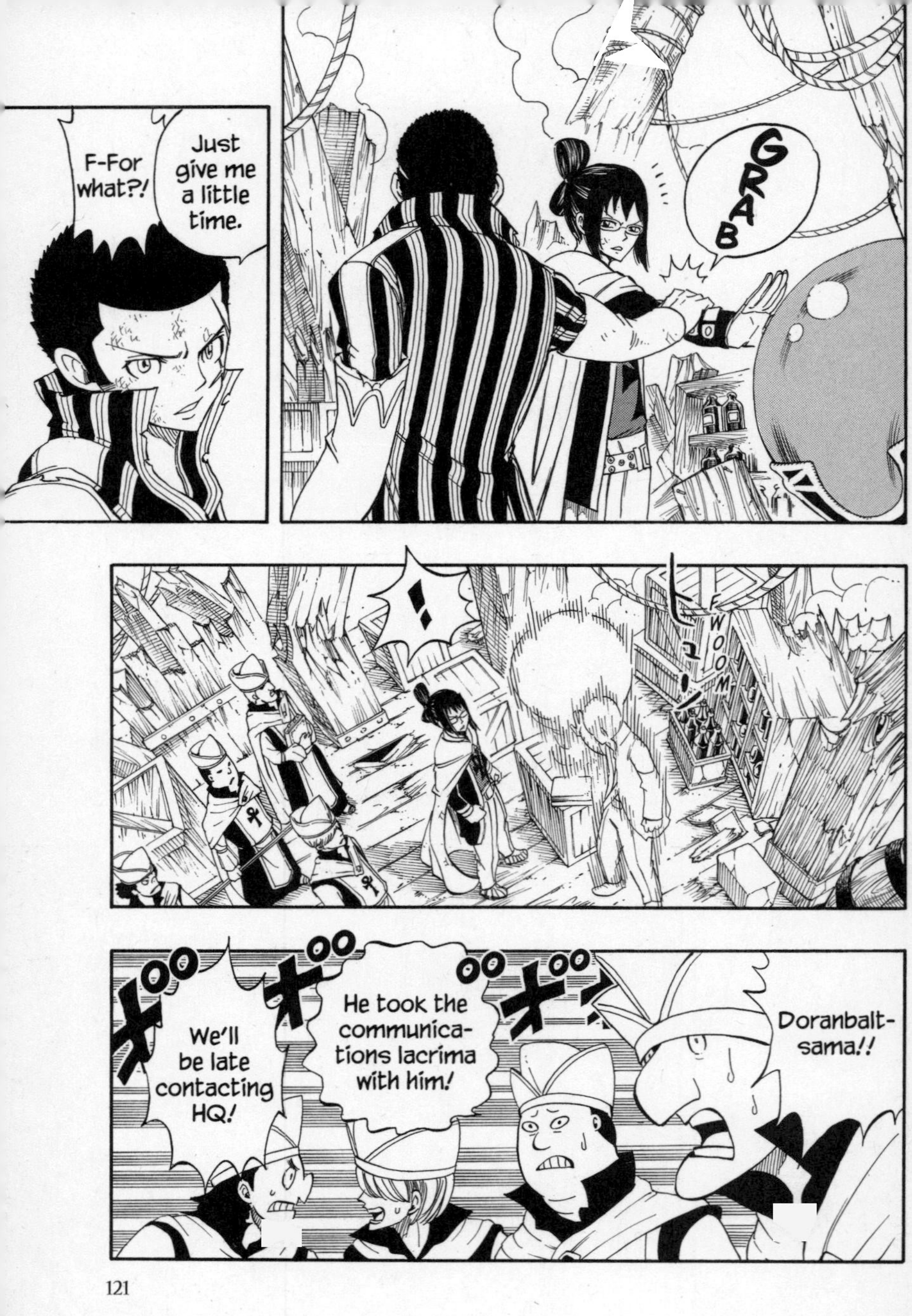
GRAB
Just give me a little time.
F-For what?!
!!
FWOOM
Doranbalt-sama!!
He took the communica-tions lacrima with him!
We'll be late contacting HQ!

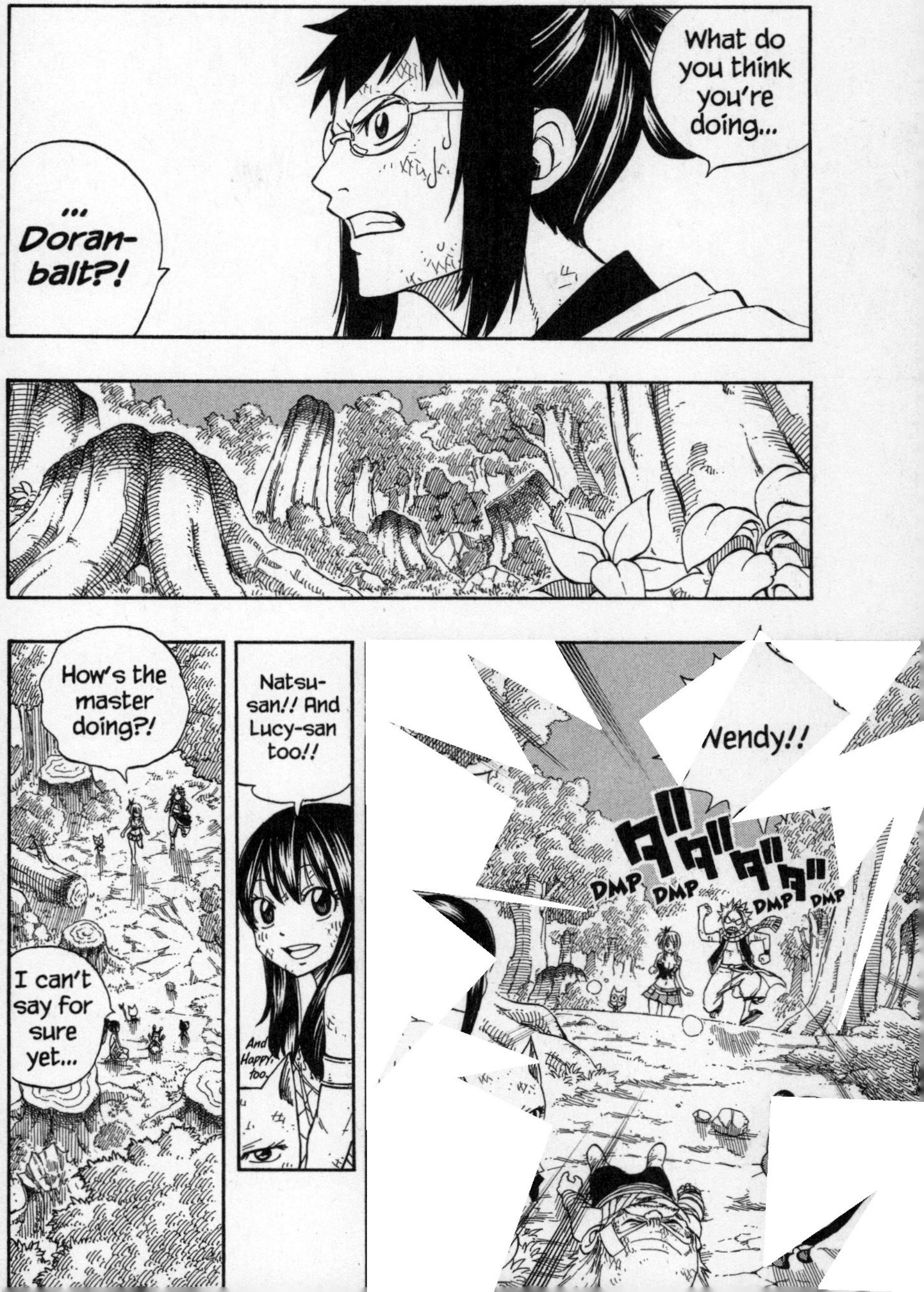
What do you think you're doing...
... Doran-balt?!
Wendy!!
DMP DMP DMP DMP
Natsu-san!! And Lucy-san too!!
And Happy, too.
How's the master doing?!
I can't say for sure yet...

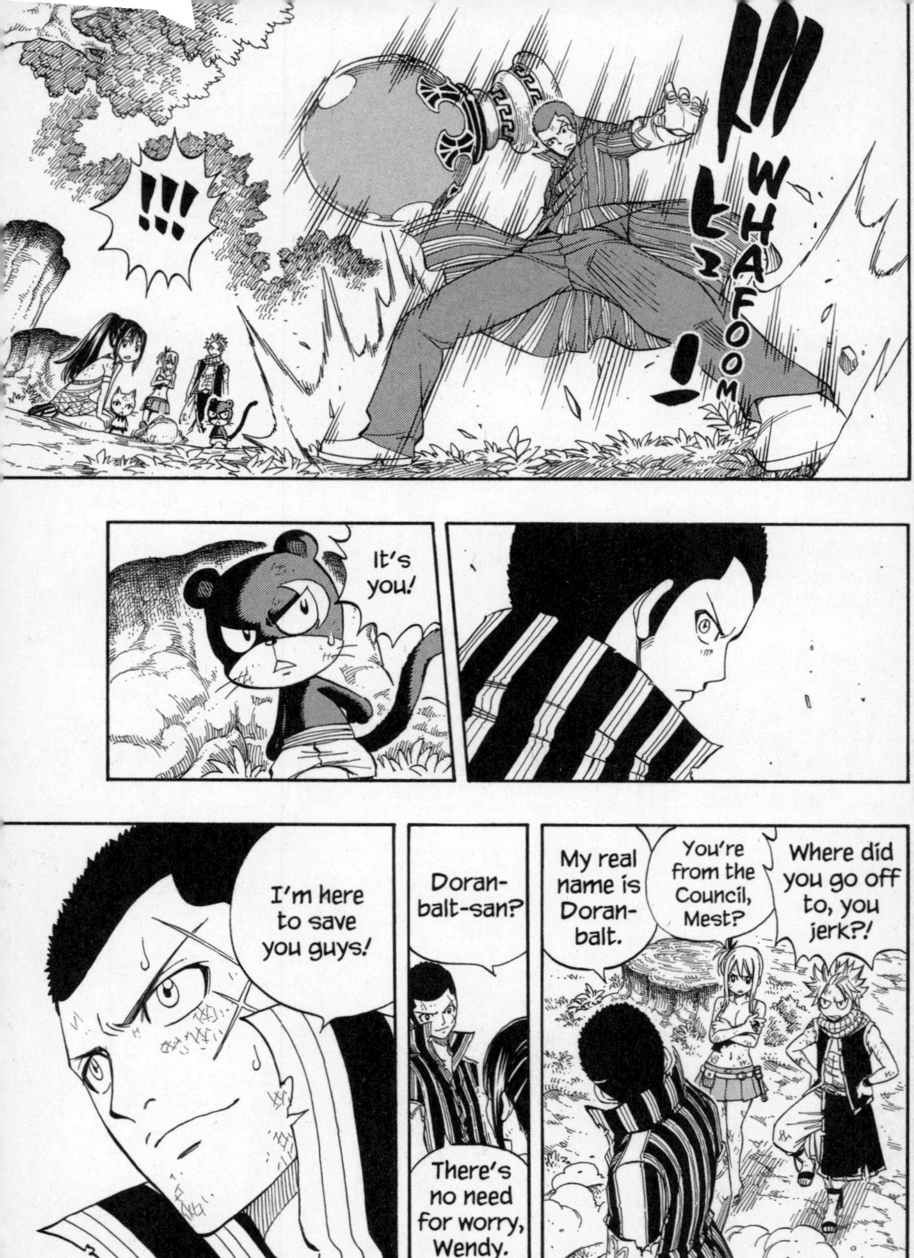
WHAFOOOM
!!!
It's you!
Where did you go off to, you jerk?!
You're from the Council, Mest?
My real name is Doran-balt.
Doran-balt-san?
There's no need for worry, Wendy.
I'm here to save you guys!

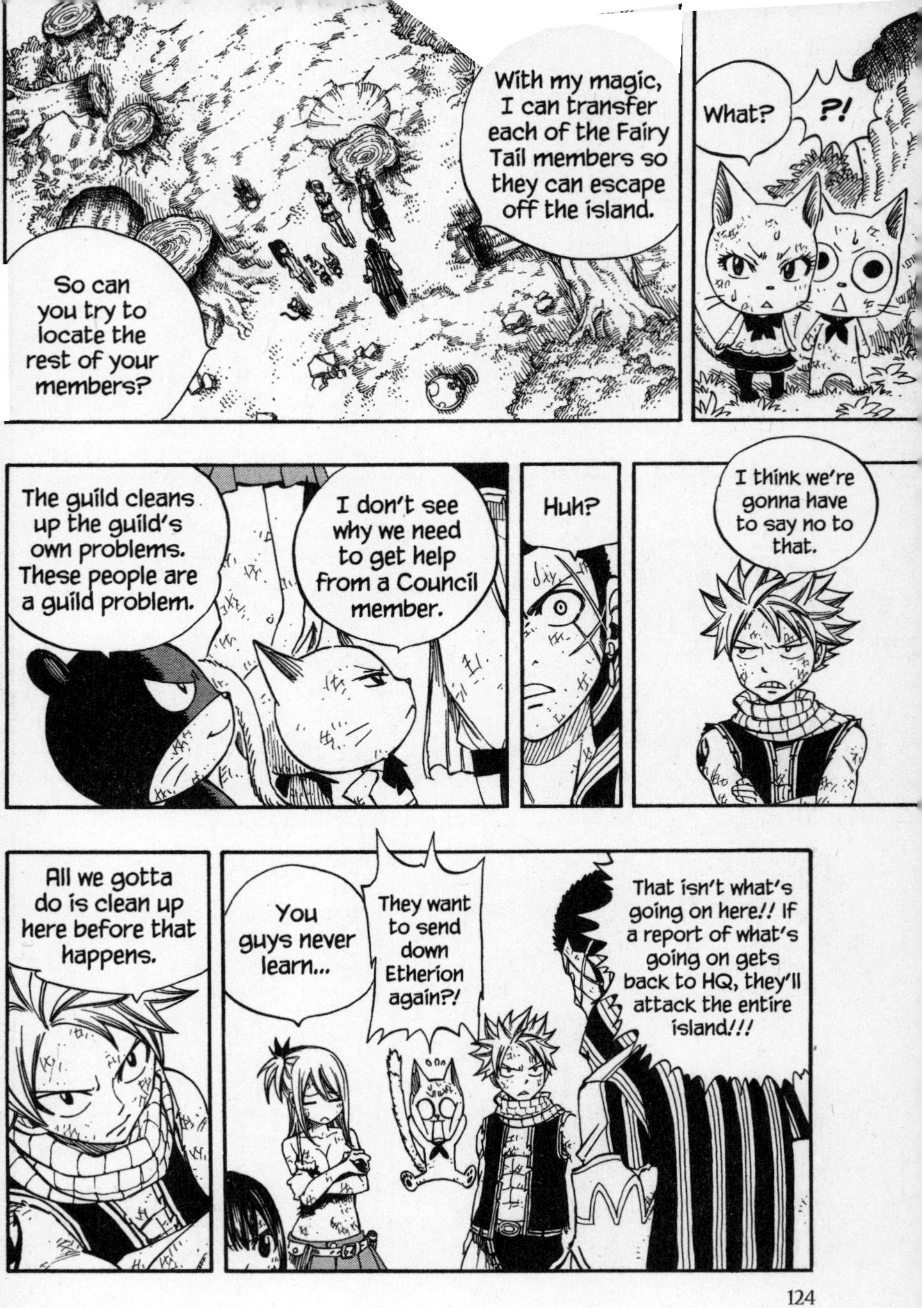
?!
What?
With my magic, I can transfer each of the Fairy Tail members so they can escape off the island.
So can you try to locate the rest of your members?
I think we're gonna have to say no to that.
Huh?
I don't see why we need to get help from a Council member.
The guild cleans up the guild's own problems. These people are a guild problem.
That isn't what's going on here!! If a report of what's going on gets back to HQ, they'll attack the entire island!!!
They want to send down Etherion again?!
You guys never learn...
All we gotta do is clean up here before that happens.

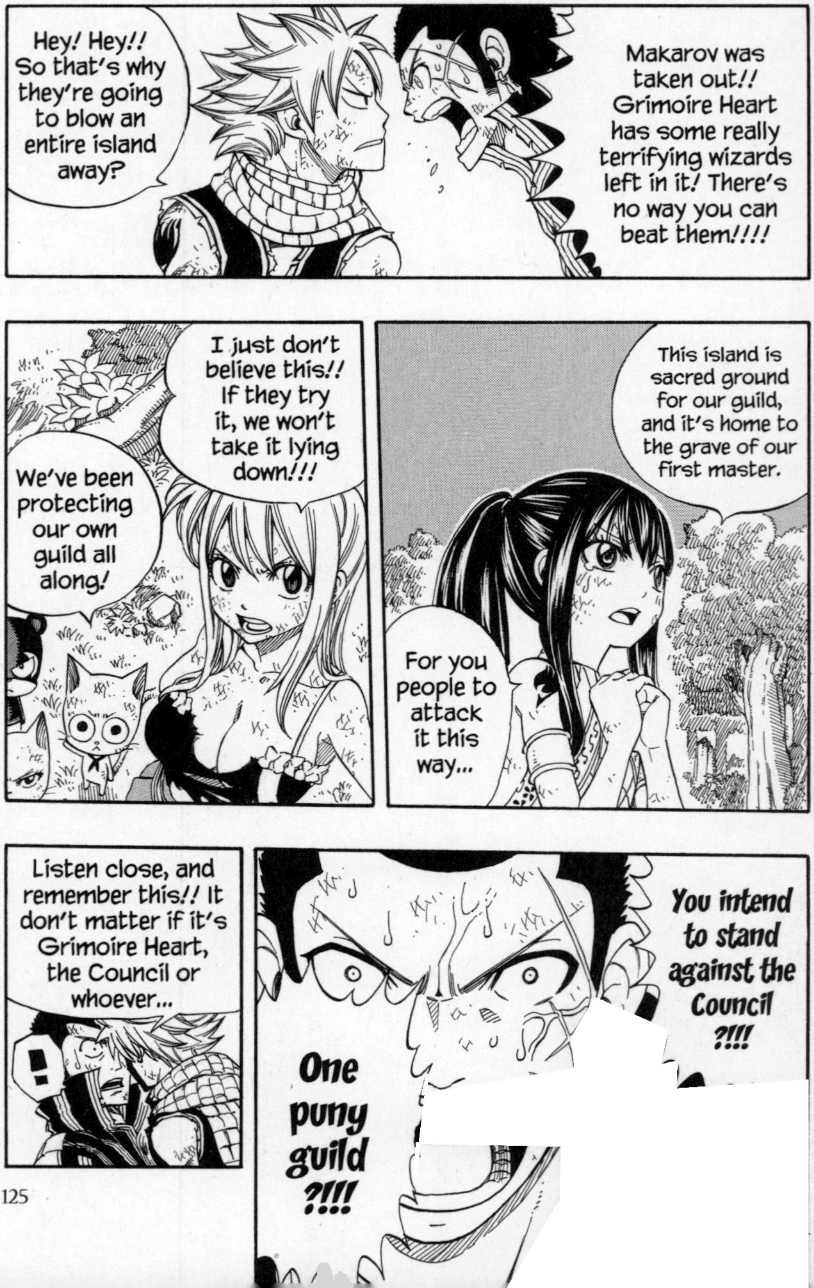
Makarov was taken out!! Grimoire Heart has some really terrifying wizards left in it! There's no way you can beat them!!!!
Hey! Hey!! So that's why they're going to blow an entire island away?
This island is sacred ground for our guild, and it's home to the grave of our first master.
For you people to attack it this way...
I just don't believe this!! If they try it, we won't take it lying down!!!
We've been protecting our own guild all along!
You intend to stand against the Council ?!!!
One puny guild ?!!!
Listen close, and remember this!! It don't matter if it's Grimoire Heart, the Council or whoever...

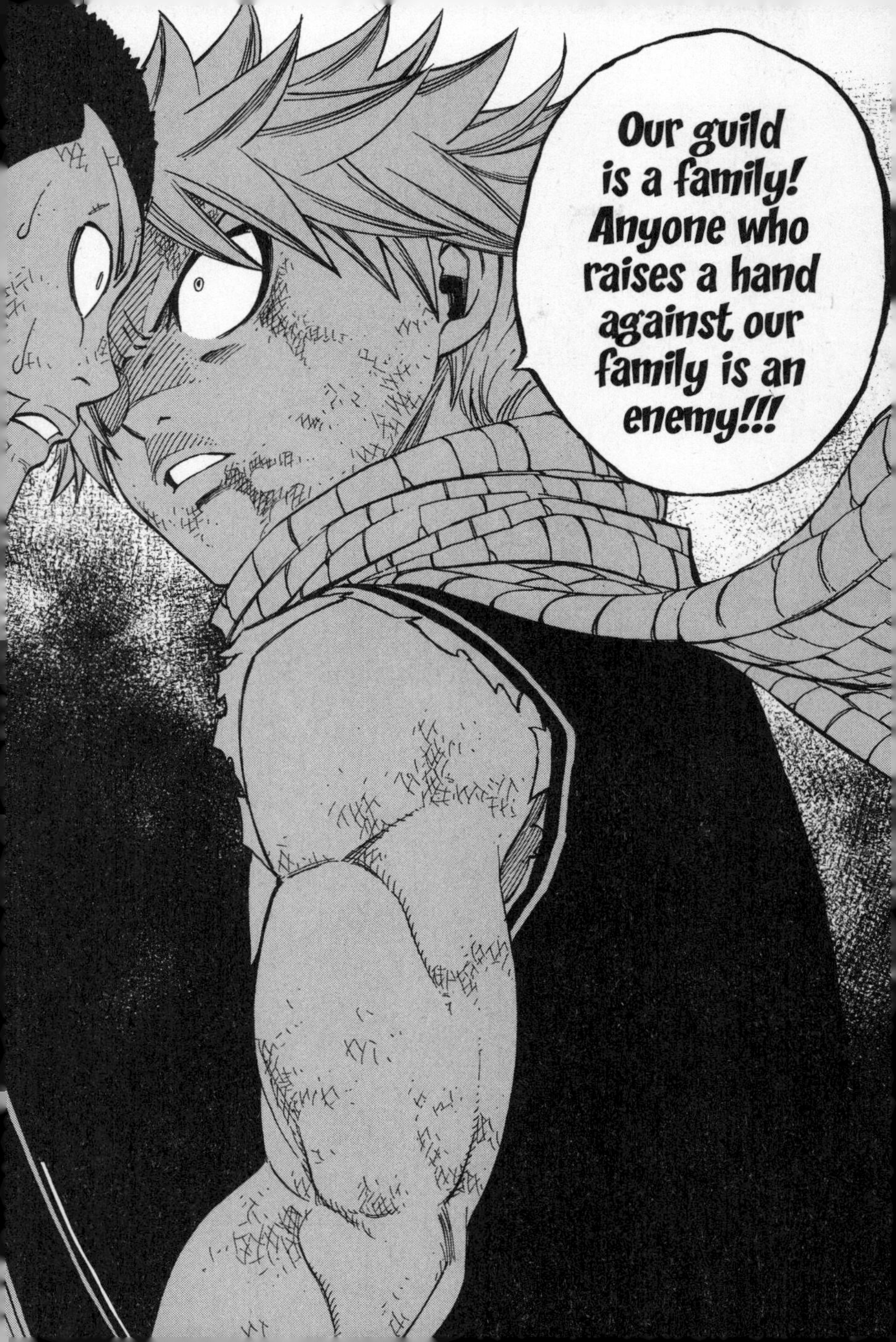
Our guild is a family! Anyone who raises a hand against our family is an enemy!!!

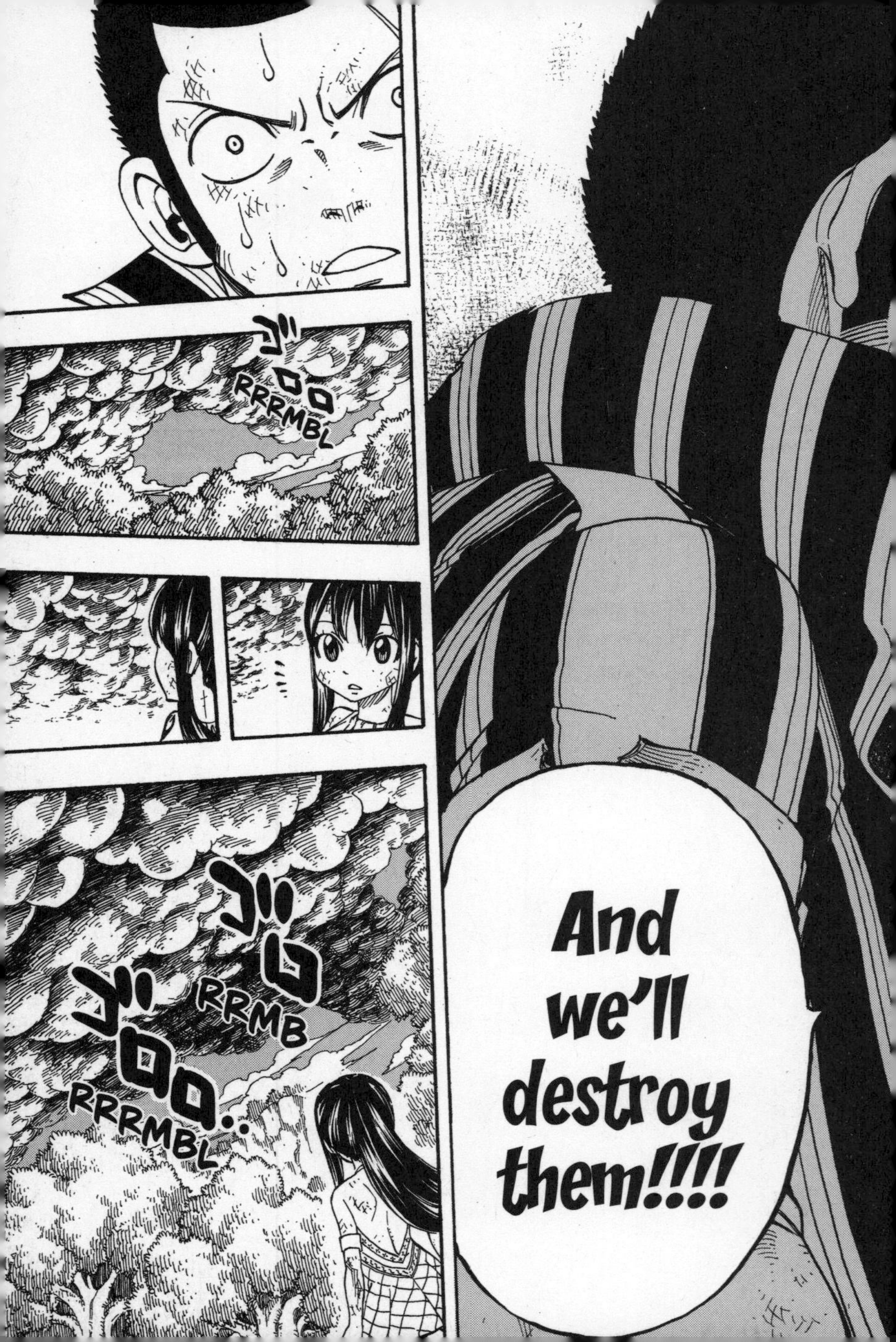
And we'll destroy them!!!!
ゴロロ
RRRMBL
ゴロ
RRMB
ゴロロ..
RRRMBL

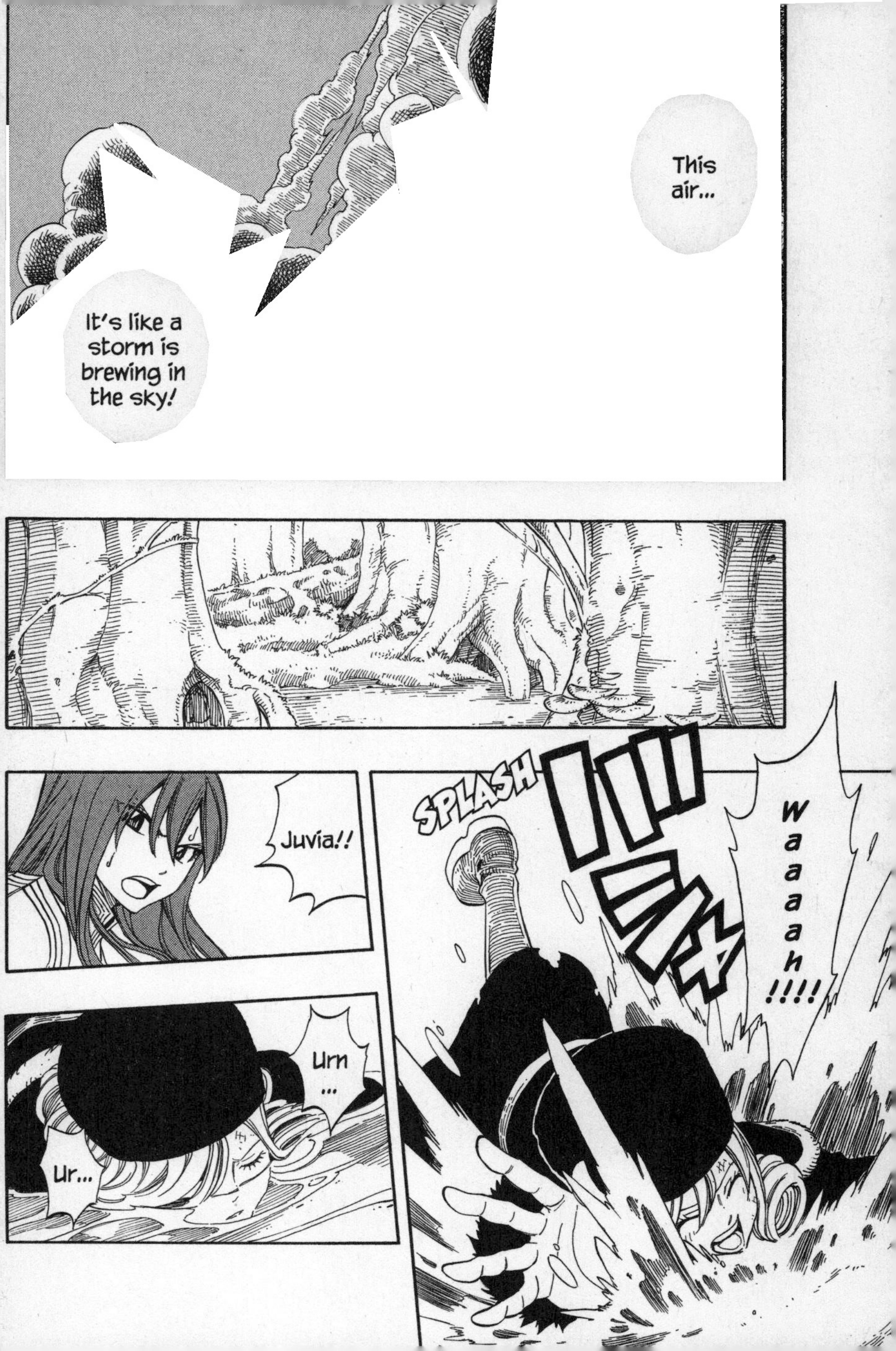
This air...
It's like a storm is brewing in the sky!
SPLASH
Waaaah!!!!
Juvia!!
Urn ...
Ur...

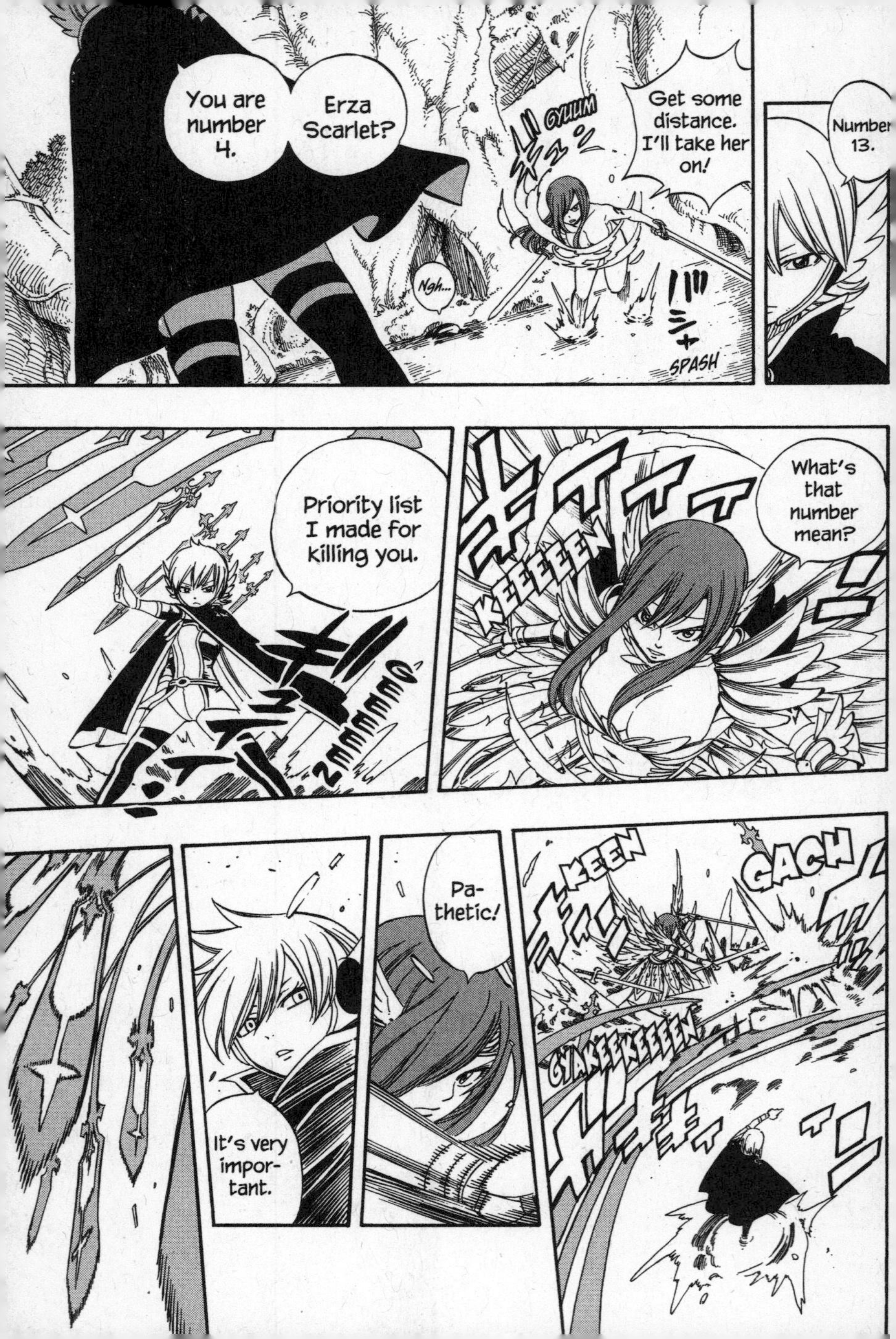

Number 13.
Get some distance. I'll take her on!
GYUUM
Erza Scarlet?
You are number 4.
Ngh...
SPASH
KEEEEEN
What's that number mean?
Priority list I made for killing you.
ZEEEEEEG
GACH
KEEN
GYAKEEKEEEEN
Pa-thetic!
It's very impor-tant.

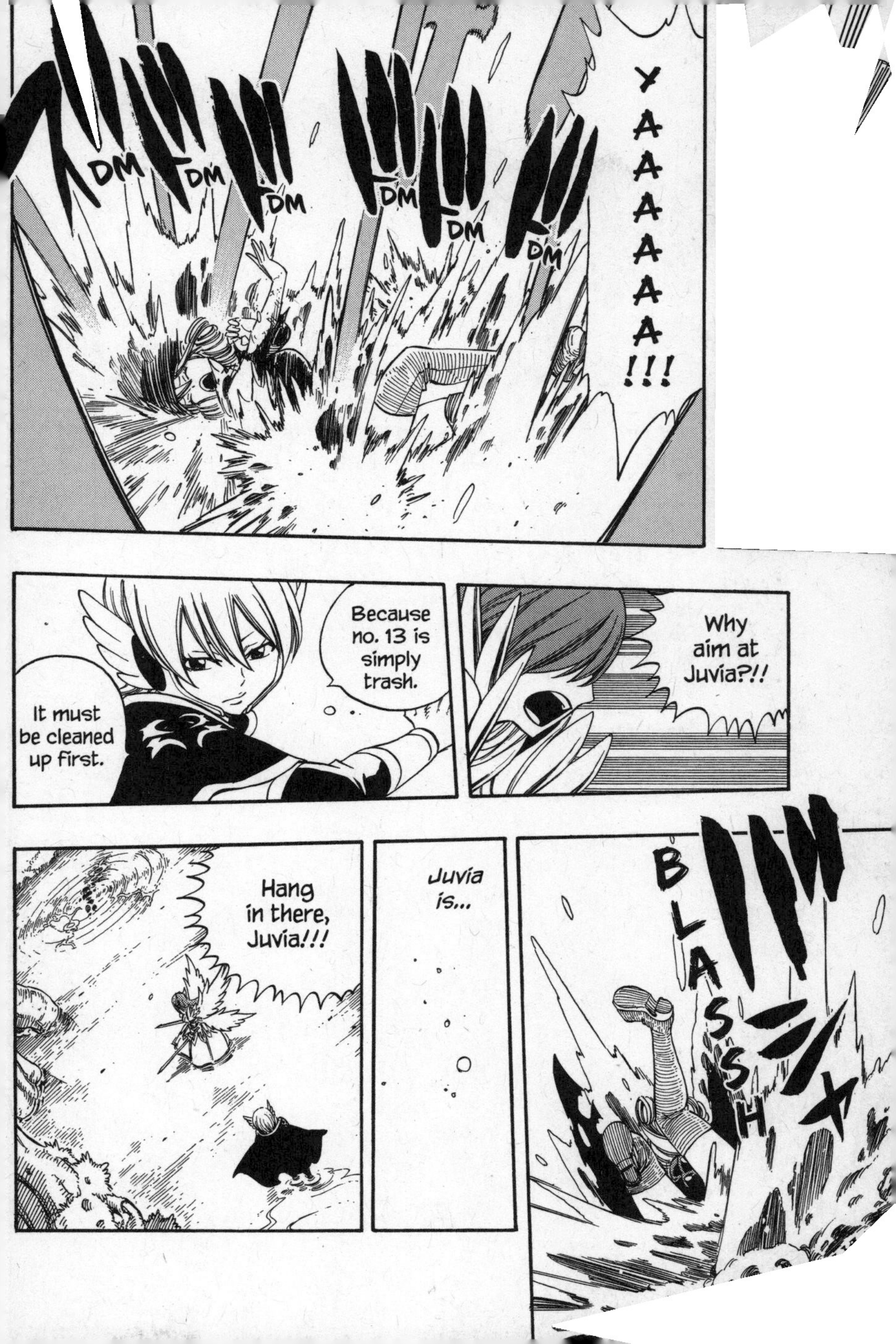
YAAAAAAA!!!
DM DM DM DM DM DM
Why aim at Juvia?!!
Because no. 13 is simply trash.
It must be cleaned up first.
BLASSH
Juvia is...
Hang in there, Juvia!!!

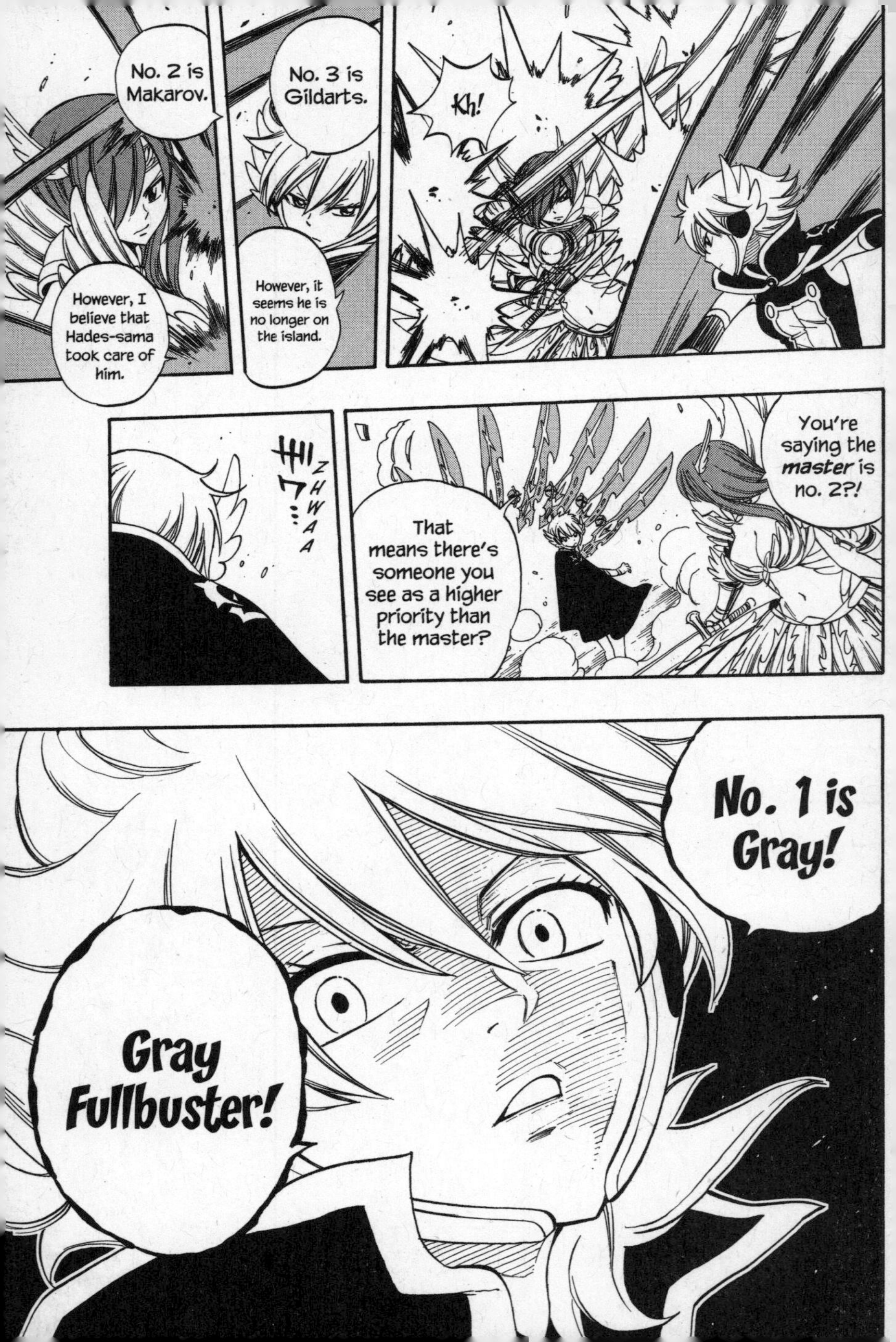
Kh!
No. 3 is Gildarts.
However, it seems he is no longer on the island.
No. 2 is Makarov.
However, I believe that Hades-sama took care of him.
You're saying the *master* is no. 2?!
That means there's someone you see as a higher priority than the master?
ZHWAA
No. 1 is Gray!
Gray Fullbuster!

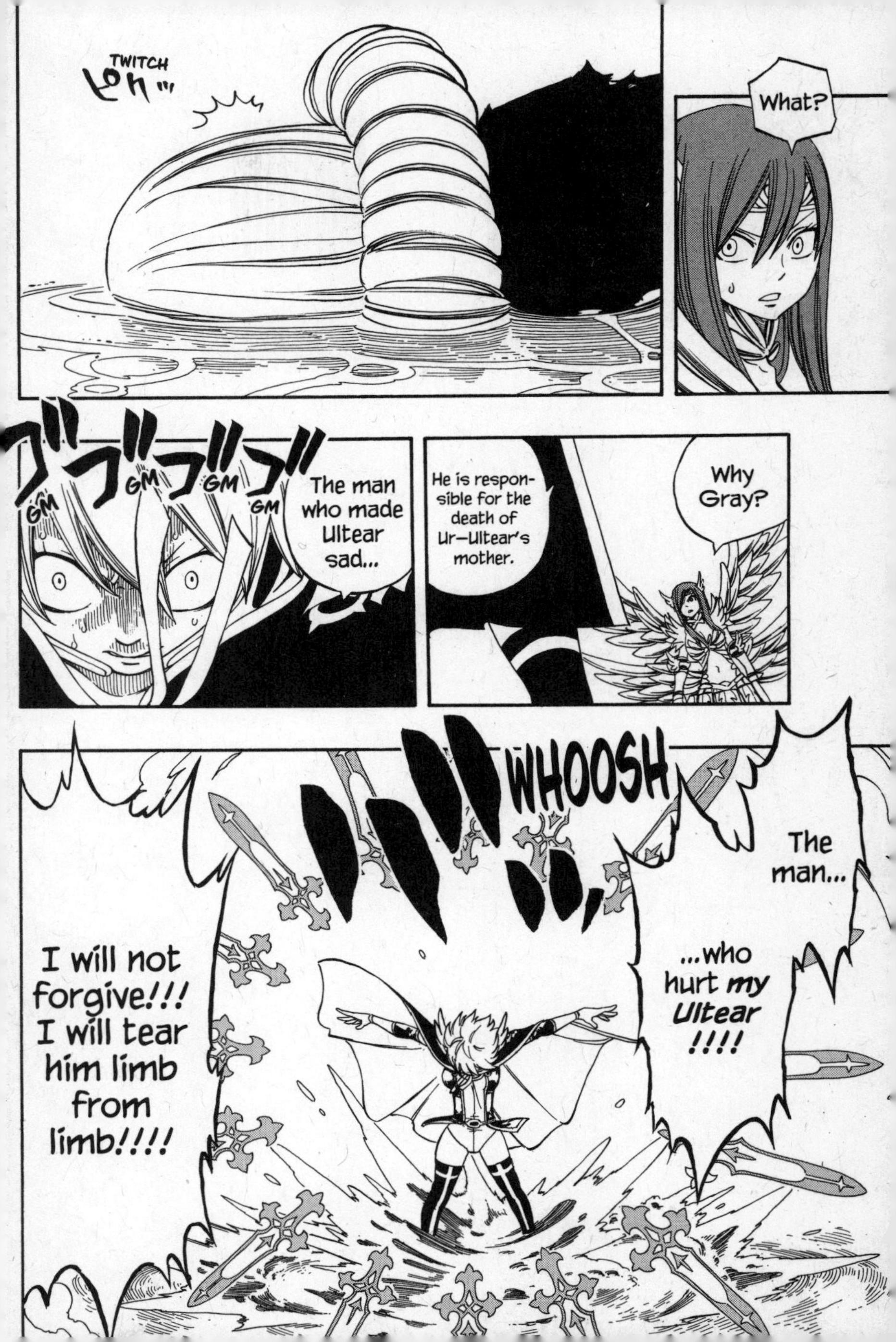
What?
TWITCH
Why Gray?
He is responsible for the death of Ur—Ultear's mother.
The man who made Ultear sad...
ゴゴゴゴ
GM GM GM GM
The man...
...who hurt *my Ultear* !!!!
WHOOSH
I will not forgive!!! I will tear him limb from limb!!!!

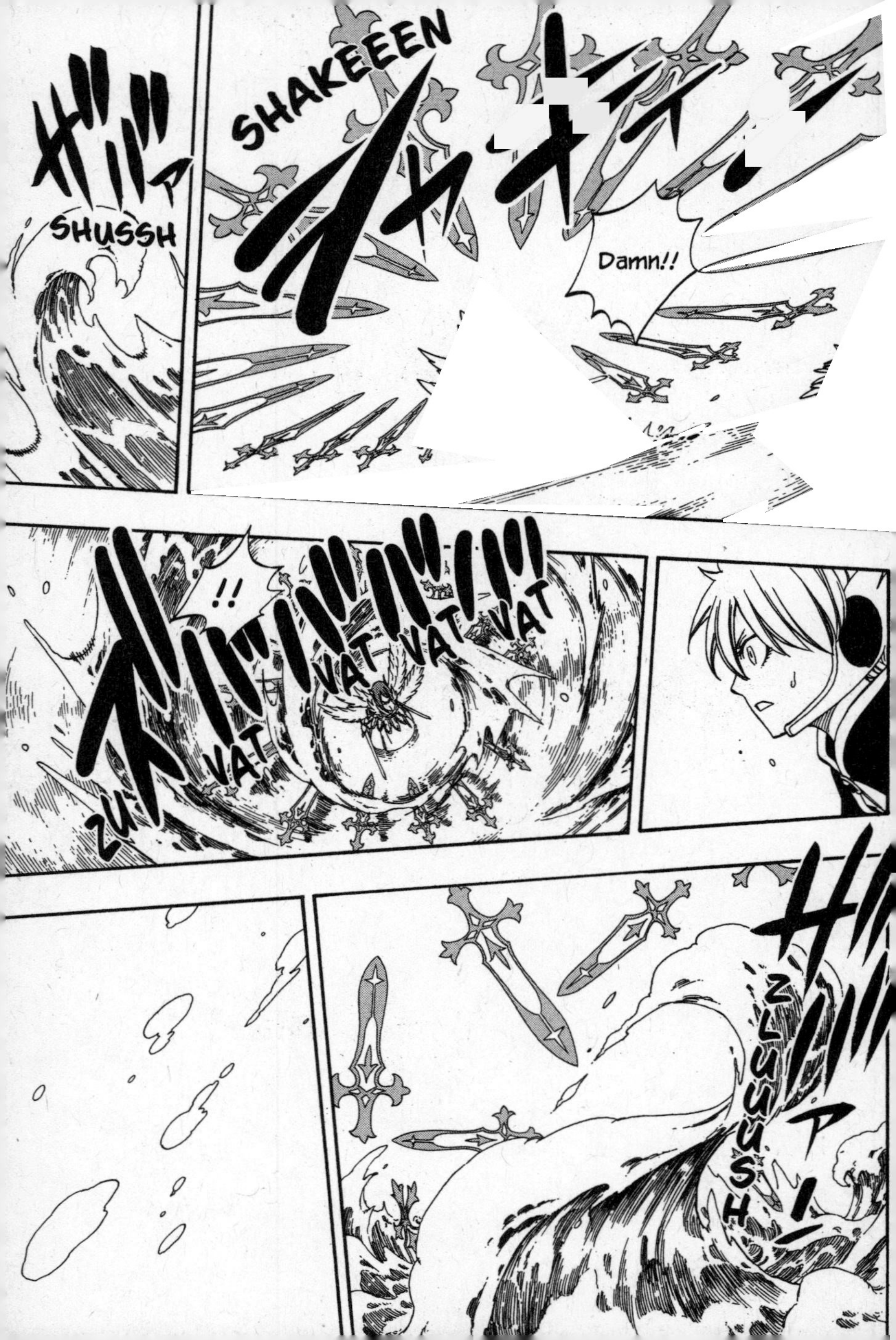
SHAKEEEN
Damn!!
SHUSSH
!!
VAT VAT VAT VAT
ZU
ZLUUUSH

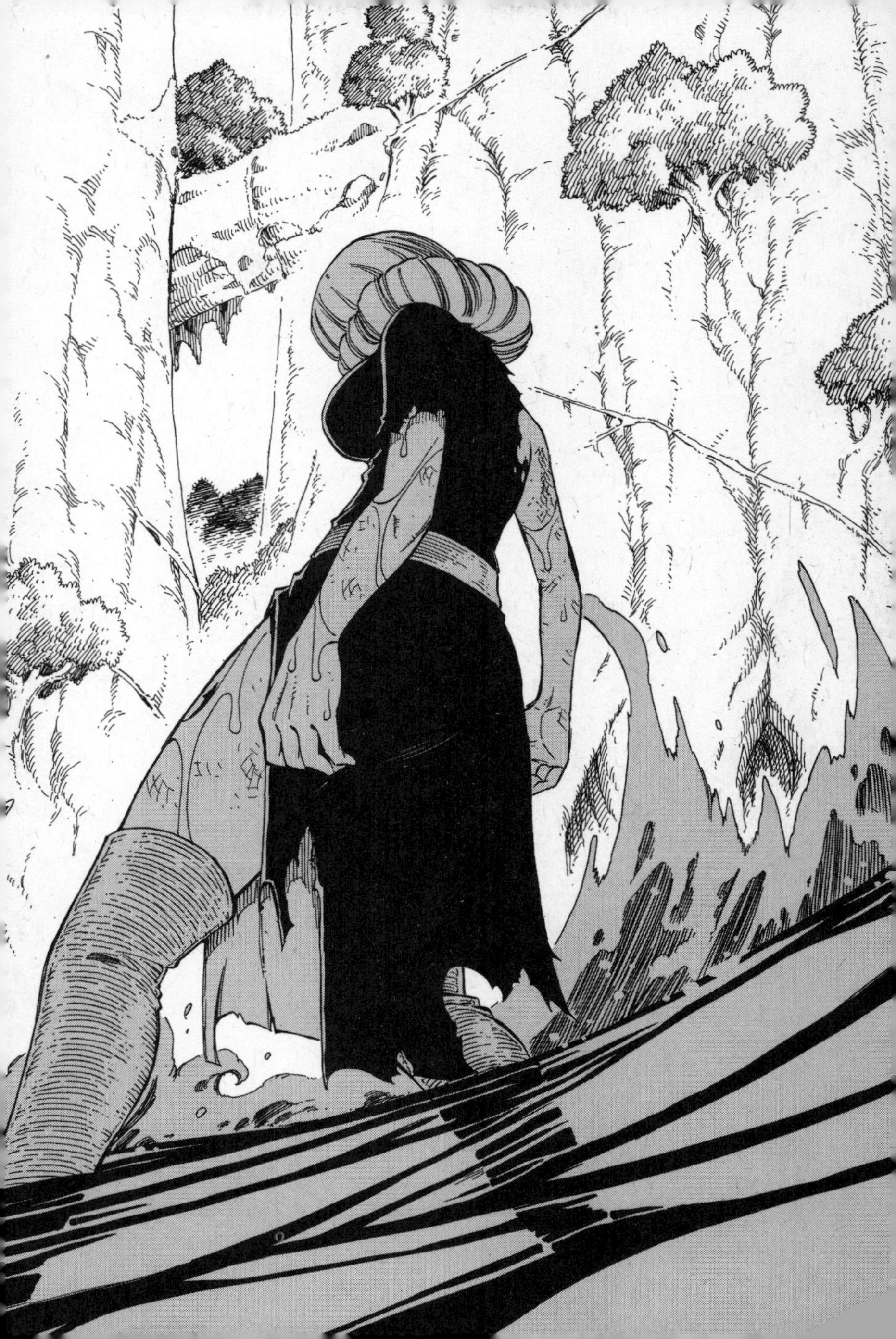

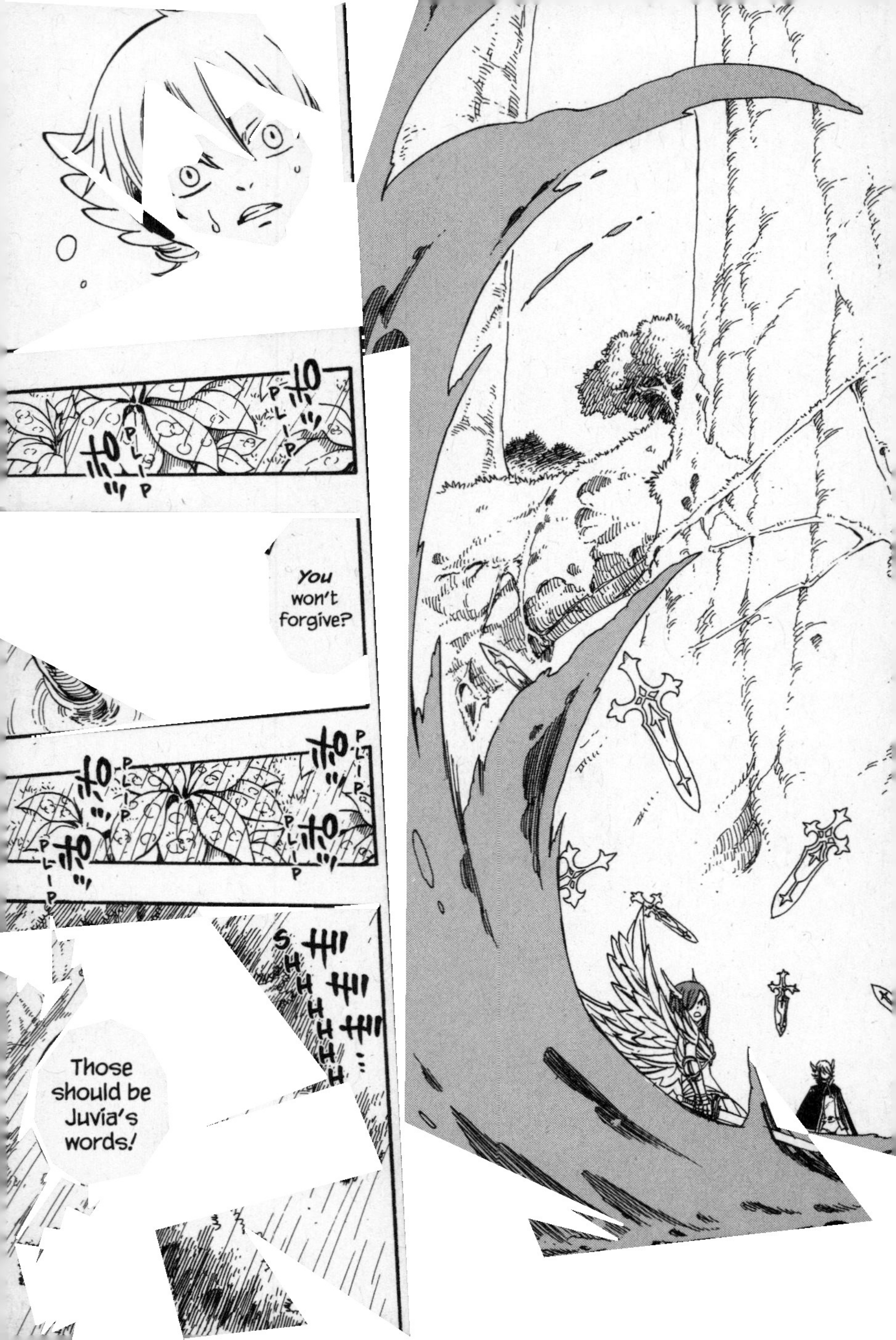
PLIP
PLIP
You won't forgive?
PLIP
PLIP
PLIP
PLIP
SHHHHHHH
Those should be Juvia's words!

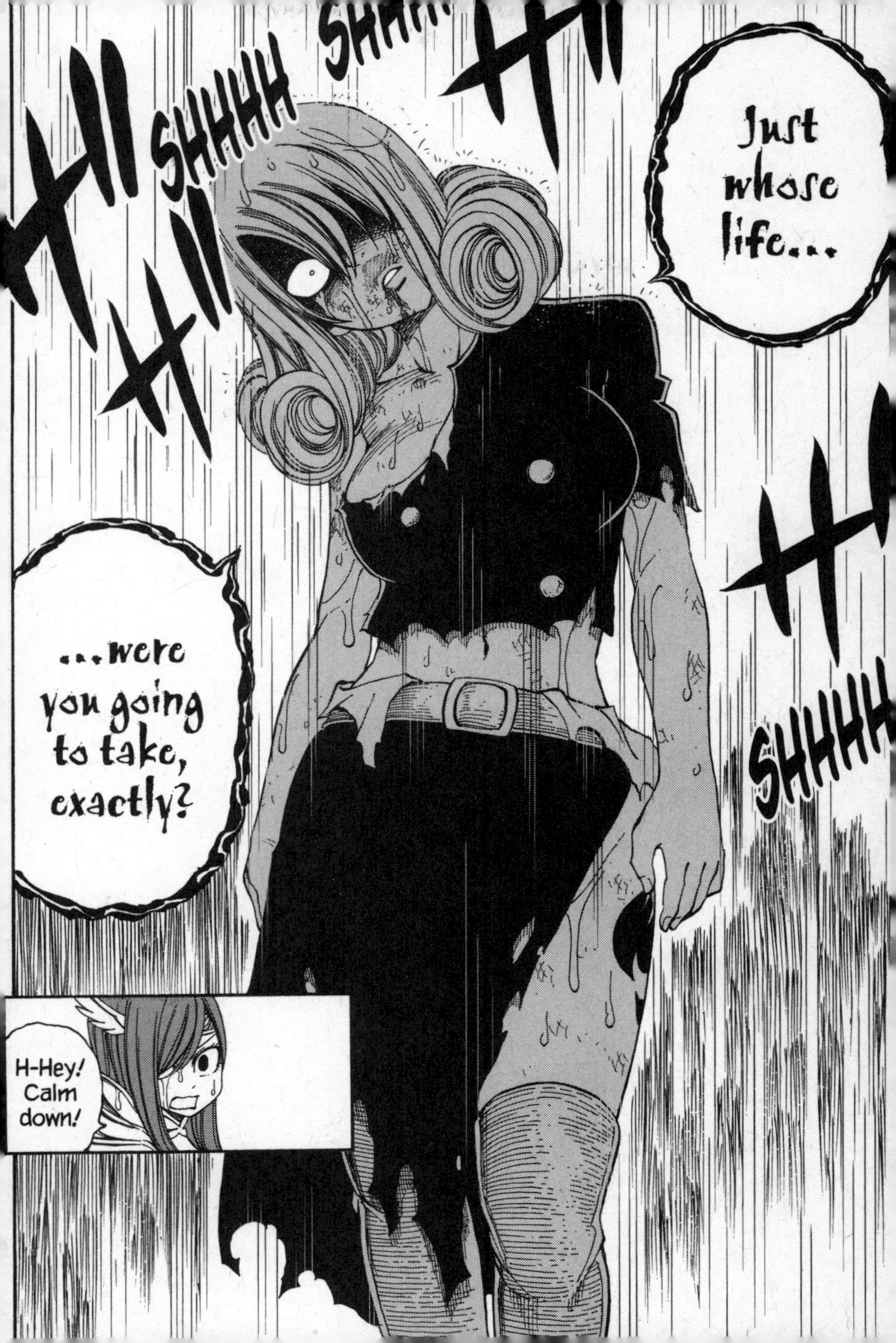
SHHHH
Just whose life...
...were you going to take, exactly?
SHHHH
H-Hey! Calm down!

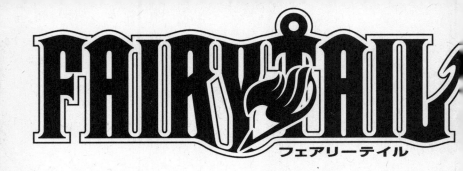

Chapter 229: Dead End of Despair

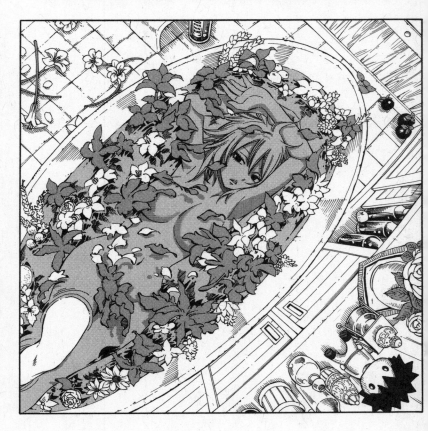

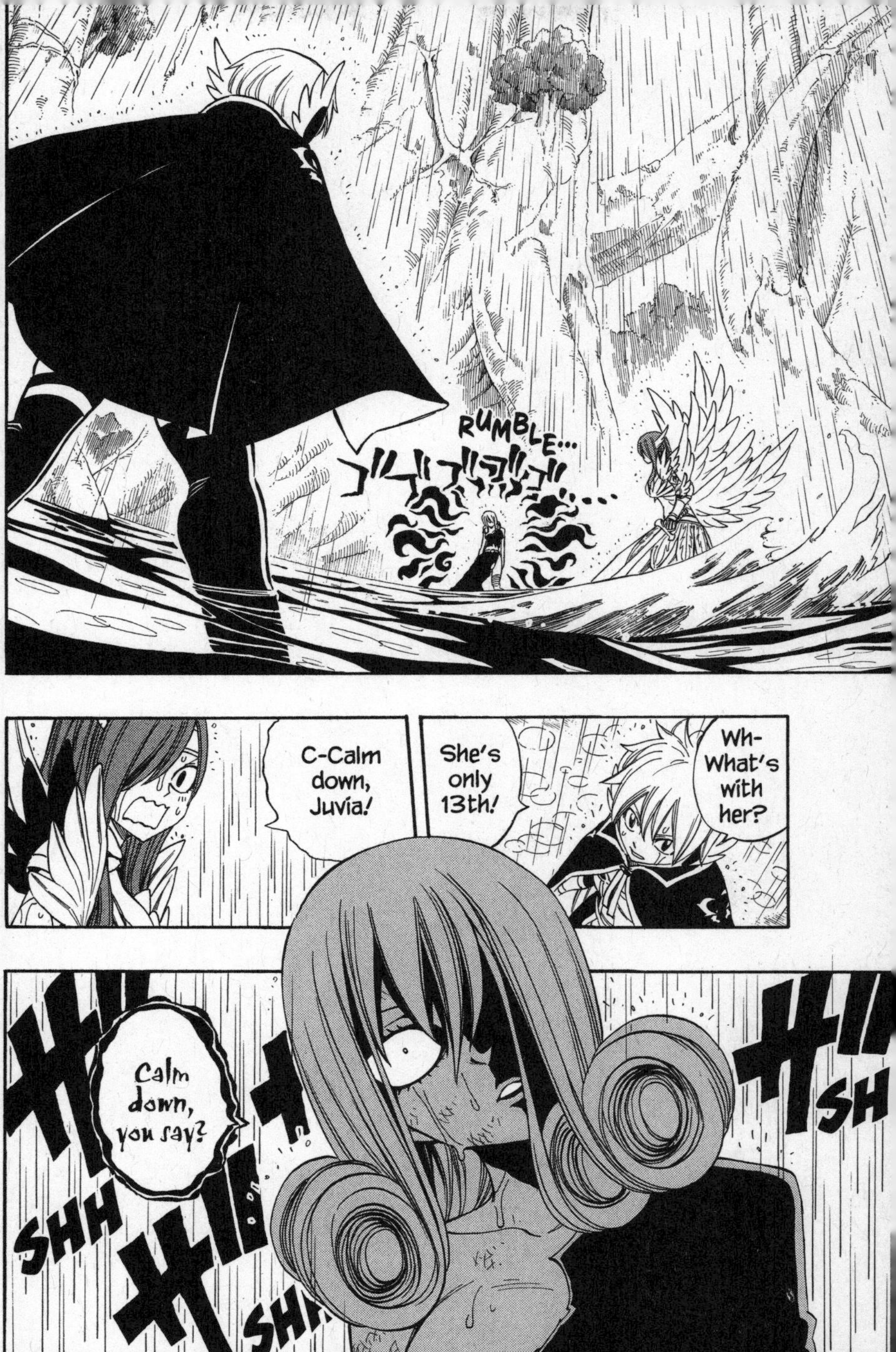
RUMBLE...
Wh- What's with her?
She's only 13th!
C-Calm down, Juvia!
SHH
Calm down, you say?
SHH
SHH

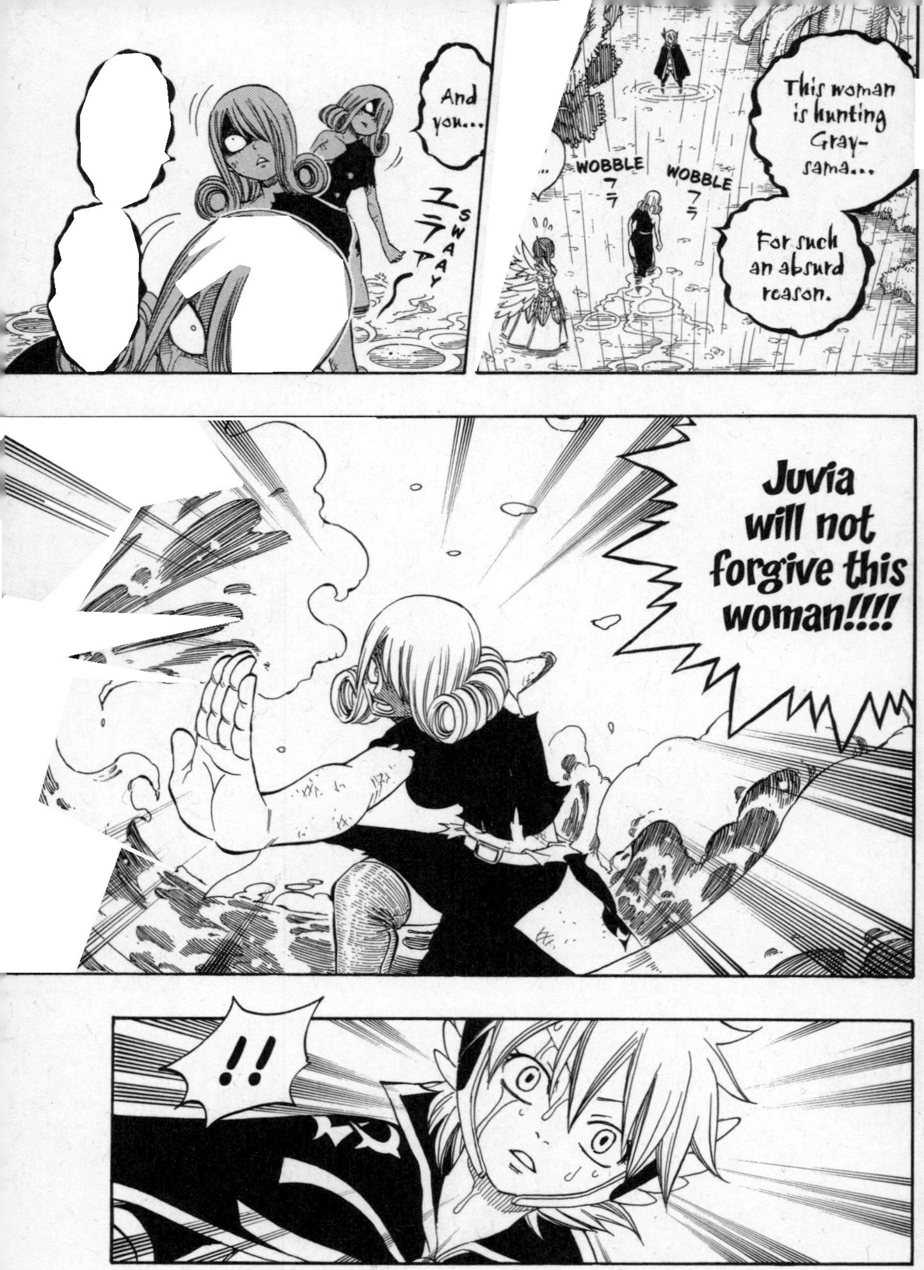
This woman is hunting Gray-sama...
For such an absurd reason.
WOBBLE フラ
WOBBLE フラ
...
And you...
SWAY ユラア
Juvia will not forgive this woman!!!!
!!

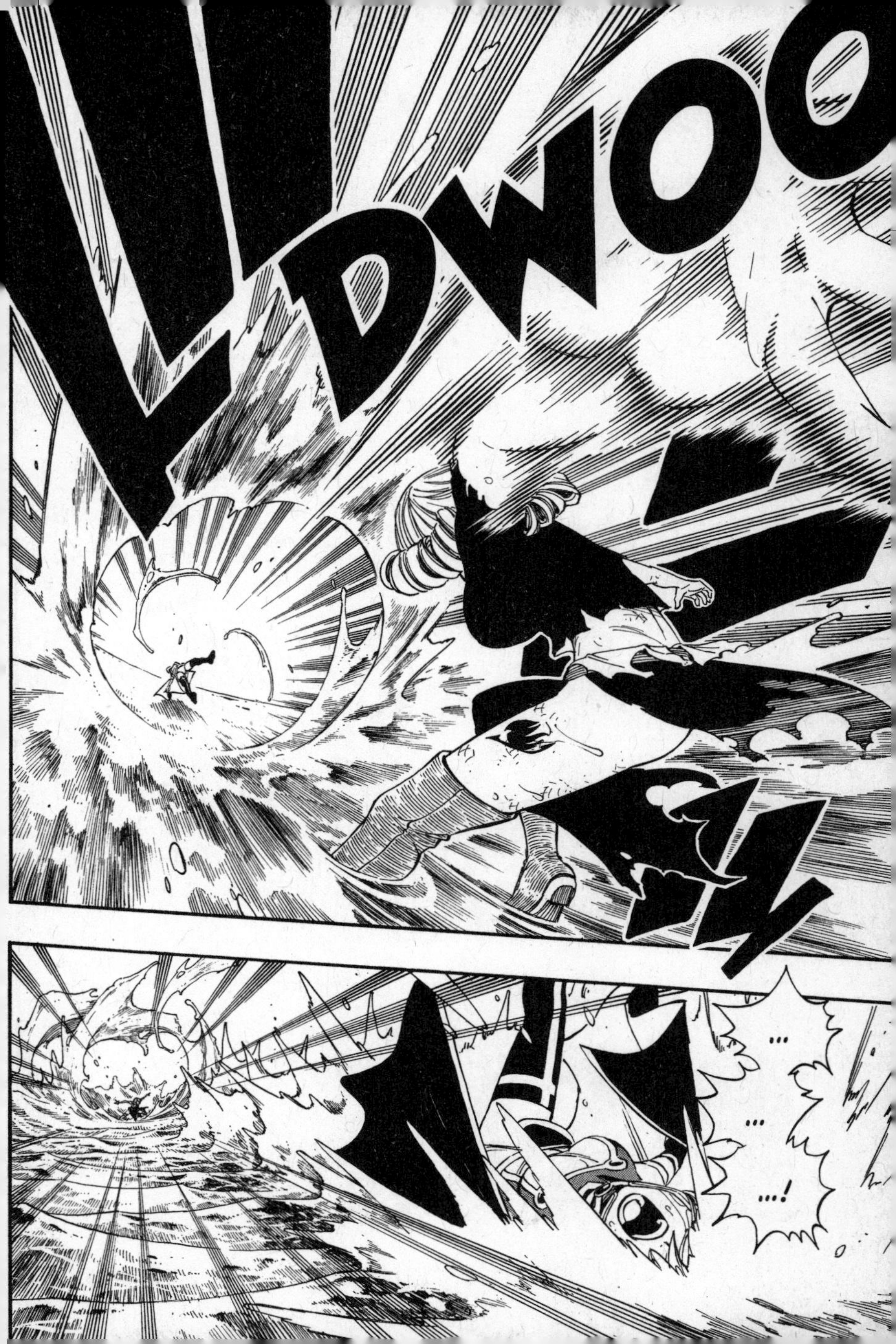
LDWOO
...
...
...!

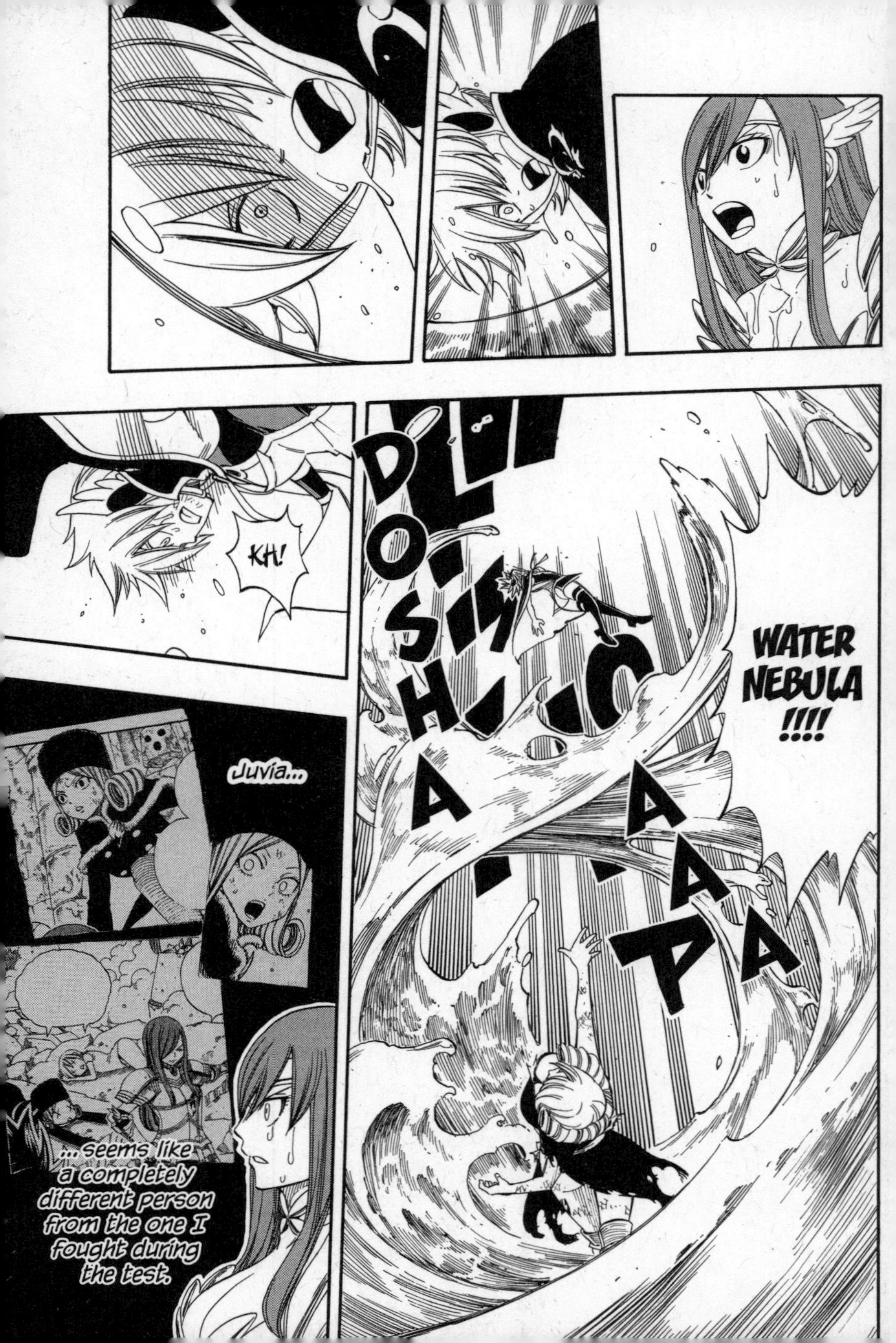
WATER NEBULA !!!!
DOSHAAAAA
KH!
Juvia...
... seems like a completely different person from the one I fought during the test.

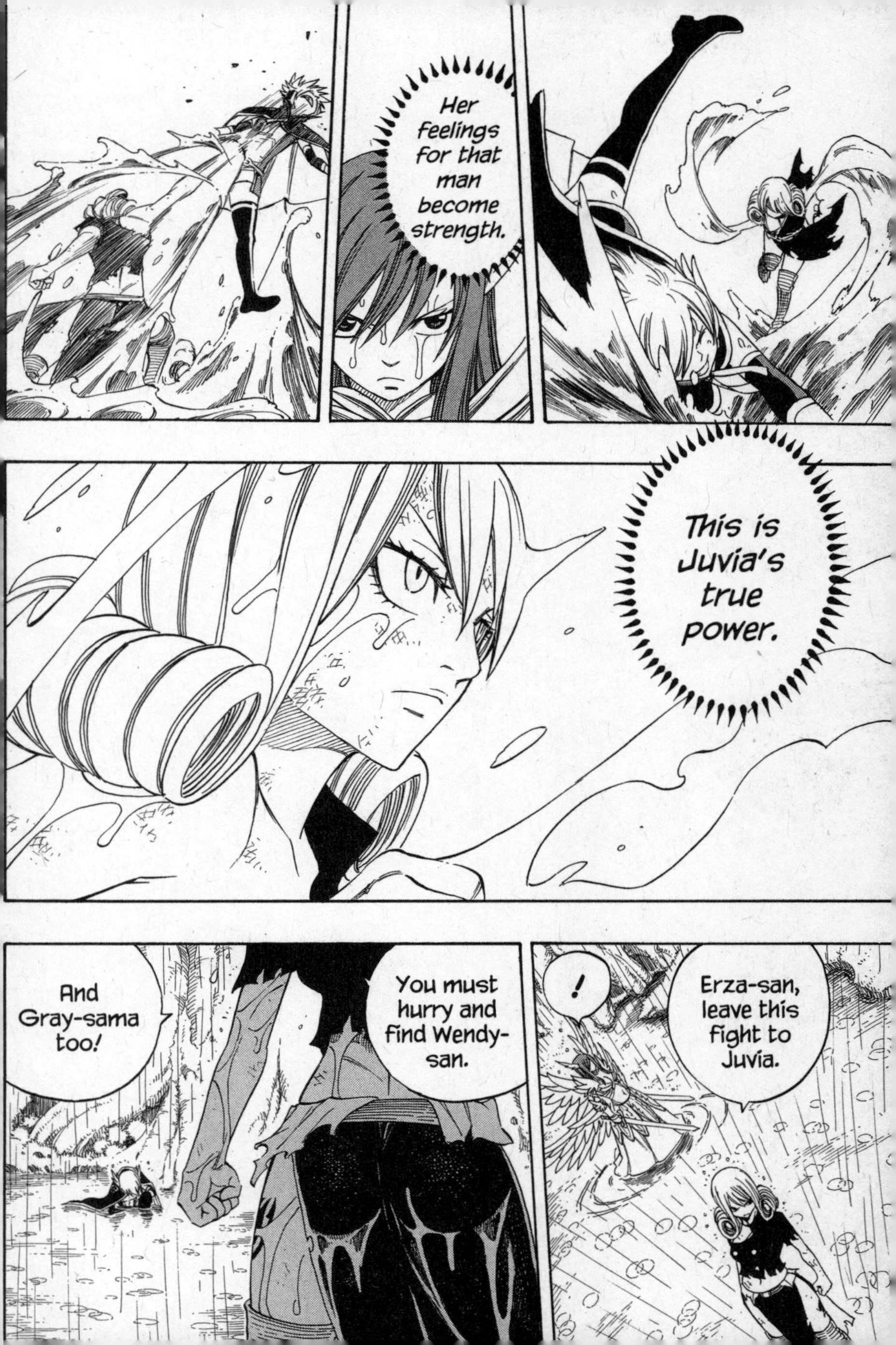
Her feelings for that man become strength.
This is Juvia's true power.
Erza-san, leave this fight to Juvia.
!
You must hurry and find Wendy-san.
And Gray-sama too!

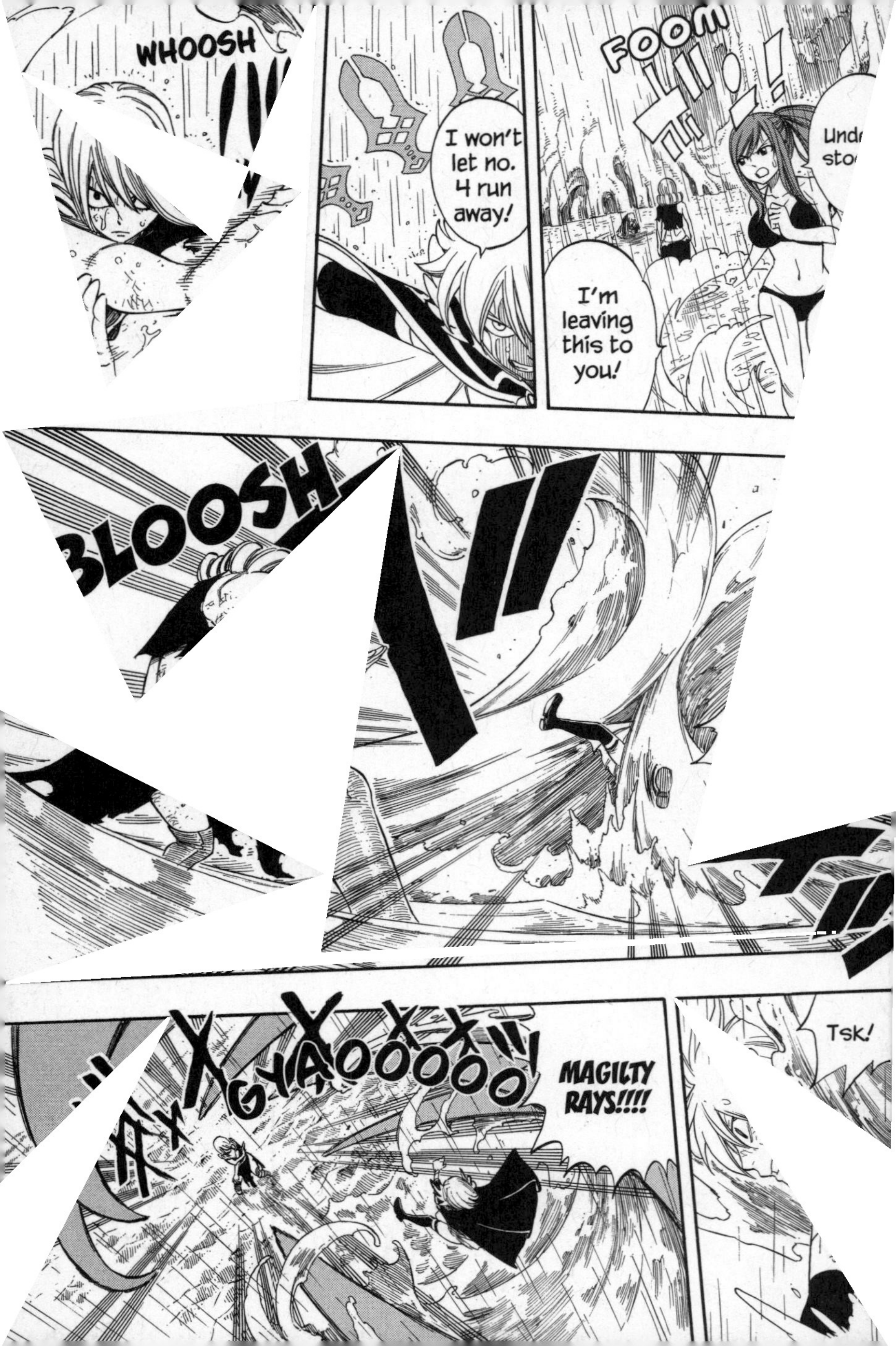
FOOM
I'm leaving this to you!
I won't let no. 4 run away!
WHOOSH
BLOOSH
Tsk!
MAGILTY RAYS!!!!
GYAAOOOOO!!

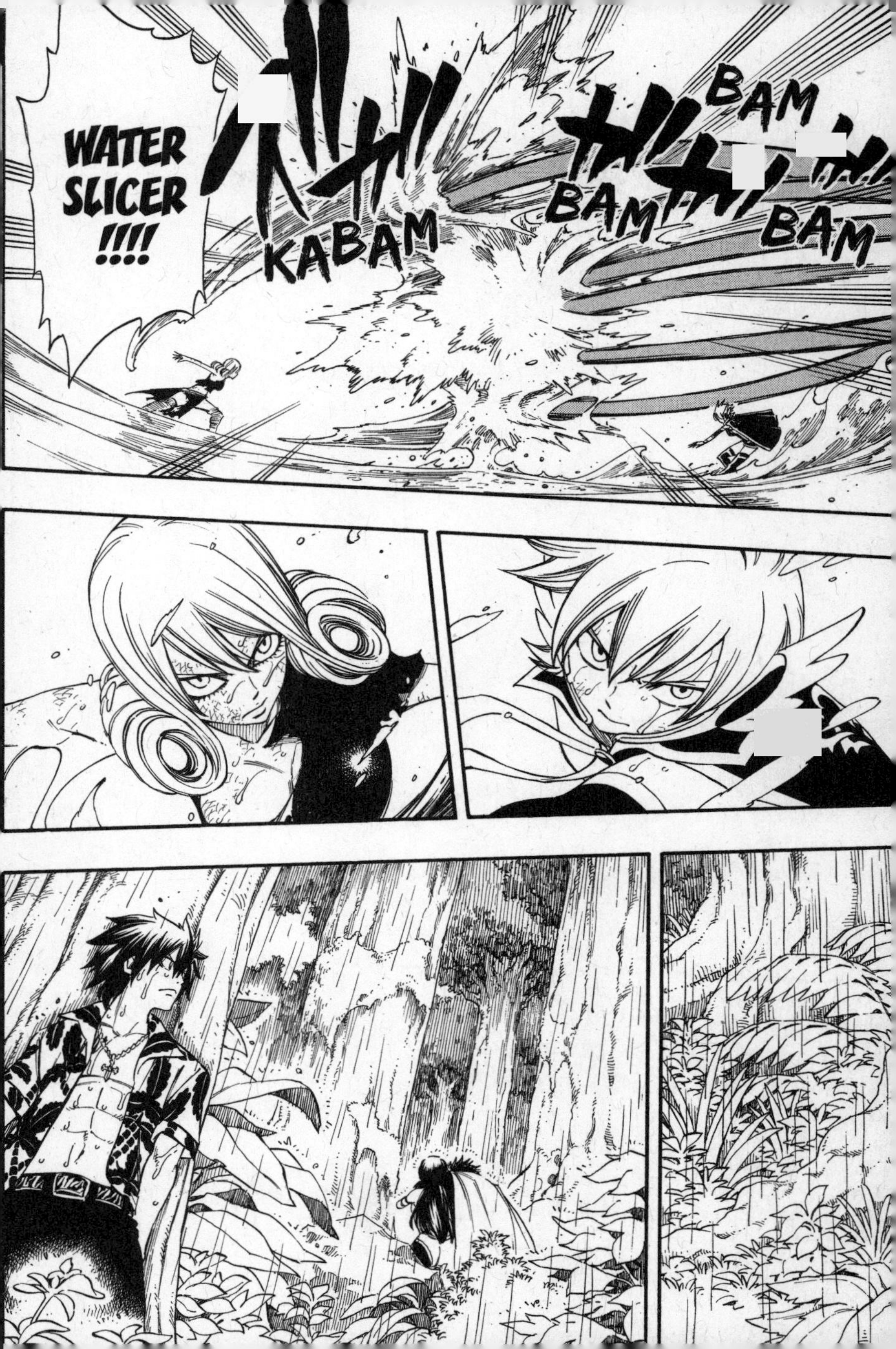
BAM
BAM
BAM
KABAM
WATER SLICER !!!!

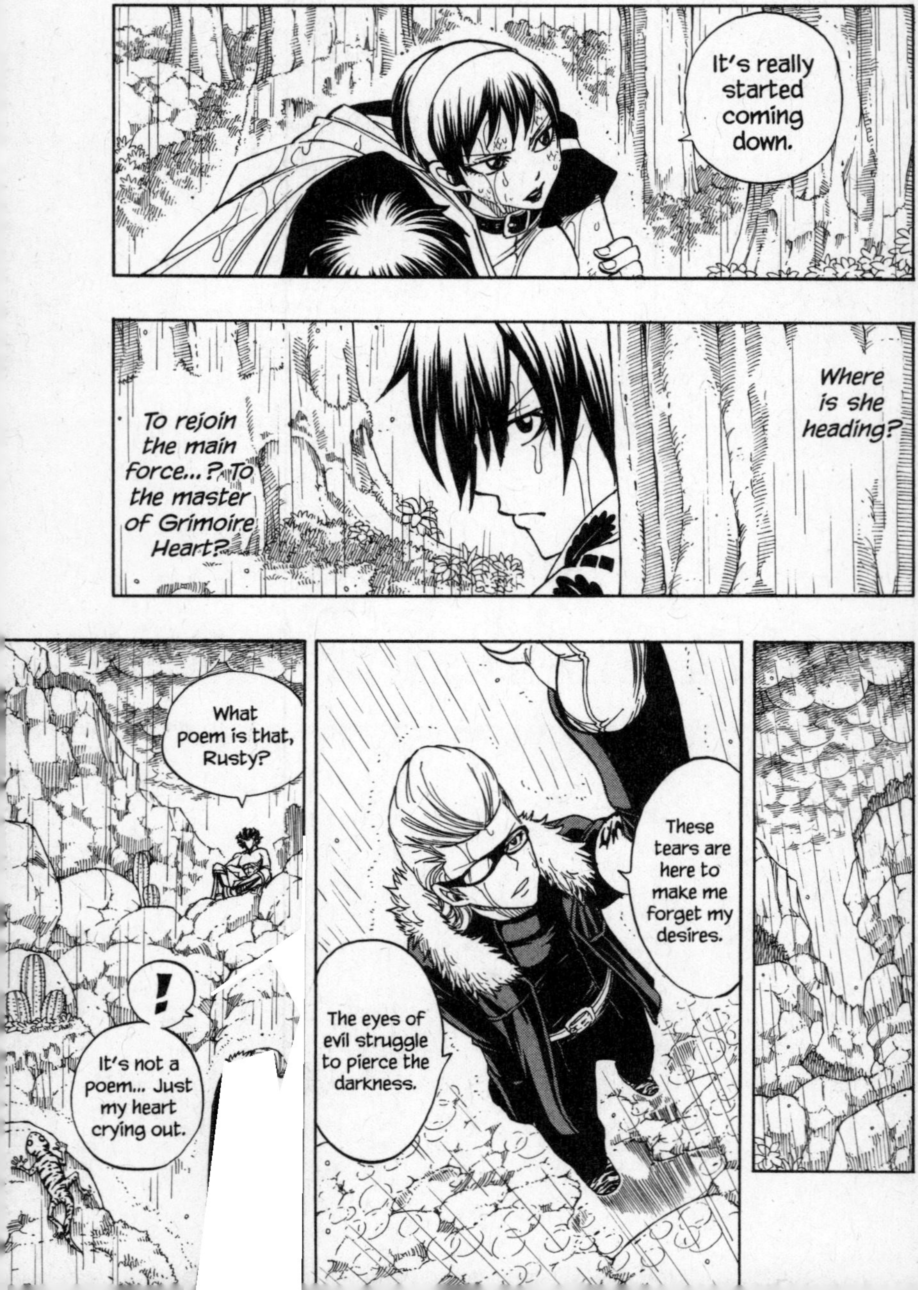
It's really started coming down.
Where is she heading?
To rejoin the main force...? To the master of Grimoire Heart?
These tears are here to make me forget my desires.
The eyes of evil struggle to pierce the darkness.
What poem is that, Rusty?
!
It's not a poem... Just my heart crying out.

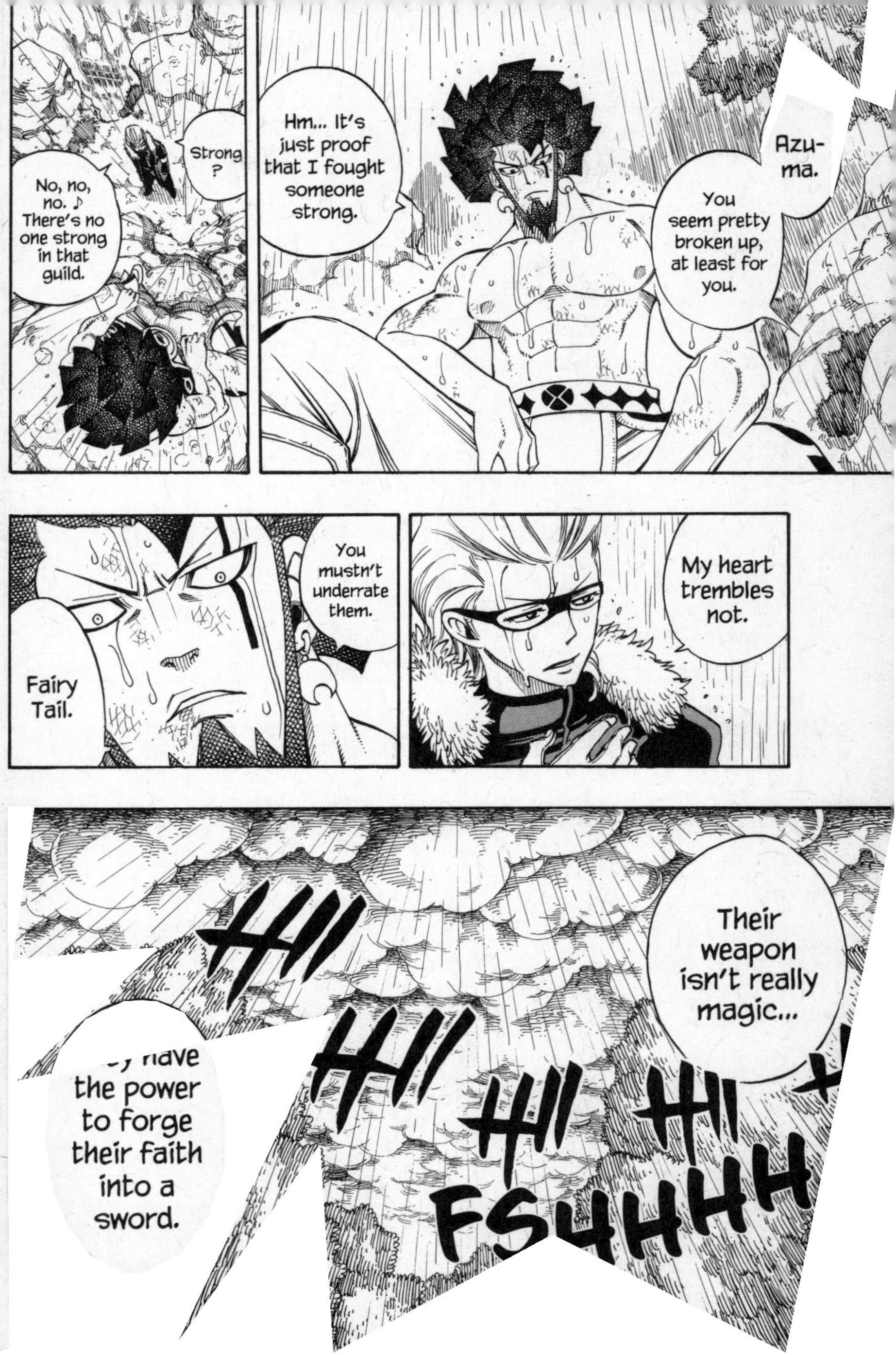
Azu-ma.
You seem pretty broken up, at least for you.
Hm... It's just proof that I fought someone strong.
Strong?
No, no, no. ♪ There's no one strong in that guild.
My heart trembles not.
You mustn't underrate them.
Fairy Tail.
Their weapon isn't really magic...
have the power to forge their faith into a sword.
FSHHHH

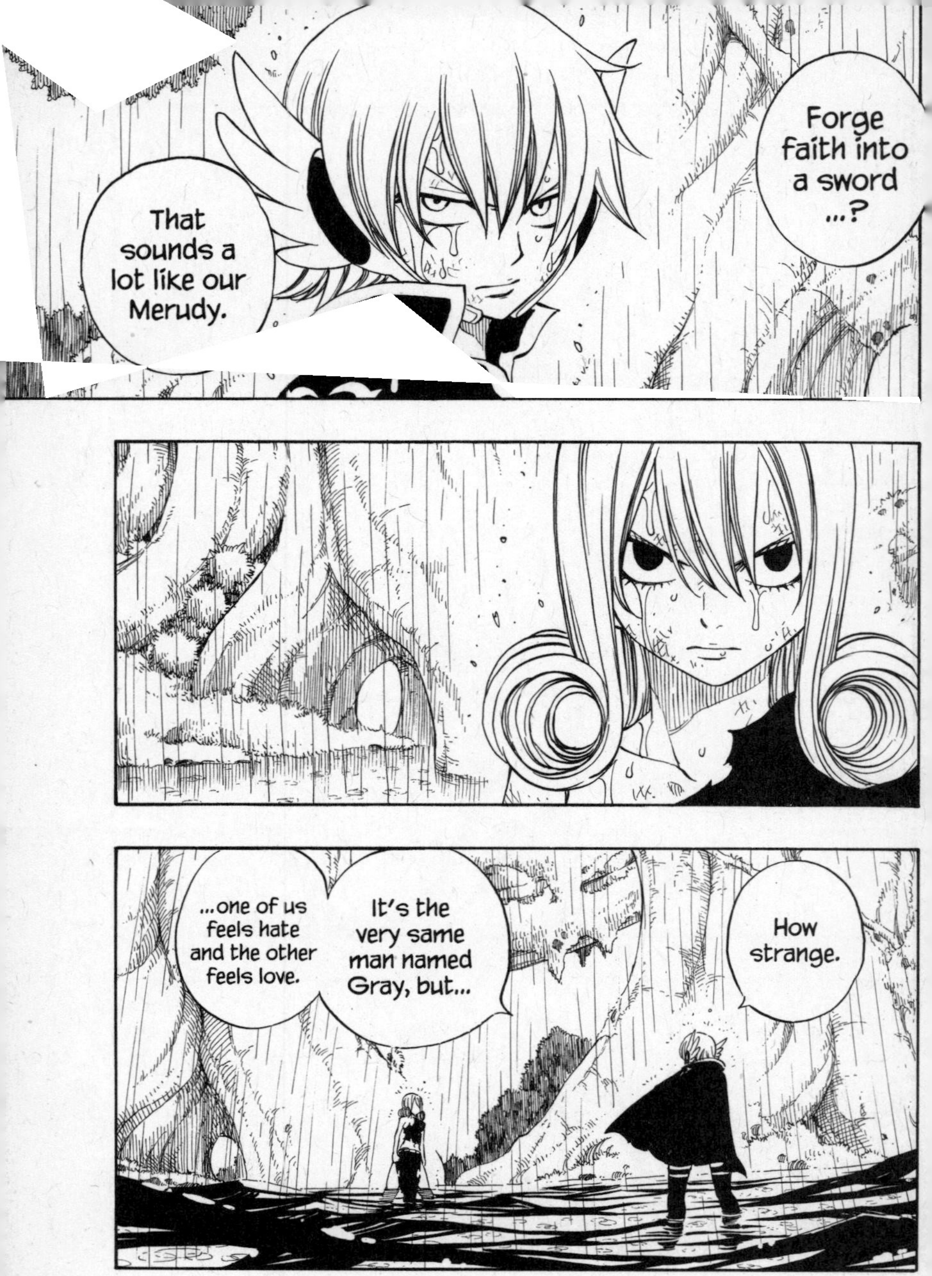
Forge faith into a sword ...?
That sounds a lot like our Merudy.
How strange.
It's the very same man named Gray, but...
...one of us feels hate and the other feels love.

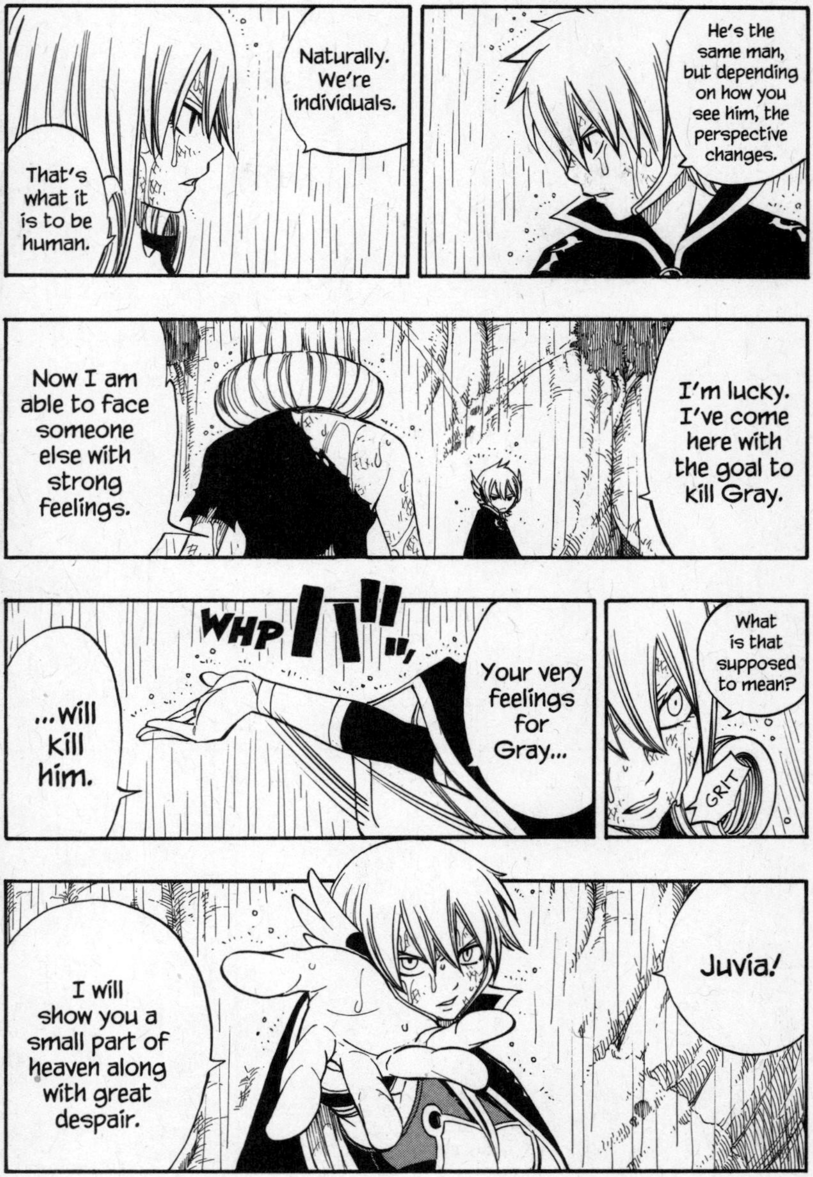
He's the same man, but depending on how you see him, the perspective changes.
Naturally. We're individuals.
That's what it is to be human.
I'm lucky. I've come here with the goal to kill Gray.
Now I am able to face someone else with strong feelings.
What is that supposed to mean?
GRIT
Your very feelings for Gray...
WHP
...will kill him.
Juvia!
I will show you a small part of heaven along with great despair.

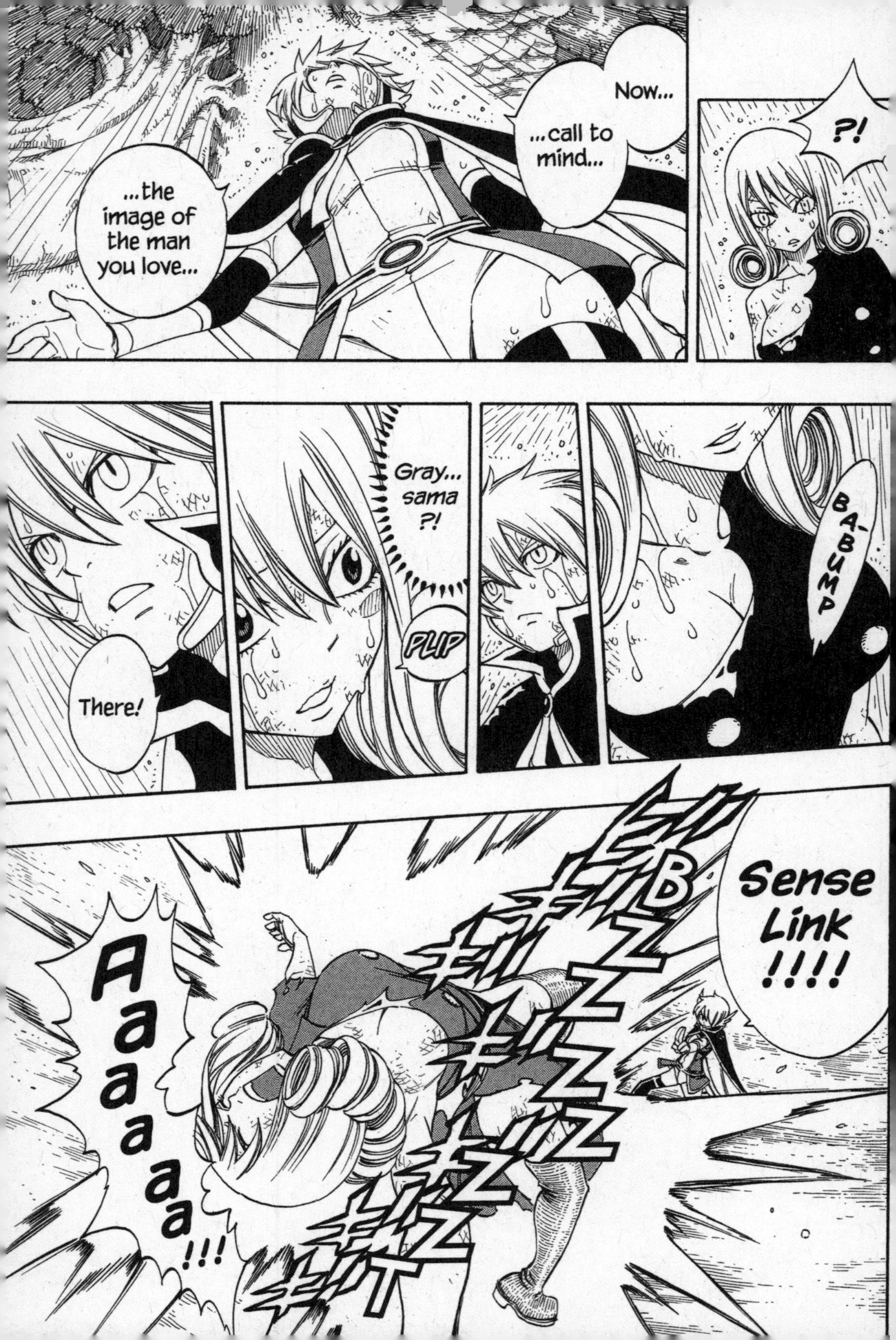
?!
Now...
...call to mind...
...the image of the man you love...
BA-BUMP
Gray... sama ?!
PLIP
There!
Sense Link !!!!
BZZZZZT
Aaaaaaa!!!

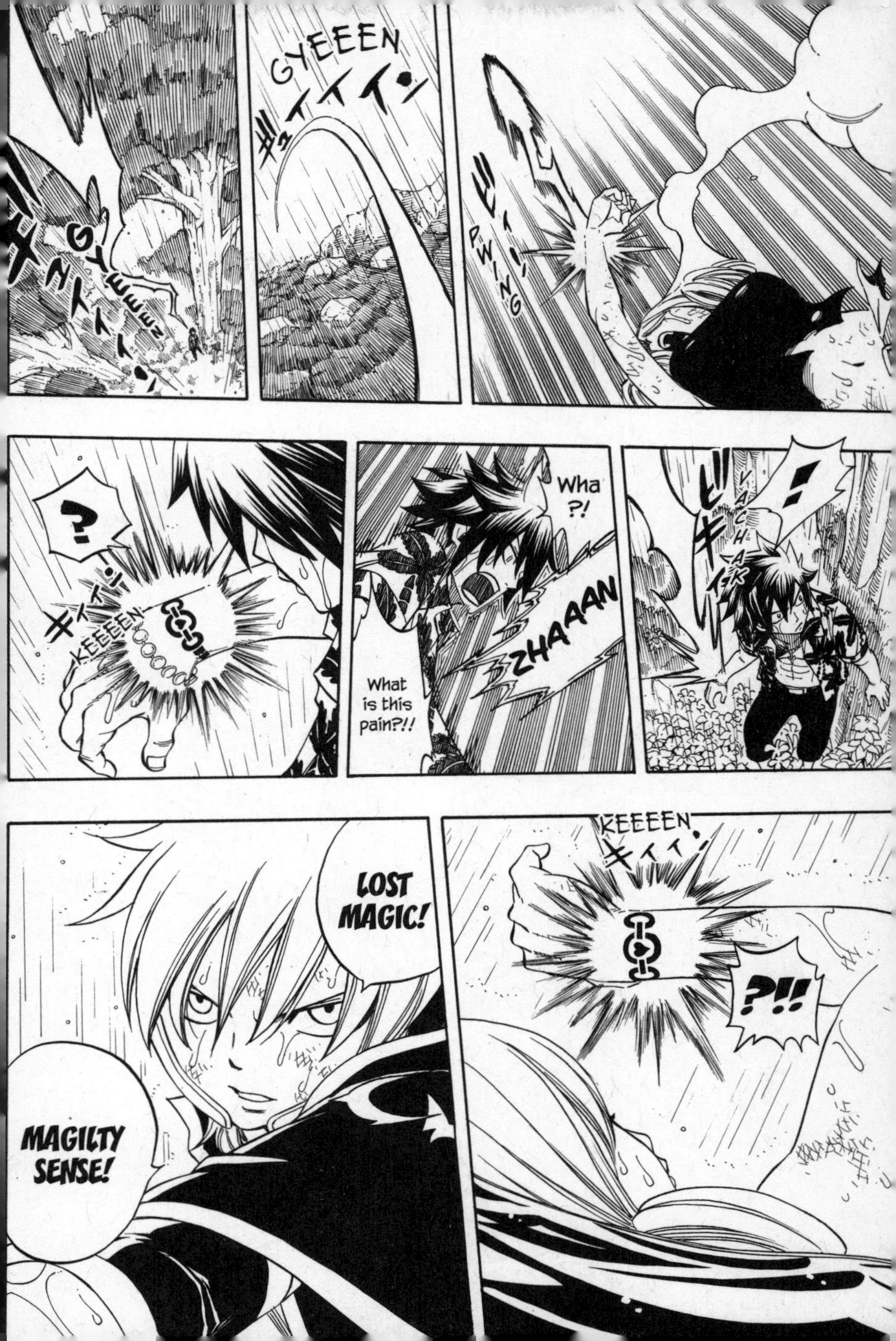
PWING
GYEEEN
GYEEEEN
VACHAK
!
Wha ?!
ZHAAAN
What is this pain?!!
?
KEEEEEN
KEEEEN
?!!
LOST MAGIC!
MAGILTY SENSE!

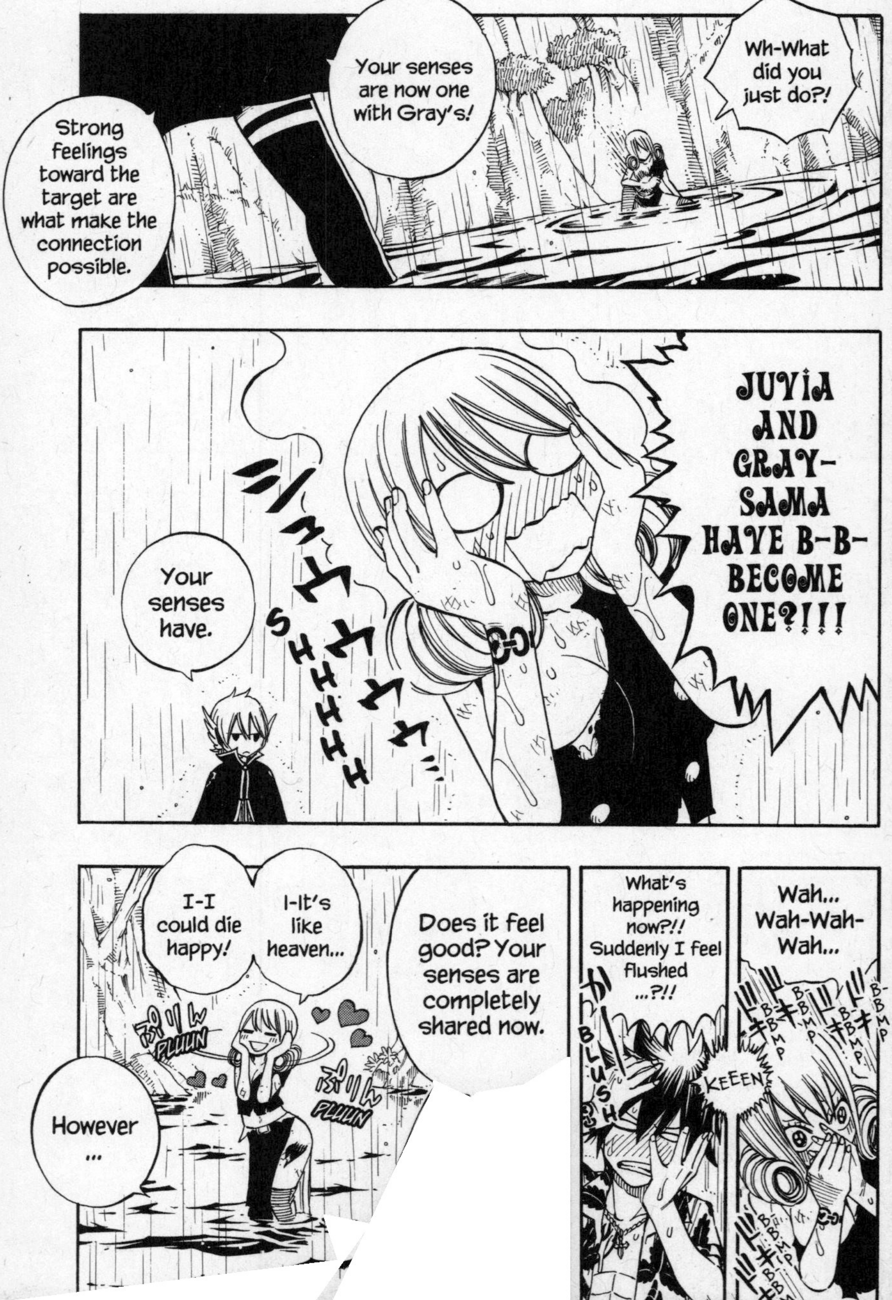
Wh-What did you just do?!
Your senses are now one with Gray's!
Strong feelings toward the target are what make the connection possible.
JUVIA AND GRAY-SAMA HAVE B-B-BECOME ONE?!!!
SHHHHHH
Your senses have.
Wah... Wah-Wah-Wah...
B-B-BMP
B-B-BMP
KEEEN
What's happening now?!! Suddenly I feel flushed ...?!!
BLUSH
Does it feel good? Your senses are completely shared now.
I-It's like heaven...
I-I could die happy!
PLUUN
PLUUN
However ...

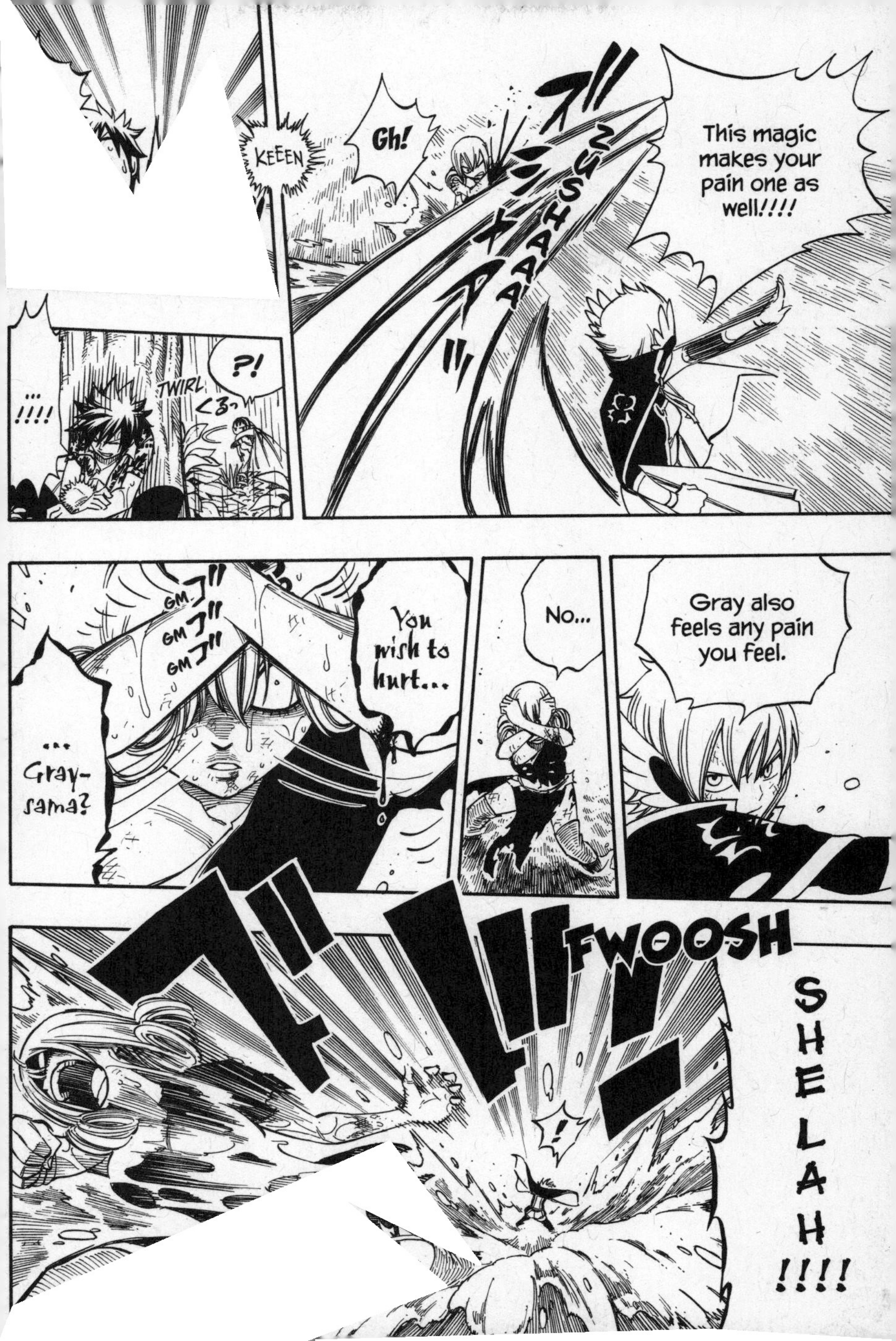

This magic makes your pain one as well!!!!
ZUSHAAAA
Gh!
KEEEN
?!
TWIRL くるっ
...!!!!
Gray also feels any pain you feel.
No...
You wish to hurt...
GM GM GM
...Gray-sama?
FWOOSH
!
SHELAH!!!!

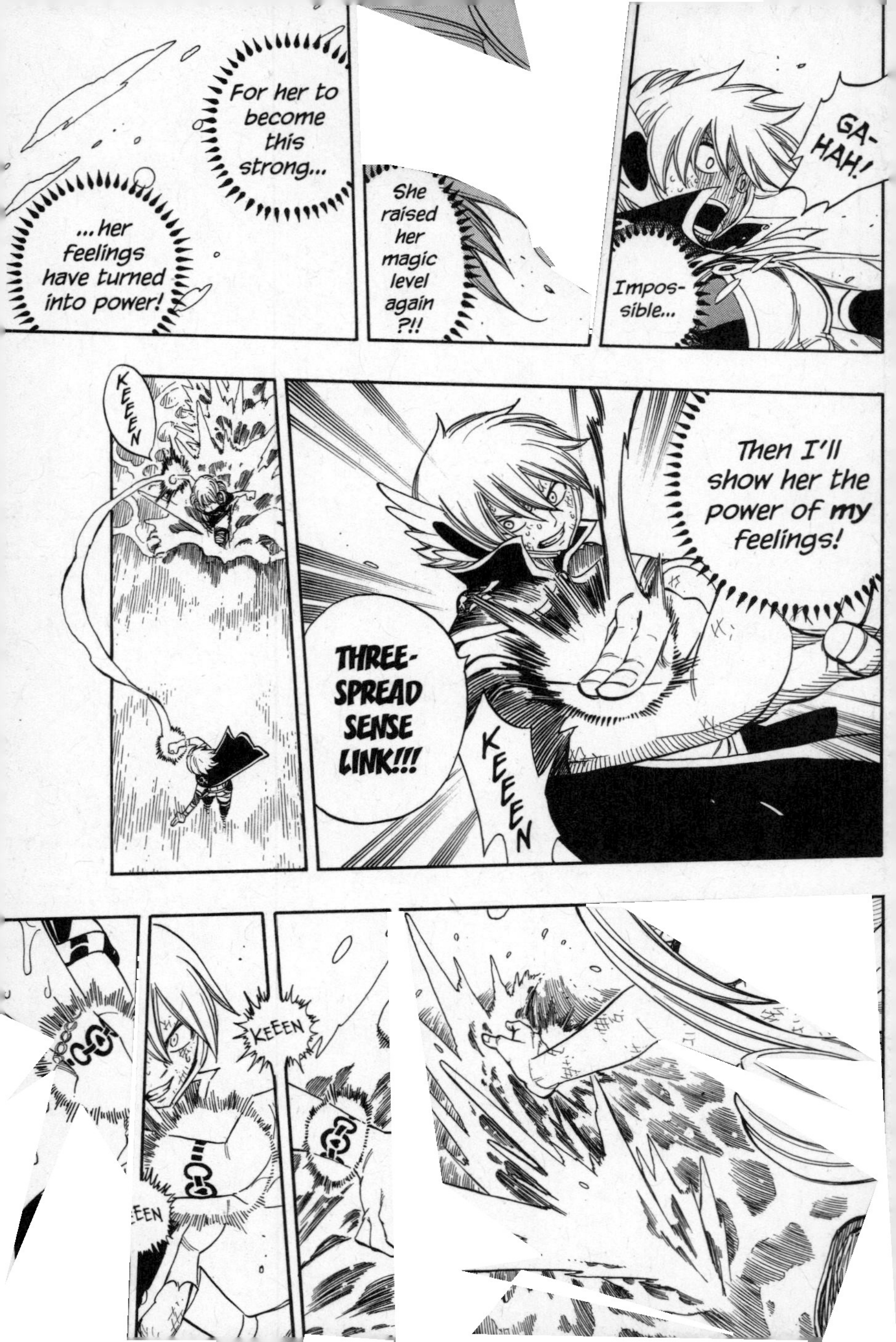
GA-HAH!
Impos-sible...
She raised her magic level again?!!
For her to become this strong...
...her feelings have turned into power!
Then I'll show her the power of **my** feelings!
THREE-SPREAD SENSE LINK!!!
KEEEN
KEEEN
KEEEN
EEEN

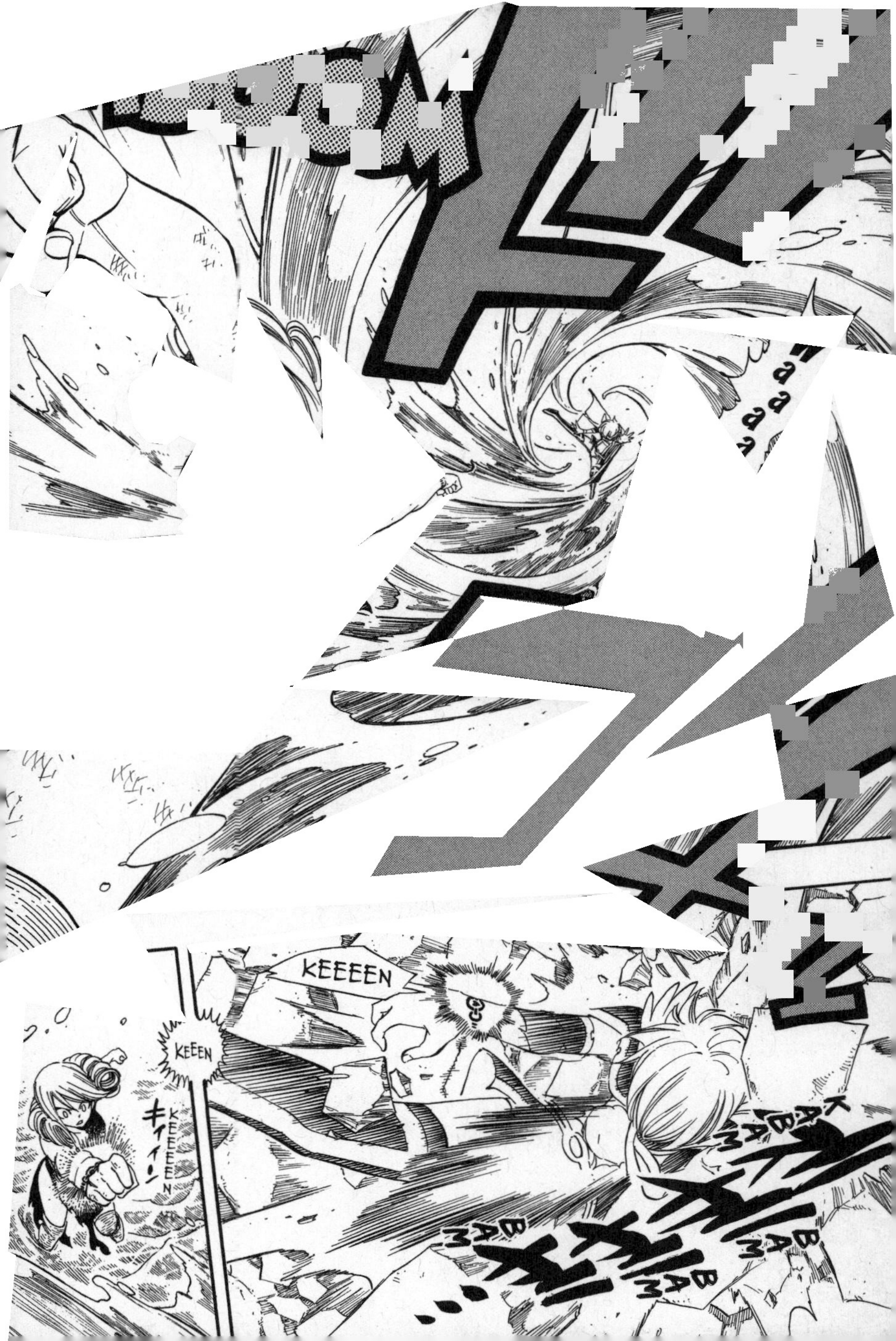
aaaa
KABAAM
BABAM
BABAM
KEEEEN
KEEEN
キイーン
KEEEEN

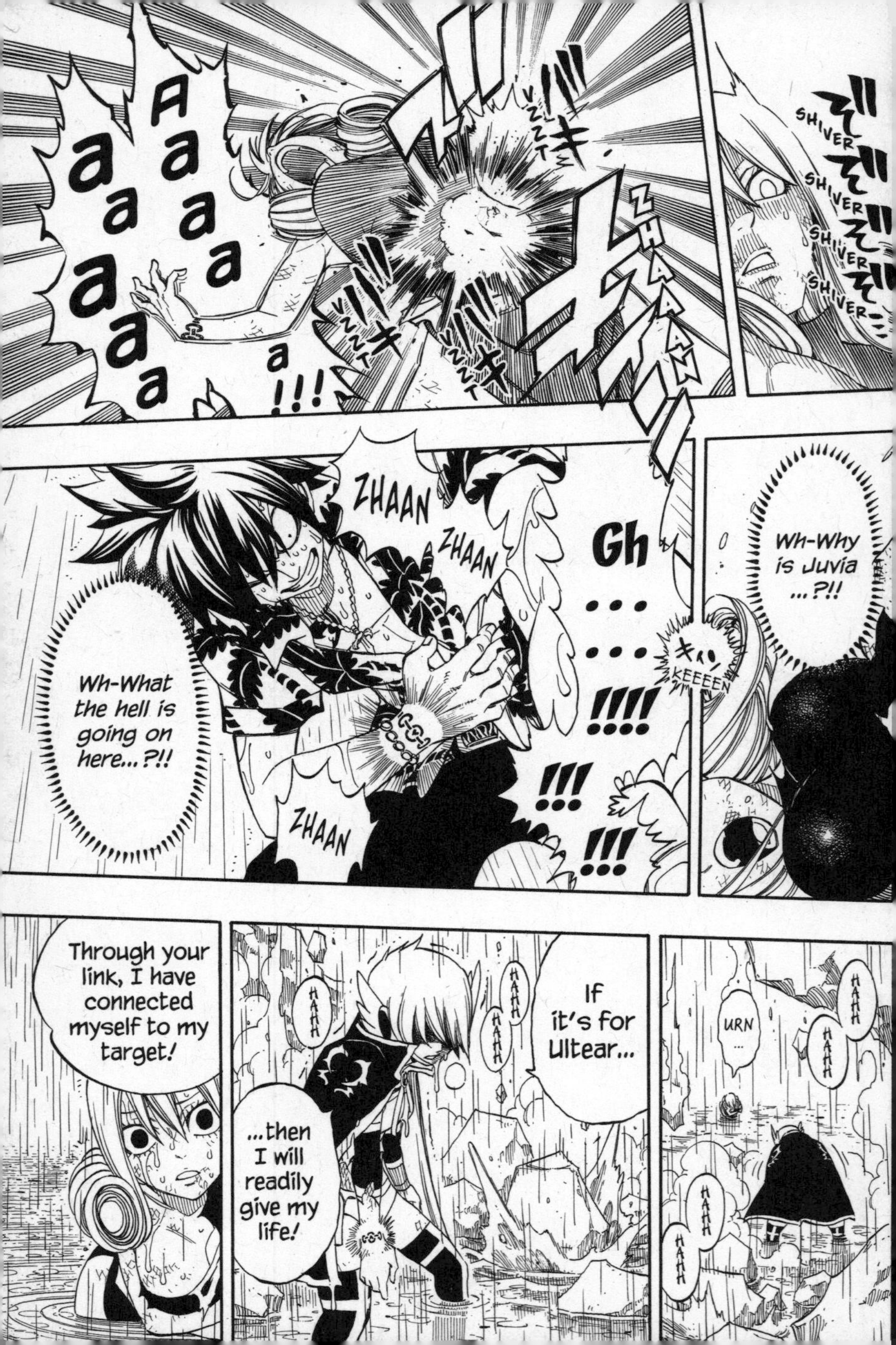
SHIVER
SHIVER
SHIVER
SHIVER
ZHAAAAN
VZZT
Aaaaaaaaaaaa!!!
VZZT
VZZT
Wh-Why is Juvia ...?!!
KEEEEN
Gh......!!!!
!!!
!!!
ZHAAN
ZHAAN
ZHAAN
Wh-What the hell is going on here...?!!
HAHH
URN ...
HAHH
HAHH
HAHH
If it's for Ultear...
...then I will readily give my life!
HAHH
HAHH
HAHH
Through your link, I have connected myself to my target!

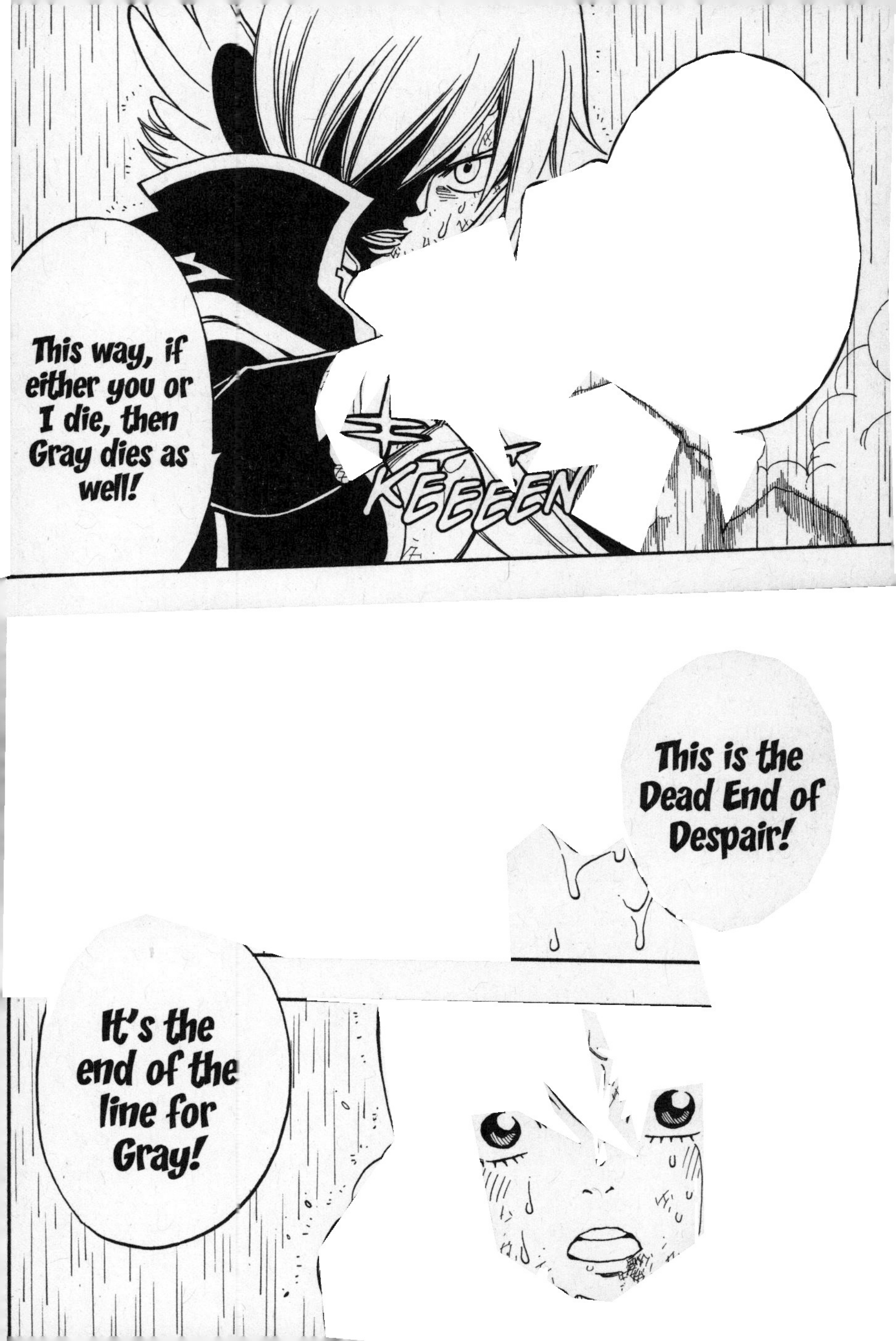
This way, if either you or I die, then Gray dies as well!
KEEEEEN
This is the Dead End of Despair!
It's the end of the line for Gray!

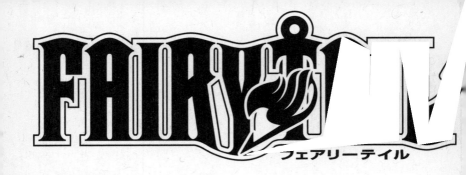

Chapter 230: Tears of Love and Vitality

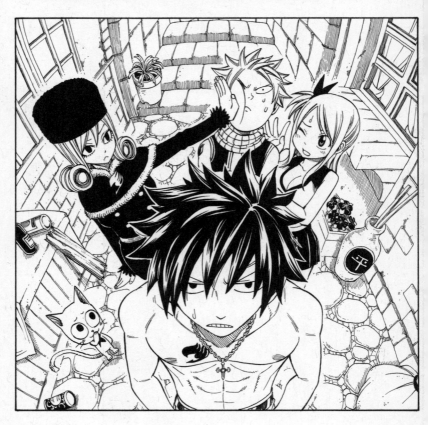

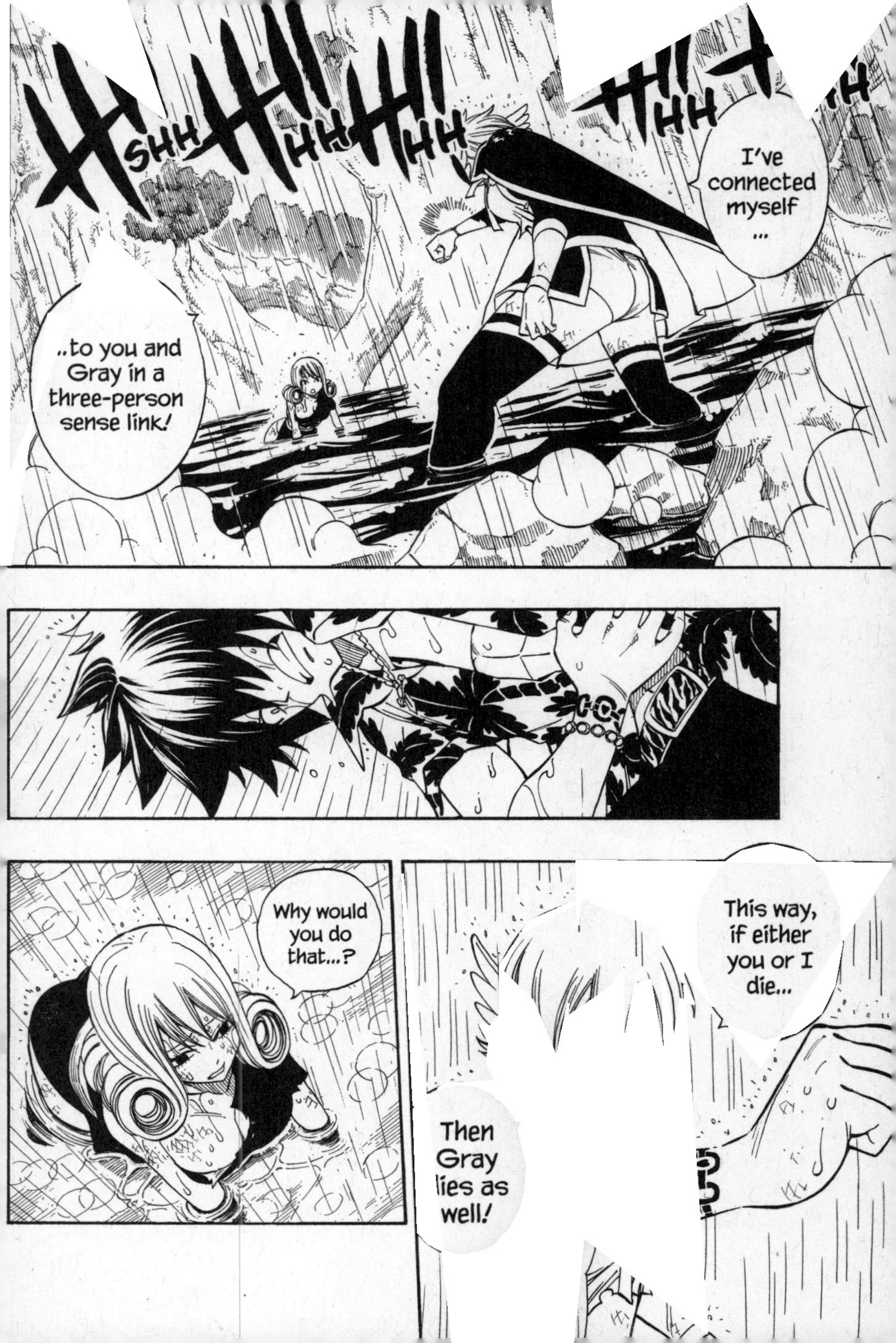
SHH
HH
HH
HH
I've connected myself ...
..to you and Gray in a three-person sense link!
This way, if either you or I die...
Then Gray dies as well!
Why would you do that...?

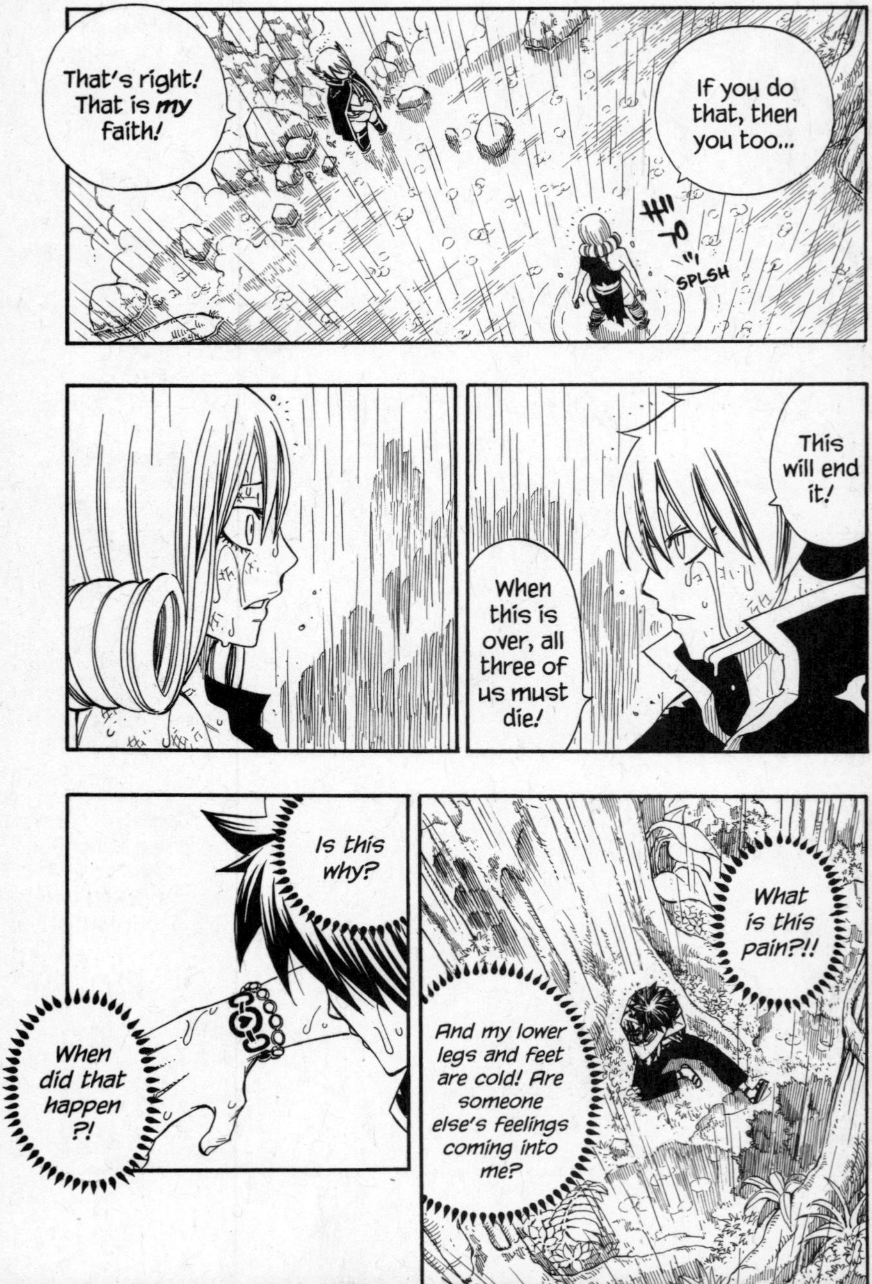
If you do that, then you too...
That's right! That is *my* faith!
SPLSH
This will end it!
When this is over, all three of us must die!
What is this pain?!!
And my lower legs and feet are cold! Are someone else's feelings coming into me?
Is this why?
When did that happen?!

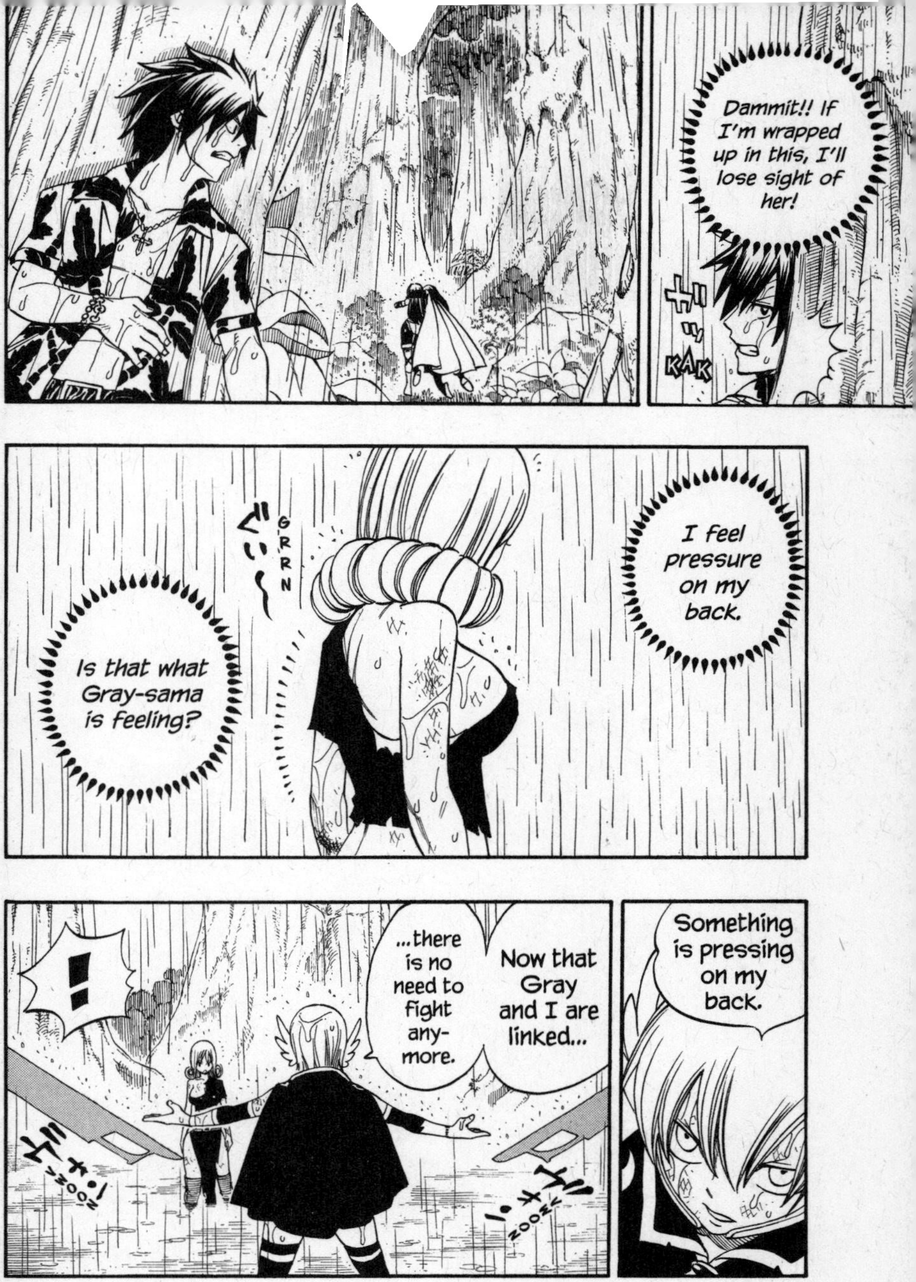
Dammit!! If I'm wrapped up in this, I'll lose sight of her!
KAK
I feel pressure on my back.
GRRN
Is that what Gray-sama is feeling?
Something is pressing on my back.
Now that Gray and I are linked...
...there is no need to fight anymore.
!
ZOOOM
ZOOOM

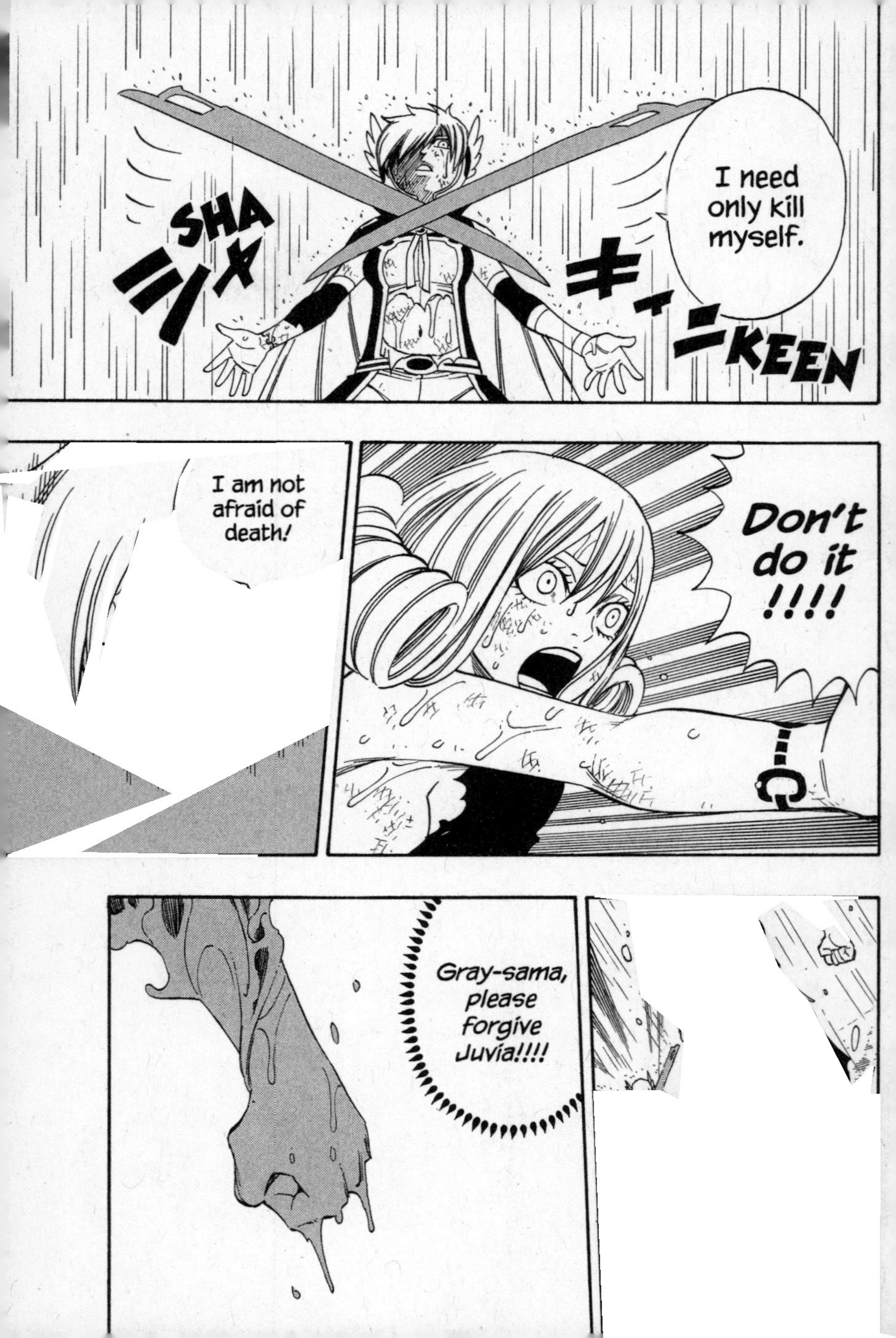
I need only kill myself.
KEEN
SHA
Don't do it!!!!
I am not afraid of death!
Gray-sama, please forgive Juvia!!!!

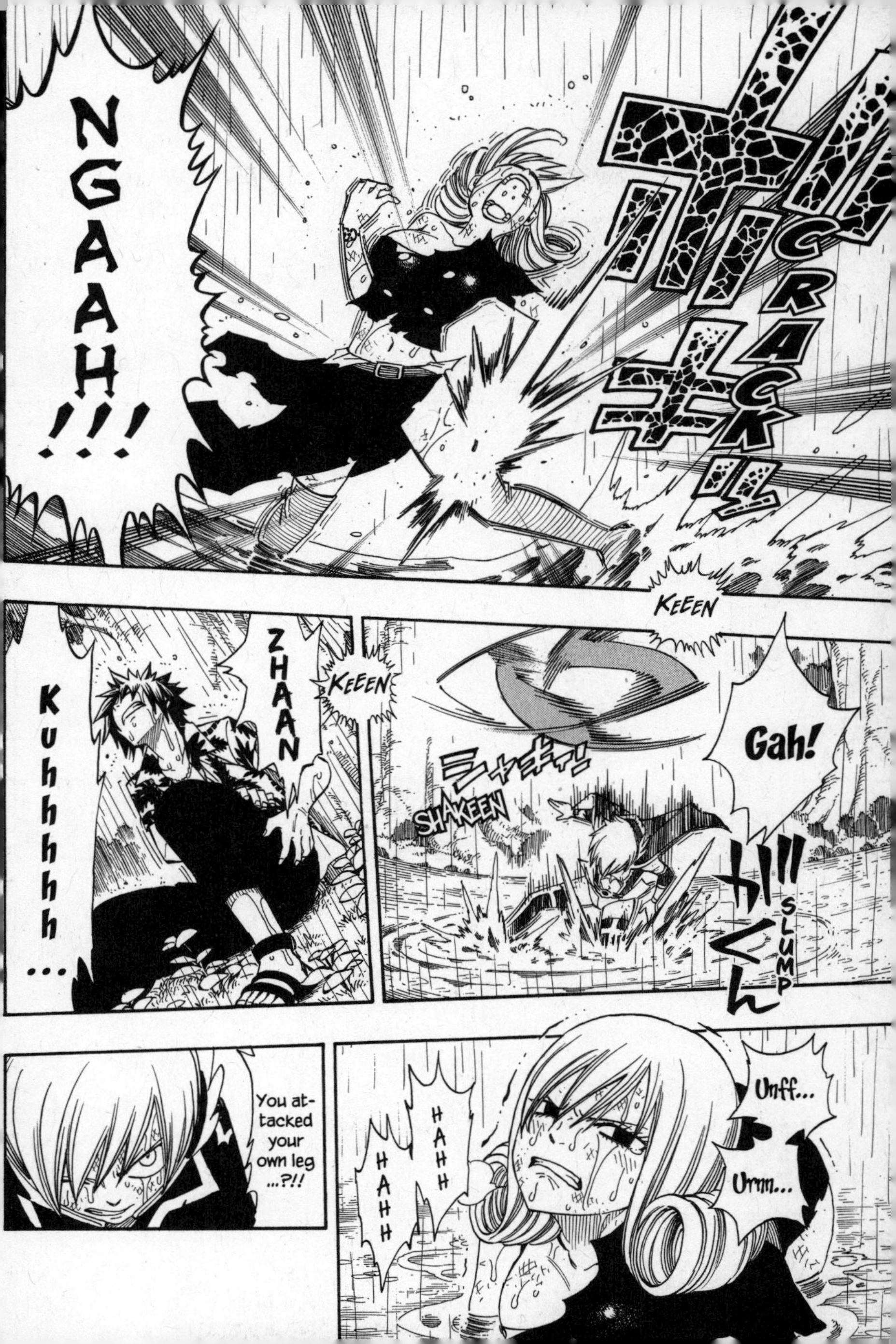
CRACK!!
NGAAH!!!
KEEEN
Gah!
SHAKEEN
SLUMP
ZHAAN
KEEEN
Kuhhhhhh...
Unff...
Urnn...
HAHH HAHH HAHH
You at-tacked your own leg ...?!!

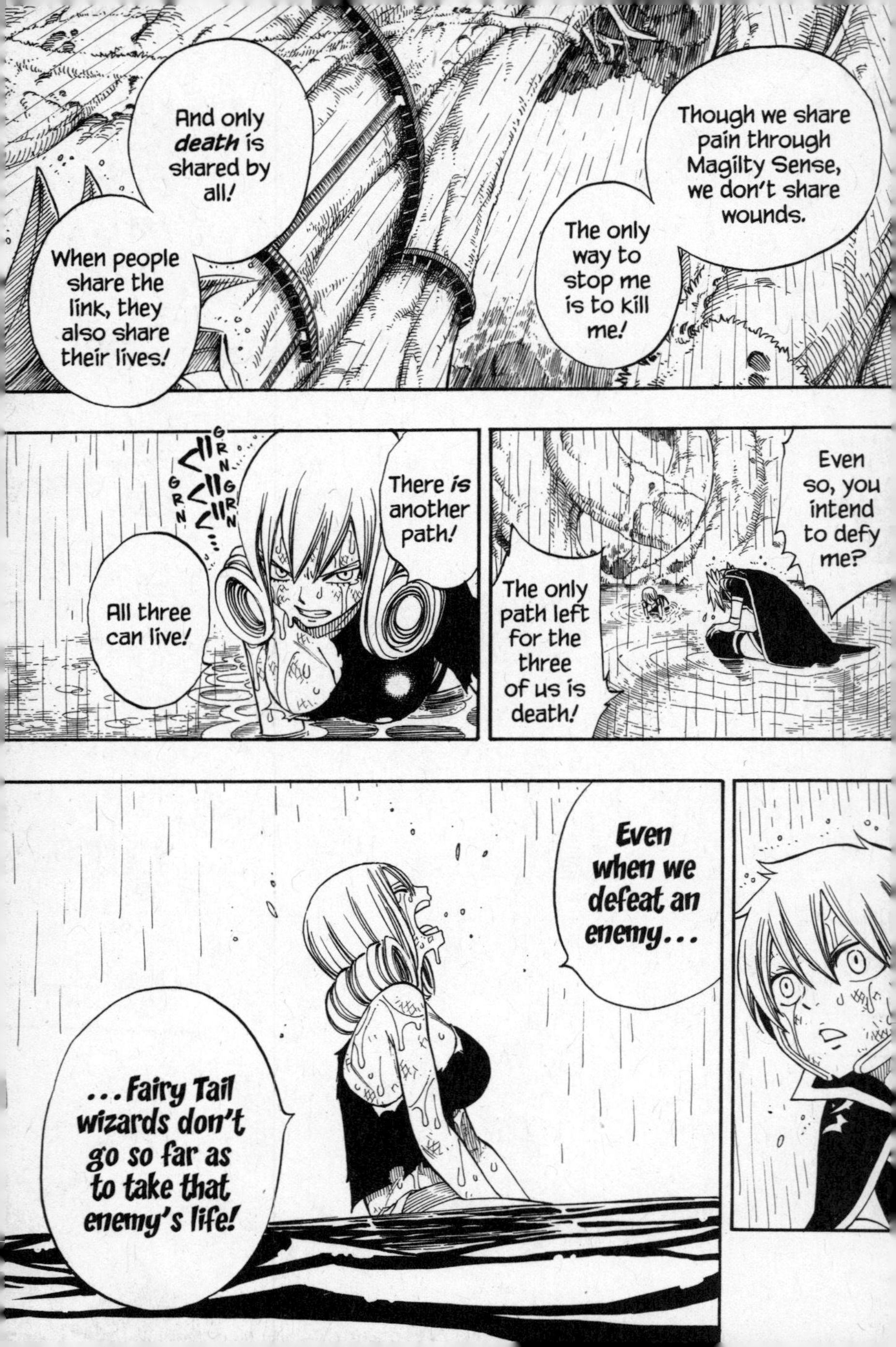

Though we share pain through Magilty Sense, we don't share wounds.
The only way to stop me is to kill me!
When people share the link, they also share their lives!
And only *death* is shared by all!
Even so, you intend to defy me?
The only path left for the three of us is death!
GRN GRN GRN
There *is* another path!
All three can live!
Even when we defeat an enemy...
...Fairy Tail wizards don't go so far as to take that enemy's life!

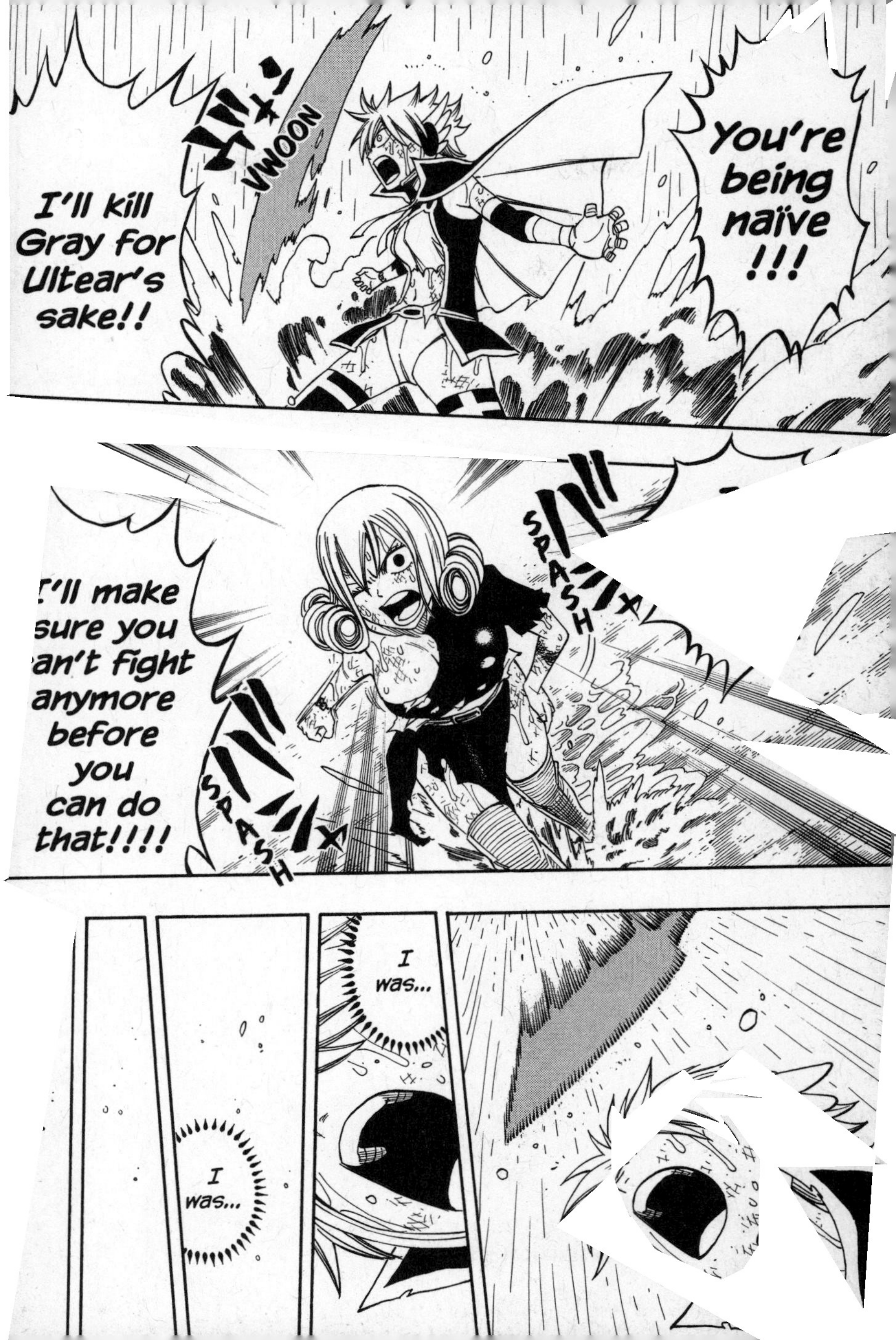
You're being naïve!!!
VWOON
I'll kill Gray for Ultear's sake!!
SPASH
SPASH
I'll make sure you can't fight anymore before you can do that!!!!
I was...
I was...

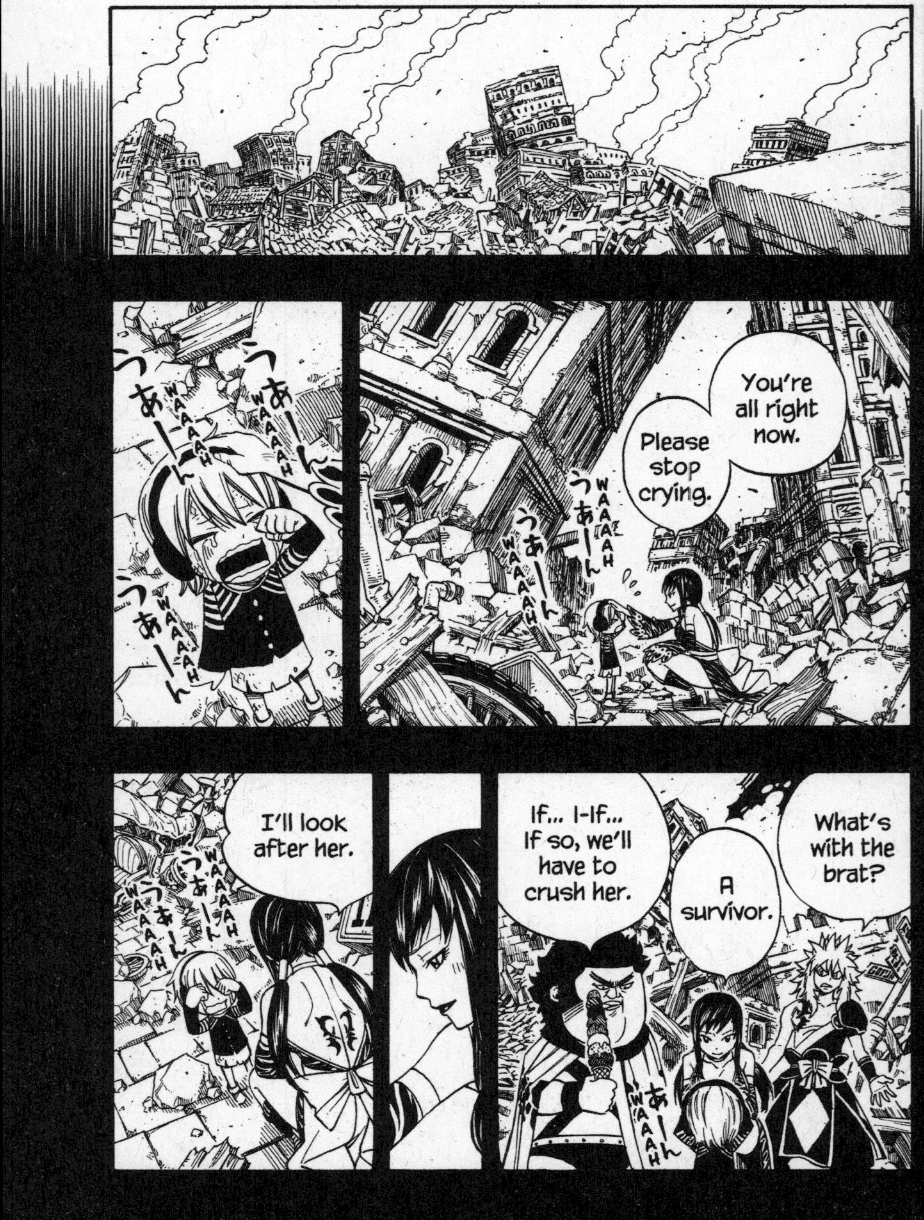
You're all right now.
Please stop crying.
うあーん WAAAAH
うあーん WAAAAH
うあーん WAAAAH
うあーん WAAAAH
うあーん WAAAAH
What's with the brat?
A survivor.
If... I-If... If so, we'll have to crush her.
あーん WAAAH
I'll look after her.
うあーん WAAAAH
うあーん WAAAAH

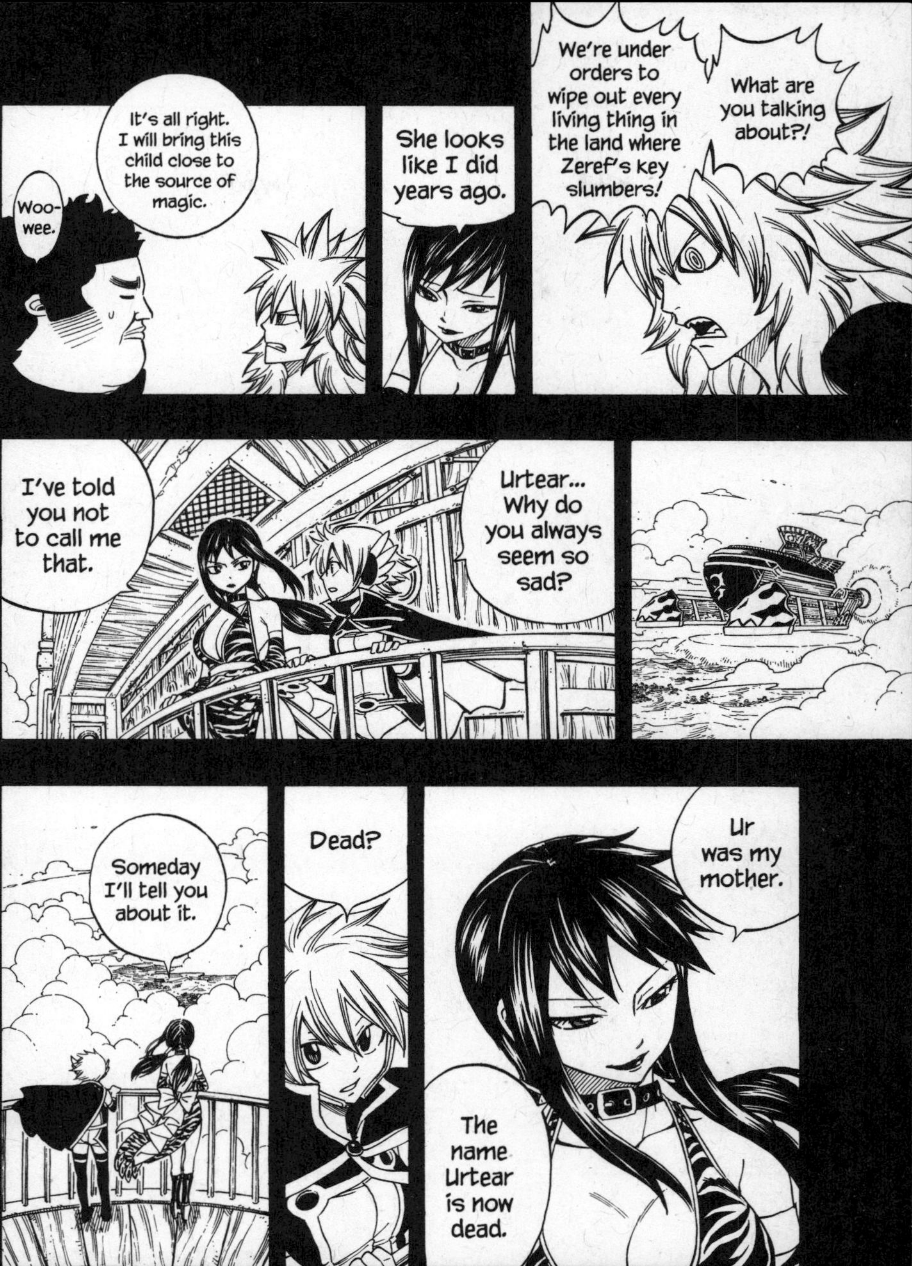
What are you talking about?!
We're under orders to wipe out every living thing in the land where Zeref's key slumbers!
She looks like I did years ago.
It's all right. I will bring this child close to the source of magic.
Woo-wee.
Urtear... Why do you always seem so sad?
I've told you not to call me that.
Ur was my mother.
The name Urtear is now dead.
Dead?
Someday I'll tell you about it.

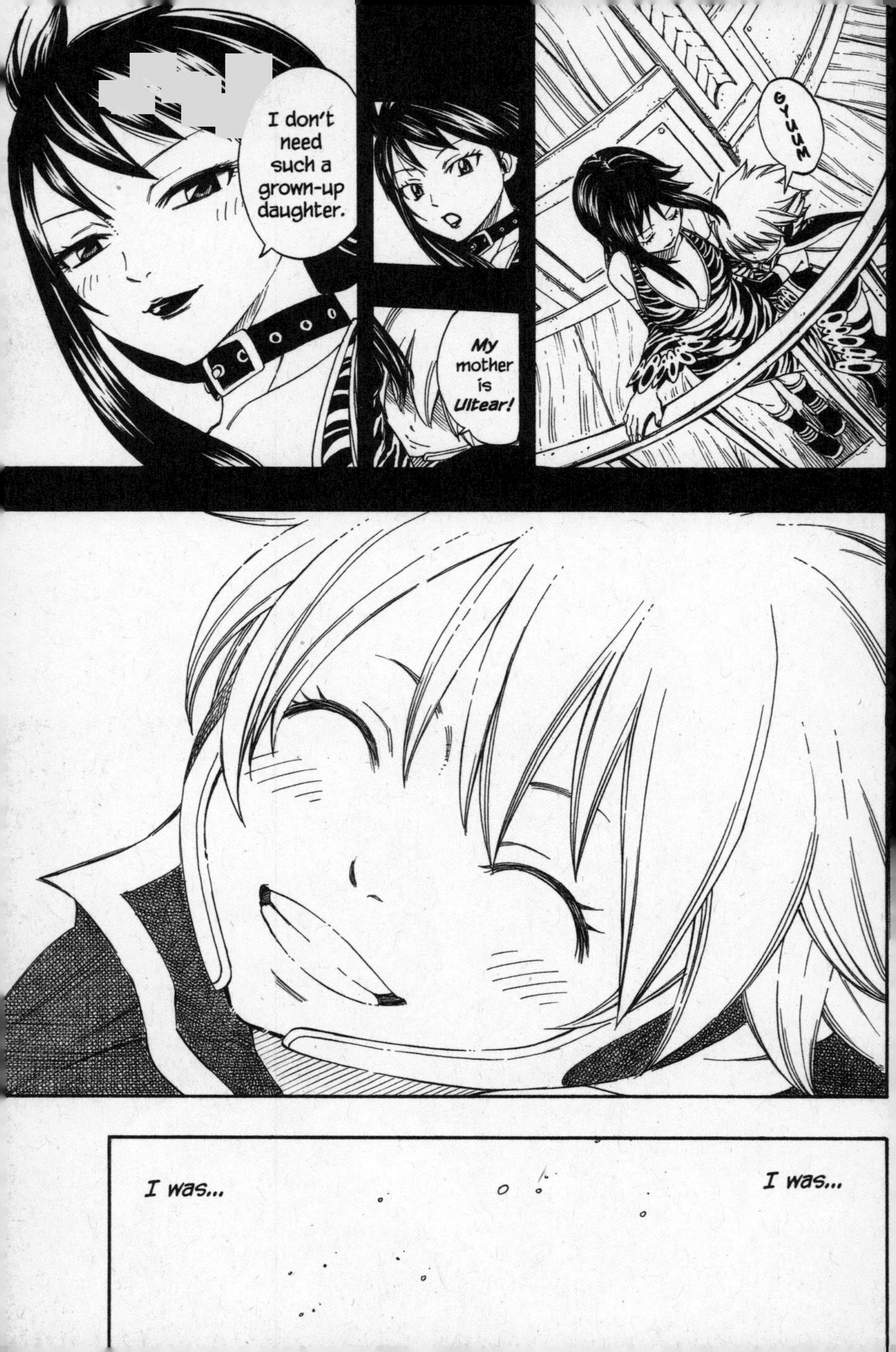
GYUUM
My mother is Ultear!
I don't need such a grown-up daughter.
I was...
I was...

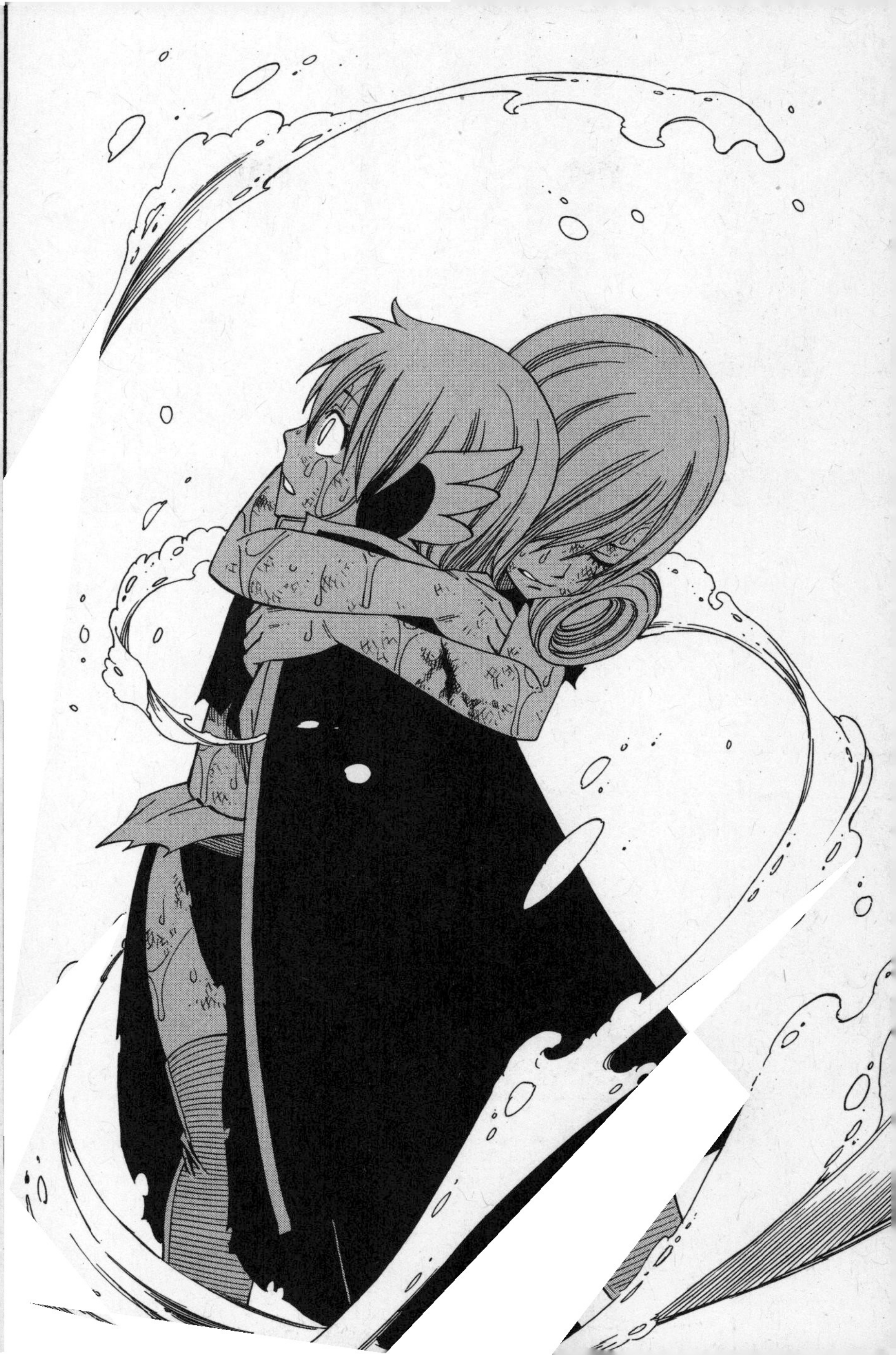

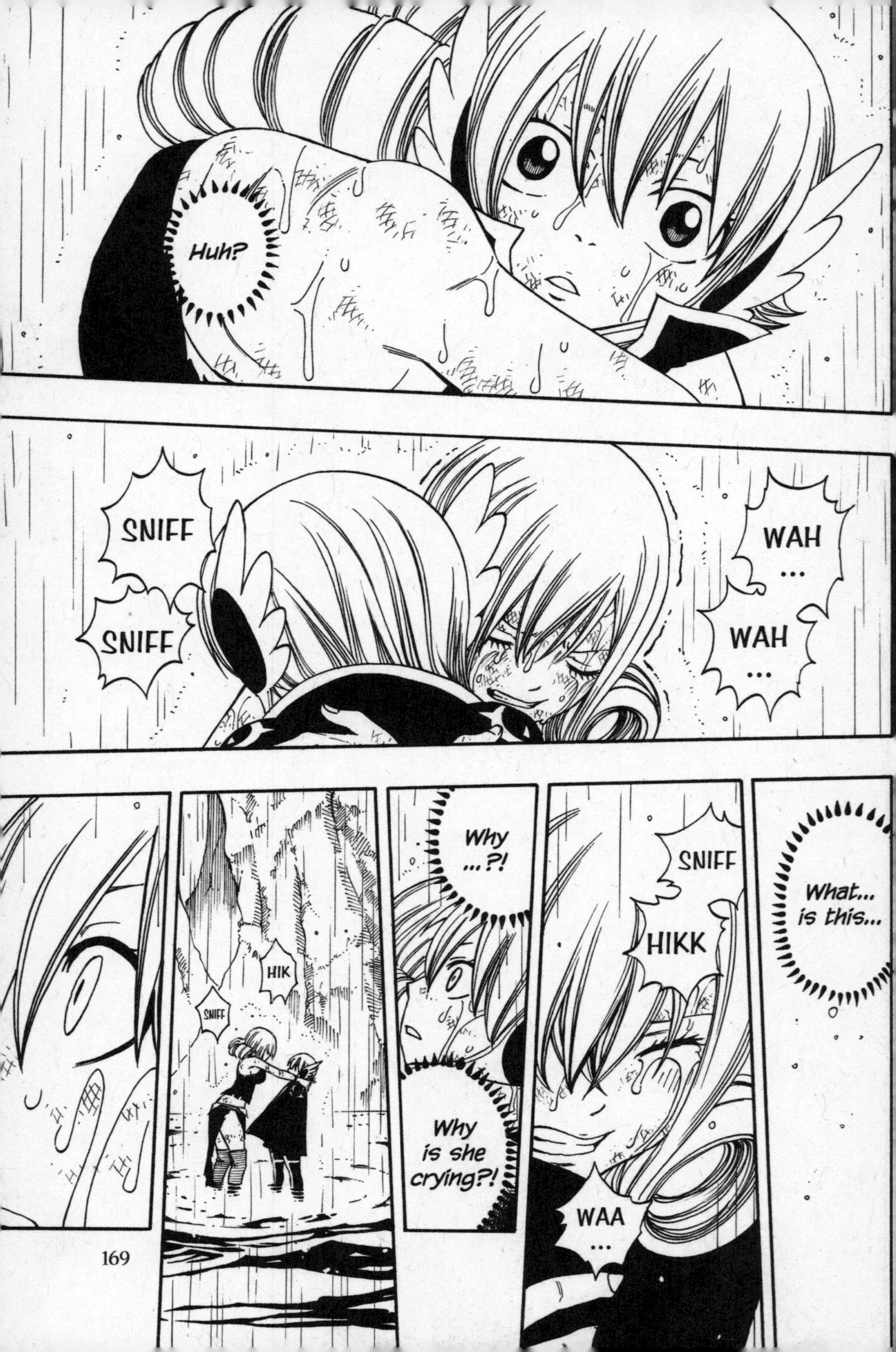
Huh?
WAH ...
WAH ...
SNIFF
SNIFF
What... is this...
SNIFF
HIKK
WAA ...
Why ...?!
Why is she crying?!
HIK
SNIFF

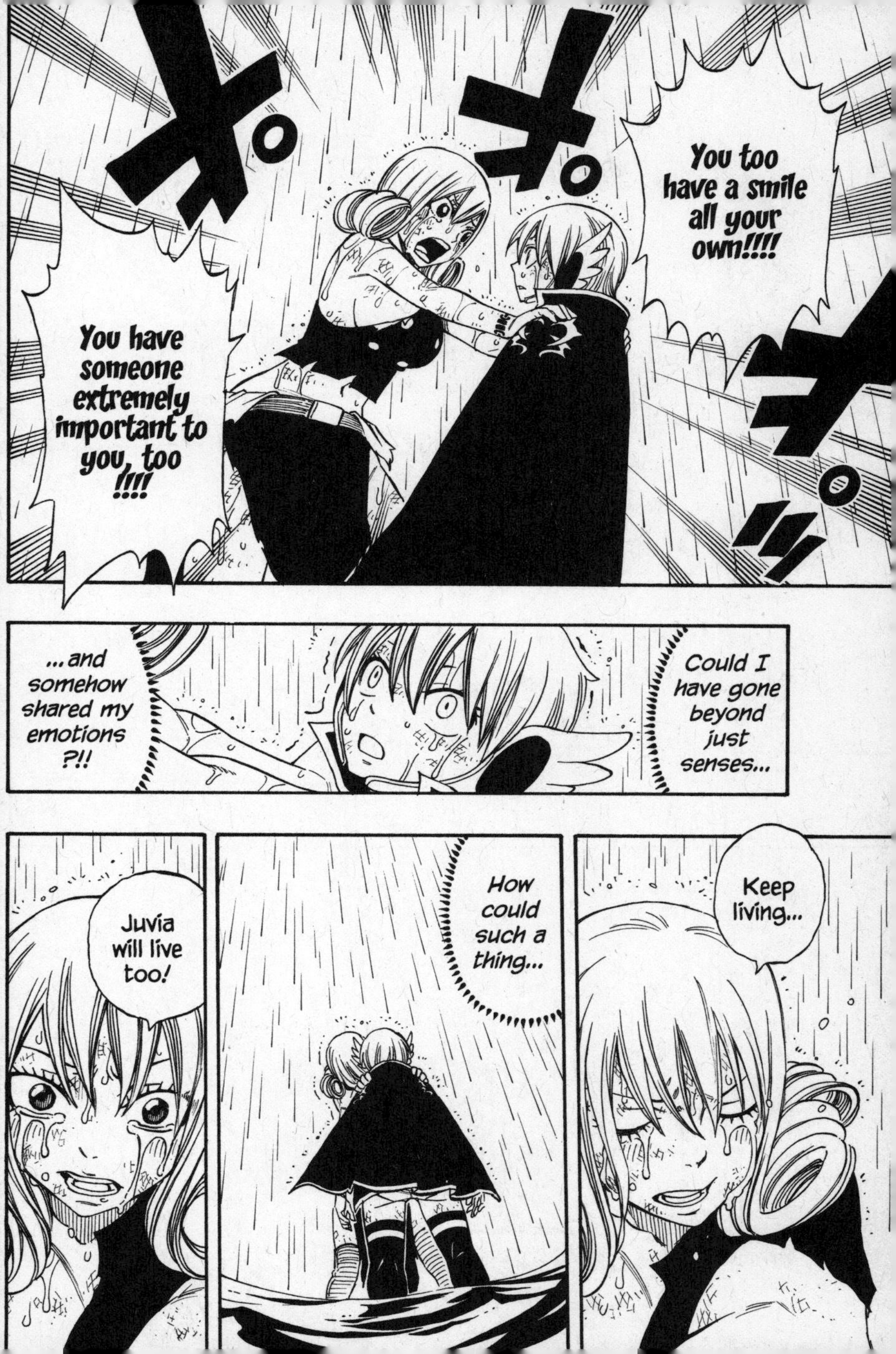
You too have a smile all your own!!!!
You have someone extremely important to you, too!!!!
Could I have gone beyond just senses...
...and somehow shared my emotions?!!
Keep living...
How could such a thing...
Juvia will live too!

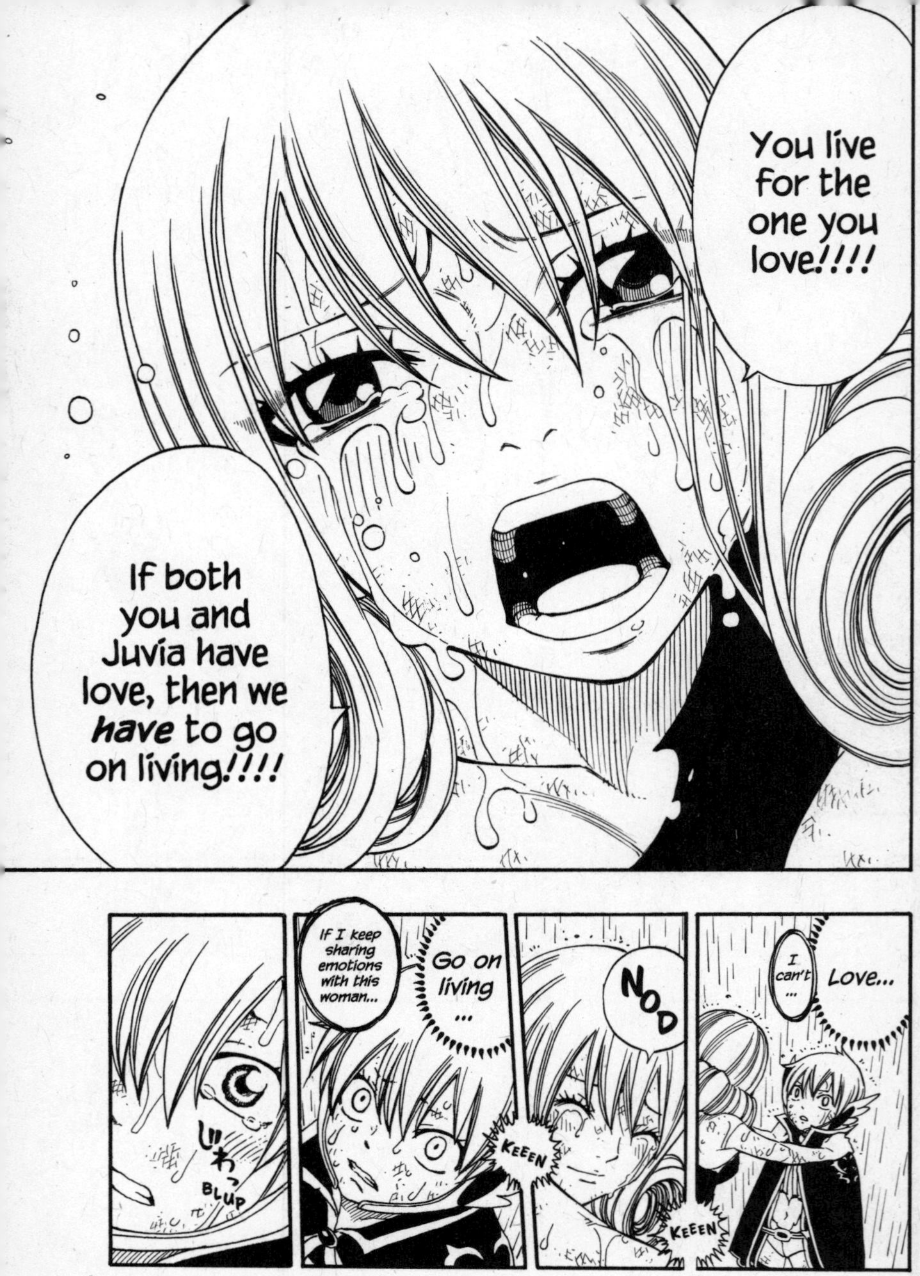
You live for the one you love!!!!
If both you and Juvia have love, then we *have* to go on living!!!!
Love...
I can't ...
NOD
KEEEN
KEEEN
Go on living ...
If I keep sharing emotions with this woman...
じわっ
BLUP

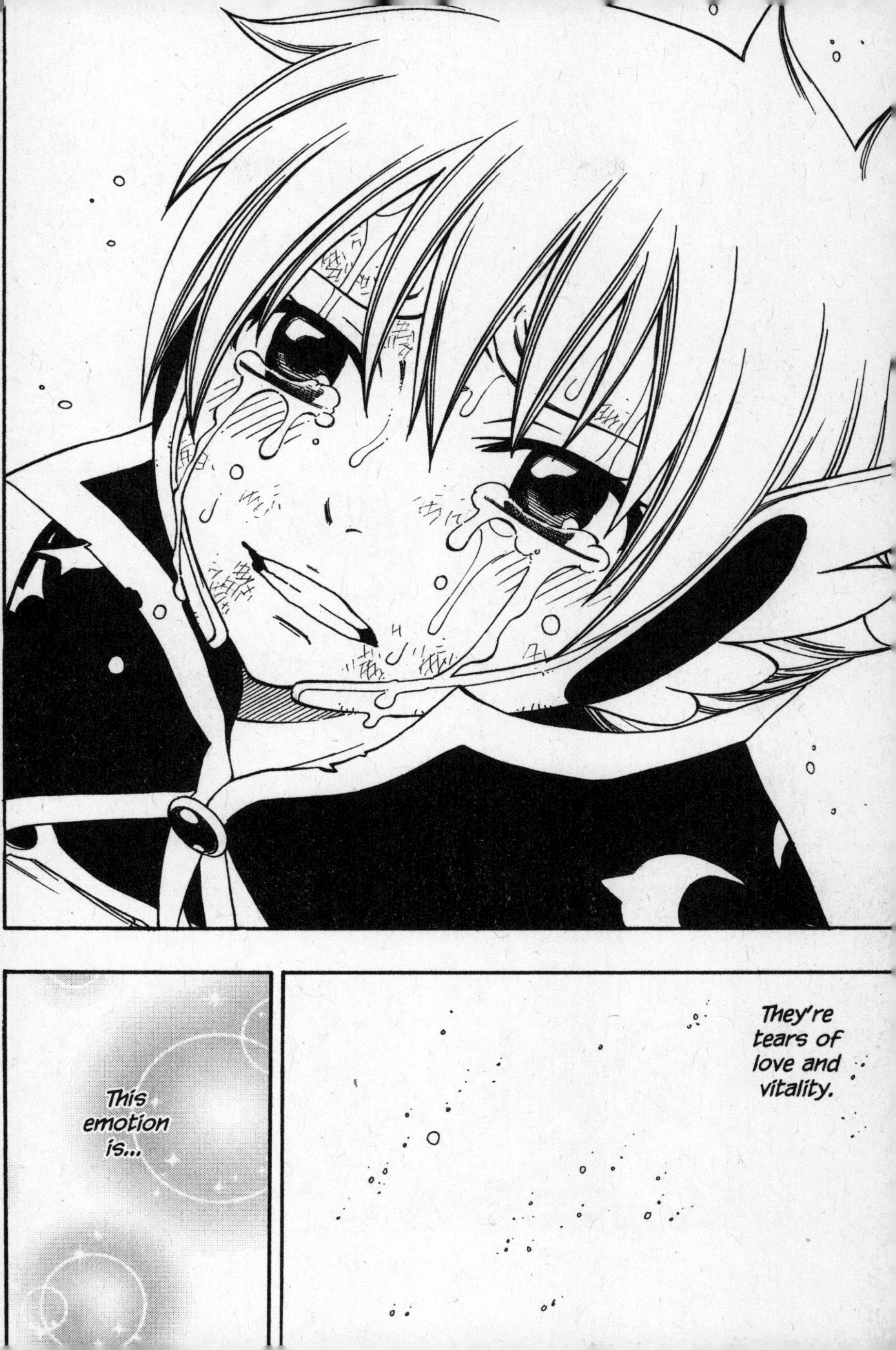
They're tears of love and vitality.
This emotion is...

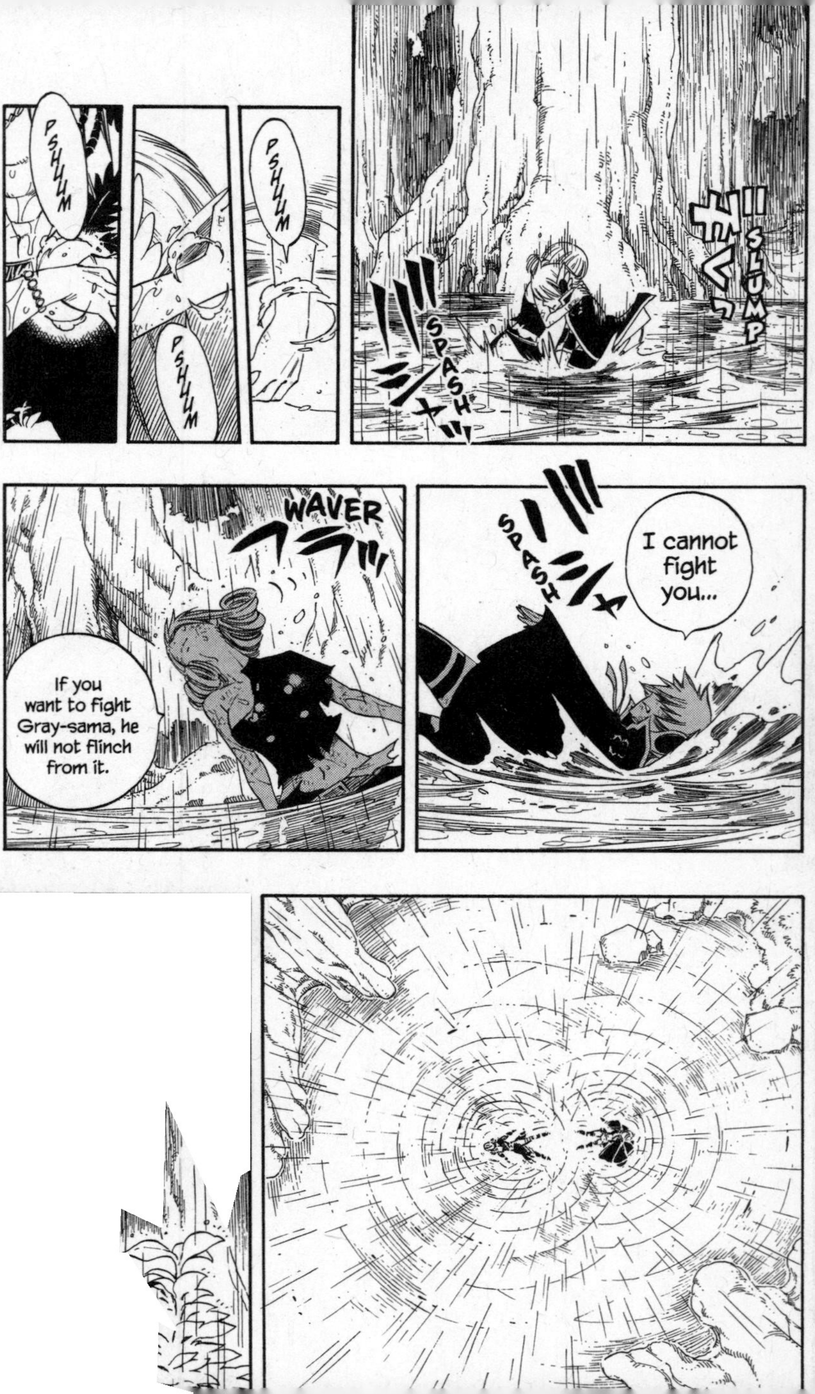
SLUMP
SPASH
PSHUUM
PSHUUM
PSHUUM
PSHUUM
SPASH
I cannot fight you...
WAVER
If you want to fight Gray-sama, he will not flinch from it.

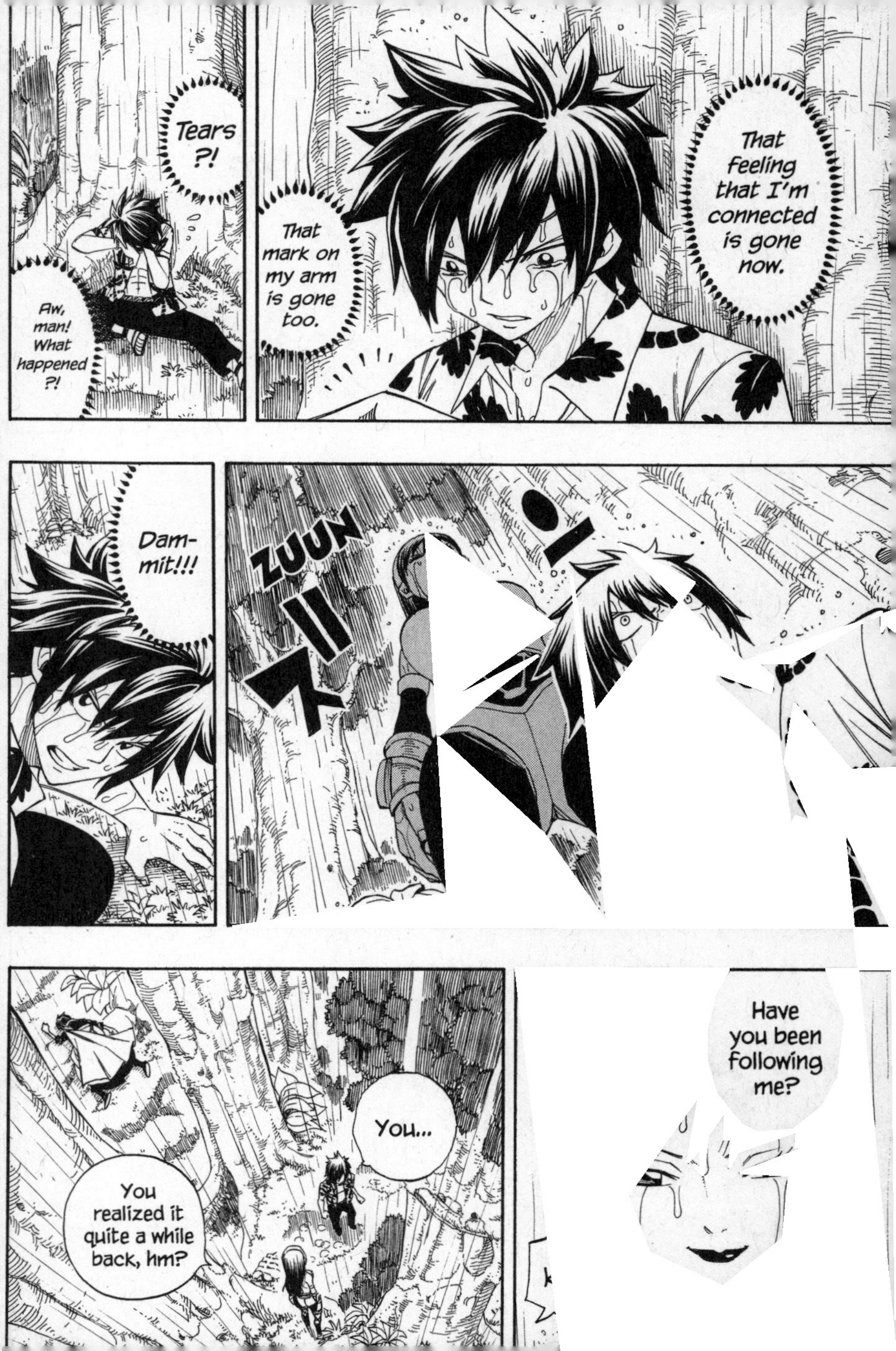
That feeling that I'm connected is gone now.
That mark on my arm is gone too.
Tears ?!
Aw, man! What happened ?!
ZUUN
Dam- mit!!!
Have you been following me?
You...
You realized it quite a while back, hm?

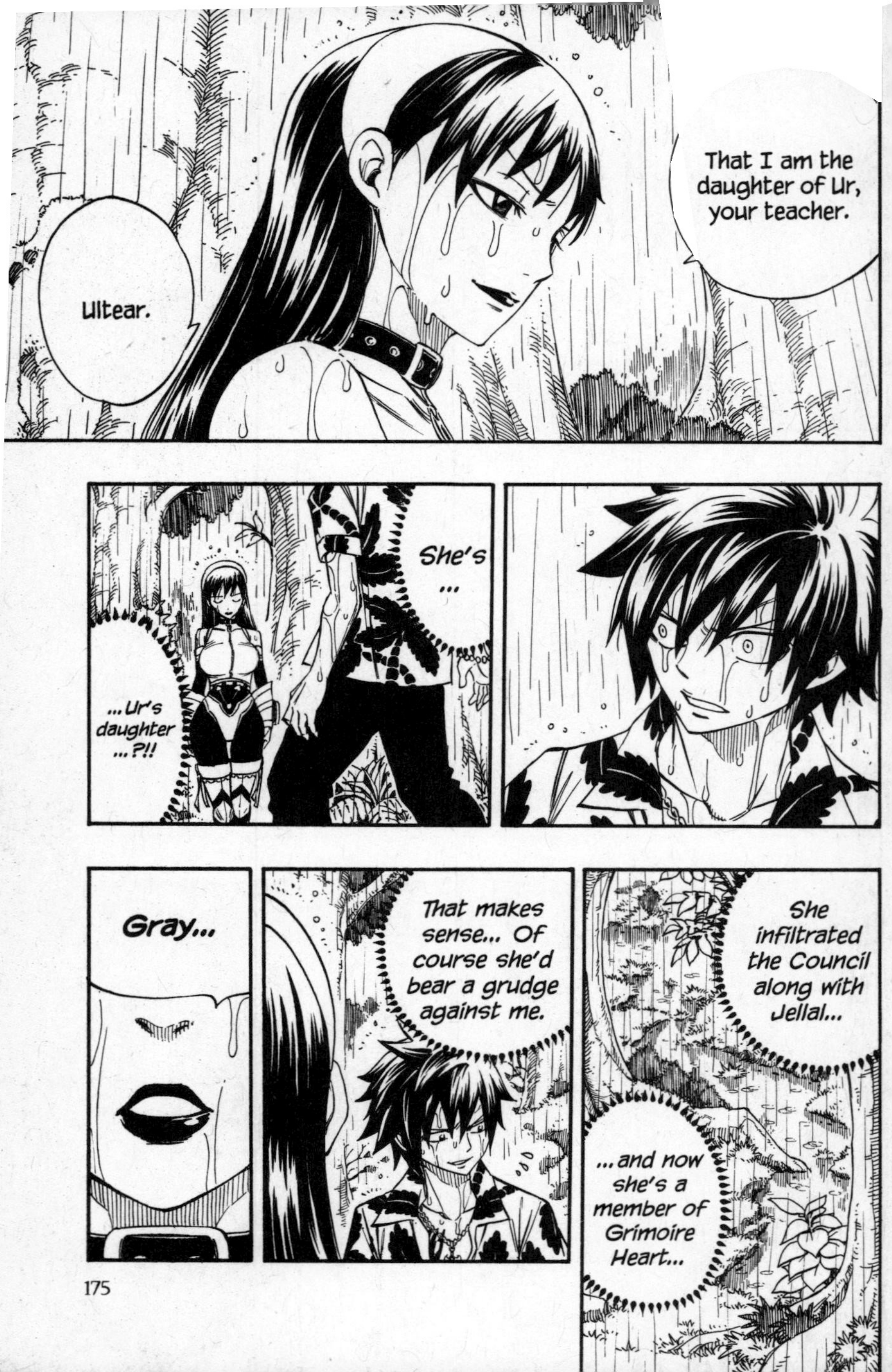
That I am the daughter of Ur, your teacher.
Ultear.
She's ...
...Ur's daughter ...?!!
She infiltrated the Council along with Jellal...
...and now she's a member of Grimoire Heart...
That makes sense... Of course she'd bear a grudge against me.
Gray...

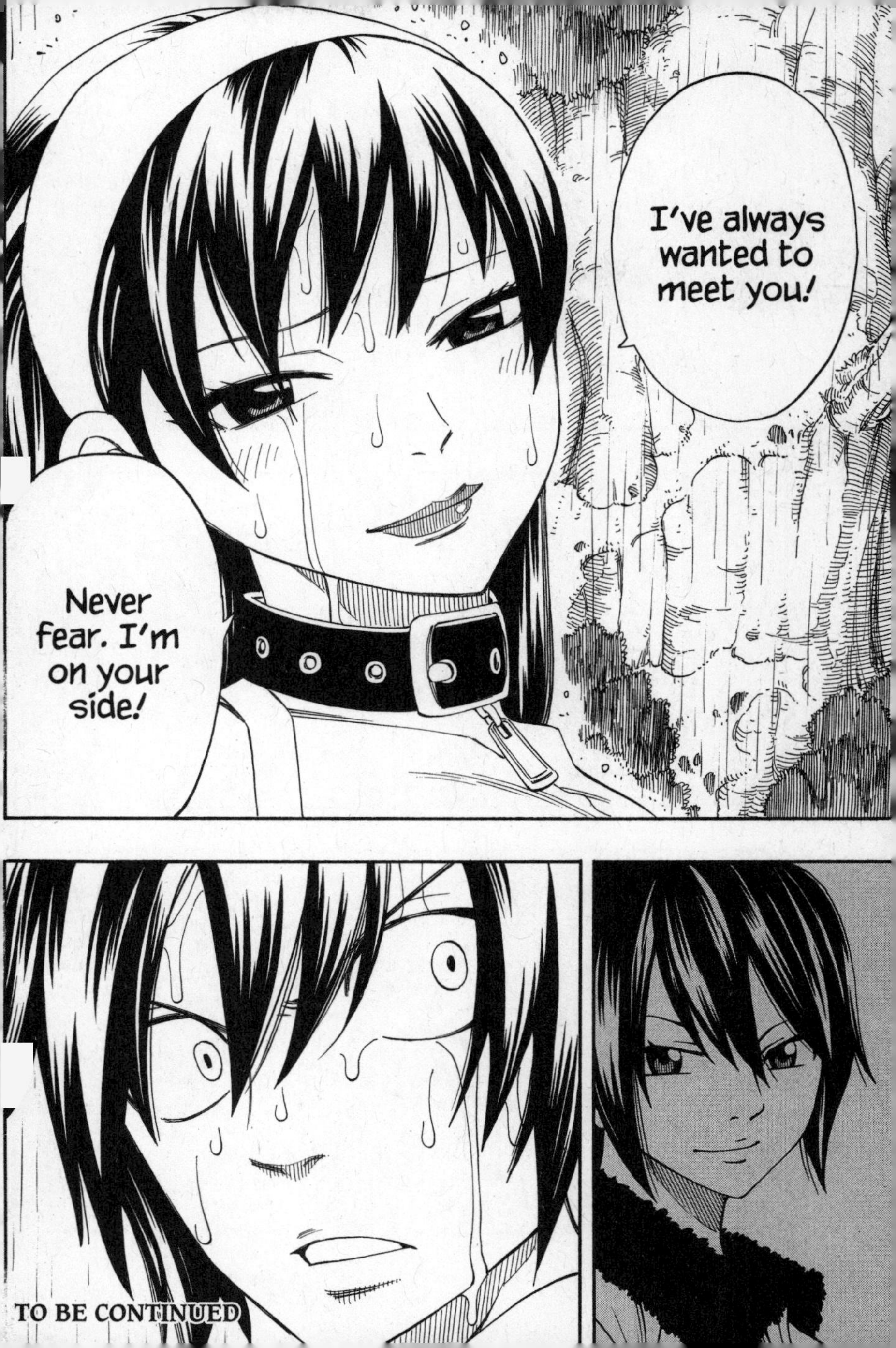
I've always wanted to meet you!
Never fear. I'm on your side!
TO BE CONTINUED

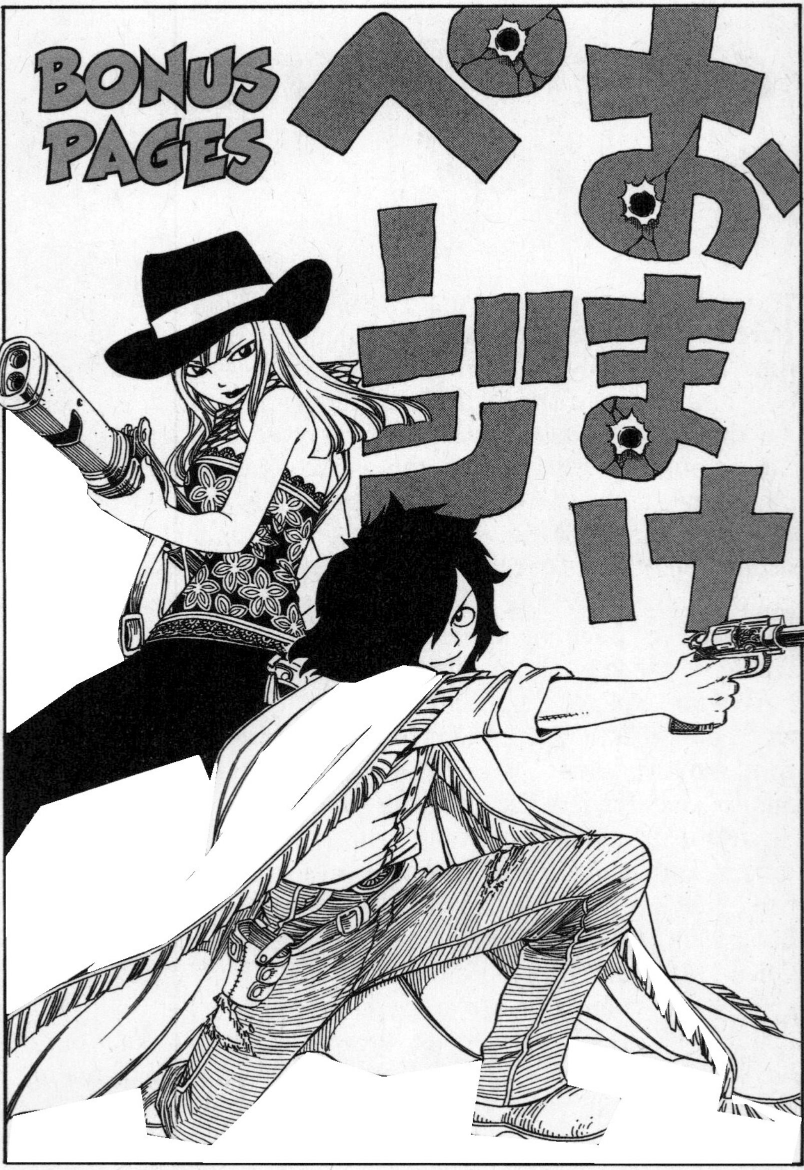
おまけページ
BONUS PAGES

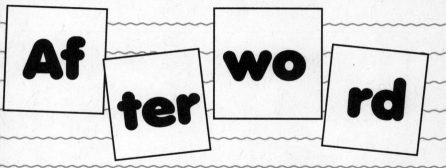

Afterword

This particular story arc is pretty long, huh? I guess my estimates were off. Usually a story arc takes about three volumes, but this time we've already gone through three volumes, and I'd say we're only about half finished with it, maybe. Hmm… Well, you could say that there are a lot more people involved this time, so the extra time is only natural, but also, things are going to heat up from here on out, so stay with us!! And I've got a really wild twist planned for the last scene of this one. Expect something big! I can't go into details, but it's one of those huge twists where the whole story, guild, and entire setting may be on the verge of changing. I can tell you that I'm chomping at the bit to draw it!

Changing the subject, I'm sure you've already noticed, but I don't have a home page, blog, Twitter account* or anything. As much as I'd like to do one, I get the feeling that I wouldn't be able to continue it very long, so I never tried. Also, I've had this nagging anxiety over readers hearing from me in my own words directly. There's a certain influence that goes along with the words of famous people like creators such as myself and TV stars, sports personalities and politicians and such. I've always thought that I don't want to blurt out something irresponsible, you know? And when I think of that, it becomes more difficult for me to do it. Even so, there are a lot of people around me using Twitter, so I've had an itch to try it myself…but I don't know how it'll turn out. Still, if I were to do a blog or Twitter, I might have less time for drawing… By the way, right now, I spend nearly all of every week drawing manga.

*Mashima-sensei has since signed up for Twitter (@hiro_mashima) and is quite active.

If-Plue

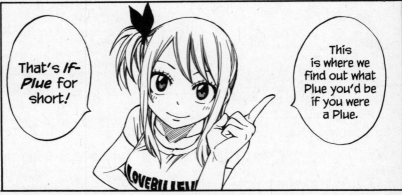

This is where we find out what Plue you'd be if you were a Plue.
That's *If-Plue* for short!

Hey everybody! If you were a Plue, what kind of Plue would you be? Have you ever thought about that? Of course not, right? We expected that. But for today, we are doing a special, "What kind of Plue would you be" column! Sure, it's dumb, but it's a fun kind of dumb to think about! How you do it is simple! Figure out the number that is derived from your name! Let's take as an example the name of Fairy Tail's Japanese editor, Mr. Matsuki.

1.) Noriaki Matsuki

(First, write out your name on a piece of paper.)

2.) N O R I A K I M A T S U K I
↓ ↓ ↓ ↓ ↓ ↓ ↓ ↓ ↓ ↓ ↓ ↓ ↓ ↓
4 5 8 9 1 1 9 3 1 0 9 1 1 9

Next, you assign numbers based on the order of the alphabet. The tens place doesn't matter for our purposes, so this is how the numbers would work.
A = 1, B = 2, C = 3, D = 4, E = 5, F = 6, G = 7, H = 8, I = 9, J = 0, K = 1, L = 2, M = 3, N = 4, O = 5, P = 6, Q = 7, R = 8, S = 9, T = 0, U = 1, V = 2, W = 3, X = 4, Y = 5, and Z = 6.

3.) 4+5+8+9+1+1+9+3+1+0+9+1+1+9
=
61
=
1

Then you add up all the numbers. When you get the total, take the ones place digit (ignoring the tens place and higher), and that becomes your Plue number. In Mr. Matsuki's example, that number is 1. Now take your Plue number you got here and check out the next page! (Just turn the page!)

Now, if you have some time to waste, give it a try!!

If-Plue 2

1. Normal Plue

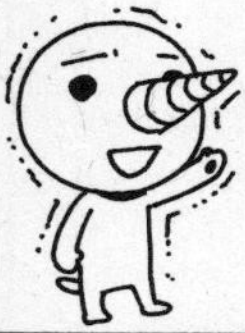

You're a normal Plue. Yes, we know you're a dog who, for some reason, walks on two legs, but you're still a normal Plue. You are the same kind of Plue you see in the manga.

2. Eating Plue

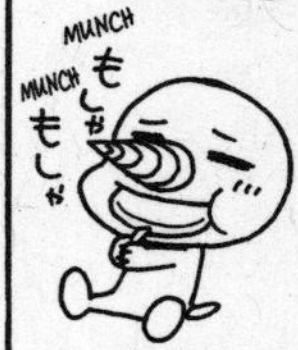
MUNCH
MUNCH

Anyway, you really like to eat! You're happiest when you're munching down on something. Just be careful you don't become a fat Plue.

3. Sleeping Plue

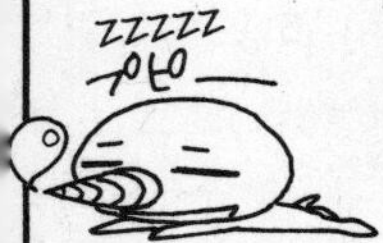
ZZZZZ

Do you find yourself running late all the time these days? Even when you've turned from human into a Plue, you still sleep all the time!

4. Happy?

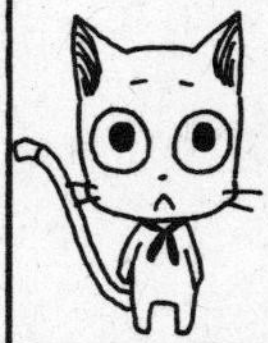

Too bad (?), but for some reason, you're not a Plue but a Happy. That's pretty rare, so you can take some pride in that.

5. ? Plue

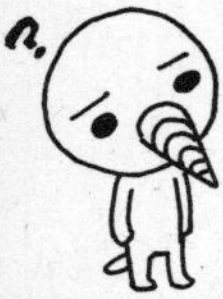

Yes, it's nice to have a burning curiosity about all sorts of things, but that can also lead to trouble, so take care with it, okay?

6. Dejected Plue

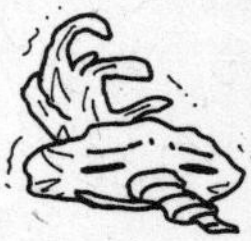

Maybe you're feeling downhearted, but you can't let it get the best of you! You'll turn out to be a fine, upstanding Plue! I know it! By the way, you really get along well with Plue Number 3!

7. Hungry Plue

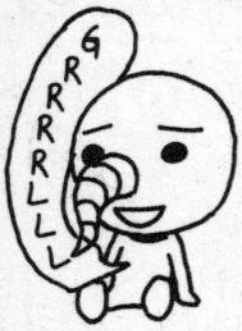
GRRRRRLLLL

Anyway, I suggest you just get a bite to eat. If you don't, it could spell trouble. You look like you could fade away. You are very compatible with Plue Number 2.

8. Crying Plue

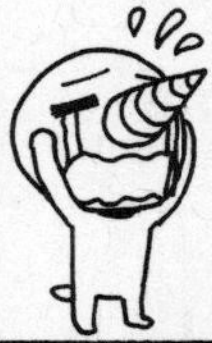

You have to be stronger! If you just keep crying, all the fun in life will run away from you! I'm sure you like to smile once in a while too, right?

9. CosPlue

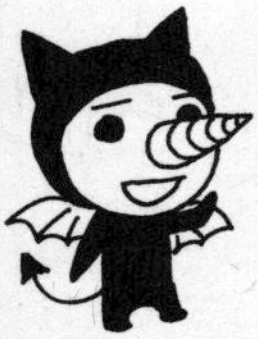

You are a Plue that loves snazzy clothing! You also blow through your money on it. You are always in pursuit of the ultimate fashion statement!

0. Dancing Plue

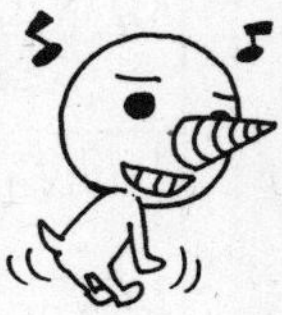

You are a Plue who loves to dance. When Lucy summons you, you can ease everyone's tension with your fancy footwork!

The Bestiary of Sirius Island

Doscadon

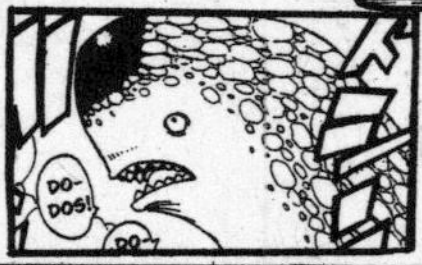
DO-DOS!

This is a giant carnivore that specializes in a head-butt attack. It crushes its prey with its head, then eats the meat.

Quly

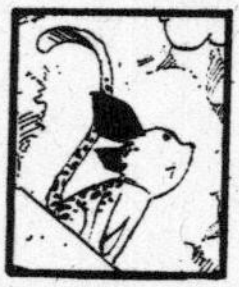

It's a native of the northern part of the island, but during winter months, it migrates to the south.

Cubina Gamal

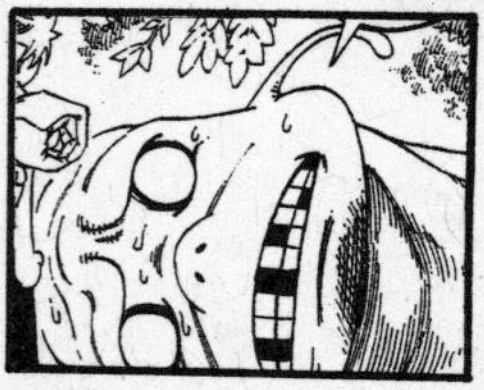

A huge herbivore 5-7 meters (16-23 feet) tall. There are rare instances where individuals can speak and understand human language.

Clipper

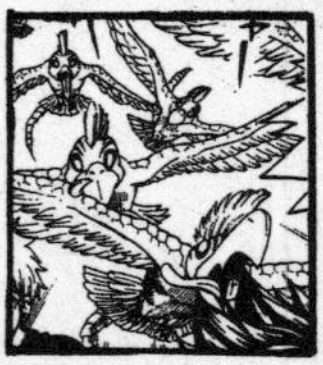

A violent-tempered bird that inhabits Sirius Island. They attack in flocks.

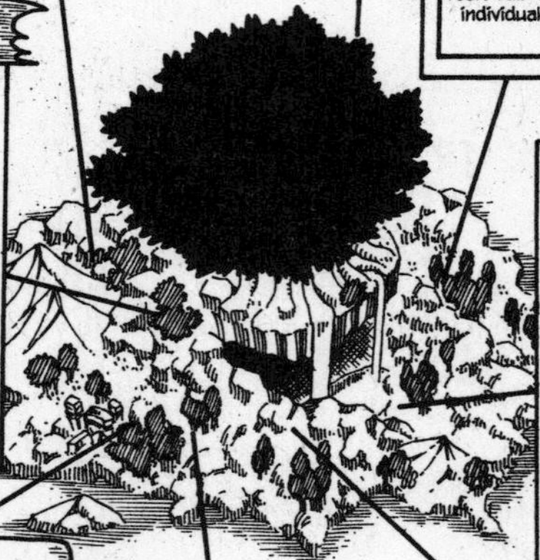

Bakshi

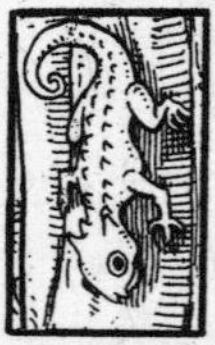

Lives in the trees or on the ground and tends to eat insects. It is unusual to catch sight of one.

Budragos

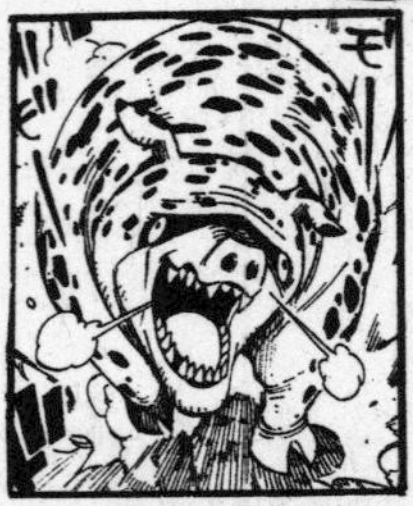

This is considered a giant member of the pig family. There are large numbers of this species in Fiore as well.

Sirius Squirrel

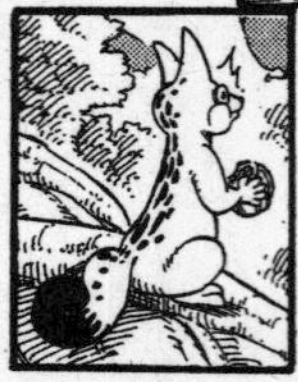

A rare member of the squirrel family that can only be found on Sirius Island. None of the world's biologists have ever seen it.

Goromajiro

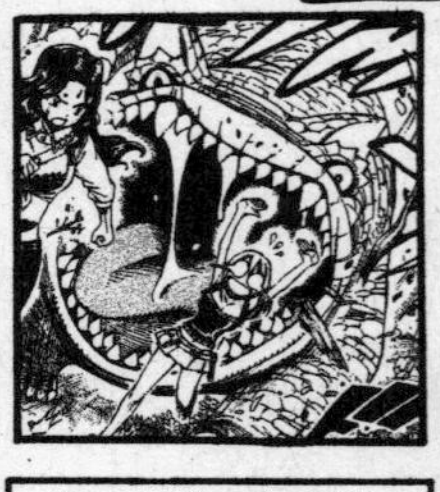

The exposed surfaces of its skin are covered in tough scales. When it is intent on battle, it can roll itself into a ball to attack.

Spot the Differences!

This artwork below is just like page 124! But if you look really closely, you can see a few differences…

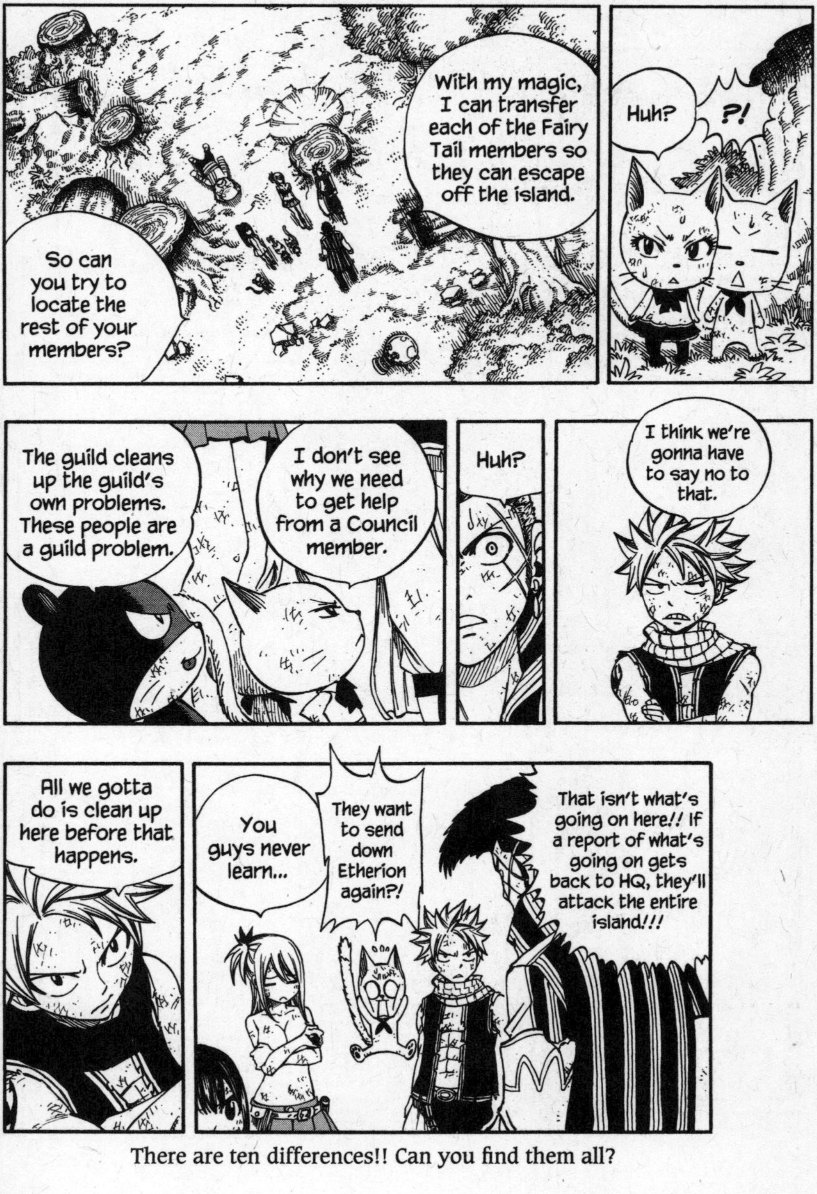

?!
Huh?
With my magic, I can transfer each of the Fairy Tail members so they can escape off the island.
So can you try to locate the rest of your members?
I think we're gonna have to say no to that.
Huh?
I don't see why we need to get help from a Council member.
The guild cleans up the guild's own problems. These people are a guild problem.
That isn't what's going on here!! If a report of what's going on gets back to HQ, they'll attack the entire island!!!
They want to send down Etherion again?!
You guys never learn...
All we gotta do is clean up here before that happens.

There are ten differences!! Can you find them all?

Hourly Scheduler

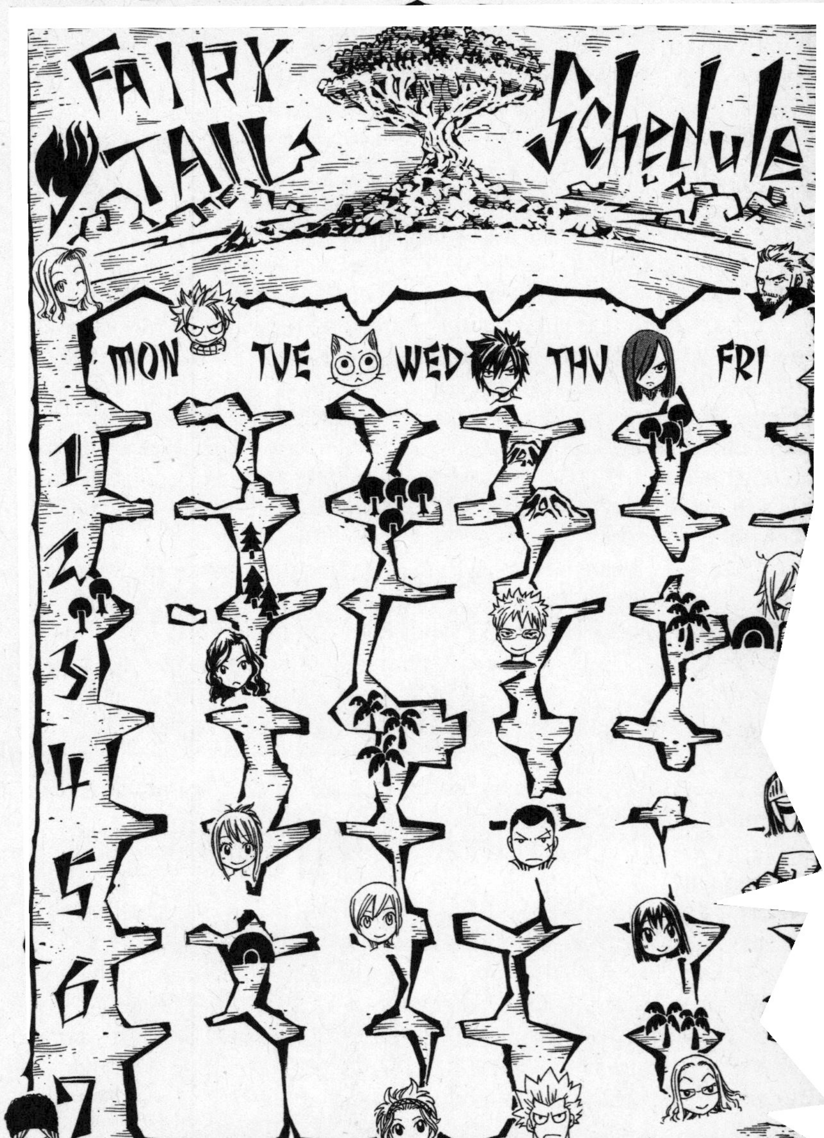
FAIRY TAIL
Schedule
MON
TUE
WED
THU
FRI
1
2
3
4
5
6
7

Copy this page and fill it in for yourself!

ABOUT THE NAMING OF THE CHARACTERS 2

It may be late to do this since there are just so many characters now, but let's go for it anyway.

Gajeel --> Kajiru, the Japanese word for "to gnaw." The Japanese sound effect for his eating is "*gaji gaji*."
Wendy --> In the first concepts, Wendy was "Water Dragon." The Japanese word for the day in the middle of the week is Suiyôbi or "water day," then I got to the English Wednesday, and from there to Wendy.
Carla (Sharuru or Charles in Japanese) --> I think this was the name of a princess character in a book I read a long time ago. But in the West, there are a lot of countries where the name is male, so the name has changed in a bunch of countries.
Fried --> He was originally supposed to be named Albion. But the rest of the Raijin Tribe had longer names, so Fried's name was shortened to give it some balance. In his original concept, he attacked with archaic words, so his name was Furui-zo! ("It's old!"), shortened to Furi-zo! to Fried.
Bickslow --> It was a mash of "Big" and "Throw."
Evergreen --> It refers to trees that don't lose their leaves in the winter. Her color is green.
Laxus --> It's based on a unit of measurement for light, "Lux."
Panther Lily --> This is a play on the name of a famous character from a certain fairy tale.
Juvia --> I don't remember about this one, but I really, really love the name!
Levy --> She was just a background character at first, so I don't really remember. But I really like her!
Lisanna --> I just get the feeling that a name ending like xxx-anna makes it sound cute!
Precht --> From the literary scholar.
Ultear --> As mentioned in the books, she's "Ur's tear."
Kain Hikaru --> The nickname of someone who was a part of my staff.
Rustyrose --> It was a riff on the name of a cocktail.
Merudy --> This just sort of came to me. (Afterwards I realized it's the name of a character in an old RPG I used to play. I regret not realizing it.)
Zancrow --> I so don't remember about this name that it surprises even me!
Caprico --> It's from Capricorn, the goat, the constellation.
Azuma --> When I was trying to think of a name, the TV celebrity Mikihisa Azuma just happened to come on.

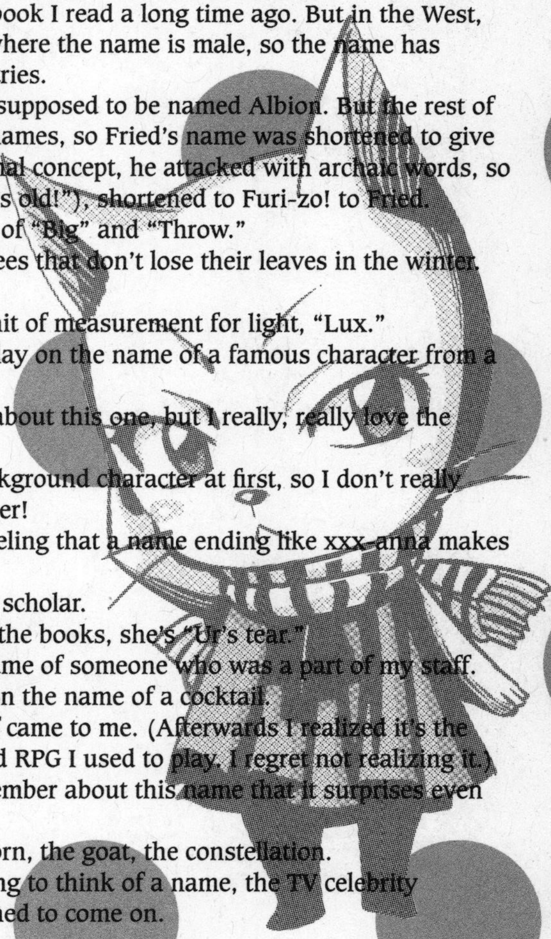

Updated for December of the year X784.

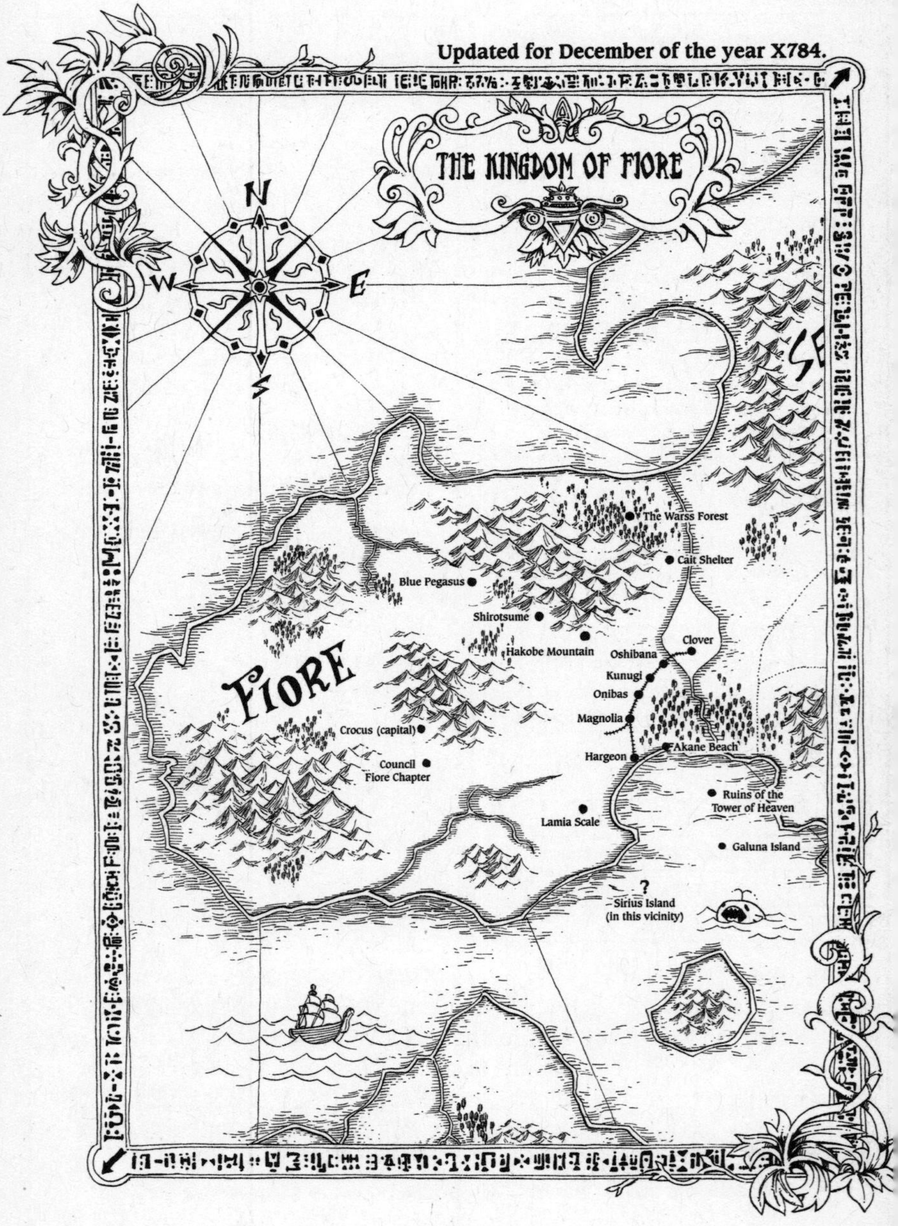
THE KINGDOM OF FIORE
N
W
E
S
FIORE
The Warss Forest
Cait Shelter
Blue Pegasus
Shirotsume
Hakobe Mountain
Clover
Oshibana
Kunugi
Onibas
Magnolia
Crocus (capital)
Hargeon
Akane Beach
Council
Fiore Chapter
Ruins of the
Tower of Heaven
Lamia Scale
Galuna Island
?
Sirius Island
(in this vicinity)

Continued from the left-hand page ⬇

Lucy: Okay, we'll just call that the reason.

Mira: There are really a lot of other detail mistakes that haven't been pointed out yet, but if we just keep quiet, nobody will ever know, so we'll not say a word!♡

Lucy: Y-Yeah, I guess...

Mira: And the next question.

If Cana failed the S-Class test four times, who were the wizards who managed to pass the test?

Lucy: I want to know that too!

Mira: Yes... Actually the truth of that is a little complicated, so let's look at a chart.

Test Year	Passed the Test	
X784	Still in Progress	Cana Takes Part
X783	No Wizard Passed	
X782	Mystogan	
X781	Mirajane (16 years old)	
X780	Erza (15 years old)	
X779	No Wizard Passed	
X778	Laxus (17 years old)	
X???	Gildarts	

Lucy: Really?

Mira: Looking at it like this, I'm reminded that I passed the year before we lost Lisanna...

Lucy: And there are times when no wizard passed, huh?

Mira: That's right. And a number of people passed between Gildarts and Laxus, but for various reasons, they're not in the guild now.

Lucy: Looking at their ages at the time, we don't know how old Gildarts was, but Erza was just 15...?

Mira: Right! She holds the record for youngest!

Lucy: That's pretty amazing...

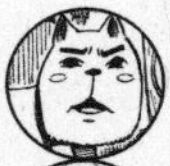
: Tswee!! Tswee!!

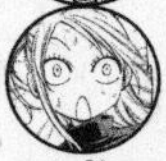
: !!

Mira: Oh, my... There you are again!

Lucy: L-Listen, Mira-san, that bark is really weird!

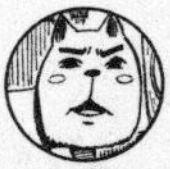
: Tswee!! Tsweetsuu!!

Mira: Really?

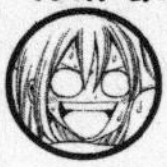
: Absolutely! Completely weird!!

Mira: I think he's better than a Lucy who barks out, "Mountain Lion Pon!"

Lucy: That isn't any kind of a bark!

Mira: Here! Here, little doggy!

Lucy: I'm just going to ask this, but what's the **breed name** of that dog?

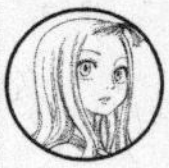
: What? I have no idea. I told you it was a stray, right? It just came to my place on its own.

Lucy: So it really *was* a stray...? (sigh)

Emergency Request! ♡

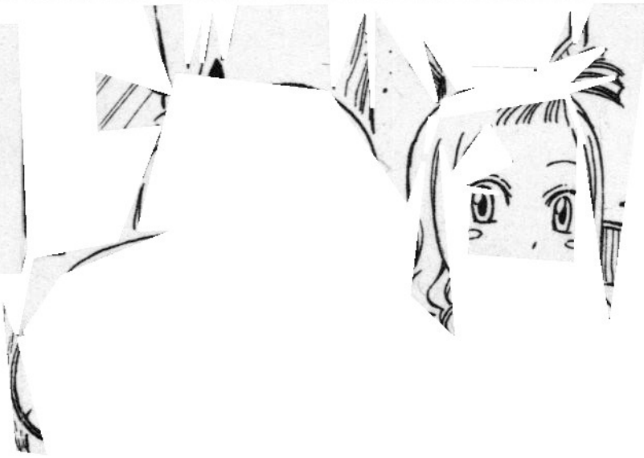

Explain the Mysteries of FT!

At Mirajane's House...

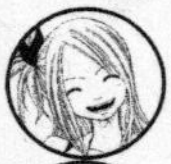: Wow!! Mirajane's house!♡

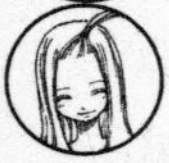: Welcome, Lucy!

Lucy: Oh! You own a dog?

Mira: He's a stray, though.

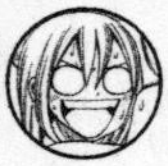: If you own him, you can't call him a stray, right?

Mira: Let's get right off to our question corner, shall we?

> ***In Volume 21, there was a scene where Edolas Natsu suddenly showed up with a scarf. What was that about?***
>
> 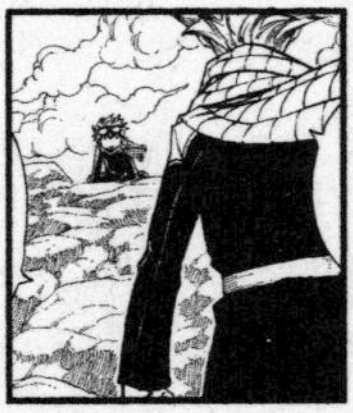

Lucy: That question... There are a lot of people pointing that out, huh?

Mira: It was nothing more than a mistake, right?

Lucy: Well manga creators are human too. I suppose there are times when they space out and make some mistakes.

Mira: Like when he ***forgets to draw your clothes, Lucy.***

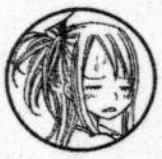: I kind of wonder why a pro would be doing that.

Mira: Speaking of questioning the professionalism of creators, there's this!

> ***In Volume 7, the guild mark was on Lisanna's left shoulder, but in the Edolas chapters it was on her left thigh. Why is that?***
>
> 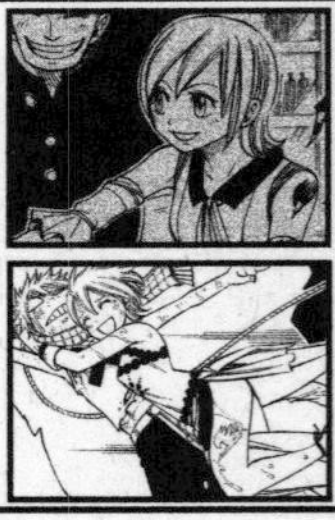

Lucy: Oh, no...!!

Mira: A lot of details being pointed out, hm?

Lucy: Another mistake?

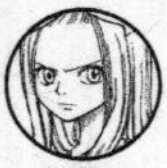: No. We actually can make up an excuse for that.

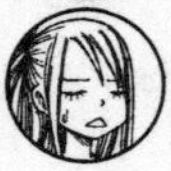: You shouldn't be saying, "excuse"...

Mira: The people of the Edolas Fairy Tail don't actually have guild marks on their bodies. That's why she moved her mark to a place where it wouldn't stand out. How's that?

Continued on the right-hand page.

TAIL d'ART

The Fairy Tail Guild is looking for illustrations! Please send in your art on a postcard or at postcard size, and do it in black pen, okay? Those chosen to be published will get a signed mini poster! ♪ Make sure you write your real name and address on the back of your illustration!

Kanagawa Prefecture, Reina Mori

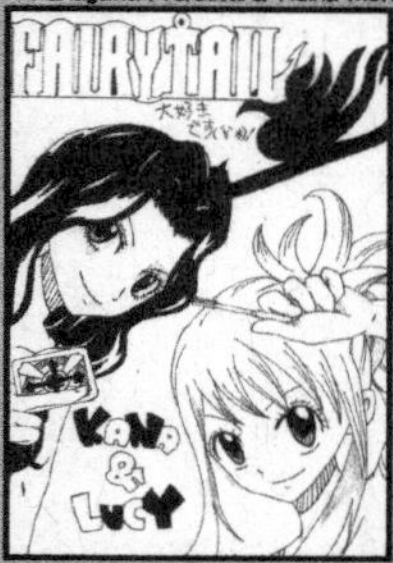
FAIRY TAIL
KANA & LUCY

▲These two were an unexpected combo! But how's their teamwork?

Fukuoka Prefecture, Nagisa ♡(Older sister)

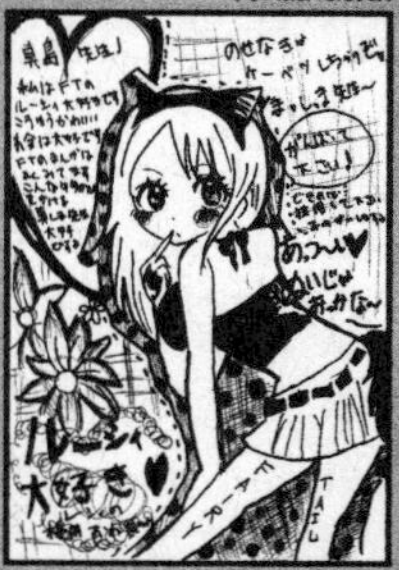

▲It's a Lucy fan! Thank you so much!

Aichi Prefecture, Misaki Tomita

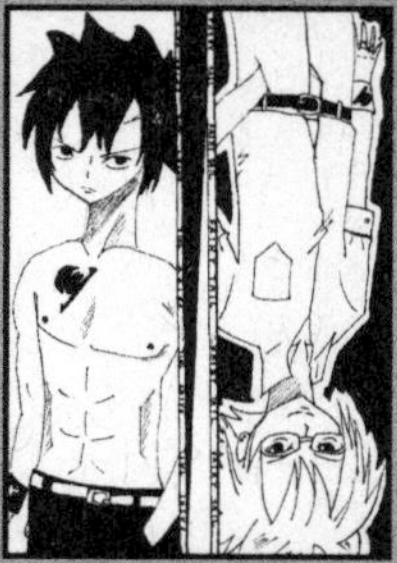

▲The men who are tagged as the hunky guys of FT. Loke really worked hard this time!

Gunma Prefecture, Hinari Akasaka

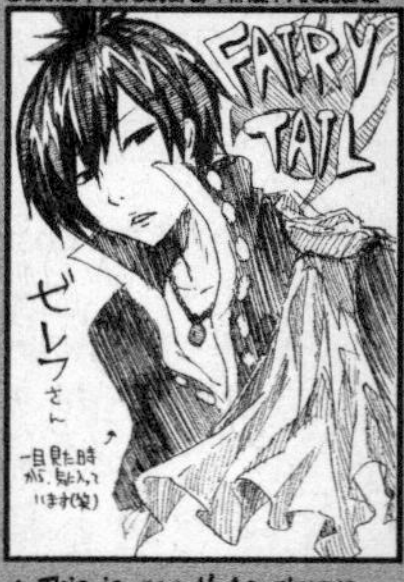
FAIRY TAIL
ゼレフさん

▲This is good! As always, Zeref is really popular, but he didn't really have a part this volume, huh?

Kanagawa Prefecture, Hōbei-Kyū

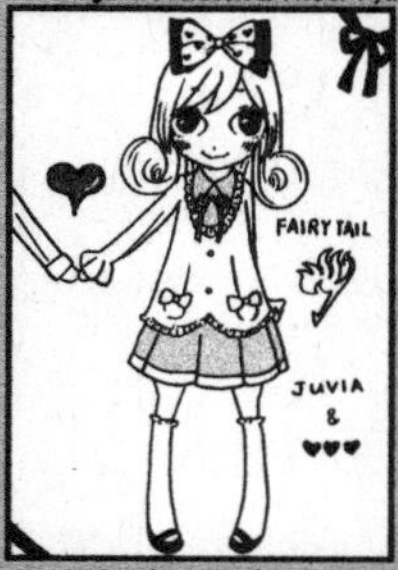
FAIRY TAIL
JUVIA & ♥♥♥

▲Juvia played a huge part this time, didn't she?

Chiba Prefecture, Yūya

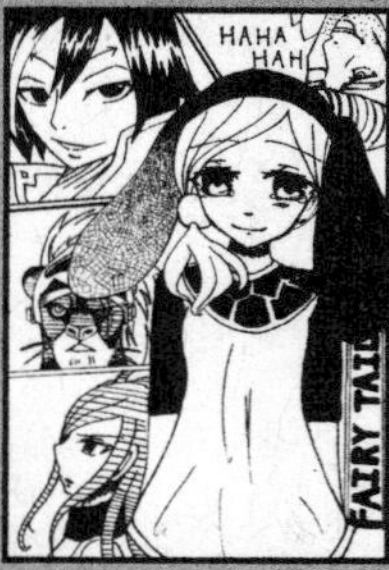
HAHA HAH
FAIRY TAIL

▲Long time, no see! Is everybody doing good?

Shizuoka Prefecture, Phantom

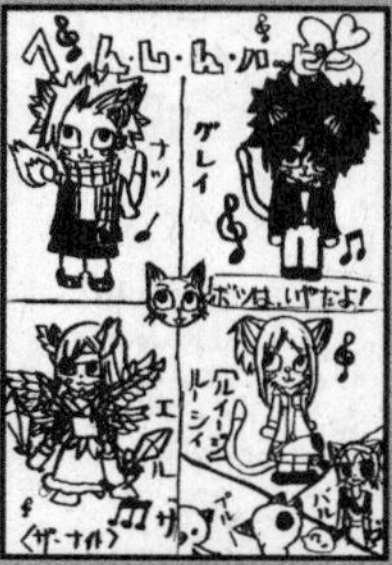
ナツ
グレイ

▲Ha haaa! Everybody with Happy's face!!

Toyama Prefecture, Yūki Izumi

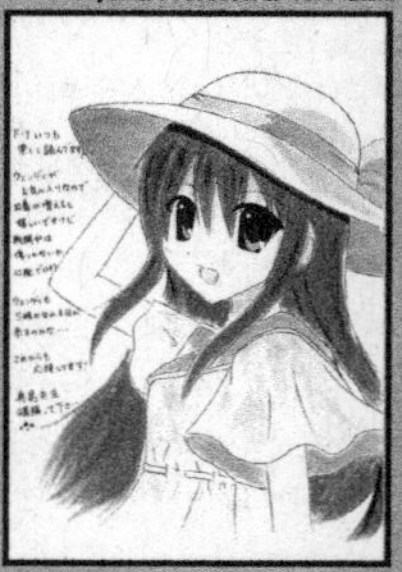

▲Thanks for the really cute picture of Wendy!

Send to Hiro Mashima, Kodansha Comics
451 Park Ave. South, 7th Floor New York, NY 10016

FAIRY GUILD

Hyogo Prefecture, Miiko

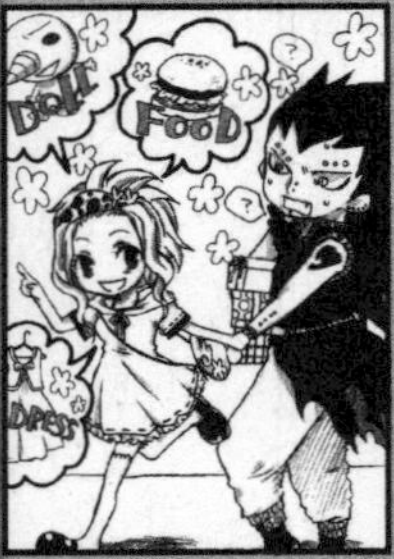
FOOD
DRESS

▲There seem to be a lot of people who are very concerned about where the relationship of these two is going.

Taiwan, Wu Yu-Jing

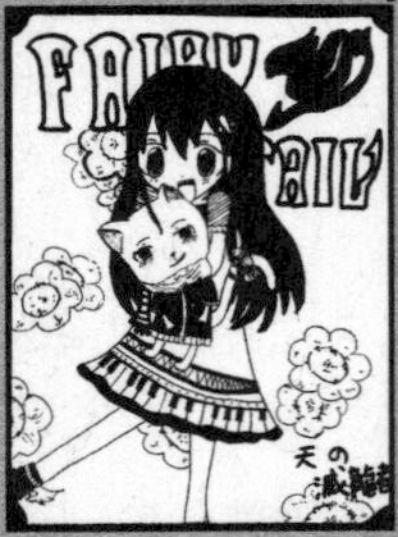
FAIRY TAIL

▲The second piece of art from Taiwan! Her skirt has a keyboard pattern! ♪

Taiwan, Ceng Heng-Min

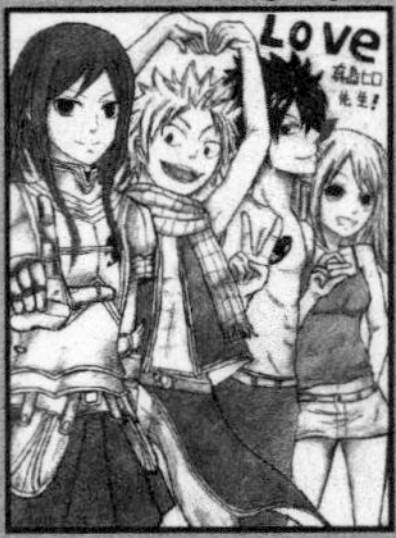
Love

▲This time, there were two pieces of work from Taiwan! Natsu's face is great!

Kanagawa Prefecture, Haruka Itō

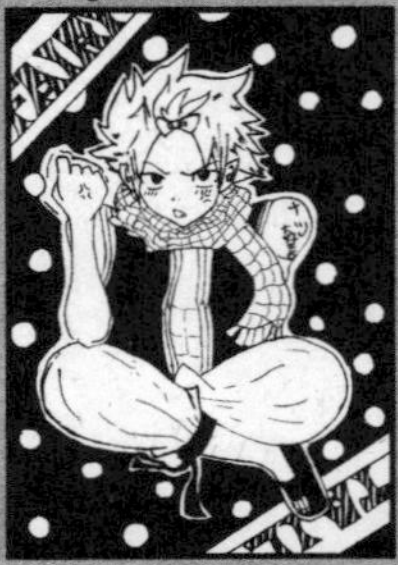

▲There's a ribbon in Natsu's hair! It looks better than expected.

Gifu Prefecture, Yūri Takagi

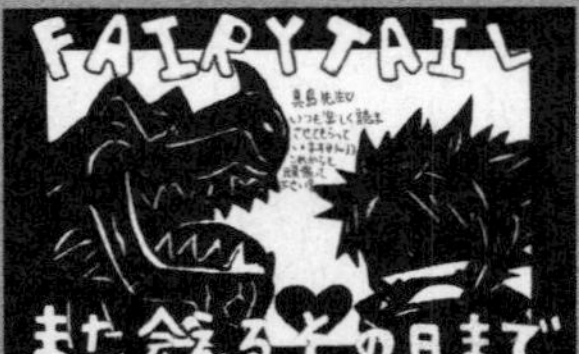
FAIRYTAIL
また会えるその日まで

◀Ohh! It's cut-out art! Wonderful!!

By sending in letters or postcards you give us permission to give your name, address, postal code and any other information you include to the author as is. Please keep that in mind.

Aichi Prefecture, Seimar

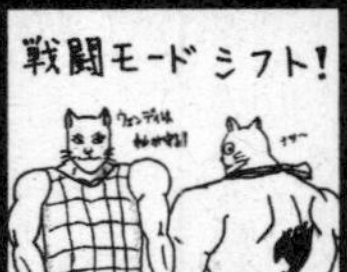
戦闘モード シフト!
シャルル & ハッピー

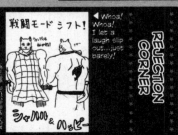

◀Whoa! Whoa! I let a laugh slip out...just barely!

REJECTION CORNER

Kyoto, Maru

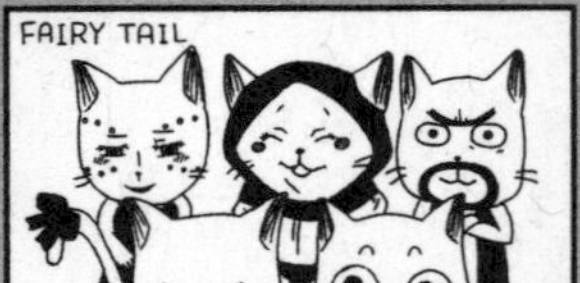
FAIRY TAIL

Happy, Carla and their families. Will we see them again?▶

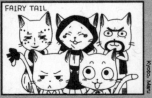

FROM HIRO MASHIMA

On the occasion of the Great Tohoku
Earthquake, I would like to offer my
support and condolences to anyone
affected by the tragedy. I have made
arrangements for any royalties I
may receive (any money sent to me)
from the sale of Japanese Volume 26,
in both normal and special editions,
to be sent to aid the victims of the
disaster. This note is to tell those who
bought Volume 26 where their money
is going and to send my fervent
wishes that smiles come back to
those who are suffering as soon as
possible.

Hiro Mashima
4/18/2011

Original Jacket Design: Hisao Ogawa

Translation Notes:

Japanese is a tricky language for most Westerners, and translation is often more art than science. For your edification and reading pleasure, here are notes on some of the places where we could have gone in a different direction with our translation of the work, or where a Japanese cultural reference is used.

Page 59, Six hours

The word for six hours in Japanese is *roku-jikan*. The word for six letters is *roku-ji*. So there was a clue (aside from simply the number 6) in Makarov's instructions as to the location of the grave. However, there was no good way to get the similarities across in the English version, since English does not use as great a variety of terms to count different things, such as hours or letters.

Page 67, Curse of Vengeance

The original Japanese refers to a specific vengeance curse called *ushi no koku mairi*. This is a trip to perform a rite during what is called the "hour of the ox" in ancient Japan, somewhere between 1 and 3 a.m., a time devoted to spirits. In modern Japanese folklore, it's usually depicted by showing a person with candles strapped to his or her forehead holding a doll made of straw, which represents the one to be cursed. The person then nails the doll to a tree to deliver the curse.

Page 71, Do-Doskoi

Dosukoi (pronounced doskoi) is a shout for which I've never heard a proper meaning. Traditionally, it's shouted at sumo matches as a taunt or an instigation from one side to the other. It can also be thought of as a wish for one to do one's best (or fight hard).

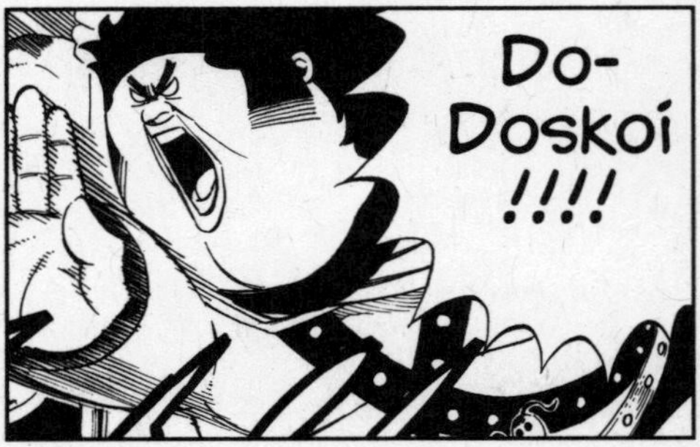
Do-
Doskoi
!!!!

Fairy Tail volume 27 is a work of fiction. Names, characters, places, and incidents are the products of the author's imagination or are used fictitiously. Any resemblance to actual events, locales, or persons, living or dead, is entirely coincidental.

A Kodansha Comics Trade Paperback Original.

Published in the United States by Kodansha Comics, an imprint of Kodansha USA Publishing, LLC, New York.

Publication rights for this English edition arranged through Kodansha Ltd., Tokyo.

First published in Japan in 2011 by Kodansha Ltd., Tokyo
ISBN 978-1-61262-269-9

Printed in the United States of America.

www.kodanshacomics.com

9 8 7 6 5 4 3

Translator: William Flanagan
Lettering: AndWorld Design